Diss. ETH № 18820

Hypervolume-Based Search for Multiobjective Optimization: Theory and Methods

A dissertation submitted to
ETH Zurich

for the degree of
Doctor of Sciences

presented by

JOHANNES M. BADER

Dipl. El.-Ing., ETH Zürich
born April 6, 1981
citizen of Basel, BS

accepted on the recommendation of
Prof. Dr. Eckart Zitzler, examiner
Prof. Dr. Günter Rudolph, co-examiner

2009

Institut für Technische Informatik und Kommunikationsnetze
Computer Engineering and Networks Laboratory

TIK-SCHRIFTENREIHE NR. 112

Johannes M. Bader

Hypervolume-Based Search for Multiobjective Optimization: Theory and Methods

Eidgenössische Technische Hochschule Zürich
Swiss Federal Institute of Technology Zurich

A dissertation submitted to
ETH Zurich
for the degree of Doctor of Sciences

Diss. ETH № 18820

Prof. Dr. Eckart Zitzler, examiner
Prof. Dr. Günter Rudolph, co-examiner
Examination date: December 18, 2009

The front cover shows a Pareto front (grass-covered surface) with 14 solutions (partially covered gray balls). For one solution, its hypervolume contribution (as introduced in Definition 3.25 on page 92) is displayed as a copper plated shape; for the remaining solutions the influence on the hypervolume contribution is depicted by metal bars.

This book was prepared and designed by the author with the XeLaTeX typesetting system. The body type is Latin Modern Roman, the math font is Computer Modern, and the sans serif font is PF Centro Sans Pro. All illustrations have been created with Adobe®Illustrator®, and Matlab®. The cover has been created by the author with 3d Studio Max®2009, V-Ray®, and Adobe®Photoshop®.

To Corinne

Contents

Abstract

Most problems encountered in practice involve the optimization of multiple criteria. Usually, some of them are conflicting such that no single solution is simultaneously optimal with respect to all criteria, but instead many incomparable compromise solutions exist. At the same time, the search space of such problems is often very large and complex, so that traditional optimization techniques are not applicable or cannot solve the problem within reasonable time.

In recent years, evidence has accumulated showing that Evolutionary Algorithms (EAs) are effective means of finding good approximate solutions to such problems. Apart from being applicable to complex problems, EAs offer the additional advantage of finding multiple compromise solutions in a single run. One of the crucial parts of EAs consists of repeatedly selecting suitable solutions. The aim thereby is to improve the current set of solutions by cleverly replacing old solutions by newly generated ones. In this process, the two key issues are as follows: first, a solution that is better than another solution in all objectives should be preferred over the latter. Second, the diversity of solutions should be supported, whereby often user preference dictates what constitutes a good diversity.

The hypervolume offers one possibility to achieve the two aspects; for this reason, it has been gaining increasing importance in recent years as selection criterion in EAs. The present thesis investigates three central topics of the hypervolume that are still unsolved:

- Although more and more EAs use the hypervolume as selection criterion, the resulting distribution of points favored by the hypervolume has scarcely been investigated so far. Many studies only speculate about this question, and in parts contradict one another.
- The computational load of the hypervolume calculation sharply increases the more criteria are considered. This hindered so far the application of the hypervolume to problems with more than about five criteria.
- Often a crucial aspect is to maximize the robustness of solutions, which is characterized by how far the properties of a solution can degenerate when

implemented in practice—for instance when manufacturing imprecisions do not allow to build perfectly the solution. So far, no attempt has been made to consider robustness of solutions within hypervolume-based search.

First, the present thesis examines how hypervolume-based search can be formalized, by proposing a new perspective on EAs which emphasizes the importance of sets rather than single solutions. Different factors are stated that need to be considered when selecting and comparing sets of solutions. In this context, a new algorithm based on this formalism is proposed. A visual comparison illustrates the different outcomes with respect to the underlying set selection method; these differences are confirmed by a new statistical procedure.

This observation leads to a rigorous mathematical investigation of the set of solutions, obtained when optimizing according to the hypervolume. A concise description of the distribution of solutions in terms of a density function not only allows to predict the outcome of hypervolume-based methods, but also enables to implement precisely user preference within the hypervolume itself.

While the foundation to articulate user preference by means of hypervolume had already be laid by previous works, no study so far considered the integration of robustness issues in hypervolume-based search. The present thesis closes this gap by extending the definition of the hypervolume to also enabling the consideration of robustness properties.

Finally, to make the hypervolume applicable to problems with many criteria a new algorithm is proposed based on a fast approximation of the hypervolume values. Thereby, importance is attached to maintain the possibility for user preference articulation, as well as the consideration or robustness issues.

Zusammenfassung

In der Praxis auftretende Optimierungsprobleme beinhalten oft mehrere
Kriterien, die berücksichtigt werden müssen. Diese Kriterien stehen dabei
meist in Konflikt zueinander, so dass bei deren gleichzeitigen Betrachtung
keine einzelne optimale Lösung resultiert, sondern mehrere Kompromisslösungen. Gleichzeitig ist der Suchraum der Probleme häufig so gross und
komplex, dass deterministische Algorithmen das Problem nicht mehr in ver-
tretbarer Zeit lösen können.

Evolutionäre Algorithmen (EAs) sind, wie sich gezeigt hat, eine leistungs-
starke Technik zur approximativen Lösung solcher Probleme. Nebst dem
Vorteil, dass EAs auch auf komplexe Probleme angewandt werden können
wo klassische Verfahren versagen, liegt ein Vorteil darin, dass sie mehrere
verschiedene Kompromisslösungen in einem Optimierungslauf finden. Eine
der Hauptpunkte eines EAs liegt dabei in der wiederholten Auswahl geeig-
neter Lösungen, d.h. die Entscheidung, welche von neu generierten Lösungen am meisten zur Verbesserung der momentanen Auswahl an Lösungen
beitragen. Dabei gilt es zwei Ziele zu berücksichtigen: Einerseits soll eine Lösung, die in allen Kriterien besser ist als eine andere Lösung, dieser
vorgezogen werden. Andererseits soll die Diversität an Lösungen möglichst
gewahrt werden, wobei häufig Anwenderpräferenzen einzubeziehen sind.

Das Hypervolumen bietet eine Möglichkeit, die zwei Kriterien zu berücksichtigen, weshalb es in den letzten Jahren vermehrt als Auswahlkriterium in
EAs eingesetzt wird. Die vorliegende Arbeit untersucht drei zentrale, noch
weitestgehend ungelöste Aspekte der Hypervolumen-basierten Suche:

- Obwohl das Hypervolumen als Selektionskriterium immer mehr an Be-
  deutung gewinnt, wurde bisher noch kaum theoretisch untersucht, welche
  Verteilung an Lösungen das Hypervolumen bevorzugt. Zu dieser Frage
  existieren bisher nur, sich zu teil widersprechende, Vermutungen.
- Der Berechnungsaufwand des Hypervolumens steigt sehr stark an, je
  mehr Kriterien betrachtet werden. Dies verhinderte bisher seinen Einsatz
  auf Problemen mit mehr als ungefähr fünf Kriterien.

- Oft ist die Robustheit einer Lösungen entscheidend; das heisst, wie stark sich die Eigenschaften der Lösung in der Praxis verschlechtern können, zum Beispiel wenn sie nicht präzise hergestellt werden kann. Bisher wurde die Berücksichtigung von Robustheit innerhalb der Hypervolumen-basierten Suche nicht angegangen.

Zunächst untersucht die vorliegende Arbeit, wie sich die Hypervolumen-basierte Suche formalisieren lässt. Dabei wird eine neue Sicht auf EAs gegeben, bei der nicht einzelne Lösungen, sondern die Menge derer im Vordergrund steht. Es werden Kriterien aufgestellt, die bei der Auswahl und beim Vergleich von Mengen zu berücksichtigen sind. In diesem Kontext wird ein Algorithmus vorgestellt, der gemäss dieser Vergleichsfunktionen optimiert. Wie ein visueller Vergleich zeigt, sind die erhaltenen Mengen an Kompromisslösungen abhängig von der zugrundeliegenden Bewertungsfunktion stark unterschiedlich, dies wird durch eine neue statistische Vergleichsmethodik bestätigt.

Diese Beobachtung führt anschliessend zu einer rigorosen Untersuchung der Menge, welche die beste Bewertung bezüglich des Hypervolumen erhält. Die genaue Beschreibung dieser Menge als Dichtefunktion erlaubt es dabei nicht nur, das Resultat von Hypervolumen-basierten Verfahren vorauszusagen, sondern hilft auch, beliebige Präferenzen des Entscheidungsträgers im Hypervolumen umzusetzen.

Während die Artikulation von Anwenderpräferenzen mittels Hypervolumen ein bekanntes Verfahren darstellt, wurde bisher die Berücksichtigung von Robustheit in der Hypervolumen-basierten Suche nicht angegangen. Die vorliegende Arbeit schliesst diese Lücke und erweitert die Definition des Hypervolumens dahingehend, dass auch Robustheitseigenschaften von Lösungen einfliessen können.

Um schliesslich den Indikator auch für Probleme mit vielen Kriterien anwendbar zu machen, wird ein neuer Algorithmus vorgestellt, welcher auf einer schnellen Approximation der Hypervolumenwerte basiert. Dabei kann der Algorithmus gleichfalls für Präferenzartikulation als auch die Berücksichtigung von Robustheit verwendet werden.

Statement of Contributions

Much of the content of the present thesis has already been published in journal articles and conference proceedings, or is accepted or submitted for publication respectively. Nonetheless, some experiments, results, and proofs have been created exclusively to complement this thesis. Additionally, the content has been completely revised and partly rewritten. Except for the results stemming from [10], the realization and evaluation of experiments were done by myself, as well as the majority of implementation work; also all illustrations (far over one hundred) are created entirely by myself, and have been redrawn to match the general style and notation of this thesis.

For writing the original papers, I benefited from strong support by various co-authors though. Except for the publications [142–144] constituting most of Chapter 2, my contribution to the writing of the paper was at least $1/n$, n denoting the number of authors.

In detail, the publications behind the individual chapters of this thesis are as follows:

Chapter 1 Almost the entire chapter is written from scratch for this thesis, some paragraphs originate from [7].

Chapter 2 The majority of this chapter is based on the work published in [142–144]. The remainder of the chapter is using material from [10].

Chapter 3 This chapter is based on [4] and [6], as well as on another article which is currently under review by a journal[1].

Chapter 4 The preliminary discussion in this chapter stem from [11], while the body is using results from [7–9].

Chapter 5 The conference proceeding [5] provided the basis for this chapter.

Chapter 6 The entire content of this chapter has been created by myself. Parts of this chapter are submitted for publication[1].

Johannes M. Bader

---

[1] as of February 2010

Acknowledgments

First of all, I would like to thank my advisor Eckart Zitzler for his constant support and encouragement; and whose expertise added considerably to my graduate experience. I also thank Günter Rudolph for agreeing to read and judge my thesis, for his comments on the manuscript and for coming to Zurich for the exam; moreover, I gratefully thank all my co-authors for fruitful and inspiring collaborations, and for contributing to this thesis. They are: Anne Auger, Dimo Brockhoff, Kalyanmoy Deb, Lothar Thiele, Samuel Welten, and Eckart Zitzler.

Moreover, I would like to thank all my colleagues at the Computer Engineering Laboratory, most notably the current and former members of the Systems Optimization Group (SOP) Dimo Brockhoff, Tim Hohm, Tamara Ulrich, and Stefan Bleuler, whom I would like to thank in particular for introducing me to SOP by supervising my semester project.

Special thanks goes to my family, Brigitte, Raphaël, Samuel and Annatina for their sincere support, and to all my friends including Patrick Bönzli, Benjamin Gertsch, Simon Hofmann, Christoph Keller, Thomas Rawyler, Andreas Stoll, Anna Stoll, Therese Stoll, Roland Studer, Philip Sturzenegger, and others.

A very special appreciation is due to my girlfriend, Corinne, for her love, encouragement and support through my PhD.

Finally, I would like to thank the Swiss National Science Foundation (SNF) for supporting my research in parts under grant IT14.

List of Symbols and Abbreviations

The following notation and abbreviations are used in this thesis:

Set-based Multiobjective Optimization

🖥, ▢, ...	Devices used in Section 1, see Table 1.1, page 4
g	Current generation of an evolutionary algorithm, page 10
g_{max}	Maximum number of generations of an evolutionary algorithm, page 10
G	Number of generations per mutation step in SPAM$^+$, page 66
X	Decision space, page 25
x	Solution, i.e., element of the decision space X, page 25
n	Number of decision variables, i.e., $x = (x_1, \ldots, x_n)$, page 25
f	Vector objective function, $f : X \to Z$, $x \mapsto f(x)$, page 25
f_i	Individual objectives, where $f = (f_1, \ldots, f_d)$, page 25
Z	Objective space, page 25
d	Number of objectives, page 25
z	Objective vector, i.e., $z = f(x)$, $z \in Z$, page 25
$\preceq$	Any preference relation on solutions, page 26
$\prec$	Strict preference on solutions, $a \prec b \equiv a \preceq b \wedge b \npreceq a$, page 27
$\equiv$	Indifference on solutions, $a \preceq b \wedge b \preceq a$, page 27
$\parallel$	Incomparability on solutions, $a \npreceq b \wedge b \npreceq a$, page 27
$\leqslant$	Any preference on objective values, page 26
$\mathrm{Min}(X, \preceq)$	Optimal solutions with respect to $\preceq$, page 27
$\mathcal{P}(X)$	Power set of X, page 29
Ψ	Set of all admissible solutions sets $A \subseteq X$, i.e., $\Psi = \mathcal{P}(X)$, page 29
$A, B, C, ...$	Sets of solutions, i.e., elements of Ψ, page 32
$\preccurlyeq$	Any preference relation on solution sets, page 29
$\prec$	Strict preference on solution sets, $A \preccurlyeq B \wedge B \npreccurlyeq A$, page 29
$\equiv$	Indifference on solution sets, $A \preccurlyeq B \wedge B \preccurlyeq A$, page 29
$\parallel$	Incomparability on solution sets, $A \npreccurlyeq B \wedge B \npreccurlyeq A$, page 29
$\mathrm{Min}(\Psi, \preccurlyeq)$	Optimal solution sets with respect to $\preccurlyeq$, page 29

$\leqq$	A preorder (reflexive and transitive), page 26
$\preceq_{\text{par}}$	Weak Pareto dominance on solutions, page 26
$\leqq_{\text{par}}$	Weak Pareto dominance on objective values, page 26
$\preccurlyeq_{\text{par}}$	Weak Pareto dominance on sets of solutions, page 29
$\preceq_{\downarrow i}$	Weak dominance in all but the ith objective, $x \preceq_{\downarrow i} y :\Leftrightarrow \forall 1 \le j \le d, j \ne i : f_j(x) \le f_j(y)$, page 119
$\preccurlyeq^{\text{mp}}$	Constructed set preference relation that combines $\preccurlyeq$ with minimum elements partitioning, page 29
S	Sequence of preference relations, $S = (\preccurlyeq^1, \preccurlyeq^2, \ldots, \preccurlyeq^k)$, page 33

Hypervolume Indicator and Sampling

$I_H(A, R)$	Original, unweighted hypervolume, page 39
λ	Lebesgue measure, page 39
R	Reference set of the hypervolume indicator, page 38
r	Reference point $r = (r_1, \ldots, r_d)$ of the hypervolume indicator, i.e., using $R = \{r\}$, page 38
$I_H^w(A, R)$	Weighted hypervolume indicator, page 39
λ_w	Weighted Lebesgue measure, page 39
w	Weight function, page 39
$C_A(x)$	Hypervolume contribution of x with respect to set A, page 92
S_x	Sampling space containing $C_A(x)$, page 118
m	Number of samples, page 137
m_i	Number of samples used to estimate $C_A(x_i)$, page 118
H_i	Number of hits in $C_A(x_i)$, page 118
$P(A_i)$	Performance score of an algorithm, page 227

Theory of the Weighted Hypervolume Indicator

μ	Number of solutions in a optimal μ-distribution, page 73
g	Biobjective Pareto front description, $f_2(x) = g(f_1(x))$, page 75
D	Domain of the front describing function g, where $D = [u_{min}, u_{max}]$, page 75
u_i	First coordinate of an objective vector of an optimal μ-distribution, page 76
u_{min}, u_{max}	Minimum and maximum value of f_1 and f_2 respectively, page 75
$I_{H,\mu}^{w*}$	Maximum hypervolume value for a given μ, weight, and Pareto front, page 77

υ_i^μ	u-coordinates of an optimal μ-distribution (letter upsilon), page 77
$\delta(u)$	Density of points on u-axis, page 84
$\delta_F(u)$	Density of points on the front, page 86
E_μ	Area dominated by the Pareto front but not the actual points multiplied by μ, page 84
e^*	Normal vector $e^* = (e_1^*, \ldots, e_d^*)$ at point z^* on the front, page 90
$\mathcal{R}$	Lower bound for the reference point to obtain the extremes, $\mathcal{R} = (\mathcal{R}_1, \mathcal{R}_2)$, page 98
$\mathcal{R}^{\text{Nadir}}$	Nadir point of the Pareto-front, i.e., $\mathcal{R}^{\text{Nadir}} = (u_{min}, g(u_{max}))$, page 107

Robustness

β	Front shape parameter of the BZ test problems., page 272
X^p	Random decision variable $X^p \in X$ describing uncertainty, page 175
$f^w(X^p)$	Objective-wise worst case of the objective values of X^p, page 176
η	Robustness constraint, page 181
$I_H^{\varphi,w}(\text{A,R})$	Robustness integrating hypervolume indicator, page 184
α_A^φ	Robustness integrating attainment function, page 183
$\varphi(r(x))$	Desirability function of the robustness $r(x)$, page 183
$\varphi_\theta(r(x), \eta)$	Constraint based desirability function of robustness, page 186
β	Number of solutions in the reserve, page 192
γ	Cooling rate of simulated annealing approaches, page 191
C	Set of robustness classes (η_i, s_i), given by constraint η_i, and size s_i., page 193
$T\ (T_0)$	(Initial) temperature of the simulated annealing approach, page 191

BZ Bader-Zitzler test problems
EA Evolutionary Algorithm
EMO Evolutionary Multiobjective Optimization
ESP Evolution Strategy with Probabilistic mutation
DTLZ Deb-Thiele-Laumanns-Zitzler test problems
HI Hypervolume Indicator
HSSP Hypervolume Subset Selection Problem
HypE Hypervolume Estimation Algorithm for Multiobjective Optimization
IBEA Indicator-Based Evolutionary Algorithm
MO-CMA-ES Multiobjective Covariance Matrix Adaptation Evolution Strategy
MOEA Multiobjective Evolutionary Algorithm
mp Minimal elements Partitioning

NSGA-II Nondominated Sorting Genetic Algorithm II

PC Personal Computer

PDA Personal Digital Assistant

RHV Regular Hypervolume-based Algorithm

rp Rank Partitioning

SBX Simulated Binary Crossover

SHV Sampling-based Hypervolume-oriented Algorithm

SMS-MOEA s-Metric Selection Multiobjective Evolutionary Algorithm

SPAM Set Preference Algorithm for Multiobjective Optimization

SPAM$^+$ Set Preference Algorithm for Multiobjective Optimization using Populations of Sets

SPEA2 modified Strength Pareto Evolutionary Algorithm

WFG Walking Fish Group test problems

ZDT Zitzler-Deb-Thiele test problems

1

Introduction

Most optimization problems encountered in practice involve multiple criteria that need to be considered. These so-called *objectives* are thereby mostly conflicting. The decision on a laptop purchase, for instance, amongst other things, maybe influenced by battery life, performance, portability, and the price. No single solution is usually simultaneously optimal with respect to all these objectives, but rather many different designs exist which are incomparable per se.

Such problems often occur in practice when dealing with the analysis and optimization of problems. The number of potential solutions, constituting the so-called *search space*, is thereby often very large, such that computer-based algorithms are the method of choice. Mimicking the principles of biological evolution, *Evolutionary Algorithms (EAs)* are one of those methods that have been successfully applied to different types of problems. A concept that has becoming increasingly popular in recent years within EAs is the *hypervolume indicator*, the preeminent theme of this thesis.

In the following, an informal introduction to the hypervolume indicator is given. The chapter is intended to provide a basic understanding of the indicator, its properties, and the research questions this thesis approaches. Mathematical notations are thereby consciously avoided; the reader is referred to Chapter 2 for a formal presentation of the hypervolume indicator.

This chapter is organized as follows. First, an introductory example is given by means of a decision making problem concerning the task of selecting the best among multiple solutions. This example introduces multiobjective optimization, and serves to illustrate the concept of hypervolume, its properties, and advantages. Thereafter, a brief introduction to Multiobjective Evolutionary Algorithms (MOEAs) is given, and an overview of hypervolume-based research is presented. Finally, the main open research questions tackled in the present thesis are stated, and an outline of the key aspects and contributions is provided.

1.1 · Introductory Example

Almost every day we are confronted with decision making problems, where one has to select the best among several alternatives. As an introductory example, consider the task of selecting a device to write text, either electronically or mechanically. Table 1.1 on page 4 lists eight devices the decision maker can choose from, along with the pictograms used in this chapter to refer to the devices. The following considerations do not tackle the task of finding or generating the solutions, but rather it is assumed that the search space consists of only the eight solutions listed in Table 1.1. The example first illustrates multiobjective problems, and their differences to single-objective ones. Next, the task of selecting the best solution(s) is approached, and in this context the hypervolume indicator is introduced.

1.1.1 · Multiobjective Problems

First, assume that the only criterion is to select the most portable solution, determined by the reciprocal value of the weight, in other words, lighter devices are preferred. As long as this is the only criterion, it is always clear which one of two gadgets is preferred, namely the lighter, more portable one.

The laptop 💻 for example is preferred over the modern Personal Computer (PC) 🖥, expressed by the notation 💻≻🖥. The smartphone and the Personal Digital Assistant (PDA) with small keyboard, on the other hand, are equivalent, denoted by 📱∼⌨, since both weigh the same hence are considered equally portable. Altogether, the order of preference for the eight solutions is: ⌨≻⌨≻(📱∼⌨) ≻💻≻🖳≻🖨≻🖥. This ranking represents a clear and total preference of the user, who in the end is usually interested only in the best device ⌨—if multiple gadgets share the same best value, any of them can be chosen arbitrarily.

As the example already indicates, mostly more than one criterion is relevant in practice. The writing comfort, for instance, is also an important characteristic of the devices. Ideally, this additional objective would correlate with the first one; in reality, however, the different objectives conflict with each other for the most part. On a stationary desktop PC, for instance, it is much easier to write text than on the small keyboard of the portable organizer. Table 1.1 on the next page lists for each device a subjective number between 1 and 10 defining the writing comfort, larger values meaning more comfortable to use. In Figure 1.1, the two objective values of the eight devices are depicted, where the inverse of the weight representing the mobility is shown as abscissa, and the writing comfort is shown as ordinate. In contrast to the single-objective scenario, two devices no longer need to be comparable in the sense that the better device can be unambiguously identified. The aforementioned PC for example is incomparable to the organizer, denoted by two parallel lines 🖥∥⌨, as the former offers more writing comfort but at the same time is less mobile. The new objective can also make indifferent alternatives comparable: while ⌨ and 📱 are indifferent with respect to weight only, the writing comfort leads to ⌨≻📱. Only if a device is *at the same time* more mobile and more convenient to use than another device, it is considered better; this is the case for instance for the laptop and the typewriter 💻≻🖨. Whenever a solution x is better than another solution y in this manner, we also say x *Pareto dominates* y. In Figure 1.1, all devices lying left and below of another device are dominated by that respective device. In detail, 🖨 is dominated to 🖳, both 🖨 and 🖳 are inferior to 💻, and 📱 is dominated to both ⌨ and ⌨. The gray shaded area in Figure 1.1 illustrates the so-called

Table 1.1 Eight devices to write text. The weight gives the mobility of an item, lighter devices being more portable. The second property is writing comfort, represented by a rating between 1 and 10, larger values meaning greater comfort. The latter depends on the keyboard size, and to a lesser extend the performance of the device.

icon	device	weight (kg)	comfort rating
🖳	PC of 2009	20.00	10
🖳	PC of 1984	7.50	7
💻	Laptop	3.00	9
📟	Typewriter	9.00	5
📱	Touchscreen Smartphone	0.11	2
🖥	PDA with large keyboard	0.09	3
🖥	PDA with small keyboard	0.11	4
🖥	Organizer with tiny keyboard	0.08	1

dominated area, any device with objectives in this region is inferior to at least one other device. On the other·hand, for the devices 🖳, 💻, 🖥, 🖥, and 🖥 no device exists which is better in terms of both mobility and weight. For example, 💻 is more comfortable to use than 📱, 🖥, 🖥, 🖥, and is more portable than the remaining devices 📟, 🖳, and 🖳. These *undominated* solutions are called *Pareto optimal*, and the set of all undominated solutions is denoted as *Pareto-optimal set* or *Pareto set* for short.

1.1.2 · Selecting the Best Solutions

While according to weight only a single solution is optimal, this is no longer the case when writing comfort is also considered—as known from everyday life, a solution can only in rare cases meet all demands optimally. Assume for instance the decision maker is a TV advert director, that wants to edit movie clips at home, and take notes while traveling to work by public transportation. To cover all these situations, having different demands on portability and performance, the decision maker would have to buy multiple solutions. For instance, she might consider the 🖳 to edit footage at home, and the 💻 and 🖥 as devices on-the-go. Usually, the number of solutions one can consider is limited. As will be shown later on, in the process of searching solutions by computer-based methods this restriction is often due to computational limitations. In our example, let financial resources allow for three devices to be bought, such that the task is: select three devices,

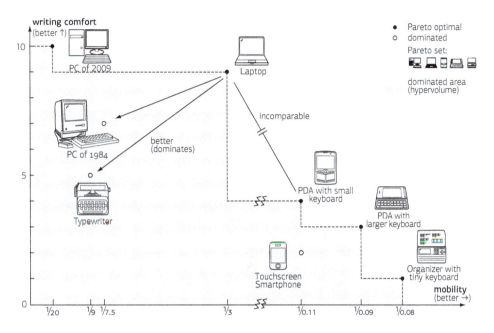

Figure 1.1 Depicts the two objective values for each device in Table 1.1. The laptop *(Pareto-)dominates* the PC from 1984, both dominating the typewriter. The touchscreen smartphone is dominated by both PDAs. The remaining five devices (solid dots) are not dominated, and therefore constitute the *Pareto-optimal set.* The gray shaded area represents the dominated area or *hypervolume,* any device with objective values in this region is dominated by at least one Pareto-optimal device.

such that in as many situations as possible a solution can be accessed providing a good compromise between performance and mobility. Given this setting, we can identify two major differences to the single-objective case:

1. With respect to one objective, the single solution ▭ is optimal, while for multiobjective problems one obtains a *set* of optimal solutions: ▭, ▭, ▭, ▭, ▭.

2. In the single-objective case, one solution ▭ is selected at the end. Considering multiple objectives, on the other hand, an additional decision has to be made which *subset of solutions* to choose. While this again can be just a single solution, the decision might also be to select multiple solutions (three in the example) to cover different situations.

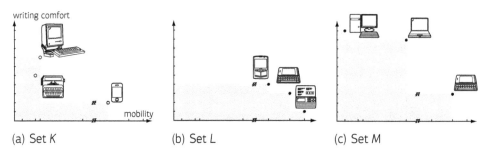

(a) Set *K*   (b) Set *L*   (c) Set *M*

Figure 1.2 Three different sets of 3 devices each. The first selection *K* is dominated by set *M* as both ⌨ and 🖥 are dominated by 💻, while 📱 is dominated by 🖥. The second set *L* is incomparable to set *M*, however, the diversity of solutions in *M* is larger than in set *L*.

A general agreement is often to neglect dominated alternatives when choosing a single solution, as at least one Pareto-optimal solution exists that can completely substitute for these device. The 💻 for instance is better than the 🖥 in terms of both mobility and performance, such that there is no reasoning (on the basis of the two objectives) to prefer the 🖥 over the 💻.

These considerations on solutions also apply to sets of solutions: the set *K* shown in Figure 1.2(a) for instance is inferior to set *M* in Figure 1.2(c), as for the devices ⌨ and 🖥 the laptop provides a better alternative in terms of both weight and comfort, and instead of 📱 one better choses 🖥. Hence, *for all situations* the best choice in set *K* is excelled by at least one solution in set *M*. This concept represents the natural extension of Pareto dominance on solutions to sets of solutions: whenever for a set *A* every element is dominated by at least one element of a second set *B*, we say *B* dominates *A* and write $B \succ A$. Again, a common agreement is to not select sets like *K* which are (Pareto-)dominated by another set.

Next, consider the selection 🖥 💻, 💻 shown in Figure 1.2(b), this set is incomparable to both sets *K* and *M*, as any set contains at least one device not dominated by the other set[1]. So how to decide between sets *K* and *M*, where Pareto dominance does not state which one is better? In this setting,

---

[1] For example, ⌨ from *K* is not dominated by set *L*, in the latter set 💻 is not dominated by any device from *K*. On the other hand, 💻 from *M* is not dominated by *L*, while 🖥 from *L* is not dominated by a device from *M*.

the preference of the decision maker is usually employed. For instance, the user might be only interested in portable solutions, then she is better of with set L. In our example, however, a large diversity of solutions is desired, to meet the demand of stationary high performance computing, and the mobility requirements when working on the way. Hence, in our setting it makes more sense to buy the greater variety of solutions constituting set M. This second criterion of choosing solutions, the *user preference*, is often much harder to formalize than Pareto dominance.

1.1.3 · The Hypervolume Indicator

In the present example, the decision maker can consider all potential sets of solutions and decide herself, which set is the best. However, as already mentioned, in reality the number of potential solutions is often very large, such that a human would be overstrained selecting solutions, or at the very least would need to dedicate to much time to this task. Furthermore, when it comes to optimization of solutions (see Section 1.2), selection decisions often have to be made repeatedly for a period of time ranging up to hours or even days. Hence, the question arises how preference as illustrated in the previous section could be formalized.

One approach is to use so-called *quality indicator functions*. These assign a value to each set representing the worthiness of the set for the decision maker. Comparing two sets then boils down to relate the indicator values—whichever set reaches a larger indicator value is preferred. The main challenge with regards to constructing quality indicator functions is to make them incorporate the two criteria stated in Section 1.1.2: first and foremost, the indicator should reflect the dominance relation between sets, so whenever a set A dominates a second set B, then the indicator value of the former is larger than of the second. Second, for two incomparable sets the indicator should prefer the set according to the user's preference, e.g., favor the more diverse set.

One quality indicator that has been gaining a lot of interest in recent years is the *hypervolume indicator*. It measures the area dominated by the Pareto-optimal solutions; for example, in Figures 1.1 and 1.2, the hypervolume corresponds to the gray area. As desired, the hypervolume of set M in Figure 1.2 on page 6 is larger than the one of K. This holds in general, i.e., the hypervolume reflects the dominance of sets. Although determining the dominance relation between sets is straightforward, constructing indicator function reflecting the dominance is not. In fact, the hypervolume indicator is the only known indicator that has this unique property. This is one of the main reasons for the popularity of the hypervolume indicator. But the hypervolume not only reflects dominance, but also promotes diverse sets. Consider for example set L, which has a smaller hypervolume than set M. The hypervolume indicator hence unifies the two criteria dominance and diversity as desired in our example. However, the hypervolume is not restricted to this type of preference. As will be shown in Chapter 5, it can also be changed to that effect, that set L (Figure 1.2(a)) is favored over set M, while still being compliant with dominance, i.e., preferring set M over K.

1.2 · Multiobjective Evolutionary Algorithms

As yet it has been established how one type of preference on sets can be expressed by using the hypervolume indicator, where the indicator has been applied to a decision making example to illustrate the concept. However, significant differences exist between the problems considered in this thesis, and the previous example: first off, the solutions the decision maker can choose from are not given in advance, but rather need to be generated first. Thereby, a vast number of potential solutions might be Pareto optimal, such that even the fastest computer systems usually can not check all solutions to determine the Pareto-optimal ones. Additionally, since the *objective functions*, i.e., the function assigning the objective values (portability and performance in the example) is usually very complex or not known, classical optimization approaches fail to determine the optimal solutions, or take too much time.

Multiobjective Evolutionary Algorithms (MOEAs) are one class of search method that can be applied to these types of problems. In the last decades

Figure 1.3 Evolutionary algorithm cycle illustrated by the example of computer devices. First, two solutions are randomly generated. By exchanging the display, the crossover operator then generates two new devices. These new solutions are then changed slightly in the process of mutation. Finally, environmental selection choses the best two solutions among the original two solutions, and the offspring generated by crossover and mutation. This process then starts over with step 2 and continues until the set of devices is satisfactory.

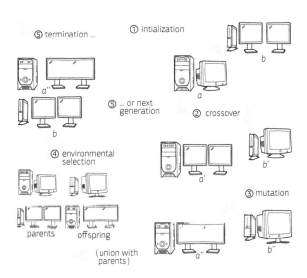

they have been shown to be well-suited for those problems in practice [37, 44]. By mimicking processes found in biological evolution, they *approximate* the Pareto-optimal set. Hence, instead of guaranteeing to find the Pareto-optimal solutions, they aim finding solutions that come as close as possible to the optimal solutions. An actual example of an MOEA is presented in Appendix E.1 on page 264. Here, again the example of electronic devices to illustrate the concept of MOEAs. Assume that each device consists of a display and a computing part.

The first step of the MOEA is to randomly generate an initial set of solutions, e.g., by assembling electronic parts given in advance. Of course, the algorithm needs rules to assure functional designs are generated. Such rules could for example state that every device needs a case, a processor, a main board, memory, etc. By analogy with natural evolution, the solutions are called *individuals* and the set of all devices is called *population*. The individuals are then modified by means of two mechanisms inspired by real evolution: *crossover* and *mutation*. The crossing over first selects two solutions from the population that represent the parents. By exchanging parts of the parents, two offspring solutions are generated. In our example, the display of the parents is swapped. Mutation, on the other hand, operates on single offspring solutions by making random modifications to change the solutions. All offspring, together with the original parent population, are then rated for fitness, i.e., the mobility and writing comfort are determined. Based on the objective values, the best devices among the parent and offspring individuals are selected by so-called *environmental selection*. The resulting individuals form the new population, which again undergoes crossover, mutation, and environmental selection. This concludes one generation of the MOEA. The process continues until the set of devices satisfies the user's need or until the maximum number of generations g_{max} is reached, see Figure 1.3 on the previous page.

Besides not needing any knowledge about the objective functions MOEAs have the major advantage of generating multiple solutions in one run, in contrast to many other approaches, most notably algorithms that aggregate the objective values into one value, such that as in the single-objective case only one solutions is optimal, see [58, 102]. This has the advantage, that the decision maker can be provided with multiple alternative he can choose from. Moreover, the decision maker does not need to give information, e.g., how to aggregate the objective functions, which requires some knowledge of the underlying problem.

The main focus in this thesis is the *environmental selection* step, i.e., the task of selecting the most promising set of solutions based on their objective values. This problem is analogous to the decision making problem stated in Section 1.1.2: given a set of solutions, a subset has to be selected that is preferred over all other feasible subsets, and which is better than the previous set. Consider for example the eight devices shown in Figure 1.4, and assume four devices need to be selected. Environmental selection then consists of comparing all $\binom{8}{4} = 70$ subsets with four devices, and choosing the one which is preferred over all others. Existing MOEAs often differ in the way, selection works. Many approaches thereby use a combination of Pareto-dominance and diversity to assess the value of an individual, for instance the Nondominated Sorting Genetic Algorithm II (NSGA-II) [50] or the modified Strength Pareto Evolutionary Algorithm (SPEA2) [139].

Figure 1.4 Hypervolume-based environmental selection, where the task is to select four out of eight devices. The set of devices is selected which reaches the largest hypervolume value (gray area) among all sets of four devices. Generally, Pareto-optimal solutions are preferred over dominated solutions by this selection procedure.

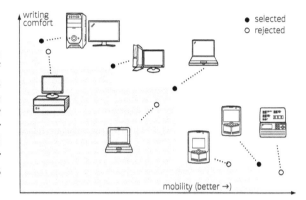

A recent trend is to use quality indicators, in particular the hypervolume indicator, to perform selection. In this context the selection process boils down to selecting the subset reaching the largest hypervolume value, see Figure 1.4.

1.3 · A Brief Review of Hypervolume-Related Research

The hypervolume indicator actually turns the multiobjective optimization problem into a single-objective one, where the only criterion is to optimize the indicator value itself. Instead of optimizing the objective functions directly, hypervolume-based algorithms therefore aim at finding a set of solutions that maximizes the underlying hypervolume value. A fundamental question is whether these two optimization goals coincide or how they differ.

The hypervolume indicator and its weighted version (see Definitions 2.20 and 2.21 on page 38) are particularly interesting, since they comply with Pareto-dominance as outlined in Section 1.1.2. Many other quality indicators do not have this property, why the hypervolume indicator is one of the most used quality indicators applied to environmental selection of MOEAs such as ESP [78], SMS-MOEA [16], MO-CMA-ES [82], and has also been suggested as optimization criterion in other methods as for instance *Simulated Annealing* [62].

The hypervolume indicator was originally proposed and employed in [136, 137] to quantitatively compare the outcomes of different MOEAs. In these two first publications, the indicator was denoted as 'size of the space covered', and later also other terms such as 'hyperarea metric' [124], 'S-metric' [133], 'hypervolume indicator' [140], and 'hypervolume measure' [16] were used. Besides the names, there are also different definitions available, based on polytopes [137], the Lebesgue measure [62, 86, 95], or the attainment function [141].

As to hypervolume calculation, the first algorithms [86, 134] operated recursively and in each recursion step the number of objectives was decremented; the underlying principle is known as 'hypervolume by slicing objectives' approach [130]. While the method used in [136, 137] was never published (only the source code is publicly available [134]), Knowles independently proposed and described a similar method in [86]. A few years later, this approach was the first time studied systematically and heuristics to accelerate the computation were proposed in [130]. All these algorithms have a worst-case runtime complexity that is exponential in the number of objectives d, more specifically $\mathcal{O}(N^{d-1})$ where N is the number of solutions considered [86, 130]. A different approach was presented by Fleischer [62] who mistakenly claimed a polynomial worst-case runtime complexity—While [128] showed that it is exponential in d as well. Recently, advanced algorithms for hypervolume calculation have been proposed, a dimension-sweep method [66] with a worst-case runtime complexity of $\mathcal{O}(N^{d-2} \log N)$, and a specialized algorithm related to the Klee measure problem [14] the runtime of which is in the worst case of order $\mathcal{O}(N \log N + N^{d/2})$. Furthermore, Yang and Ding [131] described an algorithm for which they claim a worst-case runtime complexity of $\mathcal{O}((d/2)^N)$. The fact that there is no exact polynomial algorithm available gave rise to the hypothesis that this problem in general is hard to solve, although the tightest known lower bound is of order $\Omega(N \log N)$ [15]. New results substantiate this hypothesis: Bringmann and Friedrich [28] have proven that the problem of computing the hypervolume is #P-complete, i.e., it is expected that no polynomial algorithm exists since this would imply $NP = P$.

The complexity of the hypervolume calculation in terms of programming and computation time may explain why this measure was seldom used until 2003. However, this changed with the advent of theoretical studies that provided evidence for a unique property of this indicator [62, 88, 140]: it is the only indicator known to be strictly monotonic with respect to Pareto dominance and thereby guaranteeing that the Pareto-optimal front achieves the maximum hypervolume possible, while any worse set will be assigned a worse indicator value. This property is especially desirable with many-objective problems and since classical MOEAs have been shown to have difficulties in such scenarios [126], a trend can be observed in the literature to directly use the hypervolume indicator for search.

Knowles and Corne [86, 89] were the first to propose the integration of the hypervolume indicator into the optimization process. In particular, they described a strategy to maintain a separate, bounded archive of non-dominated solutions based on the hypervolume indicator. Huband et al. [78] presented an MOEA which includes a modified SPEA2 environmental selection procedure where a hypervolume-related measure replaces the original density estimation technique. In [135], the binary hypervolume indicator was used to compare individuals and to assign corresponding fitness values within a general indicator-based evolutionary algorithm (IBEA). The first MOEA tailored specifically to the hypervolume indicator was described in [59]; it combines non-dominated sorting with the hypervolume indicator and considers one offspring per generation (steady state). Similar fitness assignment strategies were later adopted in [82, 141], and also other search algorithms were proposed where the hypervolume indicator is partially used for search guidance [103, 105]. Moreover, specific aspects like hypervolume-based environmental selection [20], cf. Section 4.2.2, and explicit gradient determination for hypervolume landscapes [60] have been investigated recently.

1.4 · Research Questions

To date, the hypervolume indicator is one of the most popular set quality measures. For instance, almost one fourth of the papers published in the proceedings of the EMO 2007 conference [106] report on the use of or are dedicated to the hypervolume indicator. However, there are still many open research questions, some of which the present thesis tackles.

1.4.1 · The Hypervolume Indicator as Set Preference Relation

As illustrated in the previous sections, the objective of hypervolume-based MOEAs is to find a set of compromise solutions, ideally a subset of the Pareto-optimal set, that maximizes the hypervolume. That means, these algorithms are focusing on *sets* rather than *single solutions*. So far, no formal description of this perspective on multiobjective problems has been given. Furthermore, while relations on solutions are well established, no general procedure to construct set preference relations, using indicator functions or by other means, exists. Given such preference relations on sets, algorithms need to be proposed to optimize according to these relations.

Secondly, using for instance the hypervolume indicator as the underlying selection criterion, the question whether the final set of solutions significantly differs from using other set preferences has to be investigated and assessed by statistical methods.

1.4.2 · Characterizing the Set Maximizing the Hypervolume

Although more and more MOEAs use the hypervolume as underlying set preference, the question, which subset of fixed size reaches the largest hypervolume value is still unsolved. Knowles and Corne [89] for instance state: *"(...) sets which are local optima of [the hypervolume] seem to be 'well distributed'. Unfortunately, at present we have found no way to quantify 'well distributedness' in this context, so this observation is not provable."* In other words, the *bias* of the hypervolume needs to be investigated.

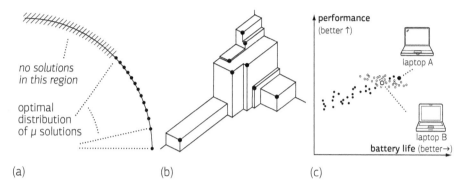

Figure 1.5 Illustration of different research questions: (a) what is the bias of the hypervolume indicator, and how can it be changed; (b) how can the hypervolume be approximated to make it applicable to problems with many objectives; (c) how can robustness issues be incorporated into hypervolume.

Interestingly, several contradicting beliefs about this bias have been reported in the literature. Zitzler and Thiele [136] for instance stated that, when optimizing the hypervolume in maximization problems, "convex regions may be preferred to concave regions", which has been also stated by Lizarraga-Lizarraga et al. [99] later on, whereas Deb et al. [53] argued that "(...) the hyper-volume measure is biased towards the boundary solutions". Beume et al. [16], claim among other things that the hypervolume focuses on knee points rather than on the extremes.

In the light of this contradicting statements, a thorough characterization of the optimal distributions for the hypervolume indicator is necessary, see Figure 1.5(a). Especially for the weighted hypervolume indicator, the bias of the indicator and the influence of the weight function in particular has not been fully understood.

1.4.3 · Considering Robustness Within Hypervolume-Based Search

So far, the hypervolume indicator has been calculated with respect to deterministic, and fixed objective values. However, the objective values of a solution when put into practice might fluctuate within certain ranges due to different perturbations. The battery life of a laptop, for example, certainly depends on different changing conditions, like the workload, or the temperature. In Figure 1.5(c), the objective values of two laptops are shown as theoretically predicted, and for different samples taken in reality.

While the foundation to articulate user preference by means of the weighted hypervolume had already been laid by previous works, no study so far considered the integration of robustness issues in hypervolume-based search. The question is, how uncertain objective values can be considered by the hypervolume indicator. Thereby, the hypervolume should be able to reproduce traditional approaches, like to consider robustness as an additional constraint [46, 47, 72, 73] or objective [32, 57, 85, 98], but also to offer new possibilities.

1.4.4 · Fast Hypervolume-Based Many-Objective Optimization

While the hypervolume indicator is easy to calculate for two objectives only, the dominated area takes more and more complex forms as the number of objectives increases. Figure 1.5(b), for instance, shows the dominated area for eight solutions with three objectives. It has been shown recently, that no algorithm exists calculating the hypervolume whose running time is polynomial with the number of objectives and number of points. In other words, calculating the hypervolume measure for many objectives is computationally highly demanding. This has so far prevented the application of existing hypervolume-based algorithms, e.g. [59, 78, 82, 90, 141], to these cases.

In order to make the hypervolume indicator applicable to problems with many objectives, a fast approximation scheme has to be derived. Thereby, the potential of incorporating user preference (by the weighted hypervolume), and considering robustness issues (by the yet to be developed generalization of the hypervolume definition) should be maintained.

1.5 · Contributions and Overview

The aforementioned four research complexes define the framework of the present thesis.

First, Chapter 2 is concerned with the concept of preference relations on sets, and formalizes them with respect to algorithm design. A general way of separating the formulation of preference and the algorithm design is proposed. This results in a high flexibility, allowing the user to focus only on the design of set preference relations, and not having to deal with the algorithm optimizing this preference. As will be demonstrated, the preference relation thereby should fulfill certain properties, where ways are shown to generate such preferences. Furthermore, a framework is proposed to use these preferences on sets for statistical performance assessment. This methodology is then applied to investigate the differences between different kinds of user preferences. Overall, the proposed methodology unifies preference articulation, algorithm design, and performance assessment, and thereby presents a new perspective on Evolutionary Multiobjective Optimization (EMO), which is used throughout this thesis[2]. Secondly, it is investigated how multiple sets can be optimized simultaneously, and whether this is advantageous over traditional approaches[3].

In Chapter 3 the focus is then on the bias of the hypervolume indicator. The chapter is primarily concerned with distributions of μ points maximizing the hypervolume. In other words, the set that is preferred over all other sets of size μ and therefore represents the optimum is characterized. The concept of density of points is thereafter introduced, that allows to assess the bias of the hypervolume indicator in a concise way. The second major contribution of Chapter 3 investigates the choice of the reference point with respect to obtaining the two extreme solutions in the optimal μ-distribution. It is shown that for some Pareto-front shapes, the extremes are never included, regardless of the choice of the reference point. For the remaining cases, a lower bound is given that guarantees to always reach the extreme solutions[4].

---

[2] These contributions are based on the papers [142–144].

[3] Loosely based on parts of Bader et al. [10].

[4] This chapter is based on [4, 6] and a paper currently (as of February 2010) under review by a journal.

Chapter 4 addresses the application of the hypervolume indicator to many objective problems. First, some preliminary consideration are presented on how to use Monte-Carlo sampling to approximate the hypervolume[5]. Second, an advanced sampling strategy called Hypervolume Estimation Algorithm for Multiobjective Optimization (HypE) is proposed. It entails an advanced fitness assignment scheme, that enhances sampling accuracy, and that can be applied to both mating and environmental selection. By adjusting the number of samples, accuracy can thereby be traded-off versus the overall computing time budget. The new algorithm HypE makes hypervolume-based search possible also for many-objective problems[6].

Next, in Chapter 5 ways to incorporate two types of user preference into hypervolume-based search are shown, using the principle of the weighted hypervolume concept by Zitzler et al. [141]. In particular, weight functions are proposed to stress extreme solutions, and to define preferred regions of the objective space in terms of so-called preference points. Both weight functions thereby allow to draw samples in a sophisticated way within HypE[7].

Finally, Chapter 6 proposes ways to consider robustness in hypervolume-based search. First, three existing approaches are translated to hypervolume, i.e., (i) modifying the objective values [21, 23, 93, 104, 107, 115, 116, 123], (ii) considering one or more additional objectives [32, 47, 57, 85, 85, 98], (iii) using at least one additional constraint [46, 47, 72, 73].

Secondly, a generalization of the hypervolume indicator is proposed that allows to realize different trade-offs between robustness and quality of solutions, including the three aforementioned approaches. To make the generalized robustness-aware indicator applicable to problems involving many objectives, HypE is extended to the new definition of the hypervolume indicator.

Altogether, Chapters 4 to 6 provide a versatile algorithm HypE, that not only allows to apply the hypervolume indicator to many objective problems,

---

[5] Building on the work in [11].

[6] The main part of Chapter 4 is based on work published in [7–9].

[7] The entire Chapter 5 is based on a conference paper [5].

but thereby also enables to incorporate different kinds of user preference, as well as to consider robustness issues.

2

Set-Based Multiobjective Optimization

Most Multiobjective Evolutionary Algorithms (MOEAs) proposed in literature are designed towards approximating the set of Parcto-optimal solutions. For instance, the first book on Evolutionary Multiobjective Optimization (EMO) by Deb [44] is mainly devoted to techniques of finding multiple trade-off solutions using evolutionary algorithms. As outlined in Chapter 1 in contrast to single-objective optimizers that look for a single optimal solution, these algorithms aim at identifying a *set* of optimal compromise solutions, i.e., they actually operate on a set problem.

This chapter introduces the set-based perspective on multiobjective optimization and the notation used throughout this thesis. In detail, first the problem of expressing and formalizing set preferences on the basis of indicators is approached, as already touched in the introductory example in Section 1.1 on page 2 and following. Then, ways to optimize according to a given relation are proposed; finally, it is demonstrated how to compare the obtained sets with respect to the underlying preference. The considerations to these questions demonstrate, why in recent year search algorithms based on indicators, in particular the hypervolume indicator, have become increasingly popular.

2.1 · Motivation

EMO in general deals with set problems: the search space Ψ consists of all potential Pareto set approximations rather than single solutions, i.e., Ψ is a set of sets. When applying an Evolutionary Algorithm (EA) to the problem of approximating the Pareto-optimal set, the population itself can be regarded as the current Pareto set approximation. The subsequent application of mating selection, variation, and environmental selection heuristically produces a new Pareto set approximation that—in the ideal case—is better than the previous one. In the light of the underlying set problem, the population represents a single element of the search space which is in each iteration replaced by another element of the search space. Consequently, selection and variation can be regarded as a mutation operator on populations resp. sets.

Somewhat simplified, one may say that a classical MOEA used to approximate the Pareto-optimal set is a $(1, 1)$-strategy on a set problem:

Definition 2.1 (($\mu \overset{+}{,} \lambda$) EA): *A $(\mu \overset{+}{,} \lambda)$-EA selects in each generation μ parent individuals, which generate λ offspring individuals by means of crossover and mutation. For the variant (μ, λ)-EA, the best μ of the λ offspring individuals are chosen as new population, hence $\lambda \geq \mu$ is required. On the other hand, for the $(\mu + \lambda)$-EA, the μ best of the $\mu + \lambda$ individuals of the union of the parent and the offspring population constitute the population of the next generation.*

Furthermore, MOEAs are usually not preference-free. The main advantage of generating methods such as MOEAs is that the objectives do not need to be aggregated or ranked a priori; but nevertheless preference information is required to guide the search, although it is usually weaker and less stringent.

In the environmental selection step, for instance, a MOEA has to choose a subset of individuals from the parents and the offspring which constitutes the next Pareto set approximation, see also Section 1.1.2. To this end, the algorithm needs to know the criteria according to which the subset should be selected, in particular when all parents and children are incomparable, i.e., mutually non-dominating. That means the generation of a new population usually relies on set preference information.

These observations led to the concept presented in this chapter which separates preference information and search method. Firstly, preference information is regarded as an appropriate order on Ψ required to fully specify the set problem—this order will here be denoted as set preference relation. A set preference relation provides the information on the basis of which the search is carried out; for any two Pareto set approximations, it says whether one set is better or not. Secondly, a general, extended $(1 + 1)$-strategy SPAM is proposed for this set problem which is only based on pairwise comparisons of sets in order to guide the search. The approach is then extended to a general $(\mu + \lambda)$ strategy SPAM$^+$ using a population of solutions sets in combination with appropriate set selection and set variation operators. Both algorithms are fully independent of the set preference relation used and thus decoupled from the user preferences.

This complete separation of concerns is the novelty of the suggested approach. It builds upon the idea presented in Zitzler and Künzli [135], but is more general as it is not restricted to a single binary quality indicator and possess in addition desirable convergence properties. Furthermore, there are various studies that focus on the issue of preference articulation in EMO, in particular integrating additional preferences such as priorities, goals, and reference points [22, 24, 41, 49, 64, 101, 111]. However, these studies mainly cover preferences on solutions and not preferences on sets, and the search procedures used are based on hard-coded preferences. Moreover, in recent years a trend can be observed to directly use specific measures such as the hypervolume indicator and the epsilon indicator in the search process [7, 53, 59, 62, 78, 82, 89, 96, 135]. Nevertheless, a *general* methodology to formalize set preferences and to use them for optimization is missing.

In the light of this discussion, three core research issues can be identified: (i) how to formalize the optimization goal in the sense of specifying what type of set is sought, (ii) how to effectively search for a suitable set to achieve the formalized optimization goal, and (iii) how to evaluate the outcomes of multiobjective optimizers with respect to the underlying set problem.

This chapter represents one step towards such an overarching methodology. It proposes

1. a theory of set preference relations that clarifies how user preferences on Pareto set approximations can be formalized on the basis of quality indicators and what criteria such formalizations must fulfill; introduces
2. a general set-preference based hillclimber that can be flexibly adapted to arbitrary types of set preference relations; proposes
3. an extension of the hillclimber to using multiple sets, i.e., an extension to a general $(\mu \mathbin{+\mkern-8mu+} \lambda)$ EA optimizing sets; and discusses
4. an approach to statistically compare the outcomes of multiple search algorithms with respect to a specific set preference relation.

The novelty of this approach is that it brings all aspects of preference articulation, multiobjective search, and performance assessment under one roof, while achieving a clear separation of concerns. This offers several benefits: (i) it provides flexibility to the decision maker as he can change his preferences without the need to modify the search algorithm, (ii) the search can be better guided which is particularly important in the context of high-dimensional objective spaces, (iii) algorithms designed to meet specific preferences can be compared on a fair basis since the optimization goal can be explicitly formulated in terms of the underlying set preference relation.

In the following, first the formal basis of set preference relations is provided, and fundamental concepts are introduced. Afterwards, set preference relations are discussed, and how to design them using quality indicators also giving some example relations. A general, set preference based multiobjective search algorithm will be proposed in Section 2.4.1, and an extension of the algorithm in Section 2.4.2. Finally, Section 2.5 presents a methodology to compare algorithms with respect to a given set preference relation and provides experimental results for selected preferences.

2.2 · A New Perspective: Set Preference Relations

As described in the motivation, multiobjective optimization will be viewed as a preference-based optimization on sets. The purpose of this section is to formally define the notation of optimization and optimality in this context, and to provide the necessary foundations for the practical algorithms described in the forthcoming sections. The *List of Symbols and Abbreviations* on page xix serves as a reference for the nomenclature introduced in the following.

2.2.1 · Basic Terms

Throughout this thesis the optimization of d objective functions $f_i : X \to Z$, $1 \le i \le d$ is considered where all f_i are, without loss of generality, to be minimized. Here, X denotes the feasible set of solutions in the decision space, i.e. the set of alternatives of the decision problem. A single alternative $x \in X$ is denoted as a decision vector or solution. The vector function $f := (f_1, \ldots, f_d)$ maps each solution $x = (x_1, \ldots, x_n)$ in the decision space X to its corresponding objective vector $z = f(x)$ in the objective space $Z \subseteq \mathbb{R}^d$, i.e., $Z = f(X) = \{y \in \mathbb{R}^d \,|\, \exists x \in X : y = f(x)\}$. Without loss of generality, in this thesis the objectives are to be minimized. For reasons of simplicity, the decision space is assumed to be finite. Nevertheless, almost all results described in the chapter hold for infinite sets also or can be generalized. Figure 2.1 illustrates a possible scenario with 7 solutions in the decision space and a two-dimensional objective space $(d = 2)$.

In order to allow for optimization in such a situation, a preference relation $a \preceq b$ on the feasible set in the decision space is needed, which states that a solution a is at least as good as a solution b[1]. The assumption is commonly

---

[1] Note, that in contrast to Chapter 1, $a \preceq b$ means a is at least as good as b and not vice versa, as in this chapter and following *minimization* problems are considered

Figure 2.1 Optimization scenario with $X = \{f, g, i, j, k, l, m\}$ and $d = 2$. In the case that the preference relation is the weak Pareto-dominance relation $\preceq_{par}$, the shaded areas represent locations of solutions that are dominated by k (dark) and that dominate k (light). Solutions m and g constitute the Pareto set.

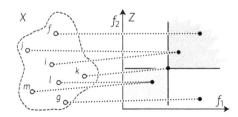

made, that preference relations are preorders, i.e., that $\preceq$ is reflexive ($a \preceq a$) and transitive $(a \preceq b \land b \preceq c) \Rightarrow (a \preceq c)$. A well known preference relation in the context of multi-objective optimization is the (weak) Pareto-dominance:

Definition 2.2 (weak Pareto dominance): *A solution $a \in X$ weakly Pareto-dominates a solution $b \in X$, denoted as $a \preceq_{par} b$, if it is at least as good in all objectives, i.e. $f(a) \leqslant_{par} f(b) \Leftrightarrow f_i(a) \leq f_i(b)$ for all $1 \leq i \leq d$.*

Note that $\preceq_{par}$ is only one example of a useful preference relation. The results described in this thesis are not restricted to the concept of Pareto-dominance but hold for any preference relation defined on the set of solutions. The situation that a solution a is at least as good as a solution b will also be denoted as a being weakly preferable to b. Moreover, the following terms will be used:

Definition 2.3 (strict Preference): *A solution a is strictly better than or preferable to a solution b—denoted as $a \prec b$—if $a \preceq b \land b \npreceq a$.*

Definition 2.4 (incomparability): *A solution a is* incomparable *to a solution b, denoted as $a \parallel b$, if $a \npreceq b \land b \npreceq a$.*

Definition 2.5 (indifference): *A solution a is equivalent or indifferent to a solution b—denoted as $a \equiv b$—if $a \preceq b \land b \preceq a$. A set of solutions is denoted as* equivalence class, *if its elements are mutually equivalent.*

Optimization may now be termed as finding a minimal element $\mathrm{Min}(X, \preceq)$ in the ordered feasible set $(X, \preceq)$:

Definition 2.6 (minimal element): *A minimal element u of an ordered set $(S, \leqq)$ with a preorder $\leqq$ satisfies: If $a \leqq u$ for some a in the set, then $u \leqq a$.*

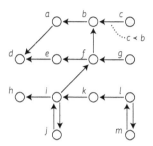

Figure 2.2 Representation of a preordered set $(X, \preceq)$ where X consists of the solutions $\{a, ..., m\}$. The optimal solutions are $\text{Min}(X, \preceq) = \{c, g, l, m\}$. $\{i, j\}$ and $\{l, m\}$ form two equivalence classes, i.e. $i \equiv j$ and $l \equiv m$. l is incomparable to m, on the other hand, c is strictly preferred over b; as $b \npreceq c$ and $c \preceq b$, one finds $c \prec b$.

In the special case of the underlying preference relation $\leqq$ being weak Pareto dominance $\preceq_{par}$, the set of minimal elements is also termed Pareto set:

Definition 2.7 (Pareto-optimal set): *The Pareto-optimal set (or Pareto set for short) of the decision space X corresponds to the set of minimal elements of $(X, \preceq_{par})$, i.e., the Pareto set consists of all elements in $u \in X$, for which no $x \in X$ exists with $x \prec_{par} u$.*

The image of the Pareto-set under the objective functions $f = (f_1, \ldots, f_d)$ is called *Pareto(-optimal) front*:

Definition 2.8 (Pareto-optimal front): *The Pareto-optimal front (or Pareto front for short) for a decision space X corresponds to the objective values of the Pareto set—which corresponds to the minimal set of $(Z, \leqq_{par})$.*

Example 2.9: Consider Figure 2.1 with Pareto dominance as preference relation. Then for solution j the following holds: $j \equiv_{par} i$ (hence also $j \preceq_{par} i$, $i \preceq_{par} j$), $j \parallel_{par} g$, $j \preceq_{par} f$, and $m \preceq_{par} j$, $l \preceq_{par} j$, $k \preceq_{par} j$. The Pareto-optimal set is $\{m, l, g\}$. ○

Preference relations can also be depicted graphically. Figure 2.2 shows a possible preordered set of solutions $X = \{a, ..., m\}$. In particular, the preferences among $\{f, g, i, k, l, m\}$ correspond directly to the scenario shown in Figure 2.1.

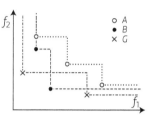

Figure 2.3 Representation of a preordered set of sets of solutions $\{A, B, G\} \in \psi$ where $\preceq_{par}$ is assumed to be the underlying solution-based preference relation. One finds $B \preccurlyeq A, G \preccurlyeq$
A and $B \parallel G$, i.e., B and G are incomparable.

2.2.2 · Approximation Of The Pareto-Optimal Set

As a preference relation $\preceq$ defined above is usually not a total order on the
feasible set[2], often many optimal solutions are obtained, i.e., many minimal
elements that reflect the different trade-offs among the objective functions.

In particular, this holds for the Pareto preference relation $\preceq_{par}$. As a result,
one may not only be interested in one of these minimal elements but in
a carefully selected subset that reflects additional preference information
of some decision maker. Traditional EMO methods attempt to solve this
problem by maintaining and improving sets of decision vectors, denoted as
populations, see upper half in Figure 2.10 on page 52. The corresponding
optimization algorithms are tuned to anticipated preferences of a decision
maker.

Thus, the underlying goal of set-based multiobjective optimization can be
described as determining a (small-sized) set of alternative solutions

1. that contains as many different decision vectors as possible that are
   minimal with respect to a preference relation *on the feasible set in the*
   decision space (for example the weak Pareto-dominance according to
   Definition 2.2), and
2. whose selection of minimal and non-minimal decision vectors reflects the
   preferences of the decision maker.

As pointed out in Section 2.1, it is the purpose of this chapter to define
set-based multiobjective optimization on the basis of these two aspects. In
contrast to previous results, the second item as defined above is made formal

---

[2]A binary relation $\leqq$ on a set S is called total, if $(a \leqq b) \vee (b \leqq a)$ holds for all $a, b \in S$.

and treated as a first class citizen in optimization theory and algorithms. This not only leads to a better understanding of classical population-based multiobjective optimization but also allows for defining set-based methods with corresponding convergence results as well as statistical tests to compare different algorithms. Finally, a new set of optimization algorithms can be obtained which can directly take preference information into account.

Therefore, the preferences of a decision maker on the subset of decision vectors needs to be formalized in an optimal set of solutions. This will be done by defining a preorder $\preccurlyeq$ on the set of all possible sets of solutions. A set of solutions P is defined as a set of decision vectors, i.e. $P \subseteq X$. A set of all admissible sets, e.g. sets of finite size, is denoted as Ψ, i.e., $P \in \Psi$.

Definition 2.10 (set-based multiobjective optimization): *Set-based multiobjective optimization is defined as finding a minimal element of the ordered set* $(\Psi, \preccurlyeq)$ *where* Ψ *is a set of admissible sets of solutions.*

The elements of a set-based multiobjective optimization problem can be summarized as follows: A set of feasible solutions X, a vector-valued objective function $f : X \to \mathbb{R}^d$, a set Ψ of all admissible sets P of decision vectors with $P \subseteq X$, and a preference relation $\preccurlyeq$ on Ψ.

In the light of the above discussion, the preference relation $\preccurlyeq$ needs to satisfy the aforementioned two conditions, whereas the first one guarantees that the objective functions are optimized actually, and the second one allows to add preferences of the decision maker. In the next section, the necessary properties of suitable preference relations are discussed, along with the concept of refinement.

2.2.3 · Preference Relations

The preference on sets $\preccurlyeq$ is constructed in two successive steps. At first, a general set-based preference relation (a set preference relation) $\preccurlyeq \subseteq \Psi \times \Psi$ will be defined that is *conforming* to a solution-based preference relation $\preceq \subseteq X \times X$. This set preference relation will then be *refined* by adding preferences of a decision maker in order to possibly obtain a total order. For a *conforming* set preference relation no solution may be excluded that could be interesting to a decision maker. In addition, if for each solution $b \in B$ there is some solution $a \in A$ which is at least as good, then A is considered at least as good as, or weakly preferable to B.

From the above considerations, the definition of a conforming set-based preference relation follows directly; it is in accordance to the formulations used in [75, 140].

Definition 2.11: *Let be given a set X and a set Ψ whose elements are subsets of X, i.e., sets of solutions. Then the preference relation $\preccurlyeq$ on Ψ conforms to $\preceq$ on X if for all $A, B \in \Psi$*

$$A \preccurlyeq B \iff (\forall b \in B : (\exists a \in A : a \preceq b))$$

As an example, Figure 2.3 shows three sets of solutions A, B and G. According to the above definition, $B \preccurlyeq_{\text{par}} A$ and $G \preccurlyeq_{\text{par}} A$. As sets B and G are incomparable, it holds $B \parallel_{\text{par}} G$.

The above preference relation is indeed suitable for optimization, as it is a preorder, see accompanying paper by the author and colleagues [144].

2.2.4 · Refinements

The set preference relation $\preccurlyeq$ according to Definition 2.11 has the disadvantage of often being sparse, i.e., for many sets A and B it is not clear, which one is preferred. This is because in order to have $A \preccurlyeq B$, *for all* elements $b \in B$ there must exist an element in A being preferred over b. Hence, the question arises how the set preference $\preccurlyeq$ can be refined, such that for more, ideally all, pairs A and B it is clear which set is preferred. Thereby, the original relation $\preccurlyeq$ needs to be taken into account, i.e., if $A \prec B$ holds, it must also hold under the refined relation.

The goal of such a refinement is twofold: At first, the given preorder should become "more total". This way, there are less incomparable sets of solutions which are hard to deal with by any optimization method. Second, the refinement will allow to explicitly take into account preference information of a decision maker. Hence, by refining set relations, preference information

Figure 2.4 Including preference information may create a total preorder that can be used for optimization. On the left, three preferences $F \preccurlyeq A$, $B \preccurlyeq G$ and $H \preccurlyeq C$ have been added to a preorder. On the other hand, cycles in the optimization can result as shown on the right, where two preferences $A \preccurlyeq F$ and $F \preccurlyeq B$ have been added.

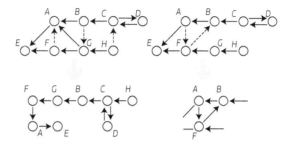

of a decision maker can be included, and optimized towards a set which contains a preferred subset of all minimal solutions, i.e., non-dominated solutions in the case of Pareto-dominance.

An example is shown in Figure 2.4 on the left, where three edges (preference relations) have been added and the resulting ordering is a total preorder with the optimal set of solutions H. Just adding an ordering among incomparable solutions potentially leads to cycles in the ordering as the resulting structure is no longer a preorder. Using such an approach in optimization will prevent convergence in general, see also right half of Figure 2.4.

Hence, for the refinement the following properties are required:

- The refinement should again be a preorder.
- If a set is minimal in the refined order for some subset of Ψ, it should also be minimal in the original order in the same subset. This way, it is guaranteed that the objective functions are optimized indeed with respect to some preference relation, e.g. Pareto-dominance.

As a result of this discussion the following definition is obtained:

Definition 2.12: *Given a set Ψ. Then the preference relation $\preccurlyeq_{ref}$ refines $\preccurlyeq$ if for all $A, B \in \Psi$*

$$(A \preccurlyeq B) \wedge (B \not\preccurlyeq A) \Rightarrow (A \preccurlyeq_{ref} B) \wedge (B \not\preccurlyeq_{ref} A)$$

All legal refinements are depicted in Figure 2.5(a). Note, that the refinement still needs to be a preorder.

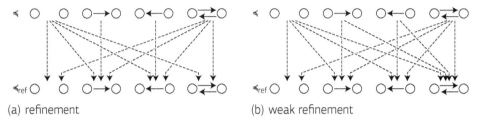

(a) refinement   (b) weak refinement

Figure 2.5 The top in both plots shows the four different possibilities between two nodes of the given preference relation: no edge (incomparable), single edge (one is better than the other) and double edge (equivalent). The bottom shows the probabilities in case of the refined relation (a), and the weakly refined relation (b). The dashed edges represent all possible changes of edges if $\preccurlyeq$ is (weakly) refined to $\preccurlyeq_{\text{ref}}$.

Using the notion of strictly better, the following condition can be derived $A \prec B \Rightarrow A \prec_{\text{ref}} B$. In other words, if in the given preference relation a set A is strictly better than a set B ($A \prec B$) then it must be strictly better in the refined relation, too ($A \prec_{\text{ref}} B$). As can be seen, refining a preference relation maintains existing strict preference relationships. If two sets are incomparable, i.e., $A \parallel B \Leftrightarrow (A \not\preccurlyeq B) \wedge (B \not\preccurlyeq A)$, then additional edges can be inserted by the refinement. In case of equivalence, i.e., $A \equiv B \Leftrightarrow (A \preccurlyeq B) \wedge (B \preccurlyeq A)$, edges can be removed.

Some of the widely used preference relations are not refinements in the sense of Definition 2.12, but satisfy a weaker condition:

Definition 2.13: *Given a set Ψ. Then the set preference relation $\preccurlyeq_{\text{ref}}$ weakly refines $\preccurlyeq$ if for all $A, B \in \Psi$ the following holds*

$$(A \preccurlyeq B) \wedge (B \not\preccurlyeq A) \Rightarrow (A \preccurlyeq_{ref} B) \ .$$

In other words, if set A is strictly better than B ($A \prec B$), then A weakly dominates B in the refined preference relation, i.e. $A \preccurlyeq_{\text{ref}} B$. Therefore, A could be incomparable to B in the refined preference relation, i.e. $A \parallel_{\text{ref}} B$. In addition, if a preference relation refines another one, it also weakly refines it. Figure 2.5(b) depicts all possibilities of a weak refinement. The weak refinement still needs to be a preorder.

The following hierarchical construction of refinement relations allows to convert a given weak refinement into a refinement. This way, a larger class of available indicators and preference relations can be used. In addition, it provides a simple method to add decision maker preference information to a given relation by adding an order to equivalent sets, thereby making a preorder 'more total'. Finally, it enables to refine a given preorder in a way that helps to speed up the convergence of an optimization algorithm, e.g. by taking into account also solutions that are worse than others in a set. This way, the successful technique of non-dominated sorting can be used in the context of set-based optimization. The construction resembles the concept of hierarchy used in [65]; however, here (a) preference relations on sets are considered, and (b) the hierarchical construction is different.

Definition 2.14: *Given a set* Ψ *and a sequence* S *of* k *preference relations over* Ψ *with* $S = (\preccurlyeq^1, \preccurlyeq^2, \ldots, \preccurlyeq^k)$, *the preference relation* $\preccurlyeq_S$ *associated with* S *is defined as follows. Let* $A, B \in \Psi$; *then* $A \preccurlyeq_S B$ *if and only if* $\exists 1 \leq i \leq k$ *such that the following two conditions are satisfied:*

(i). $(i < k \wedge (A \prec^i B)) \vee (i = k \wedge (A \preccurlyeq^k B))$
(ii). $\forall 1 \leq j < i : (A \preccurlyeq^j B \wedge B \preccurlyeq^j A)$

With this definition, the following procedure can be derived to determine $A \preccurlyeq_S B$ for two sets A and B:

- Start from the first preference relation, i.e. $j = 1$. Repeat the following step: If $A \equiv^j B$ holds (A and B are equivalent), then increase j to point to the next relation in the sequence if it exists.
- If the final j points to the last preference relation ($j = k$), then set $A \preccurlyeq_S B \Leftrightarrow A \preccurlyeq^k B$. Otherwise, set $A \preccurlyeq_S B \Leftrightarrow A \prec^k B$.

As described above, one of the main reasons to define a sequence of preference relations is to upgrade a given weak refinement to a refinement. In addition, it would be desirable to add arbitrary preorders to the sequence S. As they need not to be refinements of the given order $\preccurlyeq$, a decision maker can freely add his preferences this way. The following theorem states the corresponding results. The proof is provided in Appendix B.1 on page 227.

Figure 2.6 Representation of the hierarchical construction of refinements according to Theorem 2.15.

$$S = (\preccurlyeq^1, ..., \preccurlyeq^{k'-1}, \overbrace{\preccurlyeq^{k'}}^{\text{refinement}}, \underbrace{\preccurlyeq^{k'+1}, ..., \preccurlyeq^k}_{\text{preorder}})$$

$\underbrace{\phantom{\preccurlyeq^1, ..., \preccurlyeq^{k'-1}}}_{\substack{\text{weak}\\\text{refinement}}}$

Theorem 2.15: *Given a sequence of preference relations according to Definition 2.14. Suppose there is a $k' \leq k$ such that $\preccurlyeq^{k'}$ is a refinement of a given preference relation $\preccurlyeq$ and all relations $\preccurlyeq^j$, $1 \leq j < k'$ are weak refinements of $\preccurlyeq$. Then $\preccurlyeq_S$ is a refinement of $\preccurlyeq$. Furthermore, if all relations $\preccurlyeq^j$, $1 \leq j < k$ are preorders, so is $\preccurlyeq_S$; if all relations $\preccurlyeq^j$, $1 \leq j < k$ are total preorders, then $\preccurlyeq_S$ is a total preorder.*

All set preference relations $\preccurlyeq^j$, $k' < j \leq k$ can be arbitrary preorders that may reflect additional preferences, see also Figure 2.6. Nevertheless, the resulting preference relation $\preccurlyeq_S$ still refines $\preccurlyeq$. The previously described hierarchical construction of refinements will be applied in later sections of the chapter to construct preference relations that are useful for set-based multiobjective optimization.

2.3 · Design of Preference Relations Using Quality Indicators

This section addresses the task of building set preference relations based on quality indicator. First, an overview over different types of indicators is given, including the corresponding set preference relation. Due to its exceptional position in this thesis, the *hypervolume indicator* is thereby presented in a separate section. Thereafter, it is shown how set partitioning can be used to further refine the preference relations. The section concludes by proposing different preference relations based on indicator functions, which will be used in the experimental validation in Section 2.5.1.

2.3.1 · Overview Over Quality Indicators

Quality indicators are functions assigning a value to a predefined number of sets, usually classified according to the number of set the indicator takes as input.

Definition 2.16 (quality indicators): *An m-ary quality indicator I is a function $I : \Psi^m \to \mathbb{R}$, which maps m sets $A_1, A_2, \cdots, A_m \in \Psi$ to a real value in $\mathbb{R}$*

Unary indicators (taking one input) and binary indicators (a function of two sets) are of particular interest, while indicators considering more sets are less common.

Unary Indicators

Unary quality indicators are a possible means to construct set preference relations that on the one hand are total orders and on the other hand satisfy the refinement property, cf. Definition 2.12. They represent set quality measures that map each set $A \in \Psi$ to a real number $I(A) \in \mathbb{R}$. Given an indicator I, one can define the corresponding preference relation as

$$A \preccurlyeq_I B := I(A) \geq I(B) \tag{2.1}$$

where larger indicator values stand for higher quality, in other words, A is as least as good as B if the indicator value of A is not smaller than the one of B. By construction, the preference relation $\preccurlyeq_I$ defined above is a preorder since it is reflexive as $I(A) \geq I(A)$ and transitive as $(I(A) \geq I(B)) \wedge (I(B) \geq I(C)) \Rightarrow I(A) \geq I(C)$. Moreover, it is a total preorder because $(I(A) \geq I(B)) \vee (I(B) \geq I(A))$ holds. Note that depending on the choice of the indicator function, there may be still sets that have equal indicator values, i.e., they are indifferent with respect to the corresponding set preference relation $\preccurlyeq_I$. In this case, equivalence classes of sets may result, each one containing sets with the same indicator value. For multiobjective optimization algorithms that use indicators as their means of defining progress, sets with identical indicator values pose additional difficulties in terms of cyclic behavior and premature convergence. Later it will be shown how these problems can be circumvented by considering hierarchies of indicators.

Clearly, not all possible indicator functions realize a refinement of the orginal preference relation, e.g., weak Pareto-dominance. The following theorem provides sufficient conditions for weak refinements and refinements.

Theorem 2.17: *If a unary indicator I satisfies*

$$(A \preccurlyeq B) \wedge (B \not\preccurlyeq A) \Rightarrow (I(A) \geq I(B))$$

for all $A, B \in \Psi$, then the corresponding preference relation $\preccurlyeq_I$ according to Eq. 2.1 weakly refines the preference relation $\preccurlyeq$ according to Definition 2.13. If it holds that

$$(A \preccurlyeq B) \wedge (B \not\preccurlyeq A) \Rightarrow (I(A) > I(B))$$

then $\preccurlyeq_I$ refines $\preccurlyeq$ according to Definition 2.12.

Proof. Consider $A, B \in \Psi$ with $(A \preccurlyeq B) \wedge (B \not\preccurlyeq A)$. If $I(A) \geq I(B)$, then also $A \preccurlyeq_I B$ according to Eq. 2.1. If $I(A) > I(B)$, then $I(A) \geq I(B)$, but $I(B) \not\geq I(A)$, which implies that $A \preccurlyeq_I B$ and $B \not\preccurlyeq_I A$. $\square$

In other words, if A is strictly better than B, i.e. $A \prec B$, then the indicator value of A must be not worse or must be larger than the one of B in order to achieve a weak refinement or a refinement, respectively. In practice, this global property may be difficult to prove for a specific indicator since one has to argue over all possible sets. Therefore, the following theorem provides sufficient and necessary conditions that are only based on the local behavior, i.e., when adding a single element. The proof of the theorem is given in Appendix B.2 on page 229.

Theorem 2.19: *Let I be a unary indicator and $\preccurlyeq$ a preference relation on populations that itself conforms to a preference relation $\preceq$ on its elements (see Definition 2.11). The relation $\preccurlyeq_I$ according to Eq. 2.1 refines $\preccurlyeq$ if the following two conditions hold for all sets $A \in \Psi$ and solutions b with $\{b\} \in \Psi$:*

1. If $A \preccurlyeq \{b\}$ then $I(A \cup \{b\}) = I(A)$.
2. If $A \not\preccurlyeq \{b\}$ then $I(A \cup \{b\}) > I(A)$.

For weak refinement one needs to replace the relation $>$ by $\geq$ in the second condition. The second condition is necessary for $\preccurlyeq_I$ being a refinement (in case of $>$) or weak refinement (in case of $\geq$) of $\preccurlyeq$.

In the past decades numerous unary indicators were proposed, however, many of them do not satisfy the weak refinement property with respect to the Pareto dominance relation $\preccurlyeq_{\mathrm{par}}$, as for instance the *Generalized Distance*, the *Maximum Pareto Front Error*, the *Overall Nondominated Vector Generation* (all by Van Veldhuizen [124]) or the *Spacing Metric* of Schott [114]. Other indicators are a weak refinement of $\preccurlyeq_{\mathrm{par}}$, e.g., the *Unary Epsilon Indicator* [140] and the indicators R_1, R_2 and R_3 by Hansen and Jaszkiewicz [75] when used with preference sets. However, none of these indicators is a refinement of $\preccurlyeq_{\mathrm{par}}$. So far, the only known indicator with this property has been the *Hypervolume Indicator* which will be presented in Section 2.3.2.

Binary Indicators

In contrast to unary indicators, binary quality indicators assign a real value to ordered pairs of sets (A, B) with $A, B \in \Psi$. Assuming that larger indicator values stand for higher quality, for each binary indicator I a corresponding set preference relation can be defined as follows:

$$A \preccurlyeq_{\mathrm{I}} B := (I(A, B) \geq I(B, A))$$

Similarly to unary undicators, one can derive sufficient conditions for $\preccurlyeq_{\mathrm{I}}$ being a refinement respectively a weak refinement.

Note that the relation $\preccurlyeq_{\mathrm{I}}$ is not necessarily a preorder, and this property needs to be shown for each specific indicator separately. The binary epsilon indicator [140] does not give a preorder, see the paper by the author and colleagues [143]. Other examples of binary indicators include the $\mathcal{C}$-metric by Knowles [86] and R_1 to R_3 by Hansen and Jaszkiewicz [75]. However, one can derive valid binary indicators from unary indicators. For example, for every unary indicator I_1 a corresponding binary indicator I_2 can be defined as $I_2(A, B) := I_1(A) - I_1(B)$; it is easy to show that the property of (weak) refinement transfers from the unary indicator to the binary version. In a similar way, one could also use $I_2(A, B) := I_1(A \cup B) - I_1(B)$ as in the case of the binary hypervolume indicator, see, e.g., [133].

On the other hand, every binary indicator I_2 can be transformed into a unary indicator I_1 by using a reference set R: $I_1(A) := I_2(A, R)$[3]. Here, the refinement property is not necessarily preserved, e.g., the unary versions of the binary epsilon indicators induce only weak refinements, while the original binary indicators induce refinements of the weak Pareto-dominance relation.

n-Ary Indicators

The concept of indicators can also be extended to assigning a real value to arbitrary number of inputs, i.e., assigning a real value to vectors of sets $(A_1, \ldots, A_m)$. Examples of n-ary indicators include the n-ary Pareto dominanance indicator by Goh and Tan [69], and the G-Metric by [99]. Both these metrics calculate the indicator value of the first input with respect to the remaining sets A_2 to A_m. Defining general set preference relations from n-ary indicators is not straightforward and depends on the considered indicator.

2.3.2 · Hypervolume Indicator

All known unary indicator as of February 2010 inducing a refinement of the weak Pareto-dominance relation are based on the hypervolume indicator $I_H(A, R)$ or the weighted hypervolume indicator $I_H^w(A, R)$. The weighted hypervolume indicator has been proposed by Zitzler et al. [141]:

Definition 2.20 (weighted hypervolume indicator): *Let $A \in \Psi$ denote a set of decision vectors, then the weighted hypervolume indicator $I_H^w(A)$ corresponds to the weighted Lebesgue measure of the set of objective vectors weakly dominated by the solutions in A but not by a so-called reference set $R \in Z$.*

$$I_H^w(A, R) = \lambda_w(H(A, R))$$

where λ_w denotes the weighted Lebesgue measure, i.e.,

$$\lambda_w(H(A, R)) = \int_{\mathbb{R}^d} \alpha_A(z) w(z) dz$$

---

[3] Usually, instead of a reference set of solutions a reference set of objective vectors is given. This requires a slight modification of the indicator.

with $\alpha_A(z) = \mathbf{1}_{H(A,R)}(z)$ *where*

$$H(A, R) = \{z \mid \exists a \in A \; \exists r \in R \; : \; f(a) \leqslant z \leqslant r\}$$

and $\mathbf{1}_{H(A,r)}(z)$ *being the characteristic function of* $H(A,r)$ *that equals 1 iff* $z \in H(A,r)$ *and 0 otherwise, and* $w : \mathbb{R}^k \to \mathbb{R}_{>0}$ *is a strictly positive[4] weight function integrable on any bounded set, i.e.,* $\int_{B(0,\gamma)} w(z)dz < \infty$ *for any* $\gamma > 0$, *where* $B(0,\gamma)$ *is the open ball centered in* o *and of radius* γ. *In other words, the measure associated to* w *is assumed to be* σ-*finite.*

The definition is based on the original (non-weighted) hypervolume indicator first proposed by Zitzler and Thiele [136]:

Definition 2.21 (hypervolume indicator): *Let* $A \in \Psi$ *denote a set of objective vectors, then the hypervolume indicator* $I_H(A,R)$ *corresponds to the Lebesgue measure of the set of objective vectors weakly dominated by the solutions in* A *but not by a so-called reference set* $R \in Z$.

$$I_H(A, R) = \int_{\mathbb{R}^d} \alpha_A(z)dz$$

with $H(A,R)$ *and* $\alpha_A(z)$ *according to Definition 2.20.*

Throughout the thesis, the notation I_H refers to the non-weighted hypervolume where the weight is 1 everywhere, and the term non-weighted hypervolume is explicitly used for I_H while the weighted hypervolume indicator I_H^w is, for simplicity, referred to as hypervolume. Figure 2.7 illustrates the (weighted) hypervolume I_H^w for a biobjective problem[5].

It is easy to see that the volume is not affected whenever a weakly Pareto-dominated solution is added to a set A. Furthermore, any solution b not weakly Pareto-dominated by A covers a part of the objective space not covered by A and therefore the indicator value for $A \cup \{b\}$ is better (larger) than the one for A. These properties can be verified by looking at the

---

[4] In fact it is enough to have a strictly positive weight almost everywhere such that I_H^w is a refinement of Pareto dominance. Since there is no practical use for choosing a non positive weight in null sets, for the sake of simplicity the weight is assumed to be strictly positive everywhere.

[5] Please note, that the term "hypervolume" is used interchangeably to refer to the indicator value I_H and the dominated space $H(A,R)$

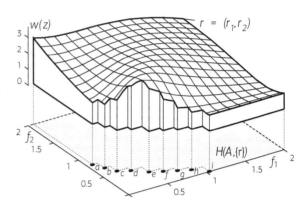

Figure 2.7 Graphical representation of the weighted hypervolume indicator for a set of solutions $A = \{a,...,i\}$ and a reference set $R = \{r\}$. The gray shaded area represents the hypervolume $H(A,R)$, the volume of the weight function $w(z)$ over the hypervolume (solid box) gives the weighted hypervolume indicator $I_H^w(A) = \lambda_w(H(A,\{r\}))$.

example shown in Figure 2.7; therefore, the hypervolume indicator induces a refinement, see also [62]. There are various other unary indicators which induce *weak* refinements, e.g., the unary R_2 and R_3 indicators [75] and the epsilon indicator [140]—the above conditions can be used to show this, see also Knowles and Corne [88] and Zitzler et al. [140] for a more detailed discussion.

The necessary condition can be used to prove that a particular indicator—when used alone—does not lead to a weak refinement or a refinement of the weak Pareto-dominance relation. That applies, for instance, to most of the diversity indicators proposed in the literature as they do not fulfill the second condition in Theorem 2.19. Nevertheless, these indicators can be useful in combination with indicators inducing (weak) refinements as will be shown in Section 2.3.4.

2.3.3 · Refinement Through Set Partitioning

The Pareto-dominance relation $\preccurlyeq_{\mathrm{par}}$ on sets is by definition insensitive to dominated solutions in a set, i.e., whether $A \in \Psi$ weakly dominates $B \in \Psi$ only depends on the corresponding minimal sets: $A \preccurlyeq_{\mathrm{par}} B \Leftrightarrow \mathrm{Min}(A, \preceq_{\mathrm{par}}) \preccurlyeq_{\mathrm{par}} \mathrm{Min}(B, \preceq_{\mathrm{par}})$. The same holds for set preference relations induced by the hypervolume indicator and other popular quality indicators. Nevertheless, preferred solutions may be of importance:

- When a Pareto set approximation is evaluated according to additional knowledge and preferences—which may be hard to formalize and therefore may not be included in the search process—then preferred solutions can become interesting alternatives for a decision maker.
- When a set preference relation is used within a (evolutionary) multiobjective optimizer to guide search, it is crucial that preferred solutions are taken into account—for reasons of search efficiency.

Accordingly, the question is how to refine a given set preference relation that only depends on its minimal elements such that also non-minimal solutions are considered.

This issue is strongly related to fitness assignment in MOEAs. Pareto-dominance based MOEAs for instance divide the population into dominance classes which are usually hierarchically organized. The underlying idea can be generalized to arbitrary set preference relations. To this end, the notion of partitions is introduced: let A denote a set of solutions, then for a partitioning P_i, $1 \leq i \leq l$, it holds $P_i \cap P_j = \emptyset \, \forall i \neq j$, and $\bigcup_{i=1}^{l} P_i = A$.

For instance, with Rank Partitioning (rp) (also called *dominance ranking* [63]) individuals which are dominated by the same number of population members are grouped into one dominance class, i.e., into the same partition:

$$P_i^{\mathrm{rp}} := \{a \in A \, : \, |\{b \in A : b \prec a\}| = i - 1\}$$

see Figure 2.8. With Minimal elements Partitioning (mp) (also called *non-dominated sorting* or *dominance depth* [70, 117]), the minimal elements are grouped into the first dominance class, and the other classes are determined by recursively applying this classification scheme to the remaining population members:

$$P_i^{\mathrm{mp}} := \begin{cases} \mathrm{Min}(X, \preceq) & \text{if } i = 1 \\ \mathrm{Min}(X \backslash \cup_{j=1}^{i-1} P_i^{\mathrm{mp}}, \preceq) & \text{else} \end{cases} . \tag{2.2}$$

For the second partitioning $P_1^{\mathrm{mp}} \prec P_2^{\mathrm{mp}} \prec \ldots \prec P_l^{\mathrm{mp}}$ holds; this is demonstrated in Figure 2.8.

Figure 2.8 Illustration of two set partitioning functions, here based on weak Pareto-dominance: mp (left) and rp (right). The light-shaded areas stand for the first partition P_1 and the darkest areas represent the last partition P_3 (left) and P_4 (right). On the left $P_1 \prec_{par} P_2 \prec_{par} P_3$ holds, while on the right $P_1 \prec_{par} P_i$ for $2 \leq i \leq 4$, $P_3 \prec_{par} P_4$, and $P_2 \parallel_{par} P_3$ as well as $P_2 \parallel_{par} P_4$.

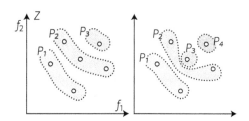

Now, given a set partitioning function 'part' giving a partitioning P_i^{part} (such as rp or mp) one can construct set preference relations that only refer to specific partitions of two sets $A, B \in \Psi$. By concatenating these relations, one then obtains a sequence of relations that induces a set preference relation according to Definition 2.14.

Definition 2.22: *Let $\preccurlyeq$ be a set preference relation and 'part' a set partitioning function where the number of partition is l. The partition-based extension of $\preccurlyeq$ is defined as the relation $\preccurlyeq^{\text{part}} := \preccurlyeq_S$ where S is the sequence $(\preccurlyeq^1_{\text{part}}, \preccurlyeq^2_{\text{part}}, \dots, \preccurlyeq^l_{\text{part}})$ of preference relations with*

$$A \preccurlyeq^i_{\text{part}} B :\Leftrightarrow P_i^A \preccurlyeq P_i^B$$

where P_i^A and P_i^B denote the ith partition of set A and B respectively.

A partition-based extension of a set preference relation $\preccurlyeq$ basically means that $\preccurlyeq$ is successively applied to the hierarchy of partitions defined by the corresponding set partition function. Given $A, B \in \Psi$, first the two first partitions of A and B are compared based on $\preccurlyeq$; if the comparison yields equivalence, then the two second partitions are compared and so forth. This principle reflects the general fitness assignment strategy used in most MOEAs.

One important requirement for such a partition-based extension is that $\preccurlyeq^{\text{part}}$ refines $\preccurlyeq$. Provided that $\preccurlyeq$ only depends on the minimal elements in the sets, both 'rp' and 'mp' induce refinements. The argument is simply that $\preccurlyeq^1_{\text{part}}$ is the same as $\preccurlyeq$ because the first partition corresponds for both functions to the set of minimal elements; that means $\preccurlyeq^1_{\text{part}}$ is a refinement of $\preccurlyeq$. Furthermore, all $\preccurlyeq_{\text{part}}^{i}$ are preorders. Applying Theorem 2.15 leads to the above statement.

Throughout this thesis, the set partitioning function 'mp' is considered and referred to as minimum elements partitioning (or non-dominated sorting in the case of Pareto-dominance). It induces a natural partitioning into sets of minimal elements where the partitions are linearly ordered according to strict preferability.

2.3.4 · Combined Preference Relations

The issue of preferred (dominated) solutions in a set $A \in \Psi$ cannot only be addressed by means of set partitioning functions, but also by using multiple indicators in sequence. For instance, one could use the hypervolume indicator I_H (to assess the minimal elements in A) in combination with a diversity indicator I_D (to assess the non-minimal elements in A); according to Theorem 2.15, the set preference relation $\preccurlyeq_{H,D}$ given by the sequence $(\preccurlyeq_H, \preccurlyeq_D)$ is a proper refinement of weak Pareto-dominance since $\preccurlyeq_H$ is a refinement (see above) and $\preccurlyeq_D$ is a preorder.

In the following, some examples are presented for combined set preference relations that illustrate different application scenarios. All of these relations are refinements of the set preference relation $\preccurlyeq_{\text{par}}$.

1. The first combination is based on the unary epsilon indicator $I_{\varepsilon 1}$ with a reference set R in objective space which is defined as $I_{\varepsilon 1}(A) = E(A, R)$ with

$$E(A, R) = \max_{r \in R} \min_{a \in A} \max\{f_i(a) - r_i \mid 1 \leq i \leq d\}$$

   where r_i is the ith component of the objective vector r. Since this indicator induces only a weak refinement of the weak Pareto-dominance relation $\preccurlyeq_{\text{par}}$, the hypervolume indicator is used to distinguish between sets indifferent with respect $I_{\varepsilon 1}$. The resulting set preference relation is denoted as $\preccurlyeq_{\varepsilon 1,H}$; it is a refinement of $\preccurlyeq_{\text{par}}$.

2. The second combination uses the R_2 indicator proposed in [75] for which the following definition is used here:

$$I_{R2}(A) = R_2(A, R) = \frac{\sum_{\lambda \in \Lambda} u^*(\lambda, R) - u^*(\lambda, f(A))}{|\Lambda|}$$

where the function u^* is a utility function based on the weighted Tchebycheff function

$$u^*(\lambda, T) = \min_{z \in T} \max_{1 \leq j \leq d} \lambda_j |z_j^* - z_j|$$

and Λ is a set of weight vectors $\lambda \in \mathbb{R}^d$, $R \subset Z$ is a reference set, and $z^* \in Z$ is a reference point. In this chapter, the reference set is $R = \{z^*\}$. Also the R_2 indicator provides only a weak refinement; as before, the hypervolume indicator is added in order to achieve a refinement. This set preference relation will be denoted as $\preccurlyeq_{R2,H}$.

3. The next set preference relation can be regarded as a variation of the above relation $\preccurlyeq_{R2,H}$. It allows a detailed modeling of preferences by means of a set of reference points $r^{(i)} \in R$ with individual scaling factors $\rho^{(i)}$ and individual sets of weight vectors $\Lambda^{(i)}$. As a starting point, the generalized epsilon-distance between a solution $a \in X$ and a reference point $r \in Z$ is defined as

$$F_\varepsilon^\lambda(a, r) = \max_{1 \leq i \leq d} \lambda_i \cdot (f_i(a) - r_i)$$

with the weight vector $\lambda \in \mathbb{R}^d$ where $\lambda_i > 0$ for $1 \leq i \leq d$. In contrast to the usual epsilon-distance given, the coordinates of the objective space are weighted which allows for choosing a preference direction.

The P indicator for a single reference point r can now be described as

$$I_P(A, r, \Lambda) = -\sum_{\lambda \in \Lambda} \min_{a \in A} F_\varepsilon^\lambda(a, r)$$

where Λ is a potentially large set of different weight vectors. The minimum operator selects for each weight vector λ the solution a with minimal generalized epsilon-distance. Finally, all these distances are summed up. In order to achieve a broad distribution of solutions and a sensitive indicator, the cardinality of $|\Lambda|$ should be large, i.e., larger than the expected number of minimum elements in A. For example, Λ may contain a large set of random vectors on a unit sphere, i.e., vectors with length 1. One may also scale the weight vectors to different lengths in order to express the preference for an unequal density of solutions.

If one has a set of reference points $r^{(i)} \in R$ with individual sets of weight vectors $\Lambda^{(i)}$ and scaling factors $\rho^{(i)} > 0$, one can simply add the individual P indicator values as follows

$$I_P(A) = \sum_{r^{(i)} \in R} \rho^{(i)} \cdot I_P(A, r^{(i)}, \Lambda^{(i)})$$

Of course, equal sets $\Lambda^{(i)}$ might be chosen for each reference point. In this case, the scaling factors $\rho^{(i)}$ can be used to give preference to specific reference points.

The P indicator as defined above provides only a weak refinement; as before, the hypervolume indicator is added in order to achieve a refinement. This set preference relation will be denoted as $\preccurlyeq_{P,H}$.

4. The previous three indicator combinations will be used together with a set partitioning function. To demonstrate that the partitioning can also be accomplished by indicators, the following sequence of indicators $S = (I_H, I_C, I_D)$ is proposed where I_C measures the largest distance of a solution to the closest minimal element in a set and I_D reflects the diversity of the solutions in the objective space. The latter two indicators, which both do not induce weak refinements of $\preccurlyeq_{\text{par}}$, are defined as follows:

$$I_C(A) = -\max_{a \in A} \min_{b \in \text{Min}(A, \preceq)} dist(f(a), f(b))$$

and

$$I_D(A) = -\max_{a \in A} \left(\frac{1}{nn_1(a, A \setminus \{a\})} + \frac{1}{nn_2(a, A \setminus \{a\})} \right)$$

with

$$nn_1(a, B) = \min_{b \in B} dist(f(a), f(b))$$

$$nn_2(a, B) = \max_{c \in B} \min_{b \in B \setminus \{c\}} dist(f(a), f(b))$$

where $nn_1(a, B)$ gives the smallest and $nn_2(a, B)$ the second smallest distance of a to any solution in B. For the distance function $dist(z^1, z^2)$, Euclidean distance is used here, i.e., $dist(z^1, z^2) = \sqrt{\sum_{1 \leq i \leq d}(z_i^1 - z_i^2)^2}$. The I_C indicator resembles the generational distance measure proposed in [125] and I_D resembles the nearest neighbor niching mechanism in the modified Strength Pareto Evolutionary Algorithm (SPEA2) [139]. The overall set preference relation is referred to as $\preccurlyeq_{H,C,D}$. According to Theorem 2.15, $\preccurlyeq_{H,C,D}$ is a refinement of $\preccurlyeq_{par}$.

It is worth mentioning that it is also possible to combine a non-total preorder such as $\preccurlyeq_{par}$ with total orders differently to the principle suggested in Definition 2.14. As has been pointed out, see e.g. right hand side of Figure 2.4, convergence may not be achievable if an optimization is not based on a preorder or if the underlying preorder is not a refinement. The following example illustrates why density-based MOEA such as the Nondominated Sorting Genetic Algorithm II (NSGA-II) and SPEA2 show cyclic behavior, see [96], in particular, when the population mainly contains incomparable solutions, e.g., when being close to the trade-off surface.

For instance, let I be a unary indicator, then one may define a set preference relation $\preccurlyeq_{par,I}$ as follows with $A, B \in \Psi$:

$$A \preccurlyeq_{par,I} B :\Leftrightarrow (A \preccurlyeq_{par} B) \vee ((A \parallel_{par} B) \wedge (A \preccurlyeq_I B))$$

Now, consider a unary diversity indicator, e.g., I_D as defined above; this type of indicator usually does not induce a weak refinement. The resulting set preference relation $\preccurlyeq_{par,I}$ is not a proper preorder as Figure 2.9 demonstrates: transitivity is violated, i.e., $A \preccurlyeq_{par,I} B$ and $B \preccurlyeq_{par,I} C$, but $A \npreccurlyeq_{par,I} C$. The relation graph of $\preccurlyeq_{par,I}$ contains cycles. However, if I stands for the hypervolume indicator I_H, then $\preccurlyeq_{par,I}$ is a set preference relation refining $\preccurlyeq_{par}$; this combination could be useful to reduce computation effort.

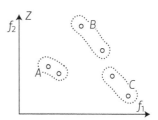

Figure 2.9 Three sets are shown in the objective space where $A \preccurlyeq_{par} B$, $A \parallel_{par} C$ and $B \parallel_{par} C$. Using a combination of Pareto-dominance and diversity results in a cyclic relation $\preccurlyeq_{par,I}$ with $A \prec_{par,I} B$, $B \prec_{par,I} C$, and $C \prec_{par,I} A$.

2.4 · Multiobjective Optimization Using Set Preference Relations

The previous two sections discussed how to design set preference relations so that the concept of Pareto dominance is preserved while different types of user preferences are included. This section presents corresponding generalized multiobjective optimizers that make use of such set preference relations in order to search for promising solution sets. First, Section 2.4.1 proposes an algorithm corresponding to classical EAs, while Section 2.4.2 extends the approach to a more general class of optimizers.

In the following, optimizers are classified according to the following definition:

Definition 2.23: *An optimizer that operates on elements of the decision space U and returns an element of V is referred to as a U/V-optimizer.*

Hence, MOEAs are, from a classical EA perspective, $X/\mathcal{P}(X)$ optimizer. On the other hand, multiobjective algorithms using aggregation are considered as X/X-optimizers. First, in Section 2.4.1 the Set Preference Algorithm for Multiobjective Optimization (SPAM) is presented which gives a new perspective on traditional MOEAs interpreting them as $\mathcal{P}(X)/\mathcal{P}(X)$ strategies. As SPAM reveals, traditional MOEAs in this light are *hillclimbers*, i.e., (1+1)-strategies, that operate on a single set[6]. Stemming from this observation, Section 2.4.2 then presents and extension of SPAM, operating on multiple sets, i.e., realizing a general (μ, λ) strategy. Finally, Section 2.4.3 discusses the relation of SPAM and SPAM$^+$ to existing MOEAs.

---

[6]Note, that strictly speaking many MOEAs employ a (1,1) strategy, i.e., the successor set is chosen no matter whether the new set is preferred over the old set. Nonetheless, these algorithms are also referred to as *hillclimbers*.

2.4.1 · SPAM–Set Preference Algorithm for Multiobjective Optimization

The classical view of MOEAs is illustrated in the upper left corner of Figure 2.10. Mating selection, mutation, crossover, and environmental selection operate on single solutions and thereby generate a new—hopefully better—set of solutions. Summarized, one can state that classical MOEAs operate on elements of X and deliver an element of $\mathcal{P}(X)$, where $\mathcal{P}(X)$ denotes the power set of X.

In the following, the Set Preference Algorithm for Multiobjective Optimization (SPAM) is introduced which can be used with any set preference relation and resembles a standard hill climber with the difference that two new elements of the search space Ψ are created using two types of mutation operators. The main part of SPAM is given by Algorithm 1.

Starting with a randomly chosen set $P \in \Psi$ of size α, first a random mutation operator is applied to generate another set P'. This operator should be designed such that every element in Ψ could be possibly generated, i.e., the neighborhood is in principle the entire search space. In practice, the operator will usually have little effect on the optimization process; however, its property of exhaustiveness is important from a theoretical perspective, in particular to show convergence, see [143].

Second, a heuristic mutation operator is employed. This operator mimics the mating selection, variation, and environmental selection steps as used in most MOEAs. The goal of this operator is to create a third set $P'' \in \Psi$ that is better than P in the context of a predefined set preference relation $\preccurlyeq$. However, since it is heuristic it cannot guarantee to improve P; there may be situations where it is not able to escape local optima of the landscape of the underlying set problem. Finally, P is replaced by P'', if the latter is weakly preferable to the former; otherwise, P is either replaced by P' (if $P' \preccurlyeq P$) or remains unchanged. Note that in the last step, weak preferability ($\preccurlyeq$) and not preferability ($\prec$) needs to be considered in order to allow the algorithm to cross landscape plateaus, cf. Brockhoff et al. [31].

For the mutation operators, Algorithms 2 and 3 are proposed. Algorithm 2 (random set mutation) randomly chooses k decision vectors from X and

1: generate initial set P of size α, i.e., randomly choose $A \in \Psi_{=\alpha}$ and set $P \leftarrow A$
2: **while** termination criterion not fulfilled **do**
3:    $P' \leftarrow randomSetMutation(P)$
4:    $P'' \leftarrow heuristicSetMutation(P)$
5:    **if** $P'' \preccurlyeq P$ **then**
6:        $P \leftarrow P''$
7:    **else if** $P' \preccurlyeq P$ **then**
8:        $P \leftarrow P'$
9: **return** P

Algorithm 1 SPAM Main Loop, given a set preference relation $\preccurlyeq$

1: randomly choose $r_1, \ldots, r_k \in X$ with $r_i \neq r_j$
2: randomly select $p_1, \ldots, p_k$ from P with $p_i \neq p_j$
3: $P' \leftarrow P \setminus \{p_1, \ldots, p_k\} \cup \{r_1, \ldots, r_k\}$
4: **return** P'

Algorithm 2 Random Set Mutation of set P

uses them to replace k elements in P.[7] Algorithm 3 (heuristic set mutation) generalizes the iterative truncation procedures used in NSGA-II [50], SPEA2 [139], and others. First, k new solutions are created based on P; this corresponds to mating selection plus variation in a standard MOEA. While the variation is problem-specific, for mating selection either uniform random selection (used in the following) or fitness-based selection can be used (using the fitness values computed by Algorithm 4). Then, these k solutions are added to P, and finally the resulting set of size $\alpha + k$ is iteratively truncated to size α by removing the solution with the worst fitness values in each step. Here, the fitness value of $a \in P$ reflects the loss in quality for the entire set P if a is deleted: the lower the fitness, the larger the loss.

To estimate how useful a particular solution $a \in P$ is, Algorithm 4 compares all sets $A_i \subset P$ with $|A_i| = |P| - 1$ to $P \setminus \{a\}$ using the predefined set preference relation $\preccurlyeq$. The fewer sets A_i are weakly preferable to $P \setminus \{a\}$, the better the set $P \setminus \{a\}$ and the less important is a. This procedure has a

---

[7]Note that for both mutation operators the same k is used here, although they can be chosen independently. The safe version ($k = a$) for the random mutation operator means that a random walk is carried out on ψ.

1: generate $r_1, \ldots, r_k \in X$ based on P
2: $P'' \leftarrow P \cup \{r_1, \ldots, r_k\}$
3: **while** $|P''| > \alpha$ **do**
4:     **for all** $a \in P''$ **do**
5:         $\delta_a \leftarrow fitnessAssignment(a,\ P'')$
6:     choose $p \in P''$ with $\delta_p = \min_{a \in P''} \delta_a$
7:     $P'' \leftarrow P'' \setminus \{p\}$
8: **return** P''

Algorithm 3 Heuristic Set Mutation of set P

1: $\delta_a \leftarrow 0$
2: **for all** $b \in P''$ **do**
3:     **if** $P'' \setminus \{b\} \preccurlyeq P'' \setminus \{a\}$ **then**
4:         $\delta_a \leftarrow \delta_a + 1$
5: **return** δ_a

Algorithm 4 Fitness Assignment given an individual a and population P''

runtime complexity of $\mathcal{O}((\alpha + k)t)$, where t stands for the runtime needed to compute the preference relation comparisons which usually depends on $\alpha + k$ and the number of objective functions. It can be made faster, when using unary indicators, see the technical report by the authors and colleagues [143], and Chapter 4 of this thesis.

2.4.2 · SPAM$^+$–Using Populations of Sets in Multiobjective Optimization

In SPAM, the individual steps (fitness assignment, mating selection, mutation/crossover, and environmental selection) of the MOEA, that lead to a modified set, are abstracted as a set mutation, see the upper right corner of Figure 2.10—they are in fact $\mathcal{P}(X)/\mathcal{P}(X)$-hillclimbers [142]. Therefore, the question arises how a general EA could be constructed where the individuals represent *sets*.

In the following, a general $\mathcal{P}(X)/\mathcal{P}(X)$ evolutionary algorithm is proposed (Set Preference Algorithm for Multiobjective Optimization using Populations of Sets (SPAM$^+$)) as it is depicted in the lower half of Figure 2.10, i.e., an algorithm operating on *multiple* sets of solutions. The question arises, how the corresponding operators (set mutation, set crossover, set mating and set environmental selection) can be created and if they are beneficial for search. To this end, set operators based on the hypervolume indicator are proposed for illustrative purpose, however, any other set preference relation can be used.

This section gives first insights on how to use the set-based view provided by SPAM to propose a general $\mathcal{P}(X)/\mathcal{P}(X)$ MOEA. It systematically investigates which extensions are needed and proposes a novel recombination scheme on sets using the hypervolume indicator as underlying set preference. To the author's knowledge, no study has used the set perspective on evolutionary algorithms explicitly, but parallel evolutionary algorithms can be considered as optimizers operating on sets, as discussed in Section 2.4.3.

Next, a general framework of a $\mathcal{P}(X)/\mathcal{P}(X)$-optimizer is presented for multi-objective optimization the basis of which is a population-based evolutionary algorithm. In contrast to SPAM, this new optimizer also uses mating selection, recombination, and environmental selection—operators of a usual EA. Before the different operators on solution sets are presented, a general framework is described.

A ($\mu\overset{+}{,}\lambda$)-EA as a $\mathcal{P}(X)/\mathcal{P}(X)$-Optimizer

Algorithm 5 shows a general $\mathcal{P}(X)/\mathcal{P}(X)$-optimizer that mainly follows the scheme of Figure 2.10. The algorithm resembles an island-based MOEA as will be discussed in Section 2.4.3 with additional mating and environmental selection. Mutation, recombination, and selection on single solutions are considered as mutations on solution sets and the migration operator is regarded as recombination operator on sets.

The algorithm starts by choosing the first population $\mathcal{S}$ of μ sets (of N solutions each) uniformly at random. Then, the optimization loop produces new sets until a certain number $g_{\max}$ of generations are performed. To this end, every set A in the population $\mathcal{S}$ is mutated to a new set by the operator *setMutate*(A) and λ pairs of sets are selected in the set mating selection step to form the parents of λ recombination operations. Note that

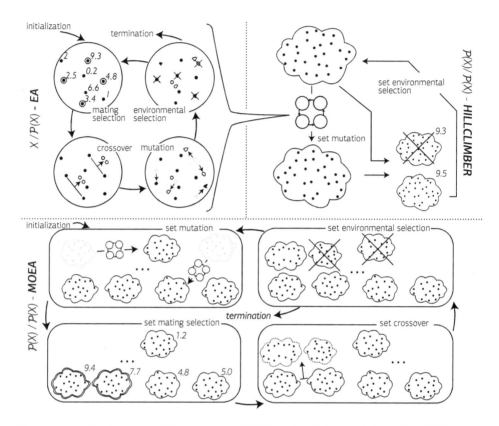

Figure 2.10 Illustration of different types of MOEAs: (top left) usual view of a MOEA where the operators work on solutions; (top right) a set-based view of the same algorithm; (bottom) an evolutionary algorithm working on sets, i.e., a $\mathcal{P}(X)/\mathcal{P}(X)$-optimizer.

the operator "$\cup$" is the union between two multisets; since the population of evolutionary algorithms usually contains duplicate solutions, the population of Algorithm 5 is not restricted to sets. In the environmental selection step, the new population is formed by selecting μ sets from the union of the previous population and the varied solution sets. Figure 2.10 illustrates the steps performed in one generation graphically.

Mutation of Solution Sets

As mutation operator on solution sets, the same operator used by SPAM is

1: $\mathcal{S} \leftarrow$ pick population $\mathcal{S}$ uniformly at random as μ sets of N solutions from X
2: $i \leftarrow 1$ (*set generation counter*)
3: **while** $i \leq g_{\text{max}}$ **do**
4:       $\mathcal{M} \leftarrow \emptyset$
5:       **for all** $A \in \mathcal{S}$ **do**
6:             $\mathcal{M} \leftarrow \mathcal{M} \cup \{setMutate(A)\}$
7:       $\mathcal{M}' \leftarrow setMatingSelection(\mathcal{M}, \lambda)$
8:       $\mathcal{M}'' \leftarrow \emptyset$
9:       **for all** $(A_p, A_q) \in \mathcal{M}'$ **do**
10:             $\mathcal{M}'' \leftarrow \mathcal{M}'' \cup \{setRecombine(A_p, A_q)\}$
11:       $\mathcal{S} \leftarrow setEnvironmentalSelection(\mathcal{S}, \mathcal{M}'')$
12:       $i \leftarrow i + 1$

Algorithm 5 A $\mathcal{P}(X)/\mathcal{P}(X)$-optimizer with ($\mu$+$\lambda$)-selection. Requires number of solution sets in population μ, number of solutions in each solution set N, number of offspring λ, maximum number of generations g_{max}.

used, see Algorithm 3. As an example, the hypervolume indicator is used with non-dominated sorting as underlying set preference. To determine the fitness of a solution, an advanced concept which will be explained in Chapter 4 is used mimicking Algorithm 4, i.e., aiming at generating the minimal element among all sets of predefined size.

Recombination of Solution Sets
Because the goal is to maximize according to the underlying set preference, (for instance the hypervolume indicator), the recombination operator on sets should also aim at producing offspring preferred over the previous set (e.g., with large hypervolume). Therefore, a new recombination operator on solution sets A and B is proposed that is targeted at generating such offspring C. As an example, the hypervolume indicator is used, see Figure 2.11 for an illustrative example. The idea behind the operator is to iteratively delete the worst solution in the first parent and add the best individual from the second parent until the new set would be no longer preferred over the previous sets, e.g., no hypervolume improvement is possible. In more detail, the process runs as described in the following.

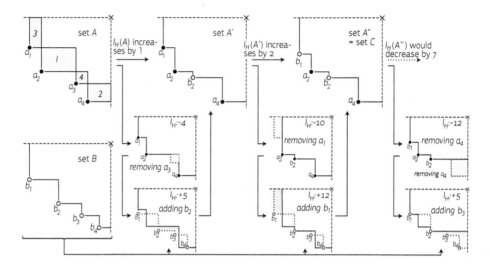

Figure 2.11 Illustration of the hypervolume-based recombination operator on solution sets: two exemplary sets A and B with four solutions each are recombined to a set C. First, the solutions in A are ranked according to their hypervolume losses. Then, iteratively, the solution in A with smallest loss is deleted (middle row) and the solution in B that maximizes the hypervolume indicator is added to A (last row) until no hypervolume improvement is possible. For each step, the changes in hypervolume are annotated in the top right corner of the corresponding figure.

In a first step, all solutions in the first set $A = \{a_1, \ldots, a_{|A|}\}$ are ranked according to their fitness as in Algorithm 4 (upper left figure in Figure 2.11). In our example, the fitness of a solution corresponds to the hypervolume that is solely dominated by this solution, in other words, its hypervolume loss. Then, the new set C results from A by iteratively removing the solution a_i with smallest fitness that is not yet removed (ties are resolved randomly, see middle row in Figure 2.11) and adding the solution $b \in B$ that leads to the minimal element, e.g., maximizes the hypervolume indicator of the new set (last row in Figure 2.11). The replacement of solutions stops before the next exchange would lead to a set which is no longer preferred over the previous set, i.e., $A'' \nprec A'$. In case of the hypervolume, the exchange would decrease the hypervolume of the new set.

An important aspect worth mentioning is the asymmetry of the recombination operator, i.e., $setRecombine(A_p, A_q) \neq setRecombine(A_q, A_p)$. This asymmetry is the reason for selecting ordered pairs in the set mating selection step of Algorithm 5.

Mating and Environmental Selection

In the following, four different variants of mating and environmental selection combinations are presented. Two variants choose sets for recombination directly from the mutated sets (denoted A-variants) whereas the other two variants choose one mutated set as the first parent and the set containing all solutions of all other sets as the second parent for recombination (called B-variants):

Variant A1 randomly selects μ pairs of sets in the mating selection step and uses (μ, μ)-selection in its environmental selection step.

Variant A2 selects all possible $\mu \cdot (\mu - 1)$ pairs of sets in mating selection and selects the best μ out of the $\mu \cdot (\mu - 1)$ new sets in environmental selection.

Variant B1 selects one pair of sets only, where the first set $A_1 \in M$ is selected uniformly at random and the second set A_2 is chosen as union of all $A \in M$ except A_1 itself. In the environmental selection step, variant B1 copies the only new set μ times to create the new population of μ identical sets.

Variant B2 selects μ pairs of sets by choosing every set of M once as the first set A_1 of a parent pair and the second set A_2 of the pair is chosen as union of all $a \in M$ except A_1 itself as in variant B1. The environmental selection of variant B2 chooses all μ newly generated sets to create the new population.

Note that all variants perform mating selection independent of the underlying preference relation, the consideration of which may improve the optimizer further.

2.4.3 · Relation of SPAM and SPAM$^+$ to Existing MOEAs

As already mentioned in Section 2.4.1, SPAM presents a new perspective on MOEAs such as NSGA-II, SPEA2 or the Indicator-Based Evolutionary

Algorithm (IBEA). On the other hand, *parallelized* MOEAs can be interpreted as a more general class of algorithm, some of them can even be considered as optimizers operating on sets like SPAM$^+$.

The first incitement to parallelization were the increasing complexity of large scale problems and the availability of large computer clusters and multiprocessor systems. The *master-slave* approach uses a master processor that performs all operations on one global population except for fitness evaluations which are delegated to different slave processors [118]. This parallelization does not change the algorithm itself, and can be either seen as a $X/\mathcal{P}(X)$-optimizer or as a $\mathcal{P}(X)/\mathcal{P}(X)$-hillclimber.

The second major category of parallel MOEAs—the *island model*—on the other hand, can be interpreted as $\mathcal{P}(X)/\mathcal{P}(X)$-optimizer that use more than one set. An island model MOEA divides the overall population into different islands or independent solution sets. Hence, when abstracting away from parallelization, the island model can be interpreted as an algorithm operating on a population of sets. Each of these sets represents one island which is optimized by a separate EA. This enables running different islands on several computers at the same time. An island model without any exchange of individuals between islands corresponds to a multi-start approach, where each island represents one run, using different seeds or even different optimization strategies [100]. Most island models, however, use a cooperative approach. Although the subpopulations evolve independently most of the time, solutions are exchanged once in a while between islands by *migration*. A well designed migration lets information of good individuals pass among islands and at the same time helps to preserve diversity by isolation of the islands. In contrast to the approaches mentioned above, this paradigm also uses recombination of sets (by migration) and can therefore be advantageous not only in terms of runtime and robustness, but also in terms of quality of the obtained Pareto-optimal solutions [37].

There exist many aspects of migration strategy: (a) the way islands are selected for migration (the set mating selection from a set based perspective), [108, 112] (b) the way the population is divided into subpopulations, [26, 76, 97], and (c) the way islands are optimized, i.e., either by the very same optimizer or by using different parameters. For more details of the different aspects of migration, refer to [37] and [120].

All island models mentioned so far do not use the concept of a set-based fitness measure and operators. Also parallel MOEAs, when interpreted as $\mathcal{P}(X)/\mathcal{P}(X)$-optimizers, usually do not perform environmental selection and select the individuals for mating according to a fixed scheme given by the neighborhood of the islands. One exception is the algorithm presented in [3], where islands are randomly selected and both mutation and recombination are applied to subpopulations rather than to single solutions. The quality of the newly generated subpopulations as well as their parents is then assessed by a fitness value and the better sets are kept (set environmental selection). However, the environmental selection only operates locally and the fitness assignment is not a true set fitness since it corresponds to the sum of single fitness values that are determined on basis of a global population.

2.5 · Experimental Validation

This section investigates both SPAM (Section 2.5.1), and SPAM$^+$ (Section 2.5.2) with respect to optimizing set preference. First, Subsection 2.5.1 tackles the question whether SPAM really optimizes the underlying set preference relation. Next, in Subsection 2.5.2 the question is explored as to whether it would be advantageous to optimize multiple sets concurrently, as done by SPAM$^+$.

2.5.1 · Experimental Validation of SPAM

First, the practicability of SPAM is investigated. The main questions are: (i) can different user preferences be expressed in terms of set preference relations, (ii) is it feasible to use a general search algorithm for arbitrary set preference relations, i.e., is SPAM effective in finding appropriate sets, and (iii) how well are set preference relations suited to guide the optimization process? However, the purpose is not to carry out a performance comparison of SPAM to existing MOEAs, but rather the separation of user preferences and search algorithm is the focus of this chapter.

Table 2.1 Overview of the set preference relations used in the experimental studies; for details, see Section 2.3.

$\preccurlyeq_H^{mp}$	hypervolume indicator I_H with reference point (12,12) resp. (12,12,12,12,12) and minimum elements partitioning
$\preccurlyeq_{P1,H}^{mp}$	preference-based quality indicator I_P with two reference points $r^{(1)}$ = (0.2, 0.9) resp. (0.2,0.9,0.9,0.9,0.9), $r^{(2)}$ = (0.8,0.5) resp. (0.8,0.5,0.5,0.5,0.5) with scaling factors $\rho^{(1)}$ = 1/3 and $\rho^{(2)}$ = 2/3, followed by the hypervolume indicator I_H with reference point (12,12) resp. (12,12,12,12,12); in addition, minimum elements partitioning is used. For I_P, the same 1 000 weights λ are used for all reference points; the weights are (once) uniformly randomly drawn from $\{(\lambda_1,\ldots,\lambda_n) \in \mathbb{R}^n \mid \lambda_i > 0 \text{ for } 1 \le i \le n, \ ||(\lambda_1,\ldots,\lambda_n)|| = 1\}$
$\preccurlyeq_{H,C,D}$	unary hypervolume indicator I_H with reference point (12,12) resp. (12,12,12,12,12) followed by the distance-to-front indicator I_C (maximum distance of any solution to the closest front member) and the diversity indicator I_D (kth-nearest neighbor approach)
$\preccurlyeq_{R2,H}^{mp}$	R_2 indicator I_{R2} with reference set $B = \{(0,0)\}$ and $\Lambda=\{(0,1), (0.01,0.99), \ldots, (0.3,0.7), (0.7,0.3), (0.71,0.29), \ldots, (1,0)\}$ in the case of two objectives* ($|\Lambda|$ = 62), followed by hypervolume indicator I_H with reference point (12,12) resp. (12,12,12,12,12); in addition, minimum elements partitioning is used
$\preccurlyeq_{\varepsilon1,H}^{mp}$	unary (additive) epsilon indicator $I_{\varepsilon1}$ with reference set $B = \{ (k\cdot0.004,0.8\text{-}k\cdot0.002) \ ; \ k \in \{0,1,\ldots,100\} \}$ resp. $B = \{(k\cdot0.004,0.8\text{-}k\cdot0.002,0.8\text{-}k\cdot0.002,0.8\text{-}k\cdot0.002,0.8\text{-}k\cdot0.002) \ ; \ k \in \{0,1,\ldots,100\} \}$, followed by the hypervolume indicator I_H with reference point (12,12) resp. (12,12,12,12,12); in addition, minimum elements partitioning is used
$\preccurlyeq_{P0,H}^{mp}$	preference-based quality indicator I_P with reference point $r^{(1)}$=(0,0) resp. (0,0,0,0,0), followed by the hypervolume indicator I_H with reference point (12,12) resp. (12,12,12,12,12); in addition, minimum elements partitioning is used. The same weights λ as in $\preccurlyeq_{P1,H}^{mp}$ are used by I_P.
$\preccurlyeq_D^{mp}$	diversity indicator I_D (kth-nearest neighbor approach) combined with minimum elements partitioning

*In the case of five objectives, overall 32·5 weight combinations are used for the set preference relation $\preccurlyeq_{R2,H}^{mp}$, cf. Table 2.1. In detail, Λ is defined as follows: $\Lambda=\{ (0,0,0,0,1), (0.01/4,0.01/4,0.01/4,0.01/4,0.99), \ldots, (0.3/4,0.3/4,0.3/4,0.3/4,0.7)\}$ $\cup \{ (0,0,0,1,0), (0.01/4,0.01/4,0.01/4,0.99,0.01/4), \ldots, (0.3/4,0.3/4,0.3/4,0.7,0.3/4) \} \cup \ldots\cup \{ (1,0,0,0,0), (0.99,0.01/4,0.01/4,0.01/4,0.01/4),\ldots, (0.7,0.3/4,0.3/4,0.3/4,0.3/4) \}$. The considered reference set was $B = \{(0,0,0,0,0)\}$

Comparison Methodology

In the following, different set preference relations are considered for integration in SPAM; they have been discussed in Section 2.3 and are listed in Table 2.1. All of them except of the last one are refinements of the set dominance relation $\preccurlyeq_{par}$; the relation $\preccurlyeq_D^{mp}$ is just used for the purpose of mimicking the behavior of dominance and density based MOEAs such as NSGA-II and SPEA2. As reference algorithms, NSGA-II [50] and IBEA[8] [135] are used; in the visual comparisons also SPEA2 [139] is included.

In order to make statements about the effectiveness of the algorithms considered, one needs to assess the generated Pareto set approximations with

---

[8]With parameters κ= 0.05 and ρ= 1.1.

regard to the set preference relation under consideration. The use of the Mann-Whitney U test is suggested to compare multiple outcomes of one algorithm with multiple outcomes of another algorithm. This is possible since all set preference relations considered in this chapter are total preorders; otherwise, the approach proposed in [91] can be applied. Thereby, one can obtain statements about whether either algorithm yields significantly better results for a specified set preference relation.

In detail, the statistical testing is carried as follows. Assuming two optimizers OA and OB, first all Pareto-set approximations generated by OA are pairwisely compared to all Pareto-set approximations generated by OB. If, e.g., 30 runs have been performed for each algorithm, then overall 900 comparisons are made. Now, let A and B be two Pareto-set approximations resulting from OA respectively OB; then, set A is considered better than set B with respect to the set preference relation $\preccurlyeq$, if $A \prec B$ holds. By counting the number of comparisons where the set of OA is better than the corresponding set of OB, one obtains the test statistics U; doing the same for OB gives U' which reflects the number of cases where OB yields a better outcome. The bigger U is compared to U', the better algorithm OA is geared towards the test relation $\preccurlyeq$ regarding OB.

As long as the entirety of the considered sets can be regarded as a large sample (e.g., 30 runs per algorithm), one can use the one-tailed normal approximation to calculate the significance of the test statistics U, correcting the variance for ties. Furthermore, multiple testing issues need to be taken into account when comparing multiple algorithms with each other; here, the significance levels are Bonferroni corrected.

Finally, the SPAM implementation used for the following experimental studies does not include the random set mutation operator, i.e., lines 3, 7, and 8 in Algorithm 1 were omitted. The reason is that every set comparison is computationally expensive—especially when the hypervolume indicator is involved—and that in practice it is extremely unlikely that random set mutation according to Algorithm 2 yields a set that is superior to the one generated by the heuristic set mutation operator. Nevertheless, a set mutation operator that in principle can generate any set in Ψ is important to

guarantee theoretical convergence. One may think of more effective operators than Algorithm 2 which preserves the convergence property; however,
this topic is subject to future work and not investigated in this chapter.

One may also ask whether the if statement at line 5 of Algorithm 1 is
actually of practical relevance. Testing SPAM with three set preference
relations, namely $\preccurlyeq_{P0,H}^{mp}$, $\preccurlyeq_{P1,H}^{mp}$, and $\preccurlyeq_{H,D}$, on a three-objective DTLZ5
(Deb-Thiele-Laumanns-Zitzler) problem instance indicates that in average
every $50th$ generation (using $\preccurlyeq_{P0,H}^{mp}$) and $100th$ generation (using $\preccurlyeq_{P1,H}^{mp}$ and
$\preccurlyeq_{H,D}$) the set produced by heuristic mutation is worse than the current set,
i.e., the current set is not replaced. One can expect and observe, though,
that this situation arises especially when being close to or on the Pareto
front (all set members are incomparable) and less frequently at the early
phase of the search process. Overall no significant differences between the
quality of the outcomes could be measured when running SPAM with and
without the check at line 5; in average, the computation time increased by
12% ($\preccurlyeq_{P0,H}^{mp}$ and $\preccurlyeq_{P1,H}^{mp}$) and 8% ($\preccurlyeq_{H,D}$). Nevertheless, it is recommended
to keep this additional check because it represents a crucial aspect of a
hill climber and prevents cycling behavior which is theoretically possible
whenever worse sets are accepted.

Results
This section provides experimental results for two test problems, namely
DTLZ2 and DTLZ5 [52] with 20 decision variables for 2 and 5 objectives.
On the one hand, visual comparisons will be provided in order to verify to
which extent the formalized user preferences have been achieved. On the
other hand, statistical tests are applied to investigate which search strategy
is best suited to optimize which user preferences; for each optimizer, 30
have been carried out. The general parameters used in the optimization
algorithms are given in Table 2.2.

Visual Comparisons of SPAM. Figure 2.12 shows the Pareto-set approximations generated by SPAM with the aforementioned set preference relations
and by the reference algorithms for the biobjective DTLZ2 problem (the

Table 2.2 Parameter settings used in section 2.5.1

Parameter	Value		continued	
set / population size a	20*,50**		η-mutation	20
newly created solutions k	20*,50**		η-recombination	20
number of generations	1 000		symmetric recombination	false
mutation probability	1		scaling	false
swap probability	0.5		tournament size	2
recombination probability	1		mating selection	uniform

* visual comparision, ** statistical testing

dotted sector of a circle represents the Pareto-front). The plots well reflect the chosen user preferences: (a) a set maximizing hypervolume, (b) a divided set close to two reference points, (c) focus on the extremes using corresponding weight combinations, (d) closeness to a given reference set, (e) a set minimizing the weighted epsilon-distance to the origin for a uniformly distributed set of weight combinations, and (f) a uniformly distributed set of solutions. This demonstrates that SPAM is in principle capable of optimizing towards the user preferences that are encoded in the corresponding set preference relation. It can also be seen that the density-based approaches by NSGA-II and SPEA2 can be imitated by using a corresponding diversity indicator—although this is not the goal of this chapter.

Usefulness for Search of SPAM. After having seen the proof-of-principle results for single runs, the question of how effective SPAM is in optimizing a given set preference relation $\preccurlyeq$ is investigated, i.e., how specific the optimization process is. The hypothesis is that SPAM used in combination with a specific $\preccurlyeq_A$ (let us say SPAM-A) yields better Pareto set approximations than if used with any other set preference relation $\preccurlyeq_B$ (let us say SPAM-B)—better here means with respect to $\preccurlyeq_A$. Ideally, for every set A generated by SPAM-A and every set B generated by SPAM-B, it would hold $A \preccurlyeq_A B$ or even $A \prec_A B$. Clearly, this describes an ideal situation. A set preference relation that is well suited for representing certain preferences may not be well suited for search per se, cf. Section 2.3.4; for instance,

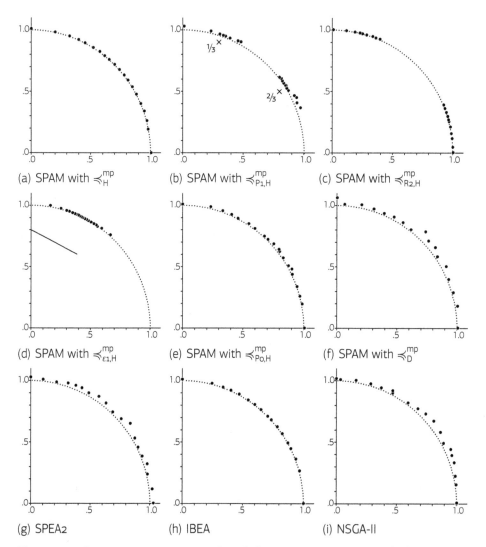

Figure 2.12 Pareto-set approximations found after 1 000 generations on a biobjective DTLZ2 problem for a set size / population size of $m = 20$. All algorithms were started with the same initial set / population.

when using a single indicator such as the hypervolume indicator refinement through set partitioning is important for effective search.

To this end, statistical comparisons of all algorithmic variants are made with respect to the six refinements listed in Table 2.1. Note that set partitioning is only used for search, not for the comparisons. The outcomes of the pairwise comparisons after Bonferroni correction are given in Tables 2.3 and 2.4. With only few exceptions, the above hypothesis is confirmed: using $\preccurlyeq_A$ in SPAM yields the best Pareto-set approximations with regard to $\preccurlyeq_A$, independently of the problem and the number of objectives under consideration. These results are highly significant at a significance level of 0.001.

Concerning the exceptions, first it can be noticed that there is no significant difference between $\preccurlyeq_H^{\mathrm{mp}}$ and $\preccurlyeq_{H,C,D}$ when used in SPAM—both times, the hypervolume indicator value is optimized. This actually confirms the assumption that set partitioning can be replaced by a corresponding sequence of quality indicators. Second, the algorithm based on the set preference relation $\preccurlyeq_{P0,H}^{\mathrm{mp}}$ using the I_P indicator with the origin as reference point performs worse than SPAM with $\preccurlyeq_H^{\mathrm{mp}}$ on DTL2; this is not suprising as it actually can be regarded as an approximation of the hypervolume-based relation. However, it is suprising that SPAM with $\preccurlyeq_{P0,H}^{\mathrm{mp}}$ is outperformed by IBEA on both DTLZ2 and DTLZ5; it seems that IBEA is more effective in obtaining a well-distributed front. This result indicates the sensitivity of $\preccurlyeq_{P0,H}^{\mathrm{mp}}$ with respect to the distribution and the number of the weight combinations chosen. The problem can be resolved by selecting a larger number of weights as discussed in Section 2.3.4.

2.5.2 · Experimental Validation of SPAM$+$

The experiments described in this section serve to compare four $\mathcal{P}(X)/\mathcal{P}(X)$-optimizer variants with SPAM[9].

---

[9]In this comparison, the tests in Lines 5 to 8 in Algorithm 1 are omitted, as in experiments considering these lines did not give statistically different results when using the $\preccurlyeq_H^{\mathrm{mp}}$ as underlying preference relation, see also the considerations made in Section 2.5.1.

Table 2.3 Pairwise statistical comparison of 30 runs per algorithm on the biobjective DTLZ2 (a) and DTLZ5 (b) after 1 000 generations. In the notation $U{:}U'$, U (resp. U') stands for the number of times a set generated by algorithm A (resp. B) beats a set of algorithm B (resp. A) with regard to the test relation associated with the corresponding row. A star next to these numbers indicates a significant difference, the few cases where this was not the case are shown in bold.

(a) 2-dimensional DTLZ2

alg A \ alg B	SPAM with set preference relation ... $\preceq^{mp}_{P_1,H}$	$\preceq^{mp}_{H}$	$\preceq^{mp}_{R_2,H}$	$\preceq^{mp}_{\varepsilon_1,H}$	$\preceq^{mp}_{Po}$	$\preceq_{H,C,D}$	IBEA	NSGA-II	test relation
SPAM with set preference ... $\preceq^{mp}_{P_1,H}$	–	900: o*	900: o*	900: o*	899: 1*	900: o*	900: o*	900: o*	$\preceq^{mp}_{P_1,H}$
$\preceq^{mp}_{H}$	900: o*	–	900: o*	900: o*	900: o*	900: o*	900: o*	900: o*	$\preceq^{mp}_{H}$
$\preceq^{mp}_{R_2,H}$	900: o*	900: o*	–	900: o*	900: o*	900: o*	900: o*	900: o*	$\preceq^{mp}_{R_2,H}$
$\preceq^{mp}_{\varepsilon_1,H}$	900: o*	900: o*	900: o*	–	889: 1*	900: o*	900: o*	900: o*	$\preceq^{mp}_{\varepsilon_1,H}$
$\preceq^{mp}_{Po}$	**60:840**	830: 70*	846: 54*	**456:444**	–	**75:835**	835: 75*	900: o*	$\preceq^{mp}_{Po}$
$\preceq_{H,C,D}$	**444:456**	900: o*	843: 57*	845: 57*	**75:835**	–	820: 80*	900: o*	$\preceq_{H,C,D}$

* preference is significant at the 0.001 level (1-tailed, Bonferroni-adjusted)

(b) 2-dimensional DTLZ5

alg A \ alg B	SPAM with set preference relation ... $\preceq^{mp}_{P_1,H}$	$\preceq^{mp}_{H}$	$\preceq^{mp}_{R_2,H}$	$\preceq^{mp}_{\varepsilon_1,H}$	$\preceq_{Po}$	$\preceq_{H,C,D}$	$\preceq^{mp}_{D}$	IBEA	NSGA-II	test relation
SPAM with set preference ... $\preceq^{mp}_{P_1,H}$	–	900: o*	900: o*	900: o*	900: o*	900: o*	900: o*	887: 13*	900: o*	$\preceq^{mp}_{P_1,H}$
$\preceq^{mp}_{H}$	900: o*	–	900: o*	900: o*	900: o*	900: o*	900: o*	900: o*	900: o*	$\preceq^{mp}_{H}$
$\preceq^{mp}_{R_2,H}$	900: o*	900: o*	–	900: o*	900: o*	900: o*	900: o*	900: o*	900: o*	$\preceq^{mp}_{R_2,H}$
$\preceq^{mp}_{\varepsilon_1,H}$	**891: 9***	900: o*	900: o*	–	900: o*	**897: 3***	900: o*	900: o*	900: o*	$\preceq^{mp}_{\varepsilon_1,H}$
$\preceq_{Po}$	**22:878**	**898: 2***	**899: 1***	**12:888**	–	**445:455**	**788:112***	**95:805**	**885: 15***	$\preceq_{Po}$
$\preceq_{H,C,D}$	**455:445**	900: o*	900: o*	900: o*	**795:105***	–	900: o*	900: o*	900: o*	$\preceq_{H,C,D}$

* preference is significant at the 0.001 level (1-tailed, Bonferroni-adjusted)

Table 2.4 Pairwise statistical comparison of 30 runs per algorithm on the five objective DTLZ2 (a) and DTLZ5 (b) after 1 000 generations. In the notation $U:U'$, U (resp. U') stands for the number of times a set generated by algorithm A (resp. B) beats a set of algorithm B (resp. A) with regard to the test relation associated with the corresponding row. A star next to these numbers indicates a significant difference, the few cases where this was not the case are shown in bold.

(a) 5-dimensional DTLZ2

alg. A \ alg. B	SPAM with set preference relation ...							IBEA	NSGA-II	test relation
	$H^{mp}_{P_1,H}$	H^{mp}_H	$H^{mp}_{R_2,H}$	$H^{mp}_{\varepsilon_1,H}$	$H^{mp}_{P_O}$	$H_{H,C,D}$	H^{mp}_D			
$H^{mp}_{P_1,H}$	–	820: 80*	820: 80*	805: 95*	838: 62*	820: 80*	900: 0*	820: 80*	900: 0*	$H_{P_1,H}$
H^{mp}_H	900: 0*	–	900: 0*	900: 0*	900: 0*	**404:496**	900: 0*	895: 5*	900: 0*	H_H
$H^{mp}_{R_2,H}$	900: 0*	900: 0*	–	900: 0*	900: 0*	900: 0*	900: 0*	900: 0*	900: 0*	$H_{R_2,H}$
$H^{mp}_{\varepsilon_1,H}$	895: 5*	895: 5*	870: 30*	–	894: 6*	895: 5*	895: 5*	895: 5*	900: 0*	$H_{\varepsilon_1,H}$
$H^{mp}_{P_O}$	880: 20*	810: 90*	871: 29*	899: 1*	–	900: 0*	898: 2*	**32:868**	900: 0*	H_{P_O}
$H_{H,C,D}$	900: 0*	**496:404**	900: 0*	900: 0*	843: 57*	–	900: 0*	900: 0*	900: 0*	$H_{H,C,D}$

* preference is significant at the 0.001 level (1-tailed, Bonferroni-adjusted)

(b) 5-dimensional DTLZ5

alg. A \ alg. B	SPAM with set preference relation ...							IBEA	NSGA-II	test relation
	$H^{mp}_{P_1,H}$	H^{mp}_H	$H^{mp}_{R_2,H}$	$H^{mp}_{\varepsilon_1,H}$	$H^{mp}_{P_O}$	$H_{H,C,D}$	H^{mp}_D			
$H^{mp}_{P_1,H}$	–	877: 23*	900: 0*	900: 0*	900: 0*	**723:177**	900: 0*	874: 26*	900: 0*	$H_{P_1,H}$
H^{mp}_H	900: 0*	–	900: 0*	900: 0*	900: 0*	**455:445**	900: 0*	900: 0*	900: 0*	H_H
$H^{mp}_{R_2,H}$	900: 0*	900: 0*	–	900: 0*	900: 0*	900: 0*	900: 0*	900: 0*	900: 0*	$H_{R_2,H}$
$H^{mp}_{\varepsilon_1,H}$	892: 8*	**618:282**	900: 0*	–	900: 0*	**626:274**	867: 33*	893: 7*	900: 0*	$H_{\varepsilon_1,H}$
$H^{mp}_{P_O}$	900: 0*	841: 59*	819: 81*	873: 27*	–	752:148*	900: 0*	**121:779**	**547:453**	H_{P_O}
$H_{H,C,D}$	900: 0*	**445:455**	900: 0*	900: 0*	900: 0*	–	900: 0*	900: 0*	900: 0*	$H_{H,C,D}$

* preference is significant at the 0.001 level (1-tailed, Bonferroni-adjusted)

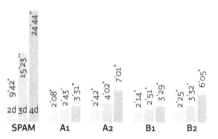

Figure 2.13 Averaged running times of the four $\mathcal{P}(X)/\mathcal{P}(X)$-optimizer variants and the standard MOEA.

Four variants of SPAM^+ are considered: A1, A2, B1, and B2 named after the used selection scheme as described in Section 2.4.2. The set mutation and set recombination operators are the same in all variants and implemented as described in Section 2.4.2. For a fair comparison, the mutation operator in SPAM is also used as set mutation operator in all four SPAM^+ variants. The mutation operator corresponds to a run of a normal hypervolume-based MOEA, as for example [16] or [82], for G generations. The used $X/\mathcal{P}(X)$-optimizer starts with a set of N solutions that is obtained from the overall $\mathcal{P}(X)/\mathcal{P}(X)$-optimizer's population. For G generations, N solutions of the current set are selected in a mating selection step, these solutions undergo SBX crossover and polynomial mutation as described in [50] and in the environmental selection step, the best solutions from the previous population and the new solutions are selected to form the new population.

Note that the implementation of the set mutation step is parallelized, i.e., the μ set mutation operations can be performed in parallel as μ independent runs of the standard MOEA if the algorithm is run on a machine with more than one core. Unless otherwise stated, the same parameters are used for all algorithms. The hypervolume indicator is computed exactly for all biobjective problems; otherwise, 10 000 samples are used to approximate it; the reference point is chosen as $(40,...,40)$ such that all solutions of the considered problems have a positive hypervolume contribution. For comparing the algorithms, the standard MOEA runs for 500 generations with a population size of 200—the $\mathcal{P}(X)/\mathcal{P}(X)$-optimizer variants use the same number of function evaluations within $g_{\max} = 25$ generations where the $\mu = 10$ sets of $N = 20$ solutions each are mutated for $G = 20$ generations of the standard MOEA.

To compare the four $\mathcal{P}(X)/\mathcal{P}(X)$-optimizer variants of Section 2.4.2 and the standard MOEA with the parameters described above, 30 runs are performed for each of the test problems DTLZ2, DTLZ5, DTLZ7 [54], as well as WFG3, WFG6, and WFG9 by the Walking Fish Group [79] with 2, 3, and 4 objectives. Table 2.5 shows the performance score and the normalized hypervolume in the last generation, i.e., the hypervolume indicator of the set containing all single solutions in the last population, see Appendix A on page 225 for an explanation of the performance score. In addition, Figure 2.13 shows the running times of the different algorithms on a 64bit AMD linux machine with 4 cores (2.6GHz) averaged over all 6 test problems.

There are two main observations: On the one hand, the $\mathcal{P}(X)/\mathcal{P}(X)$-optimizer variants are faster than the standard MOEA. On the other hand, the quality of the solution sets obtained by the $\mathcal{P}(X)/\mathcal{P}(X)$-optimizer variants are, in part, better than the standard MOEA in terms of hypervolume indicator values.

As to the running time, a speed-up is not surprising due to the parallel implementation of the $\mathcal{P}(X)/\mathcal{P}(X)$-optimizer variants. However, the speed-ups are higher than the number of cores except for the A2 variant which indicates that there will be a speed-up even on a single processor. The reason is mainly the faster hypervolume computation which depends heavily on the number of solutions to be considered.

As to the solution quality, two observations stand out: the B1 and B2 variants obtain, statistically significantly, better hypervolume values than SPAM (mimicking a standard MOEA) on all DTLZ2 and DTLZ5 instances. No general conclusion over all problems can be made for the A2, B1, and B2 variants. The A1 variant, however, yields for 16 of the 18 problems better results than SPAM (except for 4-objective DTLZ5 and 2-objective DTLZ7).

The huge differences between the DTLZ and the WFG problems for the different $\mathcal{P}(X)/\mathcal{P}(X)$-optimizer variants may be caused by the different characteristics of elitism: a good solution is more likely to be contained in *all* solution sets after recombination within the variants A2, B1, and B2 in

		SPAM	A1	A2	B1	B2
Table 2.5 Performance score P according to Appendix A of the four $\mathcal{P}(X)/\mathcal{P}(X)$ variants A1, A2, B1, B2, and SPAM introduced in Sections 2.4.2 and 2.4.1 respectively. Smaller values of P represent better algorithms. In brackets, the mean hypervolume obtained is shown, normalized to [0,1], where larger values represent better results.	**2d** DTLZ2	4 (.12)	3 (.40)	2 (.48)	0 (.87)	0 (.84)
	DTLZ5	4 (.15)	3 (.42)	2 (.50)	0 (.85)	0 (.86)
	DTLZ7	0 (1.00)	2 (.99)	4 (.81)	1 (.98)	2 (.94)
	WFG3	1 (.96)	0 (.99)	2 (.91)	3 (.79)	3 (.77)
	WFG6	1 (.84)	0 (.94)	1 (.82)	3 (.63)	4 (.56)
	WFG9	1 (.82)	0 (.88)	2 (.75)	3 (.63)	3 (.59)
	3d DTLZ2	3 (.34)	2 (.44)	3 (.31)	0 (.74)	0 (.76)
	DTLZ5	4 (.29)	2 (.34)	2 (.35)	1 (.77)	0 (.85)
	DTLZ7	2 (.98)	0 (.99)	4 (.67)	1 (.93)	1 (.94)
	WFG3	1 (.75)	0 (.87)	2 (.69)	3 (.25)	3 (.27)
	WFG6	1 (.87)	0 (.94)	1 (.89)	3 (.83)	3 (.82)
	WFG9	0 (.85)	0 (.87)	2 (.67)	3 (.49)	3 (.47)
	4d DTLZ2	4 (.39)	2 (.47)	2 (.46)	1 (.82)	0 (.89)
	DTLZ5	2 (.53)	3 (.49)	4 (.33)	0 (.76)	0 (.81)
	DTLZ7	2 (.93)	0 (.99)	4 (.60)	2 (.92)	0 (.94)
	WFG3	2 (.65)	0 (.85)	1 (.73)	3 (.57)	3 (.58)
	WFG6	3 (.57)	0 (.80)	1 (.67)	1 (.61)	1 (.68)
	WFG9	1 (.77)	0 (.88)	2 (.63)	2 (.55)	2 (.62)
	Mean P	**2**	**0.94**	**2.28**	**1.67**	**1.56**

comparison to the A1 variant, i.e., the diversity is lower. In addition, the diversity of solutions is also higher in the A1 variant because of its random mating selection. This low diversity between single solutions might be the reason why the three variants A2, B1, and B2 are not performing as good as the A1 variant on the WFG problems. For the DTLZ problems, however, the small diversity seems to cause no problems for the search, potentially due to the structure of the problems.

2.6 · Summary

This chapter has discussed EMO from a single-objective perspective that is centered around set preference relations and based on the following three observations:

1. the result of a MOEA run is usually a set of trade-off solutions representing a Pareto set approximation;
2. most existing MOEAs can be regarded as hill climbers on set problems;
3. most existing MOEAs are (implicitly) based on set preference information.

When applying an evolutionary algorithm to the problem of approximating the Pareto-optimal set, the population itself can be regarded as the current Pareto set approximation. The subsequent application of mating selection, variation, and environmental selection heuristically produces a new Pareto set approximation that—in the ideal case—is better than the previous one. In the light of the underlying set problem, the population represents a single element of the search space which is in each iteration replaced by another element of the search space. Consequently, selection and variation can be regarded as a mutation operator on populations resp. sets. Somewhat simplified, one may say that a classical MOEA used to approximate the Pareto-optimal set is a $(1, 1)$-strategy on a set problem (the successor set is chosen no matter whether the newly generated set is preferred over the old set). Furthermore, MOEAs are usually not preference-free. The main advantage of generating methods such as MOEAs is that the objectives do not need to be aggregated or ranked a priori; but nevertheless preference information is required to guide the search, although it is usually weaker and less stringent. In the environmental selection step, for instance, a MOEA has to choose a subset of individuals from the parents and the offspring which constitutes the next Pareto set approximation. To this end, the algorithm needs to know the criteria according to which the subset should be selected, in particular when all parents and children are incomparable, i.e., mutually non-dominating. That means the generation of a new population usually relies on set preference information.

The intention of the chapter was to study how set preference information can be formalized such that a total order on the set of Pareto set approximations results. To this end, it has been shown how to construct set preference relations on the basis of quality indicators and various examples have been provided. Moreover, a Set Preference Algorithm for Multiobjective Optimization (SPAM) has been presented, which is basically a hill climber and generalizes the concepts found in most modern MOEAs. SPAM can be used in combination with any type of set preference relation and thereby offers full flexibility for the decision maker. As the experimental results indicate, set preference relations can be used to effectively guide the search as well as to evaluate the outcomes of multiobjective optimizers.

SPAM has been generalized to SPAM$^+$ maintaining not just a single, but a population of multiple solution sets, such that SPAM$^+$ can be considered as a $(\mu \dotplus \lambda)$ MOEA on sets. In other words, one may think of SPAM$^+$ being a true evolutionary algorithm for set-based multiobjective optimization, one that operates on a population of multiple Pareto set approximations. The experimental results show that the approach of maintaining multiple sets is beneficial in terms of (a) the quality of the Pareto set approximations obtained, and (b) the overall computation time being reduced. As to (a), set recombination seems to play a major role, while (b) is mainly because the set mutation operating independently on subsets of the population is often faster to compute for smaller solutions sets. For instance, the hypervolume-based preference relation considered in this chapter benefits a lot from smaller sets.

Clearly, there are many open issues. Firstly, although this chapter approached how to formalize, optimize and compare set preference relation, no efforts have been made to characterize the minimal element the concepts are looking for. For instance, it is not clear what set of given size μ maximizes the hypervolume indicator. This question will be approached in the next chapter.

Secondly, the design of fast search algorithms dedicated to particular set preference relations is of high interest; SPAM and SPAM$^+$ provide flexibility, but are rather baseline algorithms that naturally cannot achieve maximum possible efficiency, these issues will be tackled in Chapter 4 to 6 of the present thesis.

3

Theory of the Weighted Hypervolume Indicator: Optimal μ-Distributions and the Choice of the Reference Point

The preceding chapter demonstrated, how preference on sets can be expressed and optimized. Quality indicators play a major role in this setting, as they inherently induce a total order which is crucial in the context of search. When using quality indicators as underlying set preference, the optimization goal changes from optimizing a set of objective functions simultaneously to the single-objective optimization goal of finding a set of points that maximizes the underlying indicator, where the number of points in the set is usually limited. Understanding the difference between these two optimization goals is fundamental when applying indicator-based algorithms in practice. On the one hand, a characterization of the inherent optimization goal of different indicators allows the user to choose the indicator that meets her preferences. On the other hand, knowledge about those sets of μ points with the optimal indicator values can be used in performance assessment if the indicator is used as a performance criterion.

Due to the unique properties of the hypervolume indicator, namely being the only known indicator as of February 2010 being a refinement of Pareto dominance (see Section 2.3.2), this chapter focuses on the weighted hypervolume indicator. Two major questions are tackled in the following: firstly, Section 3.3 addresses the question of characterizing so called *optimal* μ-*distributions* for the weighted hypervolume indicator, in other words, the optimal set of μ points reaching the largest hypervolume for a given weight function.

Secondly, in Section 3.4 a second important aspect of the weighted hypervolume is addressed, which is the influence of the reference set on the optimal distribution of points, in particular using a single reference point. This chapter provides several theoretical reasonings helping to understand the influence of the reference point, but also gives practical recommendations to be used in hypervolume-based search.

3.1 · Background

In practice, the population size $|P|$ of indicator-based algorithms is upper bounded, say $|P| \leq \mu$, with $\mu \in \mathbb{N}$, and the optimization goal changes to finding a set of μ solutions optimizing the quality indicator. Such a set is denoted as *optimal μ-distribution for the given indicator*. In this case, the additional questions arise how the number of points μ influences the optimization goal and to which set of μ objective vectors the optimal μ-distribution is mapped, i.e., which search bias is introduced by changing the optimization goal. Ideally, the optimal μ-distribution for an indicator only contains Pareto-optimal points and an increase in μ gives more and more Pareto-optimal points until the entire Pareto front is covered if μ approaches infinity. It is clear, for example by looking at Figure 2.12 on page 62, that in general, two different quality indicators yield a priori two different optimal μ-distributions, or in other words, introduce a different search bias. This has for instance been shown experimentally by Friedrich et al. [67] for the multiplicative ε-indicator and the hypervolume indicator.

In this chapter the weighted and unweighted hypervolume indicator [141] are investigated in detail as they are particularly interesting indicators being a refinement of the Pareto dominance relation, see Section 2.12 on page 31. Thus, an optimal μ-distribution contains only Pareto-optimal solutions and the set (probably unbounded in size) that maximizes the (weighted) hypervolume indicator covers the entire Pareto front [62]. Many other quality indicators do not have this property which is the main reason why the hypervolume indicator is probably the most used quality indicator applied to environmental selection of indicator-based evolutionary algorithms such as the SMS-EMOA [16], MO-CMA-ES [82], or HypE (Chapter 4). Nevertheless, it has been argued that using the (weighted) hypervolume indicator to guide search introduces a certain bias. Interestingly, several contradicting beliefs about this bias have been reported in the literature which will be discussed later on in more detail in Section 3.3. They range from stating that *convex regions may be preferred to concave regions* to the argumentation that *the hypervolume is biased towards boundary solutions*. In the light of this discussion, a thoroughly investigation of the effect of the hypervolume indicator on optimal μ-distributions is necessary.

Another important issue when dealing with the hypervolume indicator is the choice of the reference set R, in particular, choosing a reference point r as reference, i.e., $R = \{r\}$. The influence of the reference point on optimal μ-distributions has not been fully understood, especially for the weighted hypervolume indicator, and only rules-of-thumb exist on how to choose the reference point in practice. In particular, it could not be observed from practical investigations how the reference point has to be set to ensure to find the extremes of the Pareto front. Several authors recommend to use the corner of a space that is a little bit larger than the actual objective space as the reference point [16, 87]. For performance assessment, others recommend to use the estimated nadir point as the reference point [81, 109,

110]. Also here, theoretical investigations are highly needed to assist in practical applications.

This chapter should contribute to the above questions giving a better understanding of the search bias the hypervolume indicator is introducing, and providing theoretically founded recommendations on where to place the reference point in the case of two objectives.

In particular,

- the sets of μ points that maximize the (weighted) hypervolume indicator are characterized, i.e., optimal μ distributions are investigated. Besides general investigations for finite μ, a limit result for μ going to infinity is derived in terms of a density of points. Furthermore the chapter investigates
- the influence of the reference point on optimal μ-distributions, i.e., gives lower bounds for the reference point (possibly infinite) for guaranteeing the Pareto front's extreme points in an optimal μ-distribution, and investigates cases where the extremes are never contained in an optimal μ-distribution; In addition,
- it is proven in case the extremes can be obtained that for any reference point dominated by the nadir point—with any small but positive distance between the two points—there is a finite number of points μ_0 (possibly large in practice) such that for all $\mu > \mu_0$, the extremes are included in optimal μ-distributions. Last,
- the theoretical results are applied to all test problems of the ZDT [138], DTLZ [54], and WFG [79] test problem suites resulting in recommended choices of the reference point including numerical and sometimes analytical expressions for the resulting density of points on the front.

The chapter is structured as follows. First, the notations and definitions are introduced needed in the reminder of the chapter (Section 2.3.2). Then, the bias of the weighted hypervolume indicator in terms of optimal μ-distributions is considered. After characterizing optimal μ-distributions for a finite number of solutions (Section 3.3.1), results on the density of points if the number of points goes to infinity (Section 3.3.2) are derived.

Section 3.4 then investigates the influence of the reference point on optimal μ-distributions especially on the extremes.

3.2 · General Aspects and Notations

In what follows, biobjective problems are considered, i.e., two objective function f_1 and f_2 have to be minimized. The Pareto front, see Definition 2.8 on page 27, can thus be described by a one-dimensional function g mapping the image of the Pareto set (see Definition 2.7 on page 27) under the first objective f_1 onto the image of the Pareto set under the second objective f_2,

$$g : u \in D \mapsto g(u) \ ,$$

where D denotes the image of the Pareto set under the first objective. D can be, for the moment, either a finite or an infinite set. An illustration is given in Figure 3.1(a) where the function g describing the front has a domain of $D = [u_{min}, u_{max}]$.

Example 3.1: Consider the biobjective problem DTLZ2 from the DTLZ test problem suite which is defined as

$$\text{minimize} \quad f_1(x) = (1 + h(x_M)) \cos(x_1 \pi/2)$$
$$\text{minimize} \quad f_2(x) = (1 + h(x_M)) \sin(x_1 \pi/2)$$
$$h(x_M) = \sum_{x_i \in x_M} (x_i - 0.5)^2$$
$$\text{subject to} \quad 0 \le x_i \le 1 \text{ for } i = 1, \ldots n$$

where x_M denotes a subset of the decision variables $x = (x_1, \ldots, x_n) \in [0,1]^n$ with $h(x_M) \ge 0$. The Pareto front is reached for $h(x_M) = 0$, see [54]. Hence, the Pareto-optimal points have objective vectors $(\cos(x_1\pi/2), \sin(x_1\pi/2))$ with $0 \le x_1 \le 1$ which can be rewritten as points $(u, g(u))$ with $g(u) = \sqrt{1 - u^2}$ and $u \in D = [0, 1]$, see Figure 3.4(f). ○

Since g represents the shape of the trade-off surface, for minimization problems, g is strictly monotonically decreasing in D[1].

---

[1] If g is not strictly monotonically decreasing, Pareto-optimal points $(u_1, g(u_1))$ and $(u_2, g(u_2))$ exist with $u_1, u_2 \in D$ such that, without loss of generality, $u_1 < u_2$ and $g(u_1) \le g(u_2)$, i.e., $(u_1, g(u_1))$ is dominating $(u_2, g(u_2))$.

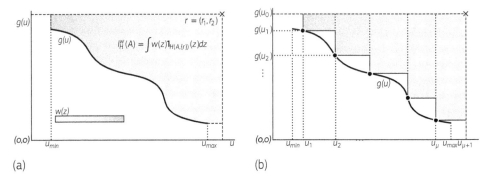

(a)   (b)

Figure 3.1 The weighted hypervolume indicator $I_H^w(A)$ corresponds to the integral of a weight function $w(z)$ over the set of objective vectors that are weakly dominated by a solution set A and in addition weakly dominate the reference point r (gray area). On the left, the set $f(A)$ is described by a function $g: [u_{min}, u_{max}] \to \mathbb{R}$. On the right, the computation of the hypervolume indicator is shown for μ solutions $(u_1, g(u_1))$, ..., $(u_\mu, g(u_\mu))$ and the reference point $r = (r_1, r_2)$ in the biobjective case as defined in Eq. 3.1.

The coordinates of a point belonging to the Pareto front are given as a pair $(u, g(u))$ with $u \in D$ and therefore, a point is entirely determined by the function g and the first coordinate $u \in D$. For μ points on the Pareto front, their first coordinates is denoted as $(u_1, \ldots, u_\mu)$. Without loss of generality, it is assumed that $u_i \leq u_{i+1}$, for $i = 1, \ldots, \mu - 1$ and for notation convenience, let $u_{\mu+1} := r_1$ and $g(u_0) := r_2$ where r_1 and r_2 are the first and second coordinate of the reference point r (see Figure 3.1(b)), i.e., $r = \{(r_1, r_2)\}$. The weighted hypervolume enclosed by these points can be decomposed into μ components, each corresponding to the integral of the weight function w over a rectangular area (see Figure 3.1(b)). The resulting weighted hypervolume writes:

$$I_H^w((u_1, \ldots, u_\mu)) := \sum_{i=1}^{\mu} \int_{u_i}^{u_{i+1}} \int_{g(u_i)}^{g(u_0)} w(u, v)\, dv\, du \ . \tag{3.1}$$

When the weight function equals one everywhere, one retrieves the expression for the non-weighted hypervolume

$$I_H((u_1, \ldots, u_\mu)) := \sum_{i=1}^{\mu} (u_{i+1} - u_i)(g(u_0) - g(u_i)) \ . \tag{3.2}$$

Please note, that in the following in order to simplify notations the indicators are defined also for *sets of u-coordinate values*, where $I_H^w((u_1, \ldots, u_\mu))$ reads as $I_H^w(\{f^{-1}(u_1, g(u_1)), \ldots, f^{-1}(u_\mu, g(u_\mu))\})$.

Remark 3.2: *Looking at Eq. 3.1 and Eq. 3.2, one sees that for a fixed g, a fixed weight w and reference point, the problem of finding a set of μ points maximizing the weighted hypervolume amounts to finding the solution of a μ-dimensional (mono-objective) maximization problem, i.e., optimal μ-distributions are the solution of a μ-dimensional problem. Here and in the remainder of the chapter, dimension refers to the dimension of the search space—as in single-objective optimization—and not to the number of objectives.*

Indicator-based evolutionary algorithms that aim at optimizing a unary indicator $I : \Psi \to \mathbb{R}$ transform a multiobjective problem into the single-objective one consisting in finding a set of points maximizing the respective indicator I. In practice, the sets of points are usually upper bounded by a constant μ, typically the population size.

Definition 3.3 (optimal μ-distribution): *For $\mu \in \mathbb{N}$ and a unary indicator I, a set of μ points maximizing I is called an optimal μ-distribution for I.*

The rest of the chapter is devoted to understand optimal μ-distributions for the hypervolume indicator in the biobjective case. The u-coordinates of an optimal μ-distribution for the hypervolume I_H^w will be denoted $(v_1^\mu, \ldots, v_\mu^\mu)$[2] and will thus satisfy

$$I_H^w(v_1^\mu, \ldots, v_\mu^\mu) \geq I_H^w((u_1, \ldots, u_\mu)) \text{ for all } (u_1, \ldots, u_\mu) \in D \times \ldots \times D .$$

Note, that the optimal μ-distribution might not be unique, and $(v_1^\mu, \ldots, v_\mu^\mu)$ therefore refers to *one* optimal μ-distribution. The corresponding value of the hypervolume will be denoted $I_{H,\mu}^{w*}$, i.e., $I_{H,\mu}^{w*} = I_H^w(v_1^\mu, \ldots, v_\mu^\mu)$.

---

[2] The optimal u-coordinates are denoted by u (greek upsilon), which looks exactly like v typeset in the serif font of this thesis.

3.3 · Characterization of Optimal μ-Distributions for Hypervolume Indicators

Whereas all sets containing μ Pareto-optimal solutions can be seen as "equally good" when the Pareto dominance relation is solely taken into account, optimizing the hypervolume indicator introduces a certain *bias*, i.e., different sets of μ Pareto-optimal solutions are associated with different hypervolume indicator values and the optimization goal changes to finding an optimal μ-distribution.

Several contradicting beliefs about this bias, the hypervolume indicator is introducing, have been reported in the literature. For example, Zitzler and Thiele [136] stated that, when optimizing the hypervolume in maximization problems, "convex regions may be preferred to concave regions", which has been also stated by Lizarraga-Lizarraga et al. [99] later on, whereas Deb et al. [53] argued that "[...] the hyper-volume measure is biased towards the boundary solutions". Knowles and Corne [89] observed that a local optimum of the hypervolume indicator "seems to be 'well-distributed'" which was also confirmed empirically [59, 90]. Beume et al. [16], in addition, state several properties of the hypervolume's bias: (i) optimizing the hypervolume indicator focuses on knee points; (ii) the distribution of points on the extremes is less dense than on knee points; (iii) only linear front shapes allow for equally spread solutions; and (iv) extremal solutions are maintained. In the light of this contradicting statements, a thorough characterization of optimal μ-distributions for the hypervolume indicator is necessary. Especially for the weighted hypervolume indicator, the bias of the indicator and the influence of the weight function w on optimal μ-distributions in particular has not been fully understood. The results, presented in this chapter provide a theoretical basis for better understanding the weighted hypervolume indicator in terms of optimal μ-distributions.

In this section, optimal μ-distributions are characterized for both the unweighted and the weighted hypervolume indicator by means of theoretical analyses. In a first part, the monotonicity in μ of the hypervolume associated with optimal μ-distributions is shown, and the existence of optimal μ-distributions for continuous fronts is proved. Then necessary conditions satisfied by optimal μ-distributions are derived. In a second part, the density associated with optimal μ-distributions when μ grows to infinity is deduced analytically.

3.3.1 · Finite Number of Points

Strict Monotonicity of Hypervolume in μ for Optimal μ-Distributions
The following proposition establishes that the hypervolume of optimal $(\mu + 1)$-distributions is strictly larger than the hypervolume of optimal μ-distributions.

Proposition 3.4: *Let $D \subseteq \mathbb{R}$, possibly finite and $g : u \in D \mapsto g(u)$ describe a Pareto front. Let μ_1 and $\mu_2 \in \mathbb{N}$ with $\mu_1 < \mu_2$, then $I_H^{w\mu_1*} < I_H^{w\mu_2*}$ holds if D contains at least $\mu_1 + 1$ elements u_i for which $u_i < r_1$ and $g(u_i) < r_2$ holds.*

Proof. To prove the proposition, it suffices to show the inequality for $\mu_2 = \mu_1 + 1$. Assume $D_{\mu_1} = \{v_1^\mu, \ldots, v_\mu^\mu\}$ with $v_i^\mu \in \mathbb{R}$ is the set of u-values of the objective vectors of the optimal μ_1-distribution for the Pareto front defined by g with a hypervolume value of $I_H^{w\mu_1*}$. Since U contains at least $\mu_1 + 1$ elements, the set $U \backslash D_{\mu_1}$ is not empty and any $u_{\text{new}} \in U \backslash D_{\mu_1}$ can be picked that is not contained in the optimal μ_1-distribution and for which $g(u_{\text{new}})$ is defined. Let $u_r := \min\{u | u \in D_{\mu_1} \cup \{r_1\}, u > u_{\text{new}}\}$ be the closest element of D_{μ_1} to the right of u_{new} (or r_1 if u_{new} is larger than all elements of D_{μ_1}). Similarly, let $g_l := \min\{r_2, \{g(u) | u \in D_{\mu_1}, u < u_{\text{new}}\}\}$ be the function value of the closest element of D_{μ_1} to the left of u_{new} (or r_2 if u_{new} is smaller than all elements of D_{μ_1}). Then, all objective vectors within $H_{\text{new}} := [u_{\text{new}}, u_r[\times[g(u_{\text{new}}), g_l[$ are (weakly) dominated by the new point $(u_{\text{new}}, g(u_{\text{new}}))$ but are not dominated by any objective vector given by D_{μ_1}. Furthermore, H_{new} is not a null set (i.e. has a strictly positive measure) since $u_{\text{new}} > u_r$ and $g_l > g(u_{\text{new}})$, and the weight w is strictly positive which gives $I_H^{w\mu_1*} < I_H^{w\mu_2*}$. $\qquad \square$

Existence of Optimal μ-Distributions

Before to further investigate optimal μ-distributions for I_H^w, a setting ensuring their existence is established. From now on assume that D is a closed interval denoted $[u_{min}, u_{max}]$ such that g writes:

$$u \in [u_{min}, u_{max}] \mapsto g(u).$$

The following theorem shows that a sufficient setting ensuring the existence of optimal distributions is the continuity of g:

Theorem 3.6 (existence of optimal μ-distributions): *If the function g describing the Pareto-front is continuous, there exists (at least) one set of μ-points maximizing the hypervolume.*

Proof. Equation 3.1 defines a μ dimensional function of $(u_1, \ldots, u_\mu)$. If g is moreover continuous, I_H^w in Eq. 3.1 is continuous and upper bounded by the hypervolume contribution of the entire front. Therefore, from the Mean Value Theorem there exists a set of μ points maximizing the hypervolume indicator.   □

Note that the previous theorem states the existence but not the uniqueness, which cannot be guaranteed in general.

Characterization of Optimal μ-Distributions for Finite μ

This section provides a general result to characterize optimal μ-distributions for the hypervolume indicator if μ is finite. The result holds under the assumption that the front g is differentiable and is a direct application of the fact that solutions of a maximization problem that do not lie on the boundary of the search domain are stationary points, i.e. points where the gradient is zero.

Theorem 3.8 (necessary conditions for optimal μ-distributions): *If g is continuous and differentiable and $(v_1^\mu, \ldots, v_\mu^\mu)$ are the u-coordinates of an optimal μ-distribution for I_H^w, then for all v_i^μ with $v_i^\mu > u_{min}$ and $v_i^\mu < u_{max}$ the following equations hold*

$$g'(v_i^\mu) \int_{v_i^\mu}^{v_{i+1}^\mu} w(u, g(v_i^\mu)) \, du = \int_{g(v_{i-1}^\mu)}^{g(v_i^\mu)} w(v_i^\mu, v) \, dv \qquad (3.3)$$

where g' denotes the derivative of g, $g(v_0^\mu) = r_2$ and $v_{\mu+1}^\mu = r_1$.

Proof. The proof idea is simple: optimal μ-distributions maximize the μ-dimensional function I_H^w defined in Eq. 3.1 and should therefore satisfy necessary conditions for local extrema of a μ-dimensional function stating that the coordinates of a local extrema lie either on the boundary of the domain (here u_{min} or u_{max}) or satisfy that the partial derivative with respect to this coordinate is zero. Hence, the partial derivatives of I_H^w has to be computed. This step is quite technical and is presented in Appendix C.1 on page 230 together with the full proof of the theorem.

The previous theorem proves an implicit relation between the points of an optimal distribution, however in certain cases of weights, this implicit relation can be made explicit as illustrated first on the example of the weight function $w(u,v) = \exp(-u)$, aiming at favoring points with small values along the first objective.

Example 3.10: If $w(u,v) = \exp(-u)$, Eq. 3.3 simplifies into the explicit relation

$$g'(v_i^\mu)(e^{-v_i^\mu} - e^{-v_{i+1}^\mu}) = e^{-v_i^\mu}\left(g(v_i^\mu) - g(v_{i-1}^\mu)\right) \qquad \circ \;(3.4)$$

Another example where the relation is explicit is given for the unweighted hypervolume I_H, stated as a corollary of the previous theorem.

Corollary 3.11 (necessary condition for optimal distributions on unweighted hypervolume): *If g is continuous, differentiable and $(v_1^\mu, \ldots, v_\mu^\mu)$ are the u-coordinates of an optimal μ-distribution for I_H, then for all v_i^μ with $v_i^\mu > u_{min}$ and $v_i^\mu < u_{max}$ the following equations hold*

$$g'(v_i^\mu)(v_{i+1}^\mu - v_i^\mu) = g(v_i^\mu) - g(v_{i-1}^\mu) \tag{3.5}$$

where g' denotes the derivative of g, $g(v_0^\mu) = r_2$ and $v_{\mu+1}^\mu = r_1$.

Proof. The proof follows immediately from setting $w = 1$ in Eq. 3.3.   □

Remark 3.13: *Corollary 3.11 implies that the points of an optimal μ-distribution for I_H are linked by a second order recurrence relation. Thus, in this case, finding optimal μ-distributions for I_H does not correspond to solving a μ-dimensional optimization problem as stated in Remark 3.2 but to a 2-dimensional one. The same remark holds for I_H^w and $w(u, v) = \exp(-u)$ as can be seen in Eq. 3.4.*

The previous Corollary can also be used to characterize optimal μ-distributions for certain Pareto fronts more generally as the following example shows.

Example 3.14: Consider a linear Pareto front, i.e., a front that can be formally defined as $g : u \in [u_{min}, u_{max}] \mapsto \alpha u + \beta$ where $\alpha < 0$ and $\beta \in \mathbb{R}$. Then, it follows immediately from Corollary 3.11 and Eq. 3.5 that the optimal μ-distribution for I_H maps to objective vectors with equal distances between two neighbored solutions:

$$\alpha(v_{i+1}^\mu - v_i^\mu) = g(v_i^\mu) - g(v_{i-1}^\mu) = \alpha(v_i^\mu - v_{i-1}^\mu)$$

for $i = 2, \ldots, \mu - 1$. Note that this result coincides with earlier results for linear fronts with slope $\alpha = -1$ (Beume et al. [15]) or the even more specific case of a front of shape $g(u) = 1 - u$ (Emmerich et al. [60]).   o

3.3.2 · Number of Points Going to Infinity

Besides for simple fronts, like the linear one, Eq. 3.3 and Eq. 3.5 cannot be easily exploited to derive optimal μ-distributions explicitly. However, one is interested in knowing how the hypervolume indicator influences the spread of points on the front, and in characterizing the bias is introduced by the hypervolume. To reply to these questions, next the number of points μ grows to infinity, and the density of points associated with optimal μ-distributions is derived. Please note, that for continuous front shapes, even if μ increases to infinity, not the whole set of solutions will be reached, as the Pareto-set is uncountable.

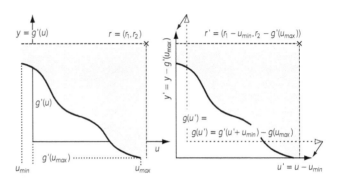

Figure 3.2 Every continuous Pareto front $g'(u)$ (left) can be described by a function $g: u' \in [0, u'_{max}] \mapsto g(u')$ with $g(u'_{max}) = 0$ (right) by a simple translation.

Density of Points on the Pareto Front

Without loss of generality let $u_{min} = 0$, and let $g : u \in [0, u_{max}] \mapsto g(u)$ with $g(u_{max}) = 0$ (Figure 3.2). Let g be continuous within $[0, u_{max}]$, differentiable and let its derivative be a continuous function g' defined in the interval $]0, u_{max}[$. An optimal μ distribution is defined as a set of μ points maximizing the weighted hypervolume indicator. However, instead of maximizing the weighted hypervolume indicator $I_H^{w\mu}$, it is easy to see that, since $r_1 r_2$ is constant, one can equivalently minimize

$$r_1 r_2 - I_H^{w\mu}((u_1^\mu, \ldots, u_\mu^\mu)) = \sum_{i=0}^{\mu} \int_{u_i^\mu}^{u_{i+1}^\mu} \int_0^{g(u_i^\mu)} w(u, v) \, dv \, du$$

with $g(u_0^\mu) = r_2$, and $u_{\mu+1}^\mu = r_1$ (see Figure 3.3, upper right). By subtracting the area below the front curve, i.e., the integral $\int_0^{u_{max}} (\int_0^{g(u)} w(u, v) \, dv) \, du$ of constant value (Figure 3.3, lower left), one sees that minimizing

$$\sum_{i=0}^{\mu} \int_{u_i^\mu}^{u_{i+1}^\mu} \int_0^{g(u_i^\mu)} w(u, v) \, dv \, du - \int_0^{u_{max}} \int_0^{g(u)} w(u, v) \, dv \, du \qquad (3.6)$$

is equivalent to maximizing the weighted hypervolume indicator (Figure 3.3, lower right).

For a fixed integer μ, consider a sequence of μ ordered points in $[0, u_{max}]$, $u_1^\mu, \ldots, u_\mu^\mu$ that lie on the Pareto front. It is assumed that the sequence converges—when μ goes to ∞—to a density $\delta(u)$ that is regular enough.

Figure 3.3 Illustration of the idea behind deriving the optimal density: Instead of maximizing the weighted hypervolume indicator $I_H^{w,\mu}((u_1^\mu,...,u_\mu^\mu))$ (upper left), one can minimize the area in the (upper right) which is equivalent to minimizing the integral between the attainment surface of the solution set and the front itself (lower left) which can be expressed with the help of the integral of g (lower right).

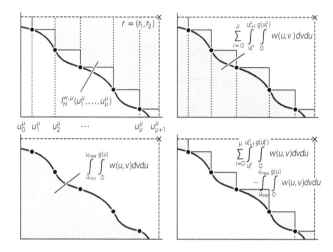

Formally, the density in $u \in [0, u_{max}]$ is defined as the limit of the number of points contained in a small interval $[u, u + h[$ normalized by the total number of points μ when both μ goes to ∞ and h to 0, i.e., $\delta(u) = \lim_{\mu\to\infty,h\to 0}\frac{1}{\mu h}\sum_{i=1}^{\mu}\mathbf{1}_{[u,u+h[}(u_i^\mu)$. As explained above, maximizing the weighted hypervolume is equivalent to minimizing Eq. 3.6, which is also equivalent to minimizing

$$E_\mu = \mu\left[\sum_{i=0}^{\mu}\int_{u_i^\mu}^{u_{i+1}^\mu}\int_0^{g(u_i^\mu)}w(u,v)\,dv\,du - \int_0^{u_{max}}\int_0^{g(u)}w(u,v)\,dv\,du\right] \quad (3.7)$$

In the following, the equivalence between minimizing E_μ and maximizing the hypervolume is assumed to also hold for μ going to infinity. Therefore, the proof consists of two steps: (i) computing the limit of E_μ when μ goes to ∞. This limit is going to be a function of a density δ. (ii) Finding the density δ that minimizes $E(\delta) := \lim_{\mu\to\infty}E_\mu$. The first step therefore consists in computing the limit of E_μ.

Lemma 3.15: *If g is continuous, differentiable with the derivative g' continuous, if $u \to w(u, g(u))$ is continuous, if $v_1^\mu, \dots, v_\mu^\mu$ converge to a continuous density δ, with $\frac{1}{\delta} \in L^2(0, u_{max})^3$, and $\exists c \in \mathbb{R}^+$ such that*

$$\mu \sup \left(\left(\sup_{0 \le i \le \mu - 1} |v_{i+1}^\mu - v_i^\mu| \right), |u_{max} - v_\mu^\mu| \right) \to c$$

then E_μ converges for $\mu \to \infty$ to

$$E(\delta) := -\frac{1}{2} \int_0^{u_{max}} \frac{g'(u)w(u, g(u))}{\delta(u)} du \ . \tag{3.8}$$

Proof. For the technical proof, see Appendix C.2 on page 232.

The limit density of μ-distribution for I_H^w, as explained before, is minimizing $E(\delta)$. It remains therefore to find the density which minimizes $E(\delta)$. This optimization problem is posed in a functional space, the Banach space $L^2(0, u_{max})$ and is also a constraint problem since the density δ has to satisfy the constraint $J(\delta) := \int_0^{u_{max}} \delta(u)du = 1$. The constraint optimization problem (P) that needs to be solved is summarized in:

$$\begin{aligned} &\text{minimize } E(\delta), \quad \delta \in L^2(0, u_{max}) \\ &\text{subject to } J(\delta) = 1 \end{aligned} \tag{P}$$

Theorem 3.17: *The density solution of the constraint optimization problem (P) equals*

$$\delta(u) = \frac{\sqrt{-g'(u)w(u, g(u))}}{\int_0^{u_{max}} \sqrt{-g'(u)w(u, g(u))}du} \ . \tag{3.9}$$

Proof. The proof is given in Appendix C.3 on page 235. □

Remark 3.19: *The previous density correspond to the density of points of the front projected onto the u-axis (first objective), and one might be interested in the density on the front δ_F. The density on the front gives for any curve*

---

[3] $L^2(0, u_{max})$ is a functional space (Banach space) defined as the set of all functions whose square is integrable in the sense of the Lebesgue measure.

on the front (a piece of the front) C, the proportion of points of the optimal μ-distribution (for μ to infinity) contained in this curve by integration on the curve: $\int_C \delta_F ds$. Since it is known that for any parametrization of C, say $t \in [a,b] \to \gamma(t) \in \mathbb{R}^2$, one has $\int_C \delta_F ds = \int_a^b \delta_F(\gamma(t))\|\gamma'(t)\|_2 dt$, one can for instance use the natural parametrization of the front given by $\gamma(t) = (t, g(t))$ giving $\|\gamma'(t)\|_2 = \sqrt{1 + g'(t)^2}$ that therefore implies that $\delta(u) = \delta_F(u)\sqrt{1 + g'(u)^2}$. Note that a small abuse of notation is used writing $\delta_F(u)$ instead of $\delta_F(\gamma(u)) = \delta_F((u, g(u)))$. one has to normalize the result from Eq. 3.9 by the norm of the tangent for points of the front, i.e., $\sqrt{1 + g'(u)^2}$. Therefore, the density on the front is

$$\delta_F(u) = \frac{\sqrt{-g'(u)w(u, g(u))}}{\int_{u_{min}}^{u_{max}} \sqrt{-g'(u)w(u, g(u))}\, du} \frac{1}{\sqrt{1 + g'(u)^2}} \;. \tag{3.10}$$

From Theorem 3.17 follows that the density of points only depends on the slope of the front and the weight function at the considered point. Figure 3.5 illustrates this dependency between the density for the unweighted hypervolume and the slope of the front. For front parts, where the tangent has a gradient of -45°, the density has its maximum. For parts where the front is parallel to the first or second objective (slope 0° and -90° respectively), the density is zero.

Example 3.20: Consider the test problem ZDT2 [138, see also Figure 3.4(b)] which is defined as

$$\text{minimize} \quad f_1(x_1) = x_1$$

$$\text{minimize} \quad f_2(x) = h(x) \cdot \left(1 - (f_1(x_1)/h(x))\right)^2$$

$$h(x) = 1 + \frac{9}{n-1}\sum_{i=2}^{n} x_i$$

$$\text{subject to} \quad 0 \le x_i \le 1 \text{ for } i = 1, \ldots n$$

for n decision variables $x = (x_1, \ldots, x_n) \in [0, 1]^n$. The Pareto front corresponds to setting $h(x) = 1$ which yields $g(u) = 1 - u^2$ with $u_{min} = 0$ and

$u_{max} = 1$ and $g'(u) = -2u$. Considering the unweighted case, the density on the u-axis according to Eq. 3.9 is

$$\delta(u) = \frac{3}{2}\sqrt{u} \qquad\qquad (3.11)$$

and the density on the front according to Eq. 3.10 is

$$\delta_F(u) = \frac{3}{2}\frac{\sqrt{u}}{\sqrt{1+4\,u^2}} \;,$$

see Figure 3.4(b) for an illustration.   ○

The density not only gives information about the bias of the hypervolume indicator for a given front, but can also be used to assess the number of solutions to be expected on a given segment of the front, as the following example illustrates.

Example 3.21: Consider again ZDT2 as in Example 3.20. The question is what fraction of points r_F of an optimal μ-distribution have first and second objectives smaller or equal 0.5 and 0.95 respectively. From $g^{-1}(v) = \sqrt{1-v^2}$ and $g^{-1}(0.95) = \sqrt{0.05}$ follows, that for the considered front segment $u \in [\sqrt{0.05}, 0.5]$ holds. Using $\delta(u)$ given in Eq. 3.11 and integrating over $[\sqrt{0.05}, 0.5]$ yields:

$$r_F = \int_{\sqrt{0.05}}^{0.5} \delta(u)du = \int_{\sqrt{0.05}}^{0.5} \frac{3}{2}\sqrt{u}du = \frac{1}{4}\sqrt{2} - 0.05^{3/4} \approx 24.78\% \;.$$

Note that for the approximated optimal μ-distribution of a finite number of $\mu = 100$ points one obtains 24 points in the considered line segment, which is close to the predicted percentage of $r_F = 24.78\%$.   ○

Comparison Between Optimal μ-Distributions and the Density
Lemma 3.15 states that the optimal distribution of μ points converges to the density $\delta(u)$ given by Theorem 3.17 when μ goes to infinity. Here, the quality of the approximation is investigated experimentally. To this end, the approximation of the optimal μ-distributions is computed exemplary for the ZDT2 test problem for $\mu = 10$, $\mu = 100$, and $\mu = 1000$, using the technique described in the paper by the author and colleagues [4]. The reference

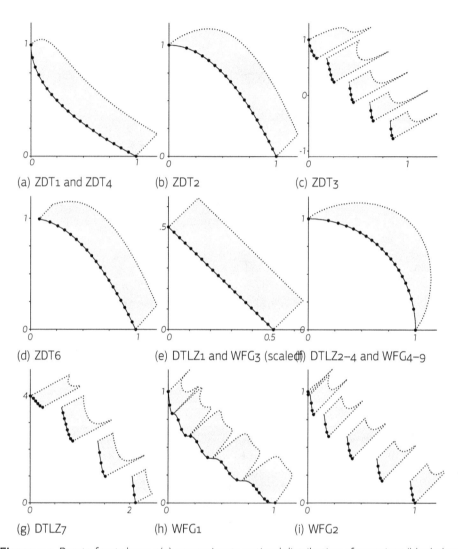

(a) ZDT1 and ZDT4   (b) ZDT2   (c) ZDT3

(d) ZDT6   (e) DTLZ1 and WFG3 (scaled)   (f) DTLZ2–4 and WFG4–9

(g) DTLZ7   (h) WFG1   (i) WFG2

Figure 3.4 Pareto front shape $g(u)$, approximate optimal distribution of 20 points (black dots), and the density $\delta_F(u)$ (gray shaded area) for the unweighted hypervolume indicator on all continuous ZDT, DTLZ and WFG test problems.

Figure 3.5 Shows the density (solid line) at different slopes of the Pareto front according to Eq. 3.10 for constant weight $w(z) \equiv 1$. The slope is expressed as the angle $a = \operatorname{atan}(f'(x))$ the front makes with the positive u-axis. Note that the density is normalized such that $\delta_F(-45°) = 1$. Additionally, the weight necessary to obtain a uniform distribution according to Example 3.24 is shown (dashed line).

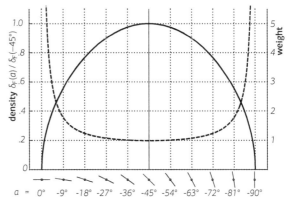

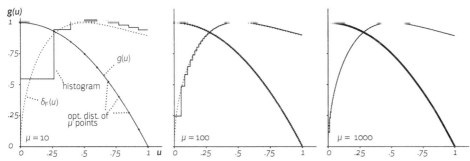

Figure 3.6 Comparison between the experimental density of points (shown as dots on the front and as a step function to compare with the theoretical density) and the theoretical prediction $\delta_F(x)$ (dashed line) of $\mu = 10$ points (left), $\mu = 100$ (middle) and $\mu = 1\,000$ (right) on the 2-objective ZDT2 problem.

point is set to $(15,15)$. Figure 3.6 shows both the experimentally observed histogram of the μ points on the front and the comparison between the theoretically derived density and the obtained experimental approximation thereof. By visual inspection, the convergence of the found μ-distribution to the density is apparent. For $\mu = 1000$ points, the theoretically derived density gives already a sufficient description of the finite optimal μ-distribution. The density is therefore not only useful to assess the bias of the hypervolume considering $\mu = \infty$, but is also helpful to accurately predict the distribution of finite number of points.

Extension to More Than Two Objectives

For more than two objectives, the increasingly complex shape of the hypervolume (see for instance Figure 1.5(b)) renders a derivation of the density hard. Nonetheless, Appendix C.4 on page 237 gives some indications how Eq. 3.10 could be extended to d objectives, leading to the following conjecture:

Conjecture 3.22: *Consider a continuous, differentiable (d-1)-dimensional Pareto front in the d dimensional objective space. Let z^* denote a Pareto-optimal point, and let $e^* = (e_1^*, \ldots, e_d^*)$ denote the unit normal vector of the front at z^*. Then the density of points $\delta_F(z^*)$ at z^* is*

$$\delta_F(z^*) = \frac{1}{C} \cdot \sqrt[d]{w(z^*) \prod_{i=1}^{d} e_i^*}$$

where $w(z^*)$ denotes the weight function at z^*, and C is constant for a given front shape.

Remark 3.23: *If Conjecture 3.22 holds, then the influence of the weight function decreases with increasing number of objectives as $\delta_F \propto \sqrt[d]{w}$. As for the biobjective case, the density is maximized on knee points where the normal vector on the front is $1/\sqrt{d}(1, \ldots, 1)$, and is zero wherever the front is parallel to at least one objective axis.*

Expressing User Preference in Terms of Density

Equation 3.10 characterizes the density $\delta_F(u)$ of points that maximize the weighted hypervolume indicator for a given weight function $w(u, v)$ and front shape $g(u)$. The result can also be interpreted in the opposite direction: given user-defined preference, expressed by a density, the corresponding weight function can be derived. This allows to model user preference in a concise manner by optimizing the weighted hypervolume indicator. Let the desired density of the user be $\delta_F'(u)$, then by rearrangig Eq. 3.10 one obtains the corresponding weight function

$$w(u, g(u)) \propto \frac{1 + g'(u)^2}{-g'(u)} \cdot \delta_F'(u)^2 \ . \tag{3.12}$$

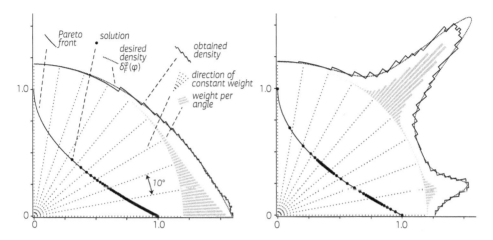

Figure 3.7 Shows the 50 solutions found optimizing the hypervolume indicator with weight function corresponding to two types of desired densities $\delta_F^\varphi(\varphi)$, according to Eq. 3.12.

Note that the weight is a strictly positive finite function if $-g'(u)$ is positive, and that it peaks to infinity if the derivate of g either goes to 0 or $-\infty$.

Example 3.24: Consider the user preference $\delta_F'(u) \equiv 1$, i.e., to obtain a uniform distribution of points. Then from Eq. 3.12 the corresponding weight is $w(u, g(u)) \propto (1 + g'(u)^2)/-g'(u)$. Figure 3.5 shows this weight with respect to different slopes of the front. The more the slope of the front approaches $0°$ or $-90°$ respectively, the more weight is needed in these regions to still achieve a uniform density.   o

In a paper by the author and colleagues [5], an evolutionary algorithm has been proposed based on Eq. 3.12. Figure 3.7 shows the distribution of 50 points obtained using this algorithm for two desired densities $\delta_F'(u)$, expressed in polar coordinate (see [5] for details). The resulting density of points comes very close to the desired density, demonstrating that Theorem 3.17 not only serves as a better theoretical understanding of the weighted hypervolume, but furthermore has also practical applications.

Equal Hypervolume Contributions
In the previous section the density of points has been derived for μ going to

infinity. In the following the *hypervolume contributions* of the points, i.e., the Lebesgue measure solely dominated by a point, is investigated.

Definition 3.25 (hypervolume contribution): *Let $A \in \Psi$ be a Pareto set approximation, let x denote a solution $x \in A$, and let $R \in Z$ be a reference set. Then the hypervolume contribution $C_A(x)$ corresponds to the hypervolume of x with respect to R, which is not dominated by any other solution $y \in A \setminus \{x\}$, i.e.,*

$$C_A(x) := H(A, R) \setminus H(A \setminus \{x\}, R) \ , \tag{3.13}$$

and the Lebesgue measure $\lambda(C_A(x))$ thereof gives the indicator value of the hypervolume contribution.

Theorem 3.26: *As the number of point μ increases to infinity, the ratio between the hypervolume contributions of any two points v_i^μ and v_j^μ of an optimal μ-distribution with both $g'(v_i^\mu)$ and $g'(v_j^\mu)$ finite goes to 1, i.e., each point has the same hypervolume contribution.*

Proof. The proof can be found in Appendix C.5 on page 240.

Example 3.28: Figure 3.8 shows the coefficient of variation c_v—the ratio of the standard deviation to the mean—of the hypervolume contributions for approximated optimal μ-distributions using the same algorithm as in Example 3.21. The considered front shape is $g(u) = 1 - u^2$. As the number of points μ increases, c_v decreases which indicates that the contributions become more and more equal as stated by Theorem 3.26.   ○

3.3.3 · Intermediate Summary

To summarize, the density follows as a limit result from the fact that the integral between the attainment function of the solution set with μ points and the front itself (lower right plot of Figure 3.3) has to be minimized and the optimal μ-distribution for finite points converges to the density when μ increases. Furthermore, one can conclude that the number of points of an optimal μ-distribution with u-values within a certain interval $[a, b]$ converges to $\int_a^b \delta(u) \, du$ if the number of points μ goes to infinity.

Instead of applying the results to specific test functions as in Example 3.20, the above results on the hypervolume indicator can also be interpreted in a much broader sense: From Theorem 3.17, it is known that it is only the weight function and the slope of the front that influences the density of the points of an optimal μ-distribution. This formally proven statement is contrary to the prevalent belief that the shape of the front, i.e., whether it is convex or concave makes a difference in the optimal distribution of solutions on the front as it was stated in [136] and [99]. Theorem 3.17 also contrasts claims in other studies, e.g., that extreme points are generally preferred [53] or the statements of Beume et al. [16] that the distribution of points on the extremes is less dense than on knee points and that extremal solutions are always maintained. Since the density of points does not depend on the position on the front but only on the gradient and the weight at the respective point, the density close to the extreme points of the front can be very high or very low—it only depends on the front shape. Section 3.4.1 will even present conditions under which the extreme points will never be included in an optimal μ-distribution for I_H^w—in contrast to the statement in [16].

Assuming a constant weight and therefore investigating the unweighted hypervolume indicator, the density has its maximum for front parts where the tangent has a gradient of $-45°$. Therefore, and compliant with the statement in [16], optimizing the unweighted hypervolume indicator stresses so-called knee-points—parts of the Pareto front decision makers believe to be interesting regions [25, 42, 45]. However, the choice of a weight that is not constant can highly change the distribution of points and makes it possible to include arbitrary user preferences into the search. With the weighted hypervolume indicator, it is now even possible to obtain sets of points that are uniformly distributed on different front shapes. With the unweighted hypervolume indicator this is—as already stated in [16] and proven in this chapter—only possible for linear fronts, i.e., for those fronts, where the slope and therefore the density is constant everywhere. Regarding the weighted hypervolume, Theorem 3.17 also complies with the original paper by Zitzler et al. [141]: the distribution of a finite set of points can be influenced by the weight function. The new result proven here is *how* the distribution

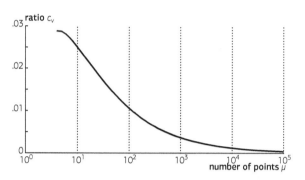

Figure 3.8 Shows the coefficient of variation c_v (the ratio of the standard deviation to the mean) of the hypervolume contributions for the approximate optimal distribution of different μ. The front shape is $g(u) = 1 - u^2$.

of points is changing: for a fixed front, it is the square root of the weight that is directly reflected in the optimal density (respectively, the dth root if Conjecture 3.22 holds).

3.4 · Influence of the Reference Point on the Extremes

Clearly, optimal μ-distributions for I_H^w are in some way influenced by the choice of the reference set R. Here, the widespread case $R = \{r\}$ is considered, i.e., the reference set being a single reference point r. The choice of the reference point influencing the outcomes of hypervolume-based algorithms is well-known from practical observations. Knowles et al. [90], for example, demonstrated the impact of the reference point on the results of selected multiobjective evolutionary algorithms based on an experimental study. How in general the outcomes of hypervolume-based algorithms are influenced by the choice of the reference point has not been investigated from a theoretical perspective though. In particular, it could not be deduced from practical investigations how the reference point has to be set to ensure to find the extremes of the Pareto front, such that theoretical investigations are highly needed to provide more concise information on the influence and choice of the reference point.

In practice, mainly rules-of-thumb exist on how to choose the reference point. Many authors recommend to use the corner of a space that is a little bit larger than the actual objective space as the reference point. Examples include the corner of a box 1% larger than the objective space in [87] or a box that is larger by an additive term of 1 than the extremal objective values obtained as in [16]. In various publications where the hypervolume indicator is used for performance assessment, the reference point is chosen as the nadir point[4] of the investigated solution set, e.g., in [81, 109, 110], while others recommend a rescaling of the objective values everytime the hypervolume indicator is computed [135].

This section tackles the question of how the reference point influences optimal μ-distributions. In particular, the section theoretically investigates whether there exists a choice for the reference point that implies that the extremes of the Pareto front are included in the optimal μ-distribution. The presented results give insights into how the reference point should be chosen, even if the weight function does not equal 1 everywhere. The main result, stated in Theorem 3.32 and Theorem 3.39, shows that for continuous and differentiable Pareto fronts an implicit lower bounds can be given on the u (objective f_1) and v (objective f_2) value for the reference point (possibly infinite depending on the Pareto front g and weight function w) such that all choices above this lower bound ensure the existence of the extremes in an optimal μ-distribution for I_H^w. For the special case of the unweighted hypervolume indicator, these lower bounds turn into explicit lower bounds (Corollaries 3.36 and 3.41). Moreover, Section 3.4.1 shows that it is necessary to have a finite derivative on the left extreme and a non-zero one on the right extreme to ensure that the extremes are contained in an optimal μ-distribution. This result contradicts the common belief that it is sufficient to choose the reference point slightly above and to the right of the nadir point or the border of the objective space to obtain the extremes as indicated above. Finally, Theorem 3.46 shows that a point slightly worse than the nadir point in all objectives starts to become a good choice for the reference point as soon as μ is large enough.

Before the results are presented recall that $r = (r_1, r_2)$ denotes the reference point and $v = g(u)$ with $u \in [u_{min}, u_{max}]$ represents the Pareto front,

---

[4]In this chapter the nadir point equals $(u_{max}, g(u_{min}))$, i.e., is the smallest objective vector that is weakly dominated by all Pareto-optimal points.

hence, $(u_{min}, g(u_{min}))$ and $(u_{max}, g(u_{max}))$ are the left and right extremal point. Since all Pareto-optimal solutions need to have a contribution to the hypervolume of the front in order to possibly be part of the optimal μ-distribution, the reference point is assumed to be dominated by all Pareto-optimal solutions, i.e. $r_1 > u_{max}$ and $r_2 > g(u_{min})$. Additionally recall that the weight function w of the weighted hypervolume indicator I_H^w is strictly positive.

3.4.1 · Finite Number of Points

For the moment, the number of points μ is considered finite. For this case, necessary and sufficient conditions are provided for the existence of a finite reference point such that the extremes are included in any optimal μ-distribution for I_H^w. In Section 3.4.2, further results are derived for μ going to infinity.

Fronts for Which It Is Impossible to Have the Extremes

A widespread belief is that choosing the reference point of the hypervolume indicator in a way, such that it is dominated by all Pareto-optimal points, is enough to ensure that the extremes can be reached by an indicator-based algorithm that aims at maximizing the hypervolume indicator. The main reason for this belief was that with such a choice of the reference point, the extremes of the Pareto front always have a positive contribution to the overall hypervolume indicator and should be therefore chosen by the algorithm's environmental selection. As will be shown in the following, however, this is only a necessary, but not sufficient, condition. The following theorem states an additional necessary condition to get the extremes:

Theorem 3.29: *Let μ be a positive integer. Assume that g is continuous on $[u_{min}, u_{max}]$, non-increasing, differentiable on $]u_{min}, u_{max}[$ and that g' is continuous on $]u_{min}, u_{max}[$ and that the weight function w is continuous and positive. If $\lim_{u \to u_{min}} g'(u) = -\infty$, the left extremal point of the front is never included in an optimal μ-distribution for I_H^w. Likewise, if $g'(u_{max}) = 0$, the right extremal point of the front is never included in an optimal μ-distribution for I_H^w.*

Proof. The idea behind the proof is to assume the extreme point to be contained in an optimal μ-distribution and to show a contradiction. In particular, the gain and loss in hypervolume if the extreme point is shifted can be computed analytically. A limit result for the case that $\lim_{u \to u_{min}} g'(u) = -\infty$ (or $g'(u_{max}) = 0$ respectively) shows that one can always increase the overall hypervolume indicator value if the outmost point is shifted, see also Figure C.3. For the technical details, including a technical lemma, refer to Appendix C.6 on page 242.

Example 3.31: Consider the test problem ZDT1 [138] for which the Pareto front is $g(u) = 1 - \sqrt{u}$ with $u_{min} = 0$ and $u_{max} = 1$, see Figure 3.4(a). The derivative $g'(u) - -1/(2\sqrt{u})$ equals $-\infty$ at the left extreme u_{min} hence the left extreme $(0, 1)$ is never included in an optimal μ-distribution for I_H^w according to Theorem 3.29. ○

Although one should keep the previous result in mind when using the hypervolume indicator, the fact that the extreme can never be obtained in the cases of Theorem 3.29 is less restrictive in practice. Due to the continuous search space for most of the test problems, no algorithm will obtain a specific solution exactly—and the extreme in particular—and if the number of points is high enough, a solution close to the extreme[5] will be found also by hypervolume-based algorithms. Nonetheless, when using the weight function in the weighted hypervolume indicator to model preferences of the user towards certain regions of the objective search, one should take Theorem C.6 into account and increase the weight drastically close to such extremes if they are desired, see also discussion in Section 3.4.3.

Lower Bound for Choosing the Reference Point to Obtain the Extremes
The previous section revealed that if the limit of the derivative of the front at the left extreme equals $-\infty$ (resp. if the derivative of the front at the right extreme equals zero) there is no finite choice of reference point that allows to have the extremes included in optimal μ-distributions for I_H^w. For this reason, in the following the case is considered that the limit of the

---

[5] Although the distance of solutions to the extremes might be sufficiently small in practice also for the scenario of Theorem 3.29, the theoretical result shows that for a finite μ, one cannot expect that the solutions approach the extremes arbitrarily close.

derivative of the front at the left extreme is finite (resp. the derivative of the front at the right extreme is not zero). For this setting, finite reference points are derived that indeed guarantee to have the extremes in any optimal μ-distribution.

Lower Bound for Left Extreme. The following theorem gives a lower bound for the reference point to obtain the left most point of the Pareto front:

Theorem 3.32 (lower bound for left extreme): *Let μ be an integer larger or equal 2. Assume that g is continuous on $[u_{min}, u_{max}]$, non-increasing, differentiable on $]u_{min}, u_{max}[$ and that g' is continuous on $]u_{min}, u_{max}[$ and $\lim\limits_{u \to u_{min}} -g'(u) < \infty$. If there exists a $\mathcal{K}_2$ such that*

$$\forall u_1 \in]u_{min}, u_{max}] : \int_{g(u_1)}^{\mathcal{K}_2} w(u_1, v)\, dv > -g'(u_1) \int_{u_1}^{u_{max}} w(u, g(u_1))\, du \ ,$$

$$(3.14)$$

then for all reference points $r = (r_1, r_2)$ such that $r_2 \geq \mathcal{K}_2$ and $r_1 > u_{max}$, the leftmost extremal point is contained in all optimal μ-distributions. In other words, defining $\mathcal{R}_2$ as

$$\mathcal{R}_2 = \inf\{\mathcal{K}_2 \text{ satisfying Eq. 3.14}\} \ ,$$

$$(3.15)$$

the leftmost extremal point is contained in all optimal μ-distributions if $r_2 > \mathcal{R}_2$, and $r_1 > u_{max}$.

The proof of the theorem requires to establish a technical proposition. Assume the reference point is dominated by the Pareto front, i.e., at least $r_1 > u_{max}$ and $r_2 > g(u_{min})$. Let consider a set of points on the front and let consider the hypervolume contribution of the leftmost point $P_1 = (u_1, g(u_1))$ (see Figure 3.9). This is a function of u_1, u_2 (the u-coordinate of the second left-most point) and r_2 (the second coordinate of the reference point). For fixed u_2 and r_2, the hypervolume contribution of the leftmost point with coordinate $u_1 \in [u_{min}, u_2[$ is denoted as $I_h^w(u_1; u_2, r_2)$ and reads

$$I_h^w(u_1; u_2, r_2) = \int_{u_1}^{u_2} \int_{g(u_1)}^{r_2} w(u, v)\, dv\, du \ .$$

$$(3.16)$$

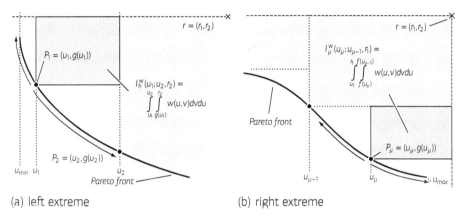

(a) left extreme $\qquad\qquad$ (b) right extreme

Figure 3.9 Shows the notation and formula to compute the hypervolume contributions of the leftmost and rightmost points P_1 and P_μ respectively.

Figure 3.10 If the hypervolume indicator is maximal for $u_1 = u_{min}$, then for any $u_2 \in$ $]u_1, u_{max}]$ the contribution is maximal for $u_1 = u_{min}$ too.

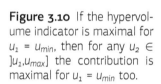 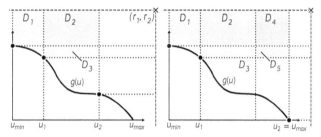

The following proposition establishes a key property of the function I_1^w.

Proposition 3.33: *If $u_1 \to I_h^w(u_1; u_{max}, r_2)$ is maximal for $u_1 = u_{min}$, then for any $u_2 \in]u_1, u_{max}]$ the contribution $I_h^w(u_1; u_2, r_2)$ is maximal for $u_1 = u_{min}$ too.*

Proof. Assume that $I_h^w(u_1; u_{max}, r_2)$ is maximal for $u_1 = u_{min}$, i.e., $I_h^w(u_{min}; u_{max}, r_2) \geq I_h^w(u_1; u_{max}, r_2)$, $\forall u_1 \in]u_{min}, u_{max}]$. Let $\{D_1, \ldots, D_5\}$ denote the weighted hypervolume indicator values of different non-overlapping rectangular areas shown in Figure 3.10. Then for all u_1 in $]u_{min}, u_{max}]$, $I_h^w(u_{min}; u_{max}, r_2) \geq I_h^w(u_1; u_{max}, r_2)$ can be rewritten using $D_1, \ldots, D_5$ as

$D_1 + D_2 + D_4 \geq D_2 + D_3 + D_4 + D_5$ which in turn implies that $D_1 + D_2 \geq D_2$ $+D_3 + D_5$. Since $D_5 \geq 0$ it follows $D_1 + D_2 \geq D_2 + D_3$, which corresponds to $I_h^w(u_{min}; u_2, r_2) \geq I_h^w(u_1; u_2, r_2)$. Hence, $I_h^w(u_1; u_2, r_2)$ is also maximal for $u_1 = u_{min}$ for any choice $u_2 \in]u_1, u_{max}]$. $\qquad\square$

Using Proposition 3.33, Theorem 3.32 can be proven:

Proof. Let u_1 and u_2 denote the u-coordinates of the two leftmost points $P_1 = (u_1, g(u_1))$ and $P_2 = (u_2, g(u_2))$. Then the hypervolume contribution of P_1 is given by Eq. 3.16. To prove that P_1 is the extremal point $(u_{min}, g(u_{min}))$ in the optimal μ-distributions, first one needs to prove that $u_1 \in [u_{min}, u_2] \mapsto I_h^w(u_1; u_2, r_2)$ is maximal for $u_1 = u_{min}$. By using Proposition 3.33, it follows that if $u_1 \to I_1^w(u_1; u_{max}, r_2)$ is maximal for $u_1 = u_{min}$ then it also follows that $I_h^w : u_1 \in [u_{min}, u_2] \mapsto I_h^w(u_1; u_2, r_2)$ is maximal for $u_1 = u_{min}$. Therefore, only the proof that $u_1 \to I_1^w(u_1; u_{max}, r_2)$ is maximal for $u_1 = u_{min}$ is needed. To do so, it will be shown that $\frac{dI_h^w(u_1; u_{max}, r_2)}{du_1} \neq 0$ for all $u_{min} < u_1 \leq u_{max}$. According to Lemma C.1, the partial derivative of the hypervolume contribution of P_1 is

$$\frac{dI_h^w(u_1; u_{max}, r_2)}{du_1} = -g'(u_1) \int_{u_1}^{u_{max}} w(u, g(u_1)) \, du - \int_{g(u_1)}^{r_2} w(u_1, v) \, dv$$

Hence, by choosing $r_2 > \mathcal{R}_2$ according to Theorem 3.32, $\frac{dI_h^w(u_1; u_{max}, r_2)}{du_1} \neq 0$. $\qquad\square$

Applying the previous theorem to the unweighted hypervolume leads to an explicit lower bound for setting the reference point so as to have the left extreme:

Corollary 3.36 (lower bound for left extreme): *Let μ be an integer larger or equal 2. Assume that g is continuous on $[u_{min}, u_{max}]$, non-increasing, differentiable on $]u_{min}, u_{max}[$ and that g' is continuous on $]u_{min}, u_{max}[$. Assume that $\lim_{u \to u_{min}} -g'(u) < \infty$. Then, if*

$$\mathcal{R}_2 = \sup\{g(u) + g'(u)(u - u_{max}) : u \in [u_{min}, u_{max}[\} , \tag{3.17}$$

is finite the leftmost extremal point is contained in optimal μ-distributions for I_H if the reference point $r = (r_1, r_2)$ is such that r_2 is strictly larger than $\mathcal{R}_2$ and $r_1 > u_{max}$.

Proof. Replacing $w(u, v)$ by 1 in Eq. 3.15 of Theorem 3.32 gives

$$\mathcal{K}_2 - g(u_1) > -g'(u_1)(u_{max} - u_1), \quad \forall u_1 \in]u_{min}, u_{max}] \tag{3.18}$$

with any $r_2 \geq \mathcal{K}_2$, the leftmost extreme is included. The previous equation writes $\mathcal{K}_2 > g(u_1) - g'(u_1)(u_{max} - u_1)$ for all $u_1 \in]u_{min}, u_{max}]$. Since $-g'(u_1)(u_{max} - u_1) = g'(u_1)(u_1 - u_{max})$, Eq. 3.18 writes as

$$\mathcal{K}_2 > g(u_1) + g'(u_1)(u_1 - u_{max}), \tag{3.19}$$

$\forall u_1 \in]u_{min}, u_{max}]$. Because $\mathcal{K}_2$ has to be larger than the right-hand side of Eq. 3.19 for all u_1 in $]u_{min}, u_{max}]$, it has to be larger than the supremum of $g(u_1) + g'(u_1)(u_1 - u_{max})$ for u_1 in $]u_{min}, u_{max}]$ and thus

$$\mathcal{K}_2 > \sup\{g(u_1) + g'(u_1)(u_1 - u_{max}) : u_1 \in [u_{min}, u_{max}[\} \tag{3.20}$$

$\mathcal{R}_2$ is defined as the infimum over $\mathcal{K}_2$ satisfying Eq. 3.20 in other words

$$\mathcal{R}_2 = \sup\{g(u) + g'(u)(u - u_{max}) : u \in [u_{min}, u_{max}[\} . \qquad \square$$

Example 3.38: Consider test problem ZDT2 with $g(u) = 1 - u^2$, $u_{min} = 0$, $u_{max} = 1$, and $g'(u) = -2u$. Then the lower bound $\mathcal{R}_2$ to obtain the left extremal point for I_H according to Corollary 3.36 is

$$\mathcal{R}_2 = \sup\{1 - u^2 - 2u(u - 1) : u \in [0, 1[\}$$
$$= \sup\{-3u^2 + 2u + 1 : u \in [0, 1[\} \tag{3.21}$$

The only critical point of $-3u^2 + 2u + 1$, obtained by setting its derivative $-6u + 2$ to zero, is $u_{crit} = 1/3$. By evaluating Eq. 3.21 at $u_{min} = 0$, $u_{max} = 1$, and $u_{crit} = 1/3$, the supremum becomes

$$= \sup\{-3u^2 + 2u + 1 : u \in \{0, 1/3, 1, \}\}$$
$$= 4/3 \tag{3.22}$$

Choosing any reference point (weakly) dominated by $(u_{max}, \mathcal{R}_2) = (1, 4/3)$ hence guarantees to obtain the left extremal point in all μ-distributions of I_H with $\mu \geq 2$. ○

Lower Bound for Right Extreme. Next the right extreme is considered, tackling the same question as for the left extreme: assuming that $g'(u_{max}) \neq 0$, is there an explicit lower bound for the left coordinate of the reference point ensuring that the right extreme is included in optimal μ-distributions.

Theorem 3.39 (lower bound for right extreme): *Let μ be an integer larger or equal 2. Assume that g is continuous on $[u_{min}, u_{max}]$, non-increasing, differentiable on $]u_{min}, u_{max}[$ and that g' is continuous on $]u_{min}, u_{max}[$ and $g'(u_{max}) \neq 0$. If there exists $\mathcal{K}_1$ such that*

$$-g'(u_\mu) \int_{u_\mu}^{\mathcal{K}_1} w(u, g(u_\mu)) \, du > \int_{g(u_\mu)}^{g(u_{min})} w(u_\mu, v) \, dv \tag{3.23}$$

then for all reference points $r = (r_1, r_2)$ such that $r_1 \geq \mathcal{K}_1$ and $r_2 > g(u_{min})$, the rightmost extremal point is contained in all optimal μ-distributions. In other words, defining $\mathcal{R}_1$ as

$$\mathcal{R}_1 = \inf\{\mathcal{K}_1 \text{ satisfying Eq. 3.23}\} \,, \tag{3.24}$$

the rightmost extremal point is contained in optimal μ-distributions if $r_1 > \mathcal{R}_2$, and $r_2 > g(u_{min})$.

Proof. The proof is similar to the proof for the left extremal point (Theorem 3.32), and is listed in Appendix C.7 on page 244.

Applying the previous theorem to the unweighted hypervolume again gives an explicit lower bound for setting the reference point so as to have the right extreme.

Corollary 3.41 (lower bound for right extreme): *Let μ be an integer larger or equal 2. Assume that g is continuous on $[u_{min}, u_{max}]$, non-increasing, differentiable on $]u_{min}, u_{max}]$ and that g' is continuous and strictly negative on $]u_{min}, u_{max}]$. Assume that $g'(u_{max}) \neq 0$. Then, if*

$$\mathcal{R}_1 = \sup\{u + \frac{g(u) - g(u_{min})}{g'(u)} : u \in]u_{min}, u_{max}]\} \tag{3.25}$$

is finite the rightmost extremal point is contained in optimal μ-distributions for I_H if the reference point (r_1, r_2) is such that r_1 is strictly larger than $\mathcal{R}_1$ and $r_2 > g(u_{min})$.

Proof. Refer to Appendix C.8 on page 245 for a proof of Corollary 3.41.

Example 3.43: Again consider test problem ZDT2 with $g(u) = 1 - u^2$, $u_{min} = 0$, $u_{max} = 1$, and $g'(u) = -2u$. Then the lower bound $\mathcal{R}_1$ to obtain the right extremal point for I_H according to Eq. 3.25 is

$$\mathcal{R}_1 = \sup\{u + \frac{1 - u^2 - (1 - 0^2)}{-2u} : u \in [0, 1[\}$$

$$= \sup\{\frac{3}{2}u : u \in [0, 1[\} = \frac{3}{2}$$

Together with result from Eq. 3.22 the lower bound $\mathcal{R} = (3/2, 4/3)$ is obtained. Choosing any reference point (weakly) dominated by $\mathcal{R}$ guarantees to obtain both extremal point in all μ-distributions of I_H with $\mu \gtrsim 2$.   ○

Table 3.1 lists the lower bound $\mathcal{R}$ of I_H for all test problems of the Zitzler-Deb-Thiele (ZDT), Deb-Thiele-Laumanns-Zitzler (DTLZ), and Walking Fish Group (WFG) suites. Note that $\mathcal{R}_1$ in Eq. 3.24, $\mathcal{R}_2$ in Eq. 3.15, as well as for the non-weighted case Eq. 3.25 and Eq. 3.17 respectively are not tight bounds. This is so because the bounds are based on the worst-case setting of $u_2 = u_{max}$ and $u_{\mu-1} = u_{min}$ respectively.

3.4.2 · Number of Points Going to Infinity

The lower bounds derived for the reference point such that the extremes are included are independent of μ. It can be seen in the proof that those bounds are not tight if μ is larger than 2. Deriving tight bounds is difficult because it would require to know for a given μ where the second point of optimal μ-distributions is located. It can be certainly achieved in the linear case, but it might be impossible in more general cases. However, this section investigates how μ influences the choice of the reference point so as to have the extremes. In this section $\mathcal{R}_1^{\text{Nadir}}$ and $\mathcal{R}_2^{\text{Nadir}}$ denote the first and second coordinates of the nadir point, namely $\mathcal{R}_1^{\text{Nadir}} = u_{max}$ and $\mathcal{R}_2^{\text{Nadir}} = g(u_{min})$.

It is first proven that for any reference point dominating the nadir point, there exists a μ_0 such that for all μ larger than μ_0, optimal μ-distributions associated to this reference point include the extremes. Before, establishing

Table 3.1 Lists for all ZDT, DTLZ, and WFG test problems and the unweighted hypervolume indicator I_H: (i) the Pareto front as $[u_{min}, u_{max}] \mapsto g(u)$, (ii) the density $\delta_F(u)$ on the front according to Eq. 3.10, and (iii) a lower bound $\mathcal{R} = (\mathcal{R}_1, \mathcal{R}_2)$ of the reference point to obtain the extremes (Eq. 3.25 and 3.17 respectively). Γ denotes the Gamma function.

name	u_{min}	u_{max}	front shape $g(u)$	density on front $\delta_F(u)$	$\mathcal{R}_1$	$\mathcal{R}_2$
ZDT1	0	1	$1-\sqrt{u}$	$3/2 \dfrac{\sqrt[4]{u}}{\sqrt{4u+1}}$	3	∞
ZDT2	0	1	$1-u^2$	$3/2\sqrt{\dfrac{u}{1+4u^2}}$	$3/2$	$4/3$
ZDT3	0	≈ 0.851	$1-\sqrt{u}-u\sin(10nu)$	$1.5589\sqrt{\dfrac{(1/2\sqrt{u}+\sin(10nu)+10u\cos(10nu)n)}{\left(1+\left(1/2\sqrt{u}+\sin(10nu)+10u\cos(10nu)n\right)^2\right)}}$	∞	∞
ZDT4			*see ZDT1*			
ZDT5			*discrete*			
ZDT6	≈ 0.280	1	$1-u^2$	$1.7622\sqrt{\dfrac{u}{1+4u^2}}$	≈ 1.461	$4/3$
DTLZ1	0	$\tfrac{1}{2}$	$\tfrac{1}{2}-u$	$\sqrt{2}$	1	1
DTLZ2-4	0	1	$\sqrt{1-u^2}$	$\dfrac{\sqrt{n}}{\Gamma(3/4)^2}\sqrt[4]{1-u^2}\sqrt{u}$	≈ 1.180	≈ 1.180
DTLZ5-6			*degenerate*			
DTLZ7	0	≈ 2.116	$4-u(1+\sin(3nu))$	$0.6566\sqrt{\dfrac{1+\sin(3nu)+3u\cos(3nu)n}{1+(1+\sin(3nu)+3u\cos(3nu)n)^2}}$	≈ 2.481	≈ 13.372
WFG1	0	1	$\dfrac{2\rho-\sin(2\rho)}{10n}-1$	$1.1570\sqrt{\dfrac{2(1-\cos(2\rho))n}{\sqrt{u(2-u)}\left(n^2-4\dfrac{(1-\cos(2\rho))^2}{u(u-2)}\right)}}$	∞	≈ 0.979
WFG2	0	1	$1-\dfrac{2(n-0.1\rho)\cos^2(\rho)}{n}$ $\rho = 10\arccos(u-1)$	$0.44607\sqrt{\dfrac{-g'(u)}{1+g'(u)^2}}$ with $g'(u)=-2\dfrac{\cos(\rho)(\cos(\rho)+20\sin(\rho)n-2\sin(\rho)\rho)}{\sqrt{u(2-u)}\,n}$	≈ 2.571	∞
WFG3	0	1	$1-u$	$1/\sqrt{2}$	2	2
WFG4-9			*see DTLZ2-4*			

a lemma saying that if there exists a reference point R^1 allowing to have the extremes, then all reference points R^2 dominated by this reference point R^1 will also allow to have the extremes.

Lemma 3.44: *Let* $R^1 = (r_1^1, r_2^1)$ *and* $R^2 = (r_1^2, r_2^2)$ *be two reference points with* $r_1^1 < r_1^2$ *and* $r_2^1 < r_2^2$. *If both extremes are included in optimal* μ-

distributions for I_H^w associated with R^1 then both extremes are included in optimal μ-distributions for I_H^w associated with R^2.

Proof. The proof is presented in Appendix C.9 on page 245. $\qquad\square$

Theorem 3.46: *Assume that g is continuous, differentiable with g' continuous on $[u_{min}, u_{max}]$ and the weight function w is bounded, i.e. there exists a $W > 0$ such that $w(u, v) \leq W$ for all (u, v). Then for all $\varepsilon = (\varepsilon_1, \varepsilon_2) \in \mathbb{R}^2_{>0}$,*

1. *there exists a μ_1 such that for all $\mu \geq \mu_1$, and any reference point R dominated by the nadir point such that $R_2 \geq \mathcal{R}_2^{\text{Nadir}} + \varepsilon_2$, the left extreme is included in optimal μ-distributions,*
2. *there exists a μ_2 such that for all $\mu \geq \mu_2$, and any reference point R dominated by the nadir point such that $R_1 \geq \mathcal{R}_1^{\text{Nadir}} + \varepsilon_1$, the right extreme is included in optimal μ-distributions.*

Proof. The proof is presented in Appendix C.10 on page 247. $\qquad\square$

As a corollary one gets the following result for obtaining both extremes simultaneously:

Corollary 3.48: *Let g be continuous, differentiable with g' continuous on $[u_{min}, u_{max}]$ and let w be bounded, i.e. there exists $W > 0$ such that $w(u, v) \leq W$ for all (u, v). For all $\varepsilon = (\varepsilon_1, \varepsilon_2) \in \mathbb{R}^2_{>0}$, there exists μ_0 such that for μ larger than μ_0 and for all reference point dominated by $(\mathcal{R}_1^{\text{Nadir}} + \varepsilon_1, \mathcal{R}_2^{\text{Nadir}} + \varepsilon_2)$, both the left and right extremes are included in optimal μ-distributions.*

Proof. The proof is straightforward taking for μ_0 the maximum of μ_1 and μ_2 in Theorem 3.46. $\qquad\square$

Theorem 3.46 and Corollary 3.48 state that for biobjective Pareto fronts which are continuous on the interval $[u_{min}, u_{max}]$ and bounded weight, one can expect to have the extremes in optimal μ-distributions for any reference point dominated by the nadir point if μ is large enough, i.e., larger than μ_0. Unfortunately, the proof does not allow to state how large μ_0 has to be chosen for a given reference point but it is expected that μ_0 depends on the reference point as well as on the front shape g and weight function w.

3.4.3 · Intermediate Summary

In summary, two cases can distinguished relevant in terms of obtaining the extremal point of an optimal μ-distribution for the unweighted hypervolume indicator I_H:

1. The derivative $g'(u)$ of the Pareto front converges to $-\infty$ as $\mu \to u_{min}$. If this holds, then the left extremal point is never contained in the optimal μ-distribution for any finite choice of μ or reference point r. Similarly, if $g'(u_{max}) = 0$ holds, the right extremal point is never contained.
2. If, on the other hand, $g'(u_{min})$ is finite and $g(u_{max}) > 0$ respectively, the extremal point can be guaranteed when choosing the reference point such that $r_2 > \mathcal{R}_1$ (for the left extreme) and choosing $r_1 > \mathcal{R}_2$ (to obtain the right extreme).

The first point (1) demonstrates, that no universal rule for the choice of the reference point exists which guarantees that extremal points are contained in the optimal set of points. Rather, in many cases one or both extremal points are never contained in the optimal set, for instances on ZDT1, 3, and 5 or WFG1 and 2. In practice, however, the implications are not restrictive. First off, due to the continuous search space for most of the test problems, no algorithm will obtain the extreme exactly anyways, and if the number of points is high enough, a solution close to the extreme will be found by hypervolume-based algorithms too. Secondly, Theorem 3.29 does not hold for the weighted hypervolume indicator in general. In fact, the following weight function w_e can be used whose corresponding indicator $I_H^{w_e}$ behaves like I_H, except for the extremal solutions:

$$w_e(u,v) := \begin{cases} I_H(A^*)\delta^2(u,v) & (u,v) \in \{(u_{min}, g(u_{min})), (u_{max}, g(u_{max}))\} \\ 1 & \text{otherwise} \end{cases}$$

$$(3.26)$$

where $\delta^2(u,v)$ denotes the two-dimensional delta function with $\int_{-\infty}^{\infty} \int_{-\infty}^{\infty} \delta^2(u,v)\,du\,dv = 1$, and $I_H(A^*)$ denotes the hypervolume of the entire Pareto set. Using Eq. 3.26 ensures, that distributions that contain both extremal points will always have a larger hypervolume indicators than those sets containing one or no extremal point.

For the remaining cases (2), i.e., when the derivative $-g'(u_{min})$ is finite and $g'(u_{max}) > 0$ respectively, this chapter provides lower bounds for the choice of the reference point for both I_H^w (Theorems 3.32 and 3.39) and as a special case for I_H (Corollaries 3.36 and 3.41). The provided bounds are not tight, though. This is not relevant in practice for two reasons: first, the reference point needs to be dominated by the objective vectors of all potential solutions in order that the hypervolume indicator induces a refinement of Pareto dominance, see Section 2.2.4. In other words, the reference points needs to lie outside the objective space, which is often more restrictive than the lower bound. For WFG3, for instance, the objective space extends to $(3, 5)$, while the lower bound for the reference point is $(2, 2)$. Secondly, the only incentive to choose the reference point not too large, is to avoid numerical problems. As Table 3.1 reveals, all (finite) lower bounds for the reference point are small and no numerical issues are expected concerning the hypervolume values.

Even though the extremal points can be reached in many cases without choosing a very large reference point, the many existing recommendations are not sufficient. Choosing the reference point a little bit larger than the actual objective space as proposed by [16, 87] for instance might not hold for DTLZ7. As μ grows to infinity, however, the reference point converges to the nadir point $\mathcal{R}^{\mathrm{Nadir}} = (u_{min}, g(u_{max}))$.

3.5 · Summary

Indicator-based Evolutionary Algorithms transform a multiobjective optimization problem into a single-objective one, that corresponds to finding a set of μ points that maximizes the underlying quality indicator. Theoretically understanding these so-called *optimal μ-distributions* for a given indicator is a fundamental issue both for performance assessment of multiobjective optimizers and for the decision which indicator to take for the optimization in practice such that the search bias introduced by the indicator meets the user's preferences.

This chapter has characterized optimal μ-distributions in different ways:

- In Theorem 3.8 a necessary condition for optimal distributions has been stated. This condition allows to directly assess, whether a distribution maybe optimal. On the other hand, it is also helpful to design fast algorithms to approximate μ-distributions, since it links the position of all optimal points by a second order recurrence relation. Therefore, finding optimal μ-distributions corresponds to solving a 2-dimensional problem regardless of the number of objectives or number of points.
- Increasing μ to infinity, optimal μ-distributions have been characterized for the weighted hypervolume indicator in case of biobjective problems. As has been demonstrated by an example, the (approximated) optimal μ-distributions and the density concur precisely already for small μ. Hence, the density allows to assess the bias of the weighted hypervolume indicator in general, but also to predict the optimal distribution for finite μ. The density is only given for biobjective problems, however, as a starting point for further research, considerations are presented leading to a conjecture for the density for arbitrary numbers objectives.
- Finally, the density formula also allows to translate user preference expressed in terms of density of points to a specific weight function.

Furthermore, the influence of the reference point on optimal μ-distributions has been investigated resulting in

- lower bounds for placing the reference point for guaranteeing the Pareto front's extreme points in an optimal μ-distribution;
- characterizing cases where the extremes are never contained in an optimal μ-distribution; and in addition,
- the belief, the best choice for the reference point corresponds to the nadir point or a point that is slightly worse in all objectives has been founded theoretically for the case of the number of points going to infinity.

All results concerning the optimal μ-distributions and the choice of the reference point have been applied to test problems of the ZDT, DTLZ, and WFG test problem suites.

The author beliefs the results presented in this chapter are important for several reasons. On the one hand, several previous beliefs were disproved concerning the bias of the hypervolume indicator and the choice of the reference point to obtain the extremes of the front. On the other hand, the results on optimal μ-distributions are highly useful in performance assessment if the hypervolume indicator is used as a quality measure. For the first time, approximations of optimal μ-distributions for finite μ allow to compare the outcome of indicator-based evolutionary algorithms to the actual optimization goal. Moreover, the actual hypervolume indicator of optimal μ-distributions (or the provided approximations) offers a way to interpret the obtained hypervolume indicator values in an absolute fashion as the hypervolume of an optimal μ-distribution is a better estimate of the best achievable hypervolume than the hypervolume of the entire Pareto front. Last, the presented results for the weighted hypervolume indicator also provide a basis for a better understanding of how to articulate user preferences with the weighted hypervolume indicator in terms of the question on how to choose the weight function in practice. This knowledge will be used in Chapter 5, where an algorithm incorporating user preference using the weighted hypervolume is proposed.

4

HypE: An Algorithm for Multiobjective Search by Sampling the Hypervolume

In the first two chapters of this thesis, the main focus was on the theoretical properties of the hypervolume indicator. Thereby, various desirable features of the indicator were observed:

1. The hypervolume indicator induces a refinement of the Pareto dominance relation, hence enables to transform a multiobjective problem into a single-objective one, see Chapter 2.
2. An unlimited variety of user preferences can be translated to a corresponding weighted hypervolume indicator, where
3. the optimal set for a given weight function and Pareto front can be described in a concise way in terms of a density function, see Chapter 3.

In this and the following chapters, these properties are put to practice. To this end, a versatile Hypervolume Estimation Algorithm for Multiobjective Optimization (HypE) is proposed; thereby, specific features addressed include the incorporation of user preference, and the consideration of robustness issues. In this chapter, the algorithm is derived for the unweighted hypervolume; while Chapter 5 extends the algorithm to the weighted hypervolume indicator to incorporate user preference; and Chapter 6 proposes an extended definition of the hypervolume indicator—and its implementation into the search algorithm HypE—to incorporate robustness issues.

As pointed out in Chapter 1, the computational effort required for hypervolume calculation increases exponentially with the number of objectives (unless P = NP), cf. Bringmann and Friedrich [28]. This has so far prevented to fully exploit the potential of this indicator; current hypervolume-based search algorithms such as SMS-MOEA [16] or MO-CMA-ES [82] are limited to problems with only a few objectives. HypE deals with this problem by approximating the hypervolume, and is also applicable to problems involving many objectives, for instance more than ten objectives.

First, Section 4.1 gives some preliminary considerations as to how hypervolume-based algorithms work by stating the Regular Hypervolume-based Algorithm (RHV). In this chapter, and generally in this thesis[1], the design of mutation and crossover operators is thereby not addressed as the hypervolume is not used in this context; instead established operators like SBX crossover and variable-wise polynomial mutation are used [44].

For the case of RHV the basic idea of Monte Carlo sampling is illustrated to approximate the fitness assignment scheme. As a result, a novel Sampling-based Hypervolume-oriented Algorithm (SHV) is presented, which has been developed by the author and colleagues and which is a predecessor of HypE. SHV serves (a) as a reference algorithm in the experimental comparisons, and (b) to demonstrate three issues, which are addressed by an advanced fitness measure shown in Section 4.2. Section 4.3 then illustrates, how to approximate this novel fitness measure. Finally, Section 4.4 proposes HypE,

---

[1] Except for the bridge problem presented in Section E.1

building on the new hypervolume-based fitness measure and the corresponding approximation procedure. Comprehensive experiments in Section 4.5 conclude the chapter, comparing HypE to RHV and SHV respectively, and to existing multiobjective evolutionary algorithms.

4.1 · Preliminary Considerations

This section first illustrates the prevalent mode of operation of hypervolume-based optimization algorithms on the basis of the Regular Hypervolume-based Algorithm (RHV). Next, a methodology based on Monte Carlo sampling is shown for RHV, the Sampling-based Hypervolume-oriented Algorithm (SHV). This algorithms was a first approach by the author and colleagues to make the hypervolume indicator applicable to problems with many objectives. It has been published in [11], where the algorithm has been discussed more thoroughly. In this thesis, SHV mainly serves to illustrate the principles of sampling, and the difficulties thereby encountered—revealed in the third part of this section. Building on the results and principles of SHV, Sections 4.2 and following then propose the more advanced HypE.

4.1.1 · General Functioning of Hypervolume-Based Optimization

As already mentioned in Chapter 1, many algorithms use the hypervolume indicator as underlying (set-)preference for search [59, 62, 82, 89, 90, 141].

The main field of application of the hypervolume in general (as is the case in the above algorithms) is environmental selection which is—from a set-based perspective—the heuristic generation of the best possible follow up set from the current set and the offspring set generated therefrom. Actually, the Set Preference Algorithm for Multiobjective Optimization (SPAM) outlined in Algorithm 1 on page 49 can be used in this context. In the following, one variant of the *heuristic set mutation* (Line 4 in Algorithm 1) is shown here specific to the hypervolume-based set preference. It is a special case of the

1: generate initial set P of size α, i.e., randomly choose $B \in \Psi_{=\mu}$ and set $P \leftarrow B$
2: **while** termination criterion not fulfilled **do**
3:     select $p_1, \ldots, p_\mu \in P$ parents from P *(mating selection)*
4:     generate $r_1, \ldots, r_\lambda \in X$ offspring from p_i by crossover and mutation
5:     $P' \leftarrow P \cup \{r_1, \ldots, r_k\}$ *(merge offspring a parent population)*
6:     determine P'^{mp}_i, $1 \le i \le l$ of P' according to Eq. 2.2   *(non-dom. sorting)*
7:     $P'' = \{\}$
8:     $s \leftarrow 1$
9:     **while** $|P''| + |P'^{\mathrm{mp}}_s| \le \alpha$ **do**
10:         $P'' \leftarrow P'' \cup P'^{\mathrm{mp}}_s$
11:         $s \leftarrow s + 1$
12:     $A \leftarrow P'_s$
13:     **while** $|A| + |P''| > \alpha$ **do**
14:         **for all** $a \in A$ **do**
15:             $d_a \leftarrow I_H(A, R) - I_H(A \setminus \{a\}, R)$
16:         choose $a \in A$ with $d_a = \min_{a \in A} d_a$
17:         $A \leftarrow A \setminus \{a\}$
18:     $P'' \leftarrow P'' \cup A$
19: **return** P''

Algorithm 6 Regular Hypervolume-based Algorithm (RHV) (iterative version). After creating an offspring population and merging it with the parent population (Lines 3 to 5), environmental selection takes place: Lines 6 to 11 perform selection according to non-dominated sorting, and Lines 13 to 17 implement the greedy procedure to fill the remaining places.

algorithm presented in Zitzler et al. [141], where indicators in general are considered.

For the specific setting of using the hypervolume indicator, the algorithm is here referred to as Regular Hypervolume-based Algorithm (RHV). Algorithm 6 outlines the steps performed by RHV: first, an initial population of α individuals is generated corresponding to potential solutions, see Line 1. Thereafter, μ parent individuals are selected (Line 3) which then generate λ offspring individuals (Line 4) by means of mutation and crossover. Mating selection is performed by selecting individuals uniformly at random from P.

After having generated offspring individuals, environmental selection aims at selecting the most promising α solutions from the multiset-union of parent

Figure 4.1 Environmental selection in hypervolume-based search: first, the parent and offspring population are merged and partitioned into P_1, to P_4 by non-dominated sorting. Secondly, P_1 is copied to P''. Within the first partition $P_2 = A$ no longer fitting into P'', a greedy procedure then approximates the subset $\{c, g\}$ maximizing the hypervolume, completing P''.

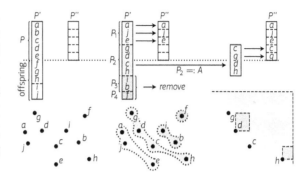

population and offspring; more precisely, it creates a new population by carrying out the following three steps, see Figure 4.1:

1. First, the union of parents and offspring is divided into disjoint partitions P_1 to P_l using the principle of non-dominated sorting [50, 70], see Section 2.3.3. This allows to assess the quality of solutions that are dominated and therefore have no influence on the indicator, see Theorem 2.19.

2. Starting with the lowest dominance depth level, the partitions are moved one by one to the new population until the first partition is reached that cannot be transferred completely (partition P_2 in Figure 4.1). This corresponds to the scheme used in most hypervolume-based multiobjective optimizers [30, 59, 78, 82].

3. For the first partition $P_i =: A$ that only fits partially into the new population (i.e., the cardinality of A exceeds the number of elements of the new population P'' that remain to be filled) the algorithm aims at finding the subset $A' \subset A$, with $|A'| = \alpha - |P''|$ which reaches the largest hypervolume. Merging A' and P'' then constitutes the population of the next generation.

The last step can be formulated as the following problem:

Definition 4.1: *Let $A \in \Psi$ be a set of solutions, let $R \subset Z$ be a reference set, and let $k \in \{0, 1, \ldots, |A|\}$. The Hypervolume Subset Selection Pro-*

blem (HSSP) is defined as the problem of finding a subset $A' \subseteq A$ with $|A'| = |A| - k$ such that the overall hypervolume loss is minimum, i.e.,

$$I_H(A', R) = \max_{\substack{A'' \subseteq A \\ |A''| = |A| - k}} I_H(A'', R)$$

If $k = 1$, then the HSSP can be solved exactly by removing that solution a from the population P with the lowest value $\lambda(H_1(a, P, R))$; this is the principle implemented in most hypervolume-based Multiobjective Evolutionary Algorithms (MOEAs) which consider one offspring per generation, e.g., [59, 82, 89]. However, it has been recently shown that exchanging only one solution in the population like in steady state MOEAs ($k = 1$) may lead to premature convergence to a local optimum in the hypervolume landscape [143]. This problem can be avoided when generating at least as many offspring as parent pairs are available, i.e., $k \geq |P|/2$.

For arbitrary k, the solution to the HSSP can be found in polynomial time for biobjective problems, using the principles of dynamic programming, see Appendix D.1 on page 255. However, the Bellman equation used by this approach no longer holds for 3 and more objectives. Whether polynomial time algorithms for the HSSP exist is subject to current research, however, due to the similar NP-hard *Maximum Coverage Problem* [38] the author assumes that the HSSP is indeed NP-hard.

For this reason, the following greedy procedure is often applied to the HSSP. Starting with the set $A' = A$, one after another solution $x \in A'$ is removed from A', until the desired size $|A'| = |A| - k$ is reached. In each step the solution is thereby removed, which causes the smallest loss in hypervolume $I_H(A', R) - I_H(A' \setminus \{x\}, R)$, also denoted the *hypervolume contribution* of solution a (see Definition 3.25 on page 92).

From Eq. 3.13 follows, that dominated solutions have no hypervolume contribution ($\lambda(C_A(x)) = 0$), for which reason the hypervolume indicator is usually combined with non-dominated sorting (see Eq. 2.2), e.g., in [59, 78, 82, 141], or is only applied to Pareto-optimal solutions [89, 90].

Please note, that the term "hypervolume contribution" is used interchange-ably to refer to both $C_A(x)$ and $\lambda(C_A(x))$—the same way the term "hyper-volume" is often used to refer to the actual indicator value.

In practice, two versions of the greedy procedure exist:

1. **Iterative:** Each time, the worst solution $x_w \in A$ is removed, the hypervol-ume contributions are recalculated with respect to the new set $A \setminus \{x\}$
2. **One shot:** The hypervolume contributions are calculated only at the beginning; and the k worst solutions are removed in one step.

Best results are usually obtained using the iterative approach, as the re-evaluation increases the quality of the generated approximation. In contrast, the one-shot approach substantially reduces the computation effort, but the quality of the resulting subset is lower. In the context of density-based MOEAs, the first approach is for instance used in the modified Strength Pareto Evolutionary Algorithm (SPEA2) [139], while the second is employed in the Nondominated Sorting Genetic Algorithm II (NSGA-II) [50].

Most hypervolume-based algorithms are similar to RHV, see Algorithm 6, in terms of both environmental selection and mating selection: The Multiob-jective Covariance Matrix Adaptation Evolution Strategy (MO-CMA-ES) of [82] uses the same greedy procedure for environmental selection, but uses a different mating selection scheme, where each individual is chosen exactly once to generate λ offspring. The s-Metric Selection Multiobjective Evo-lutionary Algorithm (SMS-MOEA) by Emmerich et al. [59] and the s-Metric Archiving approach by Knowles and Corne [89] are *steady state* EAs, i.e., a $(\mu+1)$ strategy is used where only one offspring individual being generated, see Definition 2.1 on page 22. While in [59] always the solution with the smallest contribution is removed, in [89] the offspring individual is compared with an arbitrary non-dominated solution. The SMS-MOEA uses random mating selection, while the s-Metric Archiving focuses entirely on environ-mental selection and does not address the generation of new individuals. The approach in [78] uses the hypervolume contributions as intra-ranking procedure within SPEA2 [139].

On the other hand, HypE presented from Section 4.2 onward, is different with respect to both environmental and mating selection: both are based on an extended concept of hypervolume contribution, which will be presented in Section 4.2.

All algorithms have a common disadvantage: Bringmann and Friedrich [29] have shown that calculating the hypervolume contributions is ♯P-hard like the calculation of the hypervolume of the entire set is. Therefore, hypervolume-based algorithms are not applicable to problems involving a large number of objectives. To remedy this problem, an approximation of the contributions as used by Algorithm 6 needs to be performed. The next section proposes such a methodology to estimate hypervolume contributions of solutions by means of Monte Carlo simulation.

4.1.2 · The Sampling-Based Hypervolume-Oriented Algorithm

Monte Carlo sampling is a well-known and easy-to-use approach to solve problems numerically by using random numbers. Monte Carlo sampling is used within several application areas such as atomic physics or finance. However, its most popular field of application is the computation of integrals [33]. Using Monte Carlo methods to evaluate the hypervolume indicator is not new. Everson et al. [61] for instance sampled the standard hypervolume for performance assessment.

In order to sample the contribution of a decision vector x, a sampling space $S_x \subseteq Z$ has to be defined first with the following properties: (i) the hypervolume of S can easily be computed, (ii) samples from the space S can be generated fast, and (iii) S is a superset of the domains $C_A(x) = H_i(a, P, R)$ the hypervolumes of which one would like to approximate, i.e., $C_A(x) \subseteq S_x$. Thereafter, m samples $s_i \in S_x$ are drawn at random from the sampling space, where each element of S_x is selected equally likely. Given $\{s_1, \dots, s_m\}$ the contribution is then approximated by:

$$\hat{\lambda}(C_A(x)) := \lambda(S_x)\frac{|\{s_i|s_i \in C_A(x)\}|}{m} := \lambda(S_x)\frac{H}{m} \tag{4.1}$$

where H denotes the number of samples s_i in $C_A(x)$ called *hits*.

Since the probability p of a sample s_i being a hit is independent and identically Bernoulli distributed, the estimate $\hat{\lambda}(C_A(x))$ converges to the true value with $1/\sqrt{p/(1-p) \cdot m}$. The bigger the probability of a hit p thereby is, the faster the convergence. Hence, it is crucial to choose the sampling space as small as possible while still guaranteeing $C_A(x) \subseteq S_x$ in order to maximize the number of hits, and minimize the number of samples needed to obtain a reliable estimate. In the following, a procedure to find tight sampling spaces S is addressed. To simplify drawing of samples, the shape S_x is restricted to hyperrectangles:

Definition 4.2: *Let $x \in A$ be a solution whose hypervolume contribution is to be estimated. Then the sampling hyperrectangle $S^r(x)$ of x is given by*

$$S^r(x) := \{z \in Z \mid f(x) \leqslant z \leqslant u\} \tag{4.2}$$

where $u = (u_1, \ldots, u_d)$ is

$$u_i = \min \Big\{ \{f_i(x') \mid x' \in A \setminus x \wedge x' \preceq_{|i} x\}, \\ \{r' = (r'_1, \ldots, r'_d) \in R \mid f(x) \leqslant r'\} \Big\} \tag{4.3}$$

with $x \preceq_{|i} y :\Leftrightarrow \forall 1 \leq j \leq d, j \neq i : f_j(x) \leq f_j(y)$ denoting weak dominance in all but the ith objective and where R denotes the reference set.

To simplify notation, in the following let $x_0, \ldots, x_k \in A$ denote the decision vectors with corresponding objective vectors $z^{(i)} := f(x_i)$. Furthermore, let $S_i^r := S^r(x_i)$ and $\lambda(C_i) := \lambda(C_A(x_i))$ denote the sampling hyperrectangles and contributions respectively.

To illustrate the procedure to find the sampling hyperrectangle according to Definition 4.2, the 3-dimensional hypervolume contribution of solution x_0 with objective vector $z^{(0)} = (0,0,0)$ is shown in Figure 4.2, along with the remaining eleven objective vectors. According to Eq. 4.2, the lower vertex of S_0^r corresponds to $f(x_0) = z^{(0)}$; the first coordinate u_1 of the upper vertex is $u_1 = \min\{z_1^{(1)}, z_1^{(2)}, r_1\} = 24$, the second is given by $u_2 = \min\{z_2^{(10)}, z_2^{(11)}, r_2\} = 16$, and the third is given by $u_3 = \min\{z_3^{(4)}, z_3^{(5)}, r_3\} = 9$ respectively. Hence, the sampling hyperrectangle of x_0 is $S_0^r = [0, 24] \times$

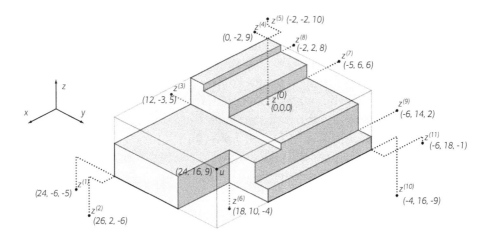

Figure 4.2 Contribution of $z^{(0)}$ (shaded polytope) in a three dimensional objective space, given eleven other incomparable objective vectors $z^{(1)}$ to $z^{(11)}$. The lower vertex of the sampling hyperrectangle (transparent box) is given by $z^{(0)}$; the upper vertex by $z_1^{(1)}$ (x-value), $z_2^{(10)}$ (y-value), and $z_3^{(4)}$ (z-value).

$[0, 16] \times [0, 9]$ (transparent box in Figure 4.2). As can be observed from Figure 4.2, the resulting sampling space is the smallest possible hyperrectangle containing the complete contribution. The following theorem shows that this holds in general, i.e., Definition 4.2 gives the optimal sampling space of hyperrectangular shape. The proof is given in Appendix on page 120.

Theorem 4.3: *The sampling hyperrectangle $S^r(x)$ according to Definition 4.2 is the minimum bounding box of the hypervolume contribution $C_A(x)$; this means (i) $S^r(x)$ contains all points that are solely dominated by x, i.e., $C_A(x) \subseteq S^r(x)$ and (ii) there exists no other hyperrectangle $\tilde{S}^r(x)$ that contains the entire contribution of x and at the same time has a smaller volume, i.e., $C_A(x) \subseteq \tilde{S}^r(x) \Rightarrow S^r(x) \subseteq \tilde{S}^r(x)$.*

Given a procedure to determine for each solution x a tight sampling space $S^r(x)$ (Eq. 4.2), and given an equation to estimate the contribution $C_A(x)$ from samples drawn from $S^r(x)$ (Eq. 4.1), the question remains, how many samples m_i should be drawn for each solution x_i. The straightforward approach is to use the same predefined number of samples m for each solution.

However, the Sampling-based Hypervolume-oriented Algorithm (SHV) uses an adaptive scheme to reduce the total number of samples. The algorithm has been published by the author and colleagues in [11]. In this thesis, the focus is on HypE, the successor of SHV. Therefore, the remaining description of the adaptive sampling strategy of SHV is moved to Appendix D.3 on page 258.

As the following section shows, SHV has a few shortcomings which will be addressed in Sections 4.2 et seq.

4.1.3 · Weaknesses of SHV

Sampling Boxes Extend to Reference Set

As Eq. 4.3 and Theorem 4.3 reveal, the sampling hyperrectangle S^r of a solution x extends in dimension i to the reference set, if no solution y exists that is better than x in all but the ith objective. Considering the objective to be independent of each other, the probability decreases that such a solution y exists which is better than x in $d-1$ out of d objectives. In other words, with increasing number of objectives, the sampling hyperrectangle S^r will more and more frequently extend up to the reference set. This is also demonstrated by the following example.

Example 4.4: Consider 50 solutions $A = \{x_1, \ldots, x_{50}\}$ whose objective values are randomly uniformly distributed on a unit simplex, i.e., $\sum_{i=1}^{d} f_i(x_j) = 1$ $\forall x_j \in A$, and let the reference set be $R = \{r\}$ with $r = \{2, 2, \ldots, 2\}$. For different numbers of objectives d, 1 000 Pareto-front approximations A are generated respectively. Then, for each front A and every solution $x_j \in A$, the volume of the corresponding hyperrectangle $\lambda(S_j^r)$ is calculated and compared to the volume of the sampling hyperrectangle $S_{max}^r(x_j)$ where u in Eq. 4.3 is set to the reference point r. In Figure 4.3, the mean ratio of $\lambda(S_j^r)$ to $\lambda(S_{max}^r(x_j))$, as well as a histogram thereof is plotted against the number of objectives d. For d larger or equal 10, the sampling hyperrectangles, and hence the contributions of the considered solution, always extend up to the reference point in all objectives (giving a ratio of 1). For as little as 6 objectives already less than 50% of the hyperrectangles volume is saved

Figure 4.3 Mean ratio between the volume of the tight sampling space S^r and the sampling space extending to the reference point S^r_{max} against the number of objectives. The gray rectangles represent a histogram of the aforementioned ratio. As the number of objectives increases, the mean ratio converges to one, meaning the sampling boxes all extend to the reference point.

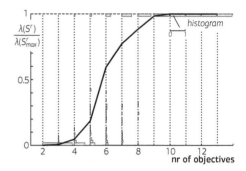

using the tightest possible choice of u (Eq. 4.3) in comparison to setting u to the reference point.   ◦

The previous example shows, that already for decent numbers of objectives $d \geq 6$, i.e., choices of d where the exact calculation of the hypervolume just starts to get too expensive, the hypervolume contributions mostly extend all up to the reference point. Hence, instead of sampling each solution separately within its own sampling hyperrectangle, a more efficient procedure would be to sample within the whole objective space up to the maximum of the reference set and thereby approximate all contributions in one pass. The samples saved sampling all contributions together instead of individually, most likely compensate for the (slightly) oversized sampling space—even when using an adaptive scheme as employed by SHV presented in Appendix D.3.

Contributions Increasingly Hard To Sample

Within the same setting used in Example 4.4, the number of samples dominated by only the considered solution has been counted, as well as the number of times $l-1$ other solutions dominated the sample. Table 4.1 reports the result for different numbers of objectives. As the number of objectives d increases, less and less samples are dominated by just the considered solutions. In other words, the number of hits decreases. The drop is very substantial at the beginning, and seems to flatten for more than 10 objectives. The same happens to the number of samples dominated by $l=2$

Table 4.1 Number of samples out of 10 000 dominated by 1, 2, 3, 4, 5, 10, and 25 or more solutions against the number of objectives d. As d increases, the number of samples dominated by just the considered solution, i.e., the number of samples giving the contribution of the solution decreases.

d	1	2	3	4	5	10	≥ 25
2	10000	0	0	0	0	0	0
3	4682	2294	1085	780	325	55	0
4	1318	1352	1104	958	814	294	487
5	198	254	290	346	354	367	2700
6	73	119	155	182	200	251	4694
7	36	58	74	87	91	131	6595
8	38	58	68	79	93	146	6432
9	29	45	62	74	87	134	6668
10	31	50	66	78	88	120	6910
25	23	40	54	66	74	113	6998
50	23	39	52	62	71	111	7046

or more solutions, however, the number of samples is generally larger the more solutions l are considered.

Estimating the contribution of a solution hence becomes more and more difficult with increasing number of objectives, which affects the accuracy of the estimate, see discussion following Eq. 4.1. It would therefore be beneficial to also use the samples dominated by 2, 3 or even more solutions.

In the following, a novel Hypervolume Estimation Algorithm for Multiobjective Optimization (HypE) is presented, that uses the entire objective space to draw samples. Additionally, both its environmental and mating selection step rely on a new fitness assignment scheme based not only on the hypervolume contribution as stated in Definition 3.25 on page 92, but also on parts of the objective space dominated by more than one solution.

A New Advanced Fitness Assignment Scheme

Using the contributions $C_A(x)$ as the fitness measure has two disadvantages: (i) the fitness is not suitable for mating selection. For instance, given two solutions x_1 and x_2 for which $f(x_1) = f(x_2)$ holds, both have no contribution, although they might be valuable parents; the same holds for dominated solutions. (ii) the contribution constitutes the loss when removing *one* solution. An advanced fitness scheme (as presented in Section 4.2.2) could also consider the hypervolume lost by removing multiple solutions to improve the greedy procedure in Algorithm 6.

The following advanced fitness assignment scheme addresses the three issues outlined in this section, which is thereafter employed by HypE.

4.2 · Hypervolume-Based Fitness Assignment

In the following, a generalized fitness assignment strategy is proposed that takes into account the entire objective space weakly dominated by a population, addressing the issue raised in Section 4.1.3. First, a basic scheme is provided for mating selection and then an extension is presented for environmental selection. Afterwards, it is briefly discussed how the fitness values can be computed exactly using a slightly modified hypervolume calculation algorithm.

4.2.1 · Basic Scheme for Mating Selection

To begin with, the hypervolume $H(A, R)$ of a set of solutions A and reference set R is further split into partitions $H(T, A, R)$, each associated with a specific subset $T \subseteq A$:

$$H(T, A, R) := [\bigcap_{t \in T} H(\{t\}, R)] \setminus [\bigcup_{a \in A \setminus T} H(\{a\}, R)]$$

The set $H(T, A, R) \subseteq Z$ represents the portion of the objective space that is jointly weakly dominated by the solutions in T and not weakly dominated by any other solution in A. It holds

$$\dot{\bigcup_{T \subseteq A}} H(T, A, R) = H(A, R) \tag{4.4}$$

which is illustrated in Figure 4.4(a). That the partitions are disjoint can be easily shown: Assume that there are two non-identical subsets S_1, S_2 of A for which $H(S_1, A, R) \cap H(S_2, A, R) \neq \emptyset$; since the sets are not identical, there exists without loss of generality an element $a \in S_1$ which is not contained in S_2; from the above definition follows that $H(\{a\}, R) \supseteq H(S_1, A, R)$ and therefore $H(\{a\}, R) \cap H(S_2, A, R) \neq \emptyset$; the latter statement leads to a contradiction since $H(\{a\}, R)$ cannot be part of $H(S_2, A, R)$ when $a \notin S_2$.

In practice, it is infeasible to determine all distinct $H(T, A, R)$ due to combinatorial explosion. Instead, a more compact splitting of the dominated objective space will be considered that refers to single solutions:

$$H_i(a, A, R) := \bigcup_{\substack{T \subseteq A \\ a \in T \\ |T| = i}} H(T, A, R) \tag{4.5}$$

According to this definition, $H_i(a, A, R)$ stands for the portion of the objective space that is jointly and solely weakly dominated by a and any $i - 1$ further solutions from A, see Figure 4.4(b). Note that the sets $H_1(a, A, R)$, $H_2(a, A, R)$, ..., $H_{|A|}(a, A, R)$ are disjoint for a given $a \in A$, i.e., $\dot{\bigcup}_{1 \leq i \leq |A|} H_i(a, A, R) = H(\{a\}, R)$, while the sets $H_i(a, A, R)$ and $H_i(b, A, R)$ may be overlapping for fixed i and different solutions $a, b \in A$. This slightly different notion has reduced the number of subspaces to be considered from $2^{|A|}$ for $H(T, A, R)$ to $|A|^2$ for $H_i(a, A, R)$.

Now, given an arbitrary population $P \in \Psi$ one obtains for each solution a contained in P a vector $(\lambda(H_1(a, P, R)), \lambda(H_2(a, P, R)), \ldots, \lambda(H_{|P|}(a, P, R)))$ of hypervolume contributions. These vectors can be used to assign fitness values to solutions; Subsection 4.2.3 describes how the corresponding values $\lambda(H_i(a, A, R))$ can be computed. While most hypervolume-based search algorithms only take the first components, i.e., $\lambda(H_1(a, P, R))$, into account, here the following scheme is proposed to aggregate the hypervolume contributions into a single scalar value.

Definition 4.5: *Let $A \in \Psi$ and $R \subset Z$. Then the function I_h with*

$$I_h(a, A, R) := \sum_{i=1}^{|A|} \frac{1}{i} \lambda(H_i(a, A, R))$$

gives for each solution $a \in A$ the hypervolume that can be attributed to a with regard to the overall hypervolume $I_H(A, R)$.

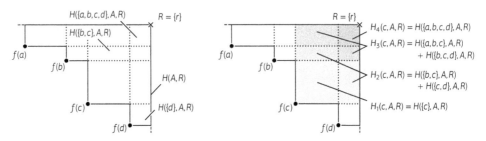

(a) The relationship between $H(A,R)$ and $H(T,A,R)$

(b) The relationship between $H(T,A,R)$ and $H_i(a,A,R)$

Figure 4.4 Illustration of the notions of $H(A,R)$, $H(T,A,R)$, and $H_i(a,A,R)$ in the objective space for a Pareto set approximation $A = \{a,b,c,d\}$ and reference set $R = \{r\}$.

Figure 4.5 Shows for an example population the selection probabilities for the population members (left). As one can see on the right, the overall selection probability for the shaded area does not change when dominated solutions are added to the population.

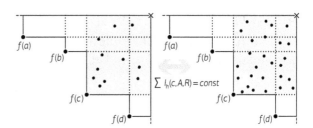

The motivation behind this definition is simple: the hypervolume contribution of each partition $H(T, A, R)$ is shared equally among the dominating solutions $t \in T$. That means the portion of Z solely weakly dominated by a specific solution a is fully attributed to a, the portion of Z that a weakly dominates together with another solution b is attributed half to a and so forth—the principle is illustrated in Figure 4.6(a). Thereby, the overall hypervolume is distributed among the distinct solutions according to their hypervolume contributions as the following theorem shows (the proof can be found in Appendix D.4 on page 260). Note that this scheme does not require that the solutions of the considered Pareto set approximation A are mutually non-dominating; it applies to non-dominated and dominated solutions alike.

Theorem 4.6: *Let* $A \in \Psi$ *and* $R \subset Z$. *Then it holds*

$$I_H(A, R) = \sum_{a \in A} I_h(a, A, R)$$

This aggregation method has some desirable properties that make it well suited to mating selection where the fitness F_a of a population member $a \in P$ is $F_a = I_h(a, P, R)$ and the corresponding selection probability p_a equals $F_a/I_H(P, R)$. As Figure 4.5 demonstrates, the accumulated selection probability remains the same for any subspace $H(\{a\}, R)$ with $a \in P$, independently of how many individuals $b \in P$ are mapped to $H(\{a\}, R)$ and how the individuals are located within $H(\{a\}, R)$. This can be formally stated in the next theorem; the proof can be found in Appendix D.5 on page 261.

Theorem 4.7: *Let* $A \in \Psi$ *and* $R \subset Z$. *For every* $a \in A$ *and all multisets* $B_1, B_2 \in \Psi$ *with* $\{a\} \preccurlyeq B_1$ *and* $\{a\} \preccurlyeq B_2$ *holds*

$$\sum_{b_1 \in \{a\} \cup B_1} I_h(b_1, \{a\} \cup B_1, R) = \sum_{b_2 \in \{a\} \cup B_2} I_h(b_2, \{a\} \cup B_2, R)$$

Since the selection probability per subspace is constant as long as the overall hypervolume value does not change, adding dominated solutions to the population leads to a redistribution of the selection probabilities and thereby implements a natural niching mechanism. Another advantage of this fitness assignment scheme is that it takes all hypervolume contributions $H_i(a, P, R)$ for $1 \leq i \leq |P|$ into account. As will be discussed in Section 4.3, this allows to more accurately estimate the ranking of the individuals according to their fitness values when using Monte Carlo simulation.

In order to study the usefulness of this fitness assignment strategy, the following experiment is considered. A standard evolutionary algorithm implementing pure non-dominated sorting fitness is applied to a selected test function (biobjective WFG1 [79] using the setting as described in Section 4.5) and run for 100 generations. Then, mating selection is carried out on the resulting population, i.e., the individuals are reevaluated using the fitness

Table 4.2 Comparison of three fitness assignment schemes: (1) constant fitness, (2) non-dominated sorting plus $\lambda(H_1(a, P, R))$, and (3) the proposed method. Each value gives the percentage of cases where the method associated with that row yields a higher hypervolume value than the method associated with the corresponding column.

versus	const. (1)	std. (2)	new (3)
const. (1)	-	44%	28%
std. (2)	56%	-	37%
new (3)	72%	63%	-

scheme under consideration and offspring are generated employing binary tournament selection with replacement and corresponding variation operators. The hypervolume of the (multi)set of offspring is taken as an indicator for the effectiveness of the fitness assignment scheme. By comparing the resulting hypervolume values for different strategies (constant fitness leading to uniform selection, non-dominated sorting plus $\lambda(H_1(a, P, R))$, and the proposed fitness according to Definition 4.5) and for 100 repetitions of this experiment, the influence of the fitness assignment strategy on the mating selection process is investigated.

The Quade test, a modification of Friedman's test which has more power when comparing few treatments [39], reveals that there are significant differences in the quality of the generated offspring populations at a signficance level of 0.01 (test statistics: $T_3 = 12.2$). Performing post-hoc pairwise comparisons following Conover [39] using the same significance level as in the Quade test provides evidence that the proposed fitness strategy can be advantageous over the other two strategies, cf. Table 4.2; in the considered setting, the hypervolume values achieved are significantly better. Comparing the standard hypervolume-based fitness with constant fitness, the former outperforms the latter significantly. Nevertheless, also the required computation resources need to be taken into account. That means in practice that the advantage over uniform selection may diminish when fitness computation becomes expensive. This aspect will be investigated in Section 4.5.

The next section will extend and generalize the fitness assignment scheme with regard to the environmental selection phase.

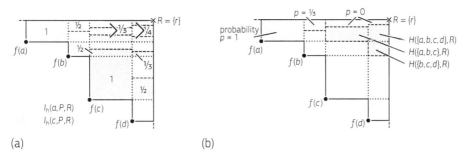

Figure 4.6 (a) Illustration of the basic fitness assignment scheme where the fitness F_a of a solution a is set to $F_a = I_h(a,P,R)$. (b) The figure is based on the previous example with $A = \{a,b,c,d\}$, $R = \{r\}$ and shows (i) which portion of the objective space remains dominated if any two solutions are removed from A (shaded area), and (II) the probabilities p that a particular area that can be attributed to $a \in A$ is lost if a is removed from A together with any other solution in A.

4.2.2 · Extended Scheme for Environmental Selection

Here, the last step of the environmental selection is considered, i.e., the task selecting $|A| - k$ of a set A maximizing the hypervolume (see Definition 4.1).

For arbitrary values of k, the greedy procedure shown in Section 4.1.1 is usually applied. The key issue with respect to this strategy is how to evaluate the usefulness of a solution. The scheme presented in Definition 4.5 has the drawback that portions of the objective space are taken into account that for sure will not change. Consider, for instance, a population with four solutions as shown in Figure 4.6(b); when two solutions need to be removed ($k = 2$), then the subspaces $H(\{a, b, c\}, P, R)$, $H(\{b, c, d\}, P, R)$, and $H(\{a, b, c, d\}, P, R)$ remain weakly dominated independently of which solutions are deleted. This observation led to the idea of considering the expected loss in hypervolume that can be attributed to a particular solution when exactly k solutions are removed. In detail, for each $a \in P$ the average hypervolume loss is considered over all subsets $T \subseteq P$ that contain a and $k - 1$ further solutions; this value can be easily computed by slightly extending the scheme from Definition 4.5 as follows.

Definition 4.8: *Let $A \in \Psi$, $R \subset Z$, and $k \in \{0, 1, \dots, |A|\}$. Then the function I_h^k with*

$$I_h^k(a, A, R) := \frac{1}{|\mathcal{T}|} \sum_{T \in \mathcal{T}} \left[\sum_{\substack{U \subseteq T \\ a \in T}} \frac{1}{|T|} \lambda(H(T, A, R)) \right] \tag{4.6}$$

where $\mathcal{T} = \{T \subseteq A \,;\, a \in T \,\wedge\, |T| = k\}$ contains all subsets of A that include a and have cardinality k gives for each solution $a \in A$ the expected hypervolume loss that can be attributed to a when a and $k - 1$ uniformly randomly chosen solutions from A are removed from A.

Notice that $I_h^1(a, A, R) = \lambda(H_1(a, A, R))$ and $I_h^{|A|}(a, A, R) = I_h(a, A, R)$, i.e., this modified scheme can be regarded as a generalization of the scheme presented in Definition 4.5 and the commonly used fitness assignment strategy for hypervolume-based search [11, 59, 82, 89]. The next theorem shows how to calculate $I_h^k(a, A, R)$ without averaging over all subsets $T \in \mathcal{T}$; the proof can be found in Appendix D.6 on page 262.

Theorem 4.9: *Let $A \in \Psi$, $R \subset Z$, and $k \in \{0, 1, \dots, |A|\}$. Then it holds*

$$I_h^k(a, A, R) = \sum_{i=1}^{k} \frac{\alpha_i}{i} \lambda(H_i(a, A, R)) \quad \text{where} \quad \alpha_i := \prod_{j=1}^{i-1} \frac{k - j}{|A| - j}$$

Next, the effectiveness of $I_h^k(a, A, R)$ is studied for approximating the optimal HSSP solution. To this end, assume that for the iterative greedy strategy $(l = 1)$ in the first round the values $I_h^k(a, A, R)$ are considered, in the second round the values $I_h^{k-1}(a, A, R)$, and so forth; each time an individual assigned the lowest value is selected for removal. For the one-step greedy method $(l = k)$, only the $I_h^k(a, A, R)$ values are considered.

Table 4.3 provides a comparison of the different techniques for 100 000 randomly chosen Pareto set approximations $A \in \Psi$ containing ten incomparable solutions, where the ten points are randomly distributed on a three dimensional unit simplex, i.e., a three objective scenario is considered. The

Table 4.3 Comparison of greedy strategies for the HSSP (iterative vs. one shot) using the new (I_h^k) and the standard hypervolume fitness (I_h^1); as a reference, purely random deletions are considered as well. The first column gives the portion of cases an optimal subset was generated; the second column provides the average difference in hypervolume between optimal and generated subset. The last two columns reflect the direct comparisons between the two fitness schemes for each greedy approach (iterative, one shot) separately; they give the percentages of cases where the corresponding method was better than or equal to the other one.

greedy strategy	optimum found	distance	better	equal
iterative with I_h^k	59.8 %	1.09 10^{-3}	30.3 %	66.5 %
iterative with I_h^1	44.5 %	2.59 10^{-3}	3.17 %	66.5 %
one shot with I_h^k	16.9 %	39.3 10^{-3}	65.2 %	23.7 %
one shot with I_h^1	3.4 %	69.6 10^{-3}	11.1 %	23.7 %
uniformly random	0.381 %	257 10^{-3}		

parameter k was set to 5, so that half of the solutions needed to be removed. The relatively small numbers were chosen to allow to compute the optimal subsets by enumeration. Thereby, the maximum hypervolume values achievable could be determined.

The comparison reveals that the new fitness assignment scheme is in the considered scenario more effective in approximating HSSP than the standard scheme. The mean relative distance (see Table 4.3) to the optimal solution is about 60% smaller than the distance achieved using I_h^1 in the iterative case and about 44% smaller in the one shot case. Furthermore, the optimum was found much more often in comparison to the standard fitness: 34% more often for the iterative approach and 497% in the one shot scenario.

Finally, note that the proposed evaluation function I_h^k will be combined with non-dominated sorting for environmental selection as for RHV, cf. Section 4.1.1, similarly to [11, 30, 59, 82, 141]. One reason is computation time: with non-dominated sorting the worst dominated solutions can be removed quickly without invoking the hypervolume calculation algorithm; this advantage mainly applies to low-dimensional problems and to the early stage of the search process. Another reason is that the full benefits of the scheme proposed in Definition 4.8 can be exploited when the Pareto

1: **procedure** *computeHypervolume*(P, R, k)
2:     $\mathcal{F} \leftarrow \bigcup_{a \in P} \{(a, 0)\}$
3:         **return** *doSlicing*($\mathcal{F}$,R,k,d,1,(∞, ∞, ..., ∞));

Algorithm 7 Hypervolume-based Fitness Value Computation. Requires a population $P \in \psi$, a reference set $R \subseteq Z$, and the fitness parameter $k \in \mathbb{N}$.

set approximation A under consideration only contains incomparable and indifferent solutions; otherwise, it cannot be guaranteed that non-dominated solutions are preferred over dominated ones.

4.2.3 · Exact Calculation of I_h^k

This subsection tackles the question of how to calculate the fitness values for a given population $P \in \Psi$. An algorithm is presented that determines the values $I_h^k(a, P, R)$ for all elements $a \in P$ and a fixed k—in the case of mating selection k equals $|P|$, in the case of environmental selection k gives the number of solutions to be removed from P. It operates according to the 'hypervolume by slicing objectives' principle [86, 130, 134], but differs from existing methods in that it allows: (i) to consider a set R of reference points and (ii) to compute all fitness values, e.g., the $I_h^1(a, P, R)$ values for $k = 1$, in parallel for any number of objectives instead of subsequently as in the work of Beume et al. [16]. Although it looks at all partitions $H(T, P, R)$ with $T \subseteq P$ explicitly, the worst-case runtime complexity is not affected by this; it is of order $\mathcal{O}(|P|^d + d|P| \log |P|)$ assuming that sorting of the solutions in all dimensions is carried out as a preprocessing step. Please note, that faster hypervolume calculation algorithms exists, most notably the algorithm by Beume and Rudolph [14].[2] Clearly, the algorithm is only feasible for a low number of objectives, and the next section discusses how the fitness values can be estimated using Monte Carlo methods.

Details of the procedure are given by Algorithms 7 and 8. Algorithm 7 just provides the top level call to the recursive function *doSlicing* and returns a

---

[2] Adjusting this method to the fitness measure I_h^k is not straightforward, hence only the extension of the basic hypervolume by slicing objectives approach is demonstrated here. A substantial speedup is expected when employing a more elaborate algorithm.

fitness assignment $\mathcal{F}$, a multiset containing for each $a \in P$ a corresponding pair (a, v) where v is the fitness value. Note that d at Line 3 denotes the number of objectives. Algorithm 8 recursively cuts the dominated space into hyperrectangles and returns a (partial) fitness assignment $\mathcal{F}'$. At each recursion level, a scan is performed along a specific objective—given by i—with u^* representing the current scan position. The vector $(z_1, \ldots, z_d)$ contains for all dimensions the scan positions, and at each invocation of *doSlicing* solutions (more precisely: their objective vectors) and reference points are filtered out according to these scan positions (Lines 2 and 3) where also dominated solutions may be selected in contrast to [86, 130, 134]. Furthermore, the partial volume V is updated before recursively invoking Algorithm 8 based on the distance to the next scan position. At the lowest recursion level $(i = 0)$, the variable V gives the hypervolume of the partition $H(A, P, R)$, i.e., $V = \lambda(H(A, P, R))$ where A stands for the remaining solutions fulfilling the bounds given by the vector $(z_1, \ldots, z_d)$—A_U contains the objective vectors corresponding to A, cf. Line 2. Since the fitness according to Definition 4.8 is additive with respect to the partitions, for each $a \in A$ the partial fitness value v can be updated by adding $\frac{\alpha_{|A_U|}}{|A_U|} V$. Note that the population is a multiset, i.e., it may contain indifferent solutions or even duplicates; therefore, all the other sets in the algorithms are multisets.

The following example illustrates the working principle of the hypervolume computation.

Example 4.10: Consider the three-objective scenario depicted in Figure 4.7 where the population contains four solutions a, b, c, d the objective vectors of which are $f(a) = (-10, -3, -2)$, $f(b) = (-8, -1, -8)$, $f(c) = (-6, -8, -10)$, $f(d) = (-4, -5, -11)$ and the reference set includes two points $r = (-2, 0, 0)$, $s = (0, -3, -4)$. Furthermore, let the parameter k be 2.

In the first call of *doSlicing*, it holds $i = 3$ and U contains all objective vectors associated with the population and all reference points. The fol-

1: **procedure** $doSlicing(\mathcal{F},\ R,\ k,\ i,\ V,\ (z_1,\dots,z_d))$
2:      $A_U \leftarrow \bigcup_{(a,v)\in\mathcal{F},\ \forall i<j\le d:\ f_j(a)\le z_j}\{f(a)\}$ *(filter out relevant solutions...)*
3:      $UR \leftarrow \bigcup_{(r_1,\dots,r_d)\in R,\ \forall i<j\le d:\ r_j\ge z_j}\{(r_1,\dots,r_d)\}$ *(... and reference points)*
4:      **if** $i=0 \wedge UR \ne \emptyset$ **then**   *(end of recursion reached)*
5:          $\alpha \leftarrow \prod_{j=1}^{|A_U|-1}(k-j)/(|\mathcal{F}|-j)$
6:          $\mathcal{F}' \leftarrow \emptyset$
7:          **for all** $(a,v)\in\mathcal{F}$ **do**   *(update hypervolumes of filtered solutions)*
8:              **if** $\forall 1\le j\le d: f_j(a)\le z_j$ **then**
9:                  $\mathcal{F}' \leftarrow \mathcal{F}' \cup \{(a, v+\frac{\alpha}{|A_U|}V)\}$
10:             **else**
11:                 $\mathcal{F}' \leftarrow \mathcal{F}' \cup \{(a,v)\}$
12:     **else if** $i>0$ **then**   *(recursion continues)*
13:         $\mathcal{F}' \leftarrow \mathcal{F}$
14:         $U \leftarrow A_U \cup UR$
15:         **while** $U \ne \emptyset$ **do**   *(scan current dimension in ascending order)*
16:             $u^* \leftarrow \min_{(u_1,\dots,u_d)\in U} u_i$
17:             $U' \leftarrow \{(u_1,\dots,u_d)\in U \mid u_i > u^*\}$
18:             **if** $U' \ne \emptyset$ **then**
19:                 $V' = V \cdot \Big((\min_{(u_1',\dots,u_d')\in U'} u_i') - u^*\Big)$
20:                 $\mathcal{F}' \leftarrow doSlicing(\mathcal{F}',\ R,\ k,\ i\text{-}1,\ V',(z_1,\dots,z_{i-1},u^*,z_{i+1},\dots,z_d)\ )$
21:             $U = U'$
22:     **return** $\mathcal{F}'$

Algorithm 8 Recursive Objective Space Partitioning. Requires the current fitness assignment $\mathcal{F}$, the reference set $R \subseteq Z$, a fitness parameter $k \in \mathbb{N}$, the recursion level i, the partial volume $V \in \mathbb{R}$, and the scan positions $(z_1, \dots, z_d) \in \mathbb{R}^d$

lowing representation shows U with its elements sorted in ascending order according to their third vector components:

$$U = \begin{array}{rl} f(d): & (-4,-5,-11)\downarrow \\ f(c): & (-6,-8,-10) \\ f(b): & (-8,-1,-8) \\ s: & (-0,-3,-4) \\ f(a): & (-10,-3,-2) \\ r: & (-2,0,0) \end{array}$$

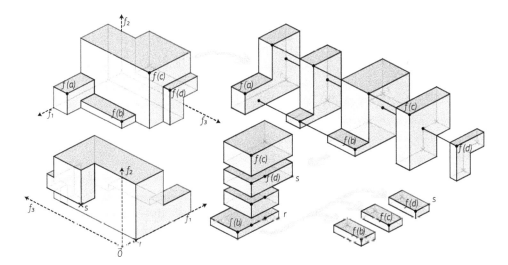

Figure 4.7 Illustration of the principle underlying Algorithm 8 where one looks from (-∞, -∞, -∞) on the front except for the lower left picture where one looks from (∞,-∞,∞) to the origin. First, the dominated polytope is cut along the third dimension leading to five slices, which are again cut along the second dimension and finally along the first dimension. In contrast to existing 'Hypervolume by Slicing Objectives' algorithms, also dominated points are carried along.

Hence, in the first two iterations of the loop beginning at Line 15 the variable u^* is assigned to $f_3(d) = -11$ resp. $u^* = f_3(c) = -10$. Within the third iteration, U is reduced to $\{f(a), f(b), r, s\}$ which yields $u^* = f_3(b) = -8$ and in turn $V' = 1 \cdot (-4 - (-8)) = 4$ with the current vector of scan positions being $(z_1, z_2, z_3) = (\infty, \infty, -8)$; these values are passed to the next recursion level $i = 2$ where U is initialized at Line 14 as follows (this time sorted according to the second dimension):

$$
U = \begin{array}{rl}
f(c): & (-6, -8, -10) \downarrow \\
f(d): & (-4, -5, -11) \\
s: & (0, -3, -4) \\
f(b): & (-8, -1, -8) \\
r: & (-2, 0, 0)
\end{array}
$$

Now, after three iterations of the loop at Line 15 with $u^* = f_2(c) = -8$, $u^* = f_2(d) = -5$, and $u^* = s_2 = -3$, respectively, U is reduced in the fourth iteration to $\{f(b), r\}$ and u^* is set to $f_2(b) = -1$. As a result, $V' = 1 \cdot 4 \cdot (0 - (-1)) = 4$ and $(z_1, z_2, z_3) = (\infty, -1, -8)$ which are the parameters for the next recursive invocation of *doSlicing* where U is set to:

$$U = \begin{array}{rl} f(b): & (-8, -1, -8) \downarrow \\ f(c): & (-6, -8, -10) \\ f(d): & (-4, -5, -11) \\ r: & (-2, 0, 0) \end{array}$$

At this recursion level with $i = 1$, in the second iteration it holds $u^* = f_1(c) = -6$ and $V' = 1 \cdot 4 \cdot 1 \cdot (-4 - (-6)) = 8$. When calling *doSlicing* at this stage, the last recursion level is reached $(i = 0)$: First, α is computed based on the population size $n = 4$, the number of individuals dominating the hyperrectangle $(|A_U| = 2)$, and the fitness parameter $k = 2$, which yields $\alpha = 1/3$; then for b and c, the fitness values are increased by adding $\alpha \cdot V / |A_U| = 1/3 \cdot 8/2 = 4/3$.

Applying this procedure to all slices at a particular recursion level identifies all hyperrectangles which constitute the portion of the objective space enclosed by the population and the reference set.   ○

4.3 · Estimating Hypervolume Contributions Using Monte Carlo Simulation

As outlined above, the computation of the proposed hypervolume-based fitness scheme is that expensive that only problems with at maximum four or five objectives are tractable within reasonable time limits. However, in the context of randomized search heuristics one may argue that the exact fitness values are not crucial and approximated values may be sufficient; furthermore, if using pure rank-based selection schemes, then only the resulting order of the individuals matters. These considerations lead to the idea of estimating the hypervolume contributions. To approximate the fitness values according to Definition 4.8, the Lebesgue measures of the domains

$H_i(a, P, R)$ need to be estimated where $P \in \Psi$ is the population. Since these domains are all integrable, their Lebesgue measure can be approximated by means of Monte Carlo simulation as in the Sampling-based Hypervolume-oriented Algorithm (SHV), see Section 4.1.2 on page 118.

For this purpose, again a sampling space $S \subseteq Z$ has to be defined. As outlined in Section 4.1.3, sampling within an axis-aligned minimum bounding box determined by the reference set makes sense, i.e.:

$$S := \{(z_1, \ldots, z_d) \in Z \,|\, \forall 1 \leq i \leq d : l_i \leq z_i \leq u_i\}$$

where

$$l_i := \min_{a \in P} f_i(a) \qquad\qquad u_i := \max_{(r_1, \ldots, r_d) \in R} r_i$$

for $1 \leq i \leq d$. Hence, the volume V of the sampling space S is given by $V = \prod_{i=1}^{d} \max\{0, u_i - l_i\}$.

Now given S, sampling is carried out as for SHV by selecting m objective vectors $s_1, \ldots, s_m$ from S uniformly at random. For each s_j it is checked whether it lies in any partition $H_i(a, P, R)$ for $1 \leq i \leq k$ and $a \in P$. This can be determined in two steps: first, it is verified that s_j is 'below' the reference set R, i.e., there exists $r \in R$ that is dominated by s_j; second, it is verified that the multiset A of those population members dominating s_j is not empty. If both conditions are fulfilled, then—given A—the sampling point s_j lies in all partitions $H_i(a, P, R)$ where $i = |A|$ and $a \in A$. This situation will be denoted as a *hit* regarding the ith partition of a. If any of the above two conditions is not fulfilled, then s_j is called a *miss*. Let $X_j^{(i,a)}$ denote the corresponding random variable that is equal to 1 in case of a hit of s_j regarding the ith partition of a and 0 otherwise.

Based on the m sampling points, an estimate for $\lambda(H_i(a, P, R))$ is obtained by simply counting the number of hits and multiplying the hit ratio with the volume of the sampling box:

$$\hat{\lambda}(H_i(a, P, R)) = \frac{\sum_{j=1}^{m} X_j^{(i,a))}}{m} \cdot V \qquad\qquad (4.7)$$

This value approaches the exact value $\lambda(H_i(a, P, R))$ with increasing m by the law of large numbers. Due to the linearity of the expectation operator, the fitness scheme according to Eq. 4.6 can be approximated by replacing the Lebesgue measure with the respective estimates given by Eq. 4.7:

$$\hat{I}_h^k(a, P, R) = \sum_{i=1}^{k} \frac{\alpha_i}{i} \cdot \left(\frac{\sum_{j=1}^{m} X_j^{(i,a))}}{m} V \right) \tag{4.8}$$

The details of the estimation procedure are described by Algorithm 9 which returns a fitness assignment, i.e., for each $a \in P$ the corresponding hypervolume estimate $\hat{I}_h^k(a, P, R)$. It will be later used by the evolutionary algorithm presented in Section 4.4. Note that the partitions $H_i(a, P, R)$ with $i > k$ do not need to be considered for the fitness calculation as they do not contribute to the I_h^k values that need to be estimated, cf. Definition 4.8.

In order to study how closely the sample size m and the accuracy of the estimates is related, a simple experiment was carried out: ten imaginary individuals $a \in A$ were generated, the objective vectors $f(a)$ of which are uniformly distributed at random on a three dimensional unit simplex, similarly to the experiments presented in Table 4.3. These individuals were then ranked on the one hand according to the estimates $\hat{I}_h^{|A|}$ and on the other hand with respect to the exact values $I_h^{|A|}$. The closer the former ranking is to the latter ranking, the higher is the accuracy of the estimation procedure given by Algorithm 9. To quantify the differences between the two rankings, the percentage is calculated of all pairs (i, j) with $1 \le i < j \le |A|$ where the individuals at the ith position and the jth position in the ranking according to $I_h^{|A|}$ have the same order in the ranking according to $\hat{I}_h^{|A|}$, see [113]. The experiment was repeated for different numbers of sampling points as shown in Table 4.4. The experimental results indicate that 10 000 samples are necessary to achieve an error below 5% and that 10 000 000 sampling points are sufficient in this setting to obtain the exact ranking.

Seeing the close relationship between sample size and accuracy, one may ask whether m can be adjusted automatically on the basis of confidence intervals. In the technical report by the author and colleagues [7] confidence intervals are derived for the sampled fitness values. Based on these,

1: **procedure** *estimateHypervolume*(P, R, k, m)
2:     **for** $i \leftarrow 1, d$ **do**   *(determine sampling box S)*
3:         $l_i = \min_{a \in P} f_i(a)$
4:         $u_i = \max_{(r_1, \ldots, r_d) \in R} r_i$
5:     $S \leftarrow [l_1, u_1] \times \cdots \times [l_d, u_d]$
6:     $V \leftarrow \prod_{i=1}^{d} \max\{0, (u_i - l_i)\}$
7:     $\mathcal{F} \leftarrow \bigcup_{a \in P}\{(a, 0)\}$ *(reset fitness assignment)*
8:     **for** $j \leftarrow 1, m$ **do**   *(perform sampling)*
9:         choose $s \in S$ uniformly at random
10:         **if** $\exists r \in R : s \leqslant r$ **then**
11:             $A_U \leftarrow \bigcup_{a \in P, \; f(a) \leqslant s}\{f(a)\}$
12:             **if** $|A_U| \leq k$ **then**   *(hit in a relevant partition)*
13:                 $\alpha \leftarrow \prod_{l=1}^{|A_U|-1} \frac{k-l}{|P|-l}$
14:                 $\mathcal{F}' \leftarrow \emptyset$
15:                 **for all** $(a, v) \in \mathcal{F}$ **do**   *(update hypervolume estimates)*
16:                     **if** $f(a) \leqslant s$ **then**
17:                         $\mathcal{F}' \leftarrow \mathcal{F}' \cup \{(a, v + \frac{\alpha}{|A_U|} \cdot \frac{V}{m})\}$
18:                     **else**
19:                         $\mathcal{F}' \leftarrow \mathcal{F}' \cup \{(a, v)\}$
20:             $\mathcal{F} \leftarrow \mathcal{F}'$
21:     **return** $\mathcal{F}$

Algorithm 9 Hypervolume-based Fitness Value Estimation. Requires a population $P \in \psi$, a reference set $R \subseteq Z$, the fitness parameter $k \in \mathbb{N}$, and the number of sampling points $m \in \mathbb{N}$

Table 4.4 Accuracy of the ranking of 10 individuals according to $\hat{I}_h^{10}$ Eq. 4.8 in comparison to I_h^{10} for different sample sizes. The percentages represent the number of pairs of individuals ranked correctly.

nr. of samples m	ranking accuracy	no of samples m	ranking accuracy
10^1	56.0%	10^5	99.2%
10^2	74.1%	10^6	99.8%
10^3	89.9%	10^7	100.0 %
10^4	96.9%		

1: initialize population P by selecting n solutions from X uniformly at random
2: $g \leftarrow 0$
3: **while** $g \leq g_{\max}$ **do**
4:     $P' \leftarrow matingSelection(P, R, n, m)$
5:     $P'' \leftarrow variation(P', n)$
6:     $P \leftarrow environmentalSelection(P \cup P'', R, n, m)$
7:     $g \leftarrow g + 1$

Algorithm 10 HypE Main Loop. Requires a reference set $R \subseteq Z$, a population size $n \in \mathbb{N}$, the number of generations g_{max}, and the number of sampling points $m \in \mathbb{N}$

an adaptive version of the sampling procedure is presented. However, the comparison to the strategy using a fixed number of samples did not reveal any advantages. Therefore, in this thesis only the version with fixed number of samples is shown, to not unnecessarily clutter this chapter by different variants of HypE (see next section).

4.4 · Using the New Fitness Assignment Scheme for Multiobjective Search

In this section, an evolutionary algorithm named HypE is described (Hypervolume Estimation Algorithm for Multiobjective Optimization) which is based on the fitness assignment schemes presented in the previous sections. When the number of objectives is small (≤ 3), the hypervolume values I_h^k are computed exactly using Algorithm 7, otherwise they are estimated based on Algorithm 9.

The main loop of HypE is given by Algorithm 10. It reflects a standard evolutionary algorithm and consists of the successive application of mating selection (Algorithm 11), variation, and environmental selection (Algorithm 12). As to mating selection, binary tournament selection is proposed here, although any other selection scheme could be used as well. The procedure *variation* encapsulates the application of mutation and recombination operators to generate λ offspring. Finally, environmental selection aims at selecting the most promising n solutions from the multiset-union of parent

1: **procedure** *matingSelection*(P,R,n,m)
2:      **if** $d \leq 3$ **then**
3:          $\mathcal{F} \leftarrow computeHypervolume(P, R, n)$
4:      **else**
5:          $\mathcal{F} \leftarrow estimateHypervolume(P, R, n, m)$
6:      $Q \leftarrow \emptyset$
7:      **while** $|Q| < n$ **do**
8:          choose $(a, v_a), (b, v_b) \in \mathcal{F}$ uniformly at random
9:          **if** $v_a > v_b$ **then**
10:              $Q \leftarrow Q \cup \{a\}$
11:          **else**
12:              $Q \leftarrow Q \cup \{b\}$
13:      **return** Q

Algorithm 11 HypE Mating Selection. Requires a population $P \in \psi$, a reference set $R \subseteq Z$, the number of offspring $n \in \mathbb{N}$, and the number of sampling points $m \in \mathbb{N}$

population and offspring; more precisely, it creates a new population by carrying out the following two steps:

1. First, the union of parents and offspring is divided into disjoint partitions using the principle of non-dominated sorting [50, 70], also known as dominance depth, see Section 2.3.3 on page 40. Starting with the lowest dominance depth level, the partitions are moved one by one to the new population as long as the first partition is reached that cannot be transfered completely. This corresponds to the scheme used in most hypervolume-based multiobjective optimizers [30, 59, 82].

2. The partition that only fits partially into the new population is then processed using the method presented in Section 4.2.2. In each step, the fitness values for the partition under consideration are computed and the individual with the worst fitness is removed—if multiple individuals share the same minimal fitness, then one of them is selected uniformly at random. This procedure is repeated until the partition has been reduced to the desired size, i.e., until it fits into the remaining slots left in the new population.

1: **procedure** *environmentalSelection(P,R,n,m)*
2:     $P' \leftarrow P$ *(remaining population members)*
3:     $Q \leftarrow \emptyset$ *(new population)*
4:     $Q' \leftarrow \emptyset$ *(current non-dominated set)*
5:     **repeat**   *(iteratively copy non-dominated sets to Q)*
6:         $Q \leftarrow Q \cup Q'$
7:         $Q', P'' \leftarrow \emptyset$
8:         **for all** $a \in P'$ **do**   *(determine current non-dominated set in P')*
9:             **if** $\forall b \in P' : b \preceq a \Rightarrow a \preceq b$ **then**
10:                 $Q' \leftarrow Q' \cup \{a\}$
11:             **else**
12:                 $P'' \leftarrow P'' \cup \{a\}$
13:         $P' \leftarrow P''$
14:     **until** $|Q| + |Q'| \geq n \vee P' = \emptyset$
15:     $k = |Q| + |Q'| - n$
16:     **while** $k > 0$ **do**   *(truncate last non-fitting non-dominated set Q')*
17:         **if** $d \leq 3$ **then**
18:             $\mathcal{F} \leftarrow computeHypervolume(Q', R, k)$
19:         **else**
20:             $\mathcal{F} \leftarrow estimateHypervolume(Q', R, k, m)$
21:         $Q' \leftarrow \emptyset$
22:         $removed \leftarrow false$
23:         **for all** $(a, v) \in \mathcal{F}$ **do**   *(remove worst solution from Q')*
24:             **if** $removed = true \vee v \neq \min_{(a,v) \in \mathcal{F}}\{v\}$ **then**
25:                 $Q' \leftarrow Q' \cup \{a\}$
26:             **else**
27:                 $removed \leftarrow true$
28:         $k \leftarrow k - 1$
29:     $Q \leftarrow Q \cup Q'$
30:     **return** Q

Algorithm 12 HypE Environmental Selection. Requires a population $P \in \psi$, a reference set $R \subseteq Z$, the number of offspring $\lambda \in \mathbb{N}$, and the number of sampling points $m \in \mathbb{N}$

Concerning the fitness assignment, the number of objectives determines whether the exact or the estimated I_h^k values are considered. If three or less objectives are involved, employing Algorithm 7 is recommended, otherwise to use Algorithm 9. The latter works with a fixed number of sampling points to estimate the hypervolume values I_h^k, regardless of the confidence of the decision to be made; hence, the variance of the estimates does not need to be calculated and it is sufficient to update for each sample drawn an array storing the fitness values of the population members.

4.5 · Experiments

This section serves two goals: (i) to investigate the influence of specific algorithmic concepts (fitness, sample size) on the performance of HypE, and (ii) to study the effectiveness of HypE in comparison to existing MOEAs. A difficulty that arises in this context is how to statistically compare the quality of Pareto-set approximations with respect to the hypervolume indicator when a large number of objectives ($d \geq 5$) is considered. In this case, exact computation of the hypervolume becomes infeasible; to this end, Monte Carlo sampling is proposed using appropriate statistical tools as summarized in the next section, and outlined in more detail in Appendix A on page 225.

4.5.1 · Experimental Setup

HypE is implemented within the PISA framework [19] and tested in two versions: the first (HypE) uses fitness-based mating selection as described in Algorithm 11, while the second (HypE*) employs a uniform mating selection scheme where all individuals have the same probability of being chosen for reproduction. Unless stated otherwise, for sampling the number of sampling points is fixed to $m = 10,000$ kept constant during a run.

HypE and HypE* are compared to three popular MOEAs, namely NSGA-II [50], SPEA2 [139], and IBEA (in combination with the ε-indicator) [135]. Since these algorithms are not designed to optimize the hypervolume, it cannot be expected that they perform particularly well when measuring the quality of the approximation in terms of the hypervolume indicator. Nevertheless, they serve as an important reference as they are considerably faster than hypervolume-based search algorithms and therefore can execute a substantially larger number of generations when keeping the available computation time fixed. On the other hand, dedicated hypervolume-based methods are included in the comparisons. The algorithms proposed in [30, 59, 82] use the same fitness assignment scheme which can be mimicked by RHV, see Section 4.1.1, where mating selection is done as in HypE but using the contributions I_h^1 as fitness value. The acronym RHV* stands for the variant that uses uniform selection for mating. However, no comparisons are provided to the original implementations of Brockhoff and Zitzler [30], Emmerich et al. [59], Igel et al. [82], because the focus is on the fitness assignment principles and not on specific data structures for fast hypervolume calculation as in [59] or specific variation operators as in [82]. Furthermore, SHV proposed in Section 4.1.2 and Appendix D.3 is used. Finally, to study the influence of the non-dominated sorting also a simple HypE variant named RS (random selection) is included where all individuals are assigned the same constant fitness value. Thereby, the selection pressure is only maintained by the non-dominated sorting carried out during the environmental selection phase.

As basis for the comparisons, the DTLZ [54], the WFG [79], and the knapsack [137] test problem suites are considered since they allow the number of objectives to be scaled arbitrarily—here, ranging from 2 to 50 objectives. For the DTLZ problem, the number of decision variables is set to 300, while for the WFG problems individual values are used, see Table 4.5. As to the knapsack problem, 400 items are used which were modified with mutation probability 1 by one-bit mutation and by one-point crossover with probability 0.5. For each benchmark function, 30 runs are carried out per algorithm using a population size of $n = 50$ and a maximum number $g_{\max} = 200$ of generations (unless the computation time is fixed). The individuals are represented by real vectors, where a polynomial distribution is used for mutation and the SBX-20 operator for recombination [44]. The recombination and mutation probabilities are set according to Deb et al. [54].

Table 4.5 Number of decision variables and their decomposition into position and distance variables as used for the WFG test functions depending on the number of objectives.

	Objective Space Dimensions (d)						
	2d	3d	5d	7d	10d	25d	50d
distance parameters	20	20	42	58	50	76	150
position parameters	4	4	8	12	9	24	49
decision variables	24	24	50	70	59	100	199

The quality of the Pareto-set approximations of all algorithms A_i are assessed using the hypervolume indicator, where for less than 6 objectives the indicator values are calculated exactly and otherwise approximated by Monte Carlo sampling. Based on the hypervolume, the performance score $P(A_i)$ is calculated as described in Appendix A on page 225.

4.5.2 · Results

In the following, the experimental results are discussed, grouped according to the foci of the investigations.

Exact Hypervolume Computation Versus Sampling

First off, HypE is compared with RHV—due to the large computation effort caused by the exact hypervolume calculation only on a single test problem, namely DTLZ2 with 2, 3, 4, and 5 objectives. Both HypE and HypE* are run with exact fitness calculation (Algorithm 7) as well as with the estimation procedure (Algorithm 9); the former variants are marked with a trailing '-e', while the latter variants are marked with a trailing '-s'. All algorithms run for 200 generations, per algorithm 30 runs were performed.

Figure 4.8 shows the hypervolume values normalized for each test problem instance separately. As one may expect, HypE beats HypE*. Moreover, fitness-based mating selection is beneficial to both HypE and RHV. The two best variants, HypE-e and RHV, reach about the same hypervolume values, independently of the number of objectives. Although HypE reaches a better hypervolume median for all four number of objectives, the difference

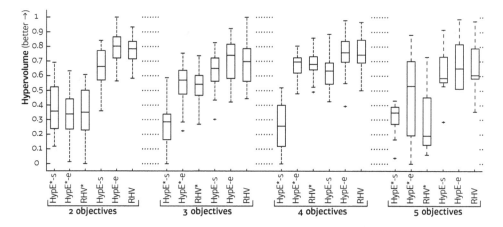

Figure 4.8 Comparison of the hypervolume indicator values for different variants of HypE and the regular hypervolume algorithm (RHV) on DTLZ2 with 2, 3, 4, and 5 objectives. For presentation reasons, the hypervolume values are normalized to the minimal and maximal values observed per problem instance.

is never significant[3]. Hence, HypE can be considered an adequate alternative to the regular hypervolume algorithms; the main advantage though becomes evident when the respective fitness measures need to be estimated, see below.

HypE Versus Other MOEAs

Now HypE and HypE* are compared, both using a constant number of samples, to other multiobjective evolutionary algorithms. Table D.1 on pages 265–268 shows the performance score and mean hypervolume on the 17 testproblems mentioned in Section 6.5.1. Except on few testproblems HypE is better than HypE*. HypE reaches the best performance score overall. Summing up all performance scores, HypE yields the best total (76), followed by HypE* (143), IBEA (171) and the method proposed in [11] (295). SPEA2 and NSGA-II reach almost the same score (413 and 421 respectively), clearly outperforming the random selection (626).

---

[3] According to the Kruskal-Wallis test described in Appendix A on page 225 with confidence level a = 0.01.

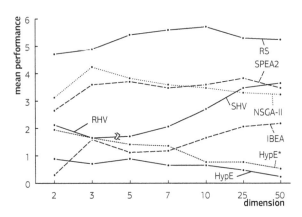

Figure 4.9 Mean performance score over all testproblems for different number of objectives. The smaller the score, the better the Pareto-set approximation in terms of hypervolume. Note, that RHV ($d \leq 3$) and SHV ($d > 3$) are plotted as one line.

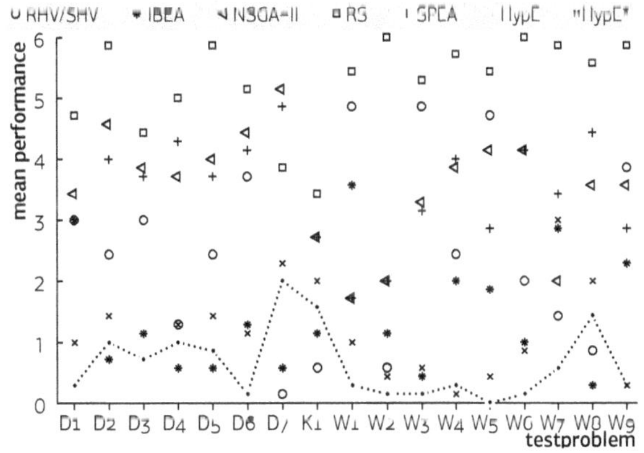

Figure 4.10 Mean performance score over all dimensions for different testproblems, namely DTLZ (Dx), WFG (Wx) and knapsack (K1). The values of HypE+ are connected by a dotted line to easier assess the score.

In order to better visualize the performance index, two figures are shown where the index is summarized for different testproblems and number of objectives. Figure 4.9 shows the average performance over all testproblems for different number of objectives. Except for two objective problems (where IBEA is better), HypE yields the best score, increasing its lead in higher dimensions. The version using uniform mating selection, HypE*, is outperformed by IBEA for two to seven objectives and only thereafter reaches a similar score as HypE. This indicates, that using non-uniform mating selection is particularly advantageous for small number of objectives.

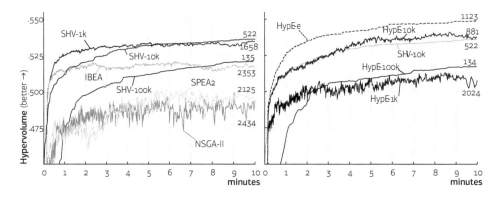

Figure 4.11 Hypervolume process over ten minutes of HypE+ for different samples sizes x in thousands (HypE-xk) as well as using the exact values (HypE-e). The test problem is WFG9 for three objectives. HypE is compared to the algorithms presented in Section 4.5, where the results are split in two figures with identical axis for the sake of clarity. The numbers at the right border of the figures indicate the total number of generations.

Next the performance score is shown for the individual testproblems. Figure 4.10 shows the average index over all number of objectives. For DTLZ2, 4, 5 and 7, knapsack and WFG8, IBEA outperforms HypE, for DTLZ7 and knapsack, SHV as well is better than HypE. On WFG4, HypE* has the lowest hypervolume. On the remaining 10 testproblems, HypE reaches the best mean performance.

Note that the above comparison is carried out for the case all algorithms run for the same number of generations and HypE needs longer execution time, e.g., in comparison to SPEA2 or NSGA-II. Therefore, in the following it is investigated, whether NSGA-II and SPEA2 will not overtake HypE given a constant amount of time. Figure 4.11 shows the hypervolume of the Pareto-set approximations over time for HypE using the exact fitness values as well as the estimated values for different samples sizes m. Although only the results on WFG9 are shown, the same experiments were repeated on DTLZ2, DTLZ7, WFG3 and WFG6 and provided similar outcomes. Even though SPEA2, NSGA-II and even IBEA are able to process twice as many generations as the exact HypE, they do not reach its hypervolume. In the three dimensional example used, HypE can be run sufficiently fast without approximating the fitness values. Nevertheless, the sampled version is used as well to show the dependency of the execution time and quality on the number of samples m. Via m, the execution time of HypE can be traded off against the quality of the Pareto-set approximation. The fewer samples are used, the more the behavior of HypE resembles random selection. On the other hand by increasing m, the quality of exact calculation can be achieved, increasing the execution time, though. For example, with $m = 1\,000$, HypE is able to carry out nearly the same number of generations as SPEA2 or NSGA-II, but the Pareto-set is just as good as when $100\,000$ samples are used, producing only a fifteenth the number of generations. In the example given, $m = 10\,000$ represents the best compromise, but the number of samples should be increased in two cases: (i) the fitness evaluation takes more time. This will affect the faster algorithm much more and increasing the number of samples will influence the execution time much less. Most real world problems, for instance, are considerably more expensive to evaluate than the DTLZ, WFG, and knapsack instances used in this thesis. Therefore, the cost of the hypervolume estimation will matter less in most applications. (ii) More generations are used. In this case, HypE using more samples might overtake the faster versions with fewer samples, since those are more vulnerable to stagnation.

4.6 · Summary

On the basis of the Regular Hypervolume-based Algorithm (RHV), this chapter has shown how the hypervolume indicator is usually employed to perform environmental selection. For this algorithm, the principle of sampling hypervolume-based fitness values has then been introduced, leading to the Sampling-based Hypervolume-oriented Algorithm (SHV) which can be applied to problems with arbitrary numbers of objective functions. Investigating SHV has illustrated different problems one is confronted with when using Monte Carlo sampling in the context of RHV.

In light of these considerations, HypE (Hypervolume Estimation Algorithm for Multiobjective Optimization) has been proposed, a novel hypervolume-based multiobjective evolutionary algorithm improving on SHV. It incorporates a new fitness assignment scheme based on the Lebesgue measure, where this measure can be both exactly calculated and estimated by means of Monte Carlo sampling. The latter allows to trade-off fitness accuracy versus the overall computing time budget which renders hypervolume-based search possible also for many-objective problems, in contrast to [30, 59, 82].

HypE was compared to various state-of-the-art MOEAs with regard to the hypervolume indicator values of the generated Pareto-set approximations—on the DTLZ [54], the WFG [79], and the knapsack [137] test problem suites. The simulations results indicate that HypE is a highly competitive multiobjective search algorithm; in the considered setting the Pareto front approximations obtained by HypE reached the best hypervolume value in 6 out of 7 cases averaged over all testproblems.

In the following Chapters, HypE will be extended in two directions: next in Chapter 5 preference incorporation is tackled, while finally Chapter 6 adds the possibility to consider robustness of solutions.

5

Articulating User Preferences in Multi-Objective Search by Sampling the Weighted Hypervolume

In Chapter 4, the Hypervolume Estimation Algorithm for Multiobjective Optimization (HypE) has been presented, which uses the unweighted hypervolume indicator to obtain Pareto-set approximations. By employing a novel fitness assignement scheme, in combination with a fast sampling method, the procedure thereby is also applicable to problems involving a large number of objectives. Experimental results have substantiated the advantages of the approach in comparison to other Multiobjective Evolutionary Algorithms (MOEAs).

As investigated in Chapter 3 for the biobjective case, the hypervolume indicator introduces a certain bias, that determines the distribution of points in the Pareto-set approximations obtained. One question that is of special interest in practice is whether and how this inherent preference of the hypervolume indicator can be changed to arbitrary user preference, e.g., towards extreme solutions or towards so-called preference points[1].

Several approaches for articulating these user preferences are known from the literature, e.g., by defining preference points [55], specifying preferred search directions [48] or defining linear minimum and maximum tradeoffs [24]. For a general overview of articulating user preferences, see [36, 102, 111]. However, none of these methods leads to a refinement of Pareto dominance.

As has been illustrated in Chapter 2, the weighted hypervolume indicator can be used to obtain such relations, and also allows to incorporate arbitrary user preference as demonstrated in Chapter 3. The weighted hypervolume indicator has been introduced in a study by Zitzler et al. [141], and has shown, theoretically and in experiments, that it is possible to articulate user preference using the hypervolume. Furthermore, the paper has shown for three different weight functions that optimizing the weighted hypervolume indicator indeed results in solutions clustered in regions with higher weight whereas regions with low weight contain only a few solutions.

However, the study inhibits two problems: (i) the proposed weight function for articulating preference points is not easily extendable to more than two objectives and (ii) the exact computation of the hypervolume indicator is expensive if the number of objectives is high, i.e., the $\#\mathcal{P}(X)$-hardness proof in [28] has theoretically shown that the hypervolume computation is exponential in the number of objectives unless $P = NP$. Another algorithm by the author and colleagues shares this two issues [6].

In this chapter, these two drawbacks are tackled by *estimating* the weighted hypervolume with HypE. In particular,

- an extension of HypE to the weighted hypervolume is introduced to avoid the exponential running time of the hypervolume indicator,

---

[1]Instead of the standard term *reference point*, see for example [102], the term *preference point* is used throughout this chapter to reduce the likelihood of confusion with the hypervolume's reference point.

- two weight functions are proposed that allow to articulate preferences towards extremes and towards predefined preference points. The distributions can be arbitrarily combined and applied to problems with any number of objectives, and
- the potential of the new approach is shown experimentally for several test problems with up to 25 objectives by means of both visual inspection and statistical tests.

5.1 · Sampling the Weighted Hypervolume Indicator

As already motivated in Chapter 4, the hypervolume indicator needs to be approximated when facing problems with many objectives, because the computational effort increases heavily. To this end, the Hypervolume Estimation Algorithm for Multiobjective Optimization (HypE) has been proposed, which relies on Monte Carlo sampling. However, only the unweighted hypervolume has been considered, which has a predefined bias—as illustrated in Chapter 3. In order to be able to realize different user preferences, in the following the weighted hypervolume indicator is used. On the one hand, this gives all the desirable properties of the unweighted hypervolume (see Chapter 2); on the other hand, it allows to accurately model user preferences, as the relationship between weight function and density of points shows (see Chapter 3).

In order to be able to use the weighted hypervolume indicator within HypE, its sampling procedure needs to be modified. The main component thereby consists of estimating $\lambda(H_i(a, P, R))$, see Eq. 4.7. By applying a weight function, the partitions $\lambda(H_i(a, P, R))$ change to the weighted Lebesgue measure $\lambda_w(H_i(a, P, R))$ where $w(z)$ denotes the weight function.

5.1.1 · Uniform Sampling

A straightforward way of approximating $\lambda_w(H_i(a, P, R))$ is to sample $s_1, \ldots, s_m$ uniformly at random as in Chapter 4. Again, let $X_j^{(i,a)}$ denote the corresponding random variable that is equal to 1 in case of a hit of s_j regarding

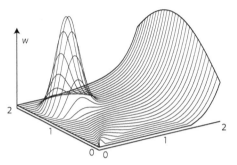
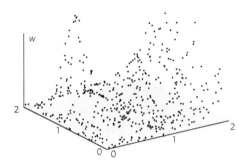

Figure 5.1 Illustrates the two sampling procedures shown in Section 5.1 when applied
to the weight distribution function shown on
the top left. In the upper left plot, 500 samples are drawn uniformly within [0,0]×[2,2]
and are thereafter multiplied by the corresponding weight. In the plot on the left, samples are generated according to the weight
distribution function, such that they do not
need to be multiplied by the weight.

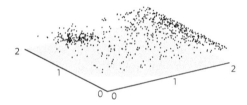

the ith partition of a and 0 otherwise. Then an estimate for $\lambda_w(H_i(a, P, R))$
is obtained by multiplying each hit by the weight at the position of the sample, summing up the results for all hits, dividing the result by the number
of samples m, and multiplying with the volume of the sampling box V:

$$\hat{\lambda}(H_i^w(a, P, R)) = \frac{\sum_{j=1}^{m} X_j^{(i,a)} w(s_j)}{m} \cdot V \tag{5.1}$$

On the top left of Figure 5.1.1, this sampling procedure is illustrated. In
this approach, however, the precision of the estimation heavily depends
on the weight distribution w: if the support of w is small, the number of
samples m needs to be large to have a reliable estimation. Using Hoeffding's
inequality [77], one can show that the length of a confidence interval for a
given confidence level is proportional to the supremum of w. In the extreme
case of a dirac "function" as suggested in [141] this would result in an infinite

length for the confidence interval—in other words, infinitely many samples
are needed to obtain any desired accuracy.

5.1.2 · Sampling According to Weight Function

Therefore, a different approach to sample the weighted hypervolume indicator, more specifically $\lambda_w(H_i(a, P, R))$ is proposed here. In this chapter, it is
thereby assumed the weight function is a distribution, i.e., $\int_{(-\infty,...,-\infty)}^r w(z)dz =$
1 holds. This causes no loss of generality, as for search only the *relative* hypervolume matters, see Line 23 in Algorithm 12, and Line 9 in Algorithm 11.
Since the weight function is also positive, it therefore constitutes a density
function. In principle, any density function can be used as w. For an
efficient way of sampling, however, w is chosen in the following such that
samples can be drawn efficiently distributed according to w. For this reason,
multivariate normal distributions and exponential distributions will be used
for sampling non-uniformly.

To give the explicit expression of the Monte Carlo estimator, let S^w denote
a random variable admitting w as probability density function. For an
extensive overview of how random samples can be generated from those
distributions, see Devroye [56]. Let $s_1^w, \ldots, s_m^w$ be m independent samples
of random variables distributed as S^w. Again, let $X_j^{(i,a)}$ be 1 if sample
s_j^w is a hit and zero otherwise. The weighted hypervolume contribution
$\lambda(H_i^w(a, P, R))$ then can be approximated by

$$\hat{\lambda}(H_i^w(a, P, R)) = \frac{\sum_{j=1}^m X_j^{(i,a)}}{m} \cdot V \ . \tag{5.2}$$

In contrast to Eq. 5.1, the samples are not multiplied by the weight, see
the lower left of Figure 5.1.1, instead, the weight distribution is implied by
the way samples are drawn. This technique of sampling according to the
weight distribution function instead of uniformly has the advantage that
the accuracy of the estimate, i.e., the confidence interval, is independent of
the weight distribution. Hoeffding's inequality implies that with probability
larger than $1 - \alpha$,

$$\lambda(H_i^w(a, P, R)) \in [\hat{\lambda}(H_i^w(a, P, R)) - t_{m,\alpha}, \ \hat{\lambda}(H_i^w(a, P, R)) + t_{m,\alpha}]$$

where $t_{m,\alpha} = \left(\frac{8}{m} \log(2/\alpha)\right)^{1/2}$ which is independent of w and which is the same confidence interval than for the non-weighted case. In other words, it is not more expensive to do a Monte Carlo integration of the weighted hypervolume than for the standard hypervolume indicator.

5.1.3 · Sampling Multiple Weight Functions

In order to sample weight distributions that are defined as a mixture of several independent distributions w_i $(1 \le i \le q)$ as proposed in Section 5.2.3, the number of samples are distributed among the different distributions in the following way: a weight distribution $w(z) = \sum_{i=1}^{q} p_i \cdot w_i(z)$ with $\sum_{1 \le i \le q} p_i = 1$ is estimated by sampling each of the distributions w_i independently with $m \cdot p_i$ samples and summing up the resulting estimates.

5.2 · Integrating User Preferences

This section presents two different weight distribution functions to express user preferences. Both distributions are continuous probability densities that enable to draw samples according to the procedure presented above. The first distribution allows to attribute importance to one objective and the second to emphasize a preference point in the objective space. The section is completed by demonstrating how any number of the two distributions can be combined, e.g., to use more than one preference point.

5.2.1 · Stressing the Extremes

One potential preference a user might have is to optimize preferably one objective, say f_s (note, that throughout the thesis minimization problems are considered). The corresponding weight distribution should therefore increase for decreasing values of f_s. In terms of the rest of the objectives, the weight distribution should stay constant for changing values in order not to introduce an additional bias.

Zitzler et al. [141] proposed to use an exponential function as the weight distribution. Here, the same distribution is represented by the probability

Figure 5.2 Illustrates the exponential distribution that corresponds to stressing the first objective (top) and the Gaussian distribution representing a preference point (buttom).   The left
parts of the two subplots indicate
the notation used along with a
contour plot at intervals of 10%
of the maximum value observed
(which occurs on the second axis
and at $\vec{\mu}$ respectively).   The right
parts of the subplots show the actual value of the distribution as a
third component.

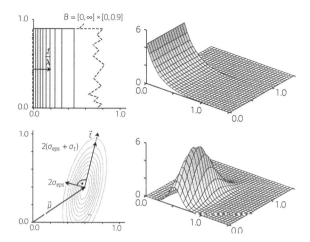

density function whose marginal distribution for objective f_s is an exponential distribution with rate parameter λ and whose marginal distributions of
the remaining objectives is a uniform distribution:

$$
w(z_1,\cdots,z_d) = \begin{cases} \left(\Pi_{i \neq s}(b_i^u - b_i^l)\right)^{-1} \lambda e^{-\lambda(z_s - b_s^l)} & z \in B \\ 0 & z \notin B \end{cases}
$$

where $B = [b_1^l, b_1^u] \times \ldots \times [b_d^l, b_d^u]$ denotes the space with non-zero probability
density.

Figure 5.2 shows the weight distribution for a biobjective problem when
stressing f_1 with an exponential distribution in f_1 ($\lambda = 5$) together with a
uniform distribution in the interval $[0, 0.95]$ in the second objective ($B = [b_s^l, b_s^u] \times [b_2^l, b_2^u] = [0, \infty] \times [0, 0.95]$).

The spread of the distribution is inversely proportional to the parameter
λ. Hence, the smaller λ the steeper the weight distribution increases at
the border of the objective space and the smaller the weight farther away
(see Figure 5.3(a) on page 161 for contour plots of the exponential weight
distribution for distinct values of λ).

5.2.2 · Preference Points

Another user preference is the *preference point* [102]. This point, as well as to a lesser extent the adjacent region, represents the most important part of the objective space for the user. Together with the location of the preference point, denoted by $\vec{\mu} = (\mu_1, \cdots, \mu_d)^T \in \mathbb{R}^d$, the user has to define a direction $\vec{t} = (t_1, \cdots, t_d)^T \in \mathbb{R}^d$. The solutions should preferably lie along this direction if the preference point cannot be reached or, on the contrary, even better solutions are found. The corresponding weight distribution function reflects this preference by having the largest values at the preference point and along $\vec{t}$ while decreasing fast perpendicular to $\vec{t}$. To this end, [141] proposes a bivariate ridge-like function that cannot be easily extended to an arbitrary number of objectives. Therefore, using the following multivariate Gaussian distribution is proposed here, which allows an efficient sampling according to Eq. 5.2 and which can be used for any number of objectives. Besides $\vec{\mu}$ and $\vec{t}$, let $\sigma_\varepsilon, \sigma_t \in \mathbb{R}$ denote standard deviations of the distribution. Then the following probability density function describes a multivariate normal distribution centered at $\vec{\mu}$

$$w(z) = \frac{1}{(2\pi)^{d/2}|C|^{1/2}} e^{-\frac{1}{2}(z-\vec{\mu})^T C^{-1}(z-\vec{\mu})}$$

where the covariance matrix $C := \sigma_\varepsilon^2 \mathbf{I} + \sigma_t^2 \vec{t}\vec{t}^T / \|\vec{t}\|^2$ is non-singular with orthogonal eigenvectors $\vec{t}, t_2, \cdots, t_d$ where the vectors $t_2, \ldots, t_d$ can be taken from an arbitrary orthogonal basis of the hyperplane orthogonal to $\vec{t}$. The eigenvalues associated to $\vec{t}, t_2, \cdots, t_d$ are $\sigma_\varepsilon^2 + \sigma_t^2, \sigma_\varepsilon^2, \cdots, \sigma_\varepsilon^2$; $|C|$ denotes the determinant of C.

The equidensity contours of the distributions are ellipsoids whose principal axis are $\vec{t}, t_2, \cdots, t_d$, see Figure 5.2. The lengths of the axes are given by the two standard deviations (i) σ_t for the axis spanned by $\vec{t}$ and (ii) σ_ε for the remaining $d - 1$ axes perpendicular to $\vec{t}$. The larger σ_t is chosen the farther the objective vectors can lie from the preference point in direction of $\pm\vec{t}$ while they are still affected by the weight distribution. At the same time, however, the number of samples near the Pareto front approximation decreases which reduces the accuracy of sampling.

The second variance, σ_ε, influences the extension of points close to the preference point. The smaller σ_ε, the less widespread the solutions are (see Figures 5.3(b) for contour plots of three different choices of σ_ε).

5.2.3 · Combinations

A mixture of q weight distributions admitting the probability density functions $w_1(z), \ldots, w_q(z)$ yields the distribution with density

$$w(z) - p_1 w_1(z) + \ldots + p_q w_q(z)$$

where the p_i are positive real numbers with $p_1 + \ldots + p_q = 1$. Though it is not possible to translate any user preference directly to a weight distribution function as in another work by the author and colleagues [6], a wide range of different user preferences can be represented by combining weight distributions. These are—in contrast to the weight distributions in [6]—also applicable to problems with more than two objectives. In the next section mixtures of the two distributions presented above will be examined.

5.3 · Experimental Validation

In order to test the approach of articulating user preferences presented in Section 5.2, the Hypervolume Estimation Algorithm for Multiobjective Optimization (HypE) as proposed in Chapter 4 using the novel sampling strategy as presented in Section 5.1.2 is evaluated. The application to different multiobjective test problems investigates three important aspects of the approach.

First, the influence of the different parameters on the distribution of the resulting Pareto front approximations are investigated visually for both approaches preferring preference points and extremes. In particular, the following is examined for a preference point: its location $\vec{\mu}$, the direction

$\vec{t}$ and the influence of the standard deviations σ_ε and σ_t; when stressing extremes, the effects of changing the parameter λ is shown.

Secondly, the weighted hypervolume approach is visually compared to existing reference algorithms that do not optimize any user preference explicitly for problems with more than two objectives. This demonstrates that the new approach is—in contrast to [141]—also applicable to problems involving more than two objectives.

Finally, a short statistical comparison on problems with up to 25 objectives is carried out to investigate whether the generated Pareto front approximations obtained by HypE, as a matter of fact, better fulfill the underlying user preference than non-dominated fronts resulting from reference algorithms.

5.3.1 · Experimental Setup

For HypE, 10 000 samples are generated according to the probability density functions presented in Section 5.2 using the corresponding built-in functions of MATLAB® version 2008a. These samples are then used to calculate a fitness value for each individual, see Chapter 4 for a detailed description of the fitness calculation of HypE.

The evolutionary multiobjective algorithms NSGA-II [50] and IBEA [135] serve as reference algorithms. For the latter, the ε-indicator has been used since preliminary experiments showed this variant to be superior to the one using the hypervolume indicator. The parameters of IBEA are set as $\kappa = 0.05$ and $\rho = 1.1$. All algorithms are run for 100 generations. New individuals are generated by the SBX crossover operator with $\eta_c = 15$ and the variable-wise polynomial mutation operator with $\eta_m = 20$ [44]. The crossover and mutation probabilities are set to 1 and $1/20$ respectively.

For the biobjective test problems both the population size and the number of offspring are set to 25 while for more objectives these numbers are doubled. For the biobjective investigations, the test problems ZDT1 (convex Pareto front), ZDT3 (discontinuous Pareto front) [138] and DTLZ2 [54] (concave Pareto front) are utilized with 20 decision variables. For higher dimensions only DTLZ2 is employed.

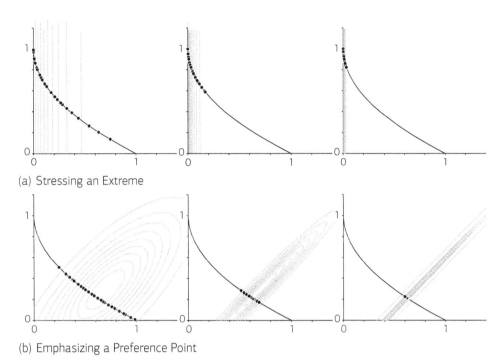

(a) Stressing an Extreme

(b) Emphasizing a Preference Point

Figure 5.3 Shows the Pareto front approximations (dots) found by HypE using different weight distribution functions, shown as contour lines at intervals of 10% of the maximum weight value. For both rows one parameter of the sampled distribution was modified, i.e., on top the rate parameter of the exponential distribution λ, on the bottom the spread σ_ε. The test problem is ZDT1 where the Pareto front is shown as a solid line.

5.3.2 · Visual Inspection of Parameter Choices

In this section, the influence of different parameters on the weight distribution functions and the resulting Pareto front approximations are investigated. Unless noted otherwise, $\sigma_t = 0.5$, $\sigma_\varepsilon = 0.05$ and $\vec{t} = (1,1)$ are used when stressing a preference point and $B = [0, \infty] \times [0, 3]$ when stressing the first objective ($f_s = f_1$). The weight distributions are indicated by contour lines at the intervals of 10% of the maximum value that arises. Hence, the contour lines do not reflect the actual weight but only the relative distribution thereof. As an example, the innermost contour line in Figure 5.3(b) corresponds to a weight that is 90% of the maximal value in

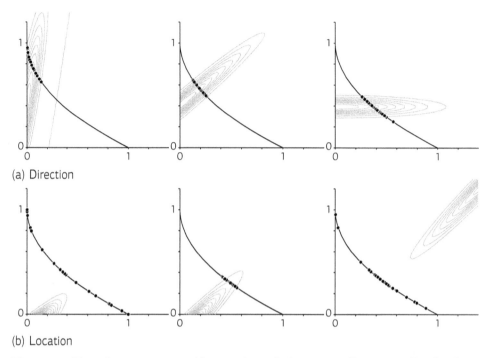

(a) Direction

(b) Location

Figure 5.4 Uses the same test problem, and visual elements as Figure 5.3. For the three figures on top the direction $\vec{t}$ is modified, and for figure on the bottom the location $\vec{\mu}$ of the preference point is changed (see text for details and the values used).

all plots. The corresponding absolute weight, however, changes from figure to figure because the maximum weight value changes due to the property $\int_{(-\infty,\ldots,-\infty)}^{r} w(z)dz = 1$. Multiple runs for each testcase were tested that led to similar results such that mostly only one run is displayed to illustrate the influence of the weight on the distribution of points.

Spread of the Distributions
Both proposed weight distribution functions have parameters that cause the weight to be more or less spread. Figure 5.3(a) shows the weight distribution and the resulting Pareto front approximation using the exponential distribution proposed in Section 5.2.1 for $\lambda = 100$ (top), $\lambda = 20$ (center) and $\lambda = 5$ (bottom). Figure 5.3(b) shows the distribution of points for a

preference point located at $\vec{\mu} = (0.7, 0.3)$ where σ_ε is set to 0.2 (top), 0.05 (middle) and 0.01 (bottom).

Direction of the Preference Point Distribution

By $\vec{t}$, the user can define the desired trade-off between the objectives for the case that either the preference point cannot be reached or that solutions dominating the preference point are obtained. In Figure 5.4(a) the preference point is positioned at $\vec{\mu} = (0, 0.4)$ which lies below the Pareto front and can therefore not be reached. In this case, the direction $\vec{t}$ predetermines where the resulting points lie. In the topmost example, a choice of $\vec{t} = (\cos(80°), \sin(80°))$ reflects a higher preference of the first objective at the expense of the second. On the other hand, the bottom figure is obtained for $\vec{t} = (1, 0)$, i.e., values of 0.4 are preferred for the second objective and only increases of the first objective are allowed. The figure in the middle presents a compromise where the focus lies close to the diagonal, $\vec{t} = (\cos(40°), \sin(40°))$.

Location of the Preference Point

Since the preference point can be placed both too optimistically (as in the previous section) or too pessimistically, the parameter σ_t allows to tune how far away the individuals can be from the preference point and still be influenced by it. For a fixed σ_t however, the location of the preference point has a high impact on the resulting distribution of solutions, see Figure 5.4(b). If none to only a few samples are dominated by the individuals (top, $\vec{\mu} = (-1.2, -1.4)$), no pressure towards the preference point is active—in fact only non-dominated sorting operates. In this case, the preference point should be combined with a uniform distribution, e.g., as in the left of Figure 5.5(a) 90% of the samples are used for the preference point and 10% to sample uniformly in the objective space within $[0, 3] \times [0, 3]$. This causes the solutions to be distributed according to the unweighted hypervolume indicator as long as the preference point has no influence.

As soon as a couple of samples are dominated, the corresponding individuals are promoted which leads to an accumulation in that area (middle, $\vec{\mu} = (-0.3, -0.5)$). If the preference point is chosen very pessimistically (bottom,

$\vec{\mu} = (1.5, 1.3))$ individuals are able to dominate all or most of the samples even if they are not located where the direction $\vec{t}$ dictates. This leads to a much ampler arrangement of solutions than expected considering the chosen σ_ε.

Combinations of Distributions

As demonstrated in Section 5.2, any number of weight distribution functions can be combined as a weighted sum, even assigning them different weights or focus. For example, the user might define different preference points he or she is interested in as depicted in the middle of Figure 5.5(a): three preference points are positioned at $\vec{\mu} = (0.2, 0.8)$, at $\vec{\mu} = (0.5, 0.5)$ and at $\vec{\mu} = (0.8, 0.2)$. The one in the middle is declared to be the most important one by assigning the largest weight $p_2 = 0.5$, the preference points to the left and right use $p_1 = 0.2$ and $p_3 = 0.3$ respectively. As expected, in this case the points are partitioned into disjoint regions around the three preference points. 10 individuals cluster around the center where the most samples emerge, 7 are associated with the preference point on the left and 8 with the one on the right.

To promote individuals at the border of the objective space, two exponential weight distributions can be added up as on the right of Figure 5.5(a) where $\lambda = 10$ with $p_1 = 0.3$ for the first objective and $p_2 = 0.7$ for the second.

Comparison Between Different Problems

In addition to ZDT1, the tests of the previous sections were also carried out for other test problems, namely ZDT3 which has a discontinuous Pareto front shape, DTLZ2 and ZDT6 (both non-convex). These three test problems are much harder to optimize and neither HypE nor the reference algorithms used were able to find Pareto optimal solutions. The points are nevertheless clustered at regions with the largest weight, see Figure 5.5(b), where one preference point with $\vec{\mu} = (0.7, 0.3)$ and $\sigma_\varepsilon = 0.1$ is used.

5.3.3 · High-Dimensional Spaces

For illustrative reasons in the previous section the sampling procedure was applied to biobjective problems. The advantage of the method, however, is

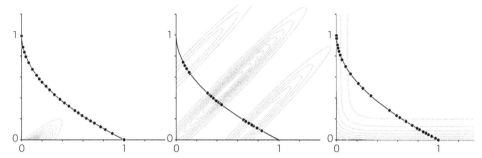

(a) On the left the same preference point is used as in the upper plot of Figure 5.4(b) but spending 10% of the samples on a uniform distribution. The Figure in the middle shows the combination of three preference points, and the Figure on the right illustrates stressing both the first and second objective.

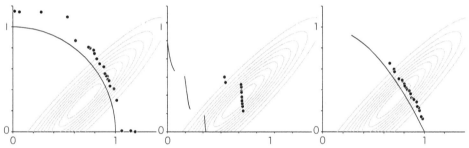

(b) Distribution of the objective vectors when applying the same preference point to different test problems, i.e., ZDT3 (only the positive part shown) (left), DTLZ2 (middle) and ZDT6 (right)

Figure 5.5 These figures use the same visual elements as Figure 5.3 which explains them in its caption.

that an arbitrary number of objectives can be tackled. Figure 5.6 shows the Pareto front and the solutions found by different algorithms on the DTLZ2 problem with 3 objectives. While NSGA-II and IBEA do not optimize any user defined preference, HypE uses two preference points at $\vec{\mu}_1 = (0.8, 0.2, 0.6)$ $(p_1 = 0.2)$ and $\vec{\mu}_2 = (0.2, 0.9, 0.5)$ $(p_2 = 0.8)$ with $\sigma_\varepsilon = 0.1$ (shown as ellipsoids). This leads to a cluster of points at each preference point.

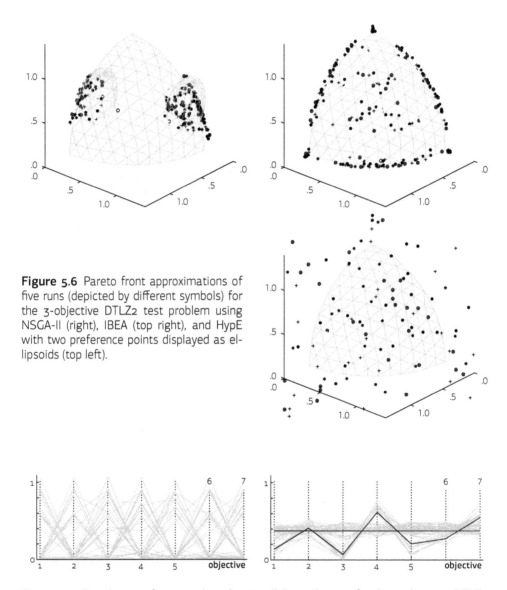

Figure 5.6 Pareto front approximations of five runs (depicted by different symbols) for the 3-objective DTLZ2 test problem using NSGA-II (right), IBEA (top right), and HypE with two preference points displayed as ellipsoids (top left).

Figure 5.7 Distribution of points, plotted in parallel coordinates, for the 7-objective DTLZ2 test problem for IBEA (a), and HypE with two preference points (solid black lines) and $\sigma_\varepsilon = 0.05$ (b).

The Pareto front approximation on DTLZ2 with 7 objectives is depicted in Figure 5.7 by means of parallel coordinates plots for IBEA and HypE with $\sigma_\varepsilon = 0.05$. The plot for NSGA-II is omitted due to space limitations; it can be noted that it looks similar to the one of IBEA except that NSGA-II does not come as close to the Pareto front as IBEA, i.e., the objective values are spread between 0 and 4.5. Both IBEA and NSGA-II generate solutions at the boundary of the objective space while only the former finds solutions near the Pareto front. To get solutions near the center of the Pareto front, HypE is applied with a preference point at $0.3780 \cdot (1, \ldots, 1)$. A second preference point is set at a random location near the Pareto front[2]. The spread σ_ε is set for both preference points to 0.05 and the probabilities of the mixture are set as 0.8 and 0.2 respectively leading to a population of solutions grouped around the two preference points (Figure 5.7).

To investigate further whether HypE actually optimizes the weight distribution used during search, five versions of HypE are run in another experiment. All versions use a different weight distribution w_{pi} with reference point p_i listed in Table 5.1. For all five versions, the spread is set to $\sigma_\varepsilon = 0.05$ and the direction to $(1, \ldots, 1)$. All versions of HypE together with IBEA and NSGA-II then optimized the DTLZ2 test problem with 10 objectives.

The Pareto front approximations for 10 independent runs of all five versions of HypE as well as of NSGA-II and IBEA are then compared in terms of the weighted hypervolume indicator with the weight distribution functions w_{p1} to w_{p5}, see Table 5.1 where larger numbers represent better hypervolume approximations. In each case, HypE with preference point p_i outperforms statistically significant the other algorithms in terms of the hypervolume indicator with w_{pi}—assessed by Kruskal–Wallis and the Conover–Inman post hoc tests with a significance level of 5% according to Appendix A on page 225. This indicates that applying the weighted integration technique during search will generate Pareto front approximations that score better on the corresponding hypervolume indicator than using general purpose algorithms with no user defined search direction.

---

[2] $\vec{\mu}$ = (0.1377, 0.4131, 0.0688, 0.6196, 0.2065, 0.2754, 0.5507)

Table 5.1 Mean hypervolume values for five different weight distribution functions that correspond to preference points at p_1 to p_5 respectively. As optimization algorithms, HypE using the aforementioned weight distribution functions, as well as IBEA and NSGA-II are used. As the bold numbers indicate, the significantly largest hypervolume for preference p_i is obtained by HypE optimizing preference p_i.

	IBEA	NSGA-II	HypE with				
			p_1	p_2	p_3	p_4	p_5
p_1	1.51	0.05	**9.64**	0.08	0.87	2.66	0.04
p_2	2.00	0.00	0.18	**9.51**	0.19	0.21	0.31
p_3	0.65	0.13	1.13	0.19	**9.09**	0.40	0.82
p_4	1.57	0.01	0.23	1.12	0.18	**6.17**	0.09
p_5	3.35	0.03	0.12	0.40	1.31	0.08	**9.64**

(Indicator — row label for the vertical axis)

p_1: $\vec{\mu} = (m_1, m_2, m_3, m_4, m_5, m_6, m_7, m_1, m_2, m_3)$; p_2: $\vec{\mu} = (m_2, m_3, m_4, m_5, m_6, m_7, m_1, m_2, m_3, m_1)$; p_3: $\vec{\mu} = (m_3, m_4, m_5, m_6, m_7, m_1, m_2, m_3, m_1, m_2)$; p_4: $\vec{\mu} = (m_4, m_5, m_6, m_7, m_1, m_2, m_3, m_1, m_2, m_3)$; p_5: $\vec{\mu} = (m_5, m_6, m_7, m_1, m_2, m_3, m_1, m_2, m_3, m_4)$ with $m_1 = 0.1377$, $m_2 = 0.4131$, $m_3 = 0.0688$, $m_4 = 0.6196$, $m_5 = 0.2065$, $m_6 = 0.2754$, $m_7 = 0.5507$

5.4 · Summary

This chapter has described two procedures to approximate the weighted hypervolume integration developed in [141] in the context of HypE. Two types of user preferences have been expressed by probability density functions that ease the fast generation of samples—one stressing certain objectives and the second emphasizing a preference point. Additionally, any combination of the two is possible. The suggested drawing of samples offers the possibility to incorporate user preferences, such that the induced preference relation is transitive and a refinement of Pareto dominance, see Section 2.2.4. Thus, cyclic behavior can be avoided, and convergence to Pareto-optimal solutions can be shown. In contrast to previous approaches based on the weighted hypervolume [6, 141] the algorithm remains applicable when increasing the number of objectives.

The new suggested drawing of samples within HypE has been applied to various test problems. It has turned out by both visual inspection and statistical tests that the generated Pareto front approximations reflect the underlying weight distribution better than methods with no user defined preference. Given the comprehensive theoretical understanding of the hypervolume indicator, derived in Chapter 3, the proposed method thereby allows to realize user preference in a very concise way, and to predict the resulting distribution of solutions in the Pareto-front approximation.

However, the proposed method first needs to prove itself in practice. In particular, it has to be investigated whether defining preference points or objectives to be stressed is (a) feasible for decision makers, and (b) offers them sufficient possibilities. The presented sampling strategy thereby only provides an initial framework, which can be easily extended to other weight distribution functions, if so desired.

6

Robustness in Hypervolume-Based Search

In the previous chapters, the main task was to approximate the set of Pareto-optimal solutions. When those are implemented in practice, however, unavoidable inaccuracies often prevent that the solutions are realized with perfect precision, which more or less degrades their objective values. Examples include the field of chemical engineering, mechanical manufacturing processes, machine constructions and others. But even for an actual realization, noise caused, for example by natural fluctuations in the environment, might lead to differing observed objective values over time.

In other words, the modeling assumption made in the previous chapters of *deterministic* decision variables being evaluated by *deterministic* objective functions no longer holds. In such cases, the decision makers are most likely interested in finding robust solutions that are less sensitive to perturbations, i.e., the optimization model in one way or another needs to consider the stochastic behavior of solutions when looked at in practice.

In this chapter, the question of incorporating robustness into hypervolume-based search is addressed. First, three common existing concepts to consider robustness are translated to hypervolume-based search. Secondly, an extension of the hypervolume indicator is proposed that not only unifies those three concepts, but also enables to realize much more general trade-offs between objective values and robustness of a solution. Finally, the approaches are compared on two test problem suites, as well as on a newly proposed real world bridge problem.

6.1 · Motivation

The vast majority of studies in the area of multiobjective optimization tackles the task of finding Pareto-optimal solutions [37, 44]. These solutions are of great theoretical interest as they achieve the best possible performance. In practice, however, for the most part their implementations suffer from inevitable, and often uncontrollable, perturbations. Solutions to engineering problems for instance can usually not be manufactured arbitrarily accurate such that the implemented solution and its objective values differ from the original specification, up to the point where they become infeasible. Designs which are seriously affected by perturbations of any kind might no longer be acceptable to a decision maker from a practical point of view—despite the promising theoretical result.

According to Beyer and Sendhoff [18] there are four different types of uncertainty affecting the objective values of a solution: (i) the environment or operating conditions change. For example, the unsteady atmospheric pressure, relative humidity, temperature, wind direction and speed influence the performance of airfoil designs; (ii) the production is only accurate up to a certain tolerance. This type of controllable perturbation directly affects the decision variables; (iii) determining the objective function is afflicted with uncertainty. For a real system, this can be due to measuring errors while for simulations this usually includes modeling errors; (iv) the underlying constraints on the decision variables might be uncertain such that the decision space changes.

This chapter focuses on the second type of uncertainty, but for the most part the derived concepts also apply to other types of uncertainty or combinations thereof. The uncertainty due to production variations needs to be taken into account within both optimization model and algorithm in order to find robust solutions that are relatively insensitive to perturbations. Ideally, there exist Pareto-optimal designs whose characteristics fluctuate within an acceptable range. Yet, for the most part robustness and quality (objective values) are irreconcilable goals, and one has to make concessions to quality in order to achieve an acceptable robustness level.

Many studies have been devoted to robustness in the context of single-objective optimization, e.g., [18, 84, 119]. Most of these approaches, however, are not applicable to multiobjective optimization. The first approaches by Kunjur and Krishnamurty [94] and Tsui [122] to consider multiple objectives in combination with robustness are based on the design of experiment approach (DOE) by Taguchi [119]; however, they aggregate the individual objective functions such that the optimization itself is no longer of multiobjective nature. Only few studies genuinely tackle robustness in multiobjective optimization: one approach by Teich [121] is to define a probabilistic dominance relation that reflects the underlying noise. A similar concept by Hughes [80] ranks individuals based on the objective values and the associated uncertainty. Deb and Gupta [46, 47] considered robustness by either adding an additional constraint or by optimizing according to a fitness averaged over perturbations. Most multiobjective optimization methods considering robustness, as well as many single-objective methods that can be extended to multiple objectives, fall into one of the following three categories:

A: **Replacing the objective values.** Among the widest-spread approaches to account for noise is to replace the objective values by a measure or statistical value reflecting the uncertainty. Parkinson et al. [107] for instance optimize the worst case. The same approach, referred to as "min max", is also employed in other studies, e.g., in [93, 115, 116]. Different studies apply an averaging approach where the mean of the objective function is used as the optimization criterion [21, 23, 123]. In Mulvey et al. [104] the objective values and a robustness measure are aggregated into a single value that serves as the optimization criterion.

B: Using one or more additional objectives. Many studies try to assess the robustness of solutions x by a measure $r(x)$, e.g., by taking the norm of the variance of the objective values $f(x)$ [85] or the maximum deviation from $f(x)$ [47]. This robustness measure is then treated as an additional objective [57, 85, 98]. A study by Burke et al. [32] fixes a particular solution (a fleet assignment of an airline scheduling problem), and only optimizes the robustness of solutions (the schedule reliability and feasibility).

C: Using at least one additional constraint. A third possibility is to restrict the search to solutions fulfilling a predefined robustness constraint, again with respect to a robustness measures $r(x)$ [46, 47, 72, 73].

Combinations of A and B are also used; Das [43] for example considers the expected fitness along with the objective values $f(x)$, while Chen et al. [35] optimize the mean and variance of $f(x)$.

In the light of the various advantages of the hypervolume indicator outlined in the previous chapters, the question arises whether the above concepts can be translated to a concept for the hypervolume indicator. On account of the only recent emergence of the hypervolume, to the author's knowledge no study has considered robustness issues in this context yet. A few studies have used the hypervolume as a measure of robustness though: Ge et al. [68] have used the indicator to assess the sensitivity of design regions according to the robust design of Taguchi [119]. A similar approach by Beer and Liebscher [12] uses the hypervolume to measure the range of possible decision variables that lead to the desired range of objective values. A study by Hamann et al. [74] applied the hypervolume in the context of sensitivity analysis.

In this chapter the following open questions concerning robustness and hypervolume are tackled: (i) how can the three existing approaches A, B, and C mentioned above be translated to hypervolume-based search; (ii) the three approaches can be seen as special ways of how to consider robustness along with objective values. The question therefore arises, as how to also consider other trade-offs between robustness and objective values; (iii) how to adjust the Hypervolume Estimation Algorithm for Multiobjective Optimization (HypE) to this generalized hypervolume indicator in order to make the new indicator applicable to problems with a large number of objectives.

The remainder of this chapter is organized as follow: in the next section, concepts to translate the three approaches (A-C) to hypervolume-based search are presented. Then, a generalization of the hypervolume indicator is proposed (Section 6.4) that unifies the three approaches but also enables to consider other trade-offs that transform the three existing approaches into one another. Then, algorithms based on these concepts are presented, and finally, in Section 6.5 an empirical comparison on different test problems and a real-world problem provides valuable insights regarding advantages and disadvantages of the presented approaches.

6.2 · Background

This section shows one possibility to extend the optimization model proposed in Chapter 2 by the consideration of robustness; robustness of a solution informally means, that the objective values scatter only slightly under real conditions. These deviations, referred to as *uncertainty*, are often not considered in multiobjective optimization. This section shows one possibility to extend the optimization model proposed in Chapter 2 by the consideration of uncertainty. As source of uncertainty, noise directly affecting the decision variable x is considered. This results in a random decision variable X^p, which is evaluated by the objective function instead of x. As distribution of X^p, this chapter considers a uniform distribution:

$$B_\delta(x) := [x_1 - \delta, x_1 + \delta] \times \ldots \times [x_n - \delta, x_n + \delta] \ . \tag{6.1}$$

The distribution according to Eq. 6.1 stems from the common specification of fabrication tolerances. Of course, other probability distributions for X^p are conceivable as well; of particular importance is the Gaussian normal distribution, as it can be used to describe many distributions observed in nature. Although not shown in this chapter, the proposed algorithms work with other uncertainties just as well.

Given the uncertainty X^p, the following definition of Deb and Gupta [46] can be used to measure the robustness of x:

$$r(x) = \frac{\|f^w(X^p) - f(x)\|}{f(x)} \tag{6.2}$$

where $f(x)$ denotes the objective values of the unperturbed solution, and $f^w(X^p)$ denotes the objective-wise worst case of all objective values of the perturbed decision variables X^p:

$$f^w(X^p) = \left(\max_{X^p} f_1(X^p), \dots, \max_{X^p} f_d(X^p) \right) \tag{6.3}$$

From the multi-dimensional interval B_δ the robustness measure $r(x)$ may be determined analytically (see Gunawan and Azarm [73]), or the interval can be used to perform interval analysis [83] as in Soares et al. [116]. If both methods are not possible, for instance because knowledge of the objective function is unavailable, random samples are generated within $B_\delta(x)$ and evaluated to obtain an estimate of the robustness measure $r(x)$.

6.3 · Concepts for Robustness Integration

As already mentioned in Section 6.1 on page 172, existing robustness integrating approaches can roughly be classified into three basic categories: (i) modifying the objective functions, (ii) using an additional objective, and (iii) using an additional constraint. In this section, these approaches are first translated to hypervolume-based search. Then, in Section 6.3.4, the three concepts are unified into a novel generalized hypervolume indicator that also enables to realize other trade-offs between robustness and quality of solutions.

To translate these approaches to hypervolume-based search, one or multiple of the three main components of hypervolume-based set preference need to be changed:

1. the preference relation is modified to consider robustness—this influences the non-dominated sorting shown in Eq. 2.2 on page 41.
2. The objective values are modified before the hypervolume is calculated.
3. The definition of the hypervolume indicator itself is changed.

Depending on how the decision maker accounts for robustness, the preference relation changes to $\preceq_{\text{rob}}$. Many different choices of $\preceq_{\text{rob}}$ are possible, however, it is assumed that the relation is consistent with both $r(x)$ and $\preceq$ according to the following definition:

Definition 6.1 (weak refinement of robustness and preference relation): *Let* r *denote a robustness measure, and let* $\preceq$ *denote the preference relation on solutions based on objective values only, e.g., weak Pareto dominance* $\preceq_{\text{par}}$. *Additionally, let* $x \preceq_{\text{ao}} y := r(x) \leq r(y) \wedge x \preceq y$ *denote the intersection of the relation induced by* $r(x)$ *and the Pareto dominance relation, see Section 6.3.2. Then a robustness integrating preference relation* $\preceq_{\text{rob}}$ *is a weak refinement of* $\preceq_{\text{ao}}$ *as stated in Section 2.13 on page 32, if for two solutions* $x, y \in X$ *the following holds:*

$$
\begin{aligned}
(r(x) \leq r(y) \wedge x \preceq y) \\
\wedge \neg(r(y) \leq r(x) \wedge y \preceq x)
\end{aligned} \Rightarrow x \preceq_{\text{rob}} y
$$

In other words, if a solution x *is preferred over* y *according to* $\preceq$, *and in addition is at least as robust as* y *(*$r(x) \leq r(y)$*) but not vice versa, then* $x \preceq_{\text{rob}} y$ *must hold.*

However, note that the relation $\preceq_{\text{rob}}$ does not need to be a subset of $\preceq$; in fact, the relation can even get reversed. For example, provided solution x is preferred over y given only the objectives $x \preceq y$, but considering robustness $y \preceq_{\text{rob}} x$ holds, for instance because y has a sufficient robustness level but x does not.

The most simple choice of dominance relation compliant with Definition 6.1 is $\preceq_{\text{rob}} \equiv \preceq_{\text{par}}$, that is to not consider robustness. This concept is used as reference in the experimental comparison in Section 6.5. Depending on the robustness of the Pareto set, optimal solutions according to $\preceq_{\text{par}}$ may or may not coincide with optimal solutions according to relations $\preceq_{\text{rob}}$ that consider robustness in some way.

In the following, other preference relations, corresponding to the approaches A,B, and C on page 173, are shown. All resulting relations $\preceq_{\text{rob}}$ thereby are not total. Therefore, to refine the relation, is is proposed to apply the general hypervolume-based procedure: first, solutions are ranked into fronts by non-dominated sorting according to Section 2.3.3 on page 40; after having partitioned the solutions, the normal hypervolume is applied on the objective values alone or in conjunction with the robustness measure (which case applies is mentioned when explaining the respective algorithm) to obtain a preference on the solutions.

First, in Sections 6.3.1, 6.3.2, and 6.3.3, it is investigated how the existing concepts can be transformed to and used in hypervolume-based search. Then, in Section 6.3.4, these three concepts are unified into a novel generalized hypervolume indicator that also enables to realize other trade-offs between robustness and quality of solutions.

6.3.1 · Modifying the Objective Functions

The first concept to incorporate robustness replaces the objective values $f(x) = (f_1(x), \ldots, f_d(x))$ by an evaluated version over all perturbations $f^p(X^p) = (f_1^p(X^p), \ldots, f_d^p(X^p))$, see Figure 6.1(a). For example, the studies by Branke [21], Branke and Schmidt [23], Tsutsui and Ghosh [123] all employ the mean over the perturbations, i.e.,

$$f_i^p(X^p) = \int_{X^p} f_i(x^p) p_{X^p}(x^p) dx^p$$

where $p_{X^p}(x^p)$ denotes the probability density function of the perturbed decision variable X^p given x. Taking the mean will smoothen the objective space, such that f^p is worse in regions where the objective values are heavily affected by perturbations; while, contrariwise, in regions where the objective values stay almost the same within the considered neighborhood, the value

(a) modifying the objectives   (b) additional objective   (c) additional constraint

Figure 6.1 Partitioning into fronts of ten solutions: a (robustness $r(a)$ = 2), b (2), c (1.4), d (1.1), e (2), f (1.2), g (1.9), h (.5), i (.9), and j (.1) for the three approaches presented in Section 6.3. The solid dots represents robust solutions at the considered level of η = 1 while the unfilled dots represent non-robust solutions.

f^p differs only slightly. Aside from the altered objective value, the search problem stays the same. The regular hypervolume indicator in particular can be applied to optimize the problem. The dominance relation implicitly changes to $\preceq_{\text{rob}} = \preceq_{\text{repl}}$ with $x \preceq_{\text{repl}} y :\Leftrightarrow f^p(x) \leqslant f^p(y)$.

6.3.2 · Additional Objective

Since the problems dealt with are already multiobjective by nature, a straight-forward way to also account for the robustness $r(x)$ is to treat the measure as an additional objective [71, 85, 98]. As for the previous approach, this affects the preference relation and thereby non-dominated sorting, but also the calculating of the hypervolume. The objective function becomes $f^{\text{ao}} = (f_1, \ldots, f_d, r)$; the corresponding preference relation $\preceq_{\text{rob}} = \preceq_{\text{oa}}$ is accordingly

$$x \preceq_{\text{ao}} y :\Leftrightarrow x \preceq_{\text{par}} y \wedge r(x) \leq r(y) \ .$$

Considering robustness as an ordinary objective value has three advantages: first, apart from increasing the dimensionality by one, the problem does not change and existing multiobjective approaches can be used. Second, different degrees of robustness are promoted, and third, no robustness level has to be chosen in advance which would entail the risk of the selected level being infeasible, or that the robustness level could be much improved with barely compromising the objective values of solutions. One disadvantage of this approach is to not focus on a specific robustness level and potentially finding many solutions whose robustness is too bad to be useful or whose objective values are strongly degraded to achieve an unnecessary large degree of robustness. A further complication is the increase in non-dominated solutions resulting from considering an additional objective, i.e., the expressiveness of the relation is smaller than the one of the previously stated relation $\preceq_{\text{repl}}$ and the relation proposed in the next section.

Figure 6.1(b) shows the partitioning according to $\preceq_{\text{ao}}$. Due to the different robustness values, many solutions which are dominated according to objective values only—that is according to $\preceq_{\text{par}}$—become incomparable and only two solutions e and g remain dominated.

6.3.3 · Additional Robustness Constraint

The third approach to embrace the robustness of a solution is to convert robustness into a constraint [46, 64, 73], which is then considered by adjusting the preference relation affecting non-dominated sorting. Here a slight modification of the definition of Deb and Gupta [46] is used by adding the additional refinement of applying weak Pareto dominance if two non-robust solutions have the same robustness value. Given the objective function $f(x)$ and robustness measure $r(x)$, an optimal robust solution then is

Definition 6.2 (optimal solution under a robustness constraint): *A solution $x^* \in X$ with $r(x^*)$ and $f(x^*)$ denoting its robustness and objective values respectively, both of which are to be minimized, is optimal with respect to the robustness constraint η, if it fulfills $x^* \in \{x \in X \mid \forall y \in X : x \preceq_{\text{con}} y\}$ where*

$$x \preceq_{\text{con}} y :\Leftrightarrow \begin{matrix} r(x) \leq \eta \wedge r(x) > \eta & \vee \\ x \preceq_{\text{par}} y \wedge (r(x) \leq \eta \wedge r(y) \leq \eta \vee r(x) = r(y)) & \vee \\ r(x) < r(y) \wedge r(x) > \eta \wedge r(y) > \eta \end{matrix} \quad (6.4)$$

denotes the preference relation for the constrained approach under the robustness constraint η.

This definition for single solutions can be extended to sets using the principle stated in Definition 2.11 on page 30:

Definition 6.3 (optimal set under a robustness constraint): *A set $A^* \in \Psi$ with $|A^*| \leq \alpha$ is optimal with respect to the robustness constraint η, if it fulfills*

$$A^* \in \{A \in \Psi \,|\, \forall B \in \Psi \ with \ |B| \leq \alpha : A \preccurlyeq_{con} B\}$$

where $\preccurlyeq_{con}$ denotes the extension of the relation $\preceq_{con}$ (Eq. 6.4) to sets, see Definition 2.11 on page 30.

In the following, a solution x whose robustness $r(x)$ does not exceed the constraint, i.e., $r(x) \leq \eta$, is referred to as robust and to all other solutions as non-robust [51].

Figure 6.1(c) on page 179 shows the allocation of solutions to fronts according to $\preceq_{con}$. The robustness constraint is set to $\eta = 1$, rendering all solutions with $r(x) \leq 1$ robust and with $r(x) > 1$ non robust, i.e., only h,i, and j are robust. In cases where solutions are considered robust or share the same robustness (a, b, and e), the partitioning corresponds to weak Pareto dominance on objective values. In all the remaining cases, partitioning is done according to the robustness value which leads to fronts independent of the objectives and containing only solutions of the same robustness $r(x)$.

6.3.4 · Extension of the Hypervolume Indicator to Integrate Robustness Considerations

The three approaches presented above all allow to consider robustness in a way that is inherent to the algorithm. The first two approaches (Sections 6.3.1 and 6.3.2) have a—predefined—way of trading off the robustness with the objective values. On the other hand, the constraint approach (Section 6.3.3) does not trade-off robustness, but rather optimizes with respect to a given robustness constraint. In this section a new approach is presented, which offers a larger degree of flexibility with respect to two important points: firstly, the concept allows to realize different trade-offs, which are not inherent to the concept, but rather can be defined by the decision maker, and secondly, even when trading-off robustness with objective values the optimization can be focused on a target robustness level.

The three approaches presented so far rely on modifying the dominance relation or the objective values to account for robustness. On solutions which are incomparable, the hypervolume indicator on the objective values is then used to refine the respective dominance relation. That means, the robustness of solutions is not directly influencing the hypervolume calculation. In the following, a new concept is proposed based not solely on modifying the dominance relation, but more importantly also on an extension of the regular hypervolume indicator. The novel *robustness integrating hypervolume indicator* $I_H^{\varphi,w}(A, R)$ is based on the objective values of solutions in A, but also on the robustness values of the solutions. An additional desirability function thereby allows to trade-off robustness and quality of solutions in almost any way, including the three existing approaches presented in Sections 6.3.1 to 6.3.3, as well as not considering robustness at all. This offers the possibility to trade-off robustness with quality of solutions given by the objective values, but at the same time to optimize with respect to a target robustness level.

Methodology

The idea behind $I_H^{\varphi,w}$ is to modify the attainment function $\alpha_A(z)$ of the original hypervolume indicator definition, see Definition 2.20 on page 38, in such a way that it reflects the robustness of solutions. In the original definition of the attainment function, $\alpha_A(z)$ is either 0 or 1; for any objective vector z not dominated by A, the attainment function is zero, while for a dominated vector z, $\alpha_A(z) = 1$ holds. Hence, a solution $x \in A$ always contributes 100% to the overall hypervolume, regardless of the robustness of the solution. To integrate robustness, the codomain of $\alpha_A(z)$ is extended to all values between 0 and 1. The new robustness integrating attainment function α_A^φ thereby is still zero for any objective vector z not dominated by A. In contrast to Definition 2.20, however, dominated objective vectors z are accounted based on the most robust solution dominating z. A desirability function of robustness φ determines the value of solutions, ranging from 0 (no contribution) to 1 (maximum influence)[1].

Definition 6.4 (Desirability function of robustness): *Given a solution $x \in A$ with robustness $r(x) \in \mathbb{R}_{\geq 0}$, the desirability function $\varphi : \mathbb{R}_{\geq 0} \to [0,1]$ assesses the desirability of a robustness level. A solution x with $\varphi(r(x)) = 0$ thereby represents a solution of no avail due to insufficient robustness. A solution y with $\varphi(r(y)) = 1$, on the other hand, is of maximum use, and further improving the robustness would not increase the value of the solution.*

Provided a function φ, the attainment function can be extended in the following way to integrate robustness:

Definition 6.5 (robustness integrating attainment function α_A^φ): *Given a set of solutions $A \in \Psi$, the robustness integrating attainment function $\alpha_A^\varphi : Z \to [0,1]$ for an objective vector $z \in Z$, and a desirability function $\varphi : r(x) \mapsto [0,1]$ is*

$$\alpha_A^\varphi(z) := \begin{cases} \varphi(\min_{x \in A, f(x) \leqslant z} r(x)) & \text{if } A \preccurlyeq \{z\} \\ 0 & \text{otherwise} \end{cases}$$

Hence, the attainment function of z correspond to the desirability of the most robust solution dominating z; and is 0 if no solution dominates z.

Finally, the robustness integrating hypervolume indicator corresponds to the established definition except for the modified attainment function according to Definition 6.5:

Definition 6.6 (robustness integrating hypervolume indicator): *The robustness integrating hypervolume indicator $I_H^{\varphi,w} : \Psi \to \mathbb{R}_{\geq 0}$ with reference set R, weight function $w(z)$, and desirability function φ is given by*

$$I_H^\varphi(A) := \int_{\mathbb{R}^d} \alpha_A^\varphi(z) w(z) dz \tag{6.5}$$

where $A \in \Psi$ is a set of decision vectors.

---

[1]The definition of desirabilty function used in this chapter is compliant with the definition known from statistical theory, cf. Abraham [1].

In the following, $I_H^{\varphi,w}$ is used to refer to the robustness integrating hypervolume indicator, not excluding an additional weight function to also incorporate user preference. The desirability function φ not only serves to extend the hypervolume indicator, but implies a robustness integrating preference relation:

Definition 6.7: *Let $x, y \in X$ be two solutions with robustness $r(x)$ and $r(y)$ respectively. Furthermore, let φ be a desirability function $\varphi : r(x) \mapsto \varphi(r(x))$. Then x weakly dominates y with respect to φ, denoted $x \preceq_\varphi y$, iff $x \preceq_{\mathrm{par}} y$ and $\varphi(r(x)) \geq \varphi(r(y))$ holds.*

Since a solution x can be in relation $\preceq_\varphi$ to y only if $\preceq_\varphi$ holds, $\preceq_\varphi$ is a subrelation of $\preceq_{\mathrm{par}}$, and generally increases the number of incomparable solutions. In order that $\preceq_\varphi$ is a reasonable relation with respect to Pareto dominance and robustness according to Definition 6.1, φ has to be monotonically decreasing as stated in the following Theorem:

Theorem 6.8: *As long as φ is a (not necessarily strictly) monotonically decreasing function, and smaller robustness values are considered better, the dominance given in Definition 6.7 is a weak refinement according to Definition 6.1. Furthermore, the corresponding robustness integrating hypervolume indicator given in Definition 6.6 (a) induces a refinement of the extension of $\preceq_\varphi$ to sets, and (b) is sensitive to any improvement of non dominated solutions x with $\varphi(r(x)) > 0$ in terms of objective values or the desirability of its robustness.*

Proof. Part 1: φ is compliant with Definition 6.1: let x and y be two solutions for which $x \preceq_{\mathrm{par}} y$ and $r(x) \leq r(y)$ holds. By the monotonicity property of φ if follows $\varphi(r(x)) \geq \varphi(r(y))$. Since also $x \preceq_{\mathrm{par}} y$, it follows $x \preceq_\varphi y$.

Part 2: the robustness integrating hypervolume is compliant with the extension of $\preceq_\varphi$ to sets: let $A, B \in \Psi$ denote two sets with $A \preceq_{\mathrm{rob}} B$. More specifically this means, for all $y \in B \; \exists x \in A$ such that $x \preceq_{\mathrm{par}} y$ and $r(x) \leq r(y)$. Now let $y'_B(z) := \arg\min_{y \in B, f(y) \leqslant z} r(y)$. Then $\exists x'_A(z) \in A$ with $x'_A(z) \preceq_{\mathrm{rob}} y'_B(z)$. This leads to $f(x'_A(z)) \leqslant f(y'_B(z)) \leqslant z$ and

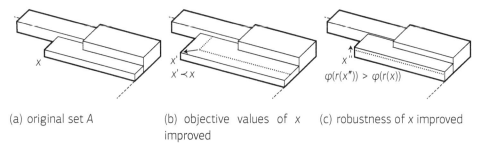

(a) original set A (b) objective values of x improved   (c) robustness of x improved

Figure 6.2 The robustness integrating hypervolume indicator is sensitive to improvements of objective values (b) as well as to increased robustness desirability (c).

$r(x'_A) \leq r(y'_B)$. The latter boils down to $\varphi(r(x'_A)) \geq \varphi(r(y'_B))$, hence $\alpha_A^{\varphi}(z) \geq \alpha_B^{\varphi}(z)$ for all $z \in Z$, and therefore $I_H^{\varphi,w}(A) \geq I_H^{\varphi,w}(B)$ holds.

Part 3: Definition 6.6 is sensitive to improvements of objective values and desirability: let $x \in A$ denote the solution which is improved, see Figure 6.2(a). First, consider the case where in a second set A', x is replaced by x' with $r(x') = r(x)$ and $x' \prec_{\text{par}} x$. Then there exists a set of objective vectors W which is dominated by $f(x')$ but not by $f(x)$. Because of $\varphi(r(x)) > 0$, the gained space W increases the overall hypervolume, see Figure 6.2(b). Second, if x is replaced by x'' with the same objective values but a higher desirability of robustness, $\varphi(r(x'')) > \varphi(r(x))$, the space solely dominated by x'' has a larger contribution due to the larger attainment value in this area, and again the hypervolume indicator increases, see Figure 6.2(c).   □

Note that choices of φ are not excluded for which the attainment function $\alpha_A^{\varphi}(z)$ can become 0 even if a solution $x \in A$ dominates the respective objective vector z—namely if all solution dominating z are considered infeasible due to their bad robustness. Provided that φ is chosen monotonically decreasing, many different choices of desirability are possible. Here, the following class of functions is proposed, tailored to the task of realizing the approaches presented above. Besides the robustness value, the function takes the constraint η introduced in Section 6.3.3 as an additional argument. A parameter θ defines the shape of the function and its properties:

$$\varphi_\theta(r(x), \eta) = \begin{cases} \left(\frac{r(x)}{r_{max}} - 1\right)\theta + (1+\theta)H_1(\eta - r(x)) & \theta \leq 0 \\ \exp\left(3 \cdot \frac{r(x) - \eta}{\eta \log(1-\theta)}\right) & 0 < \theta < 1, r(x) > \eta \\ 1 & \text{otherwise} \end{cases}$$

(6.6)

where $H_1(x)$ denotes the Heaviside function[2], and r_{max} denotes an upper bound of the robustness measure. The factor 3 in the exponent is chosen arbitrarily, and only serves the purpose of producing a nicely shaped function. By changing the shape parameter θ, different characteristics of φ can be realized that lead to different ways of trading off robustness and objective values, see Figure 6.3:

① $\theta = 1$: For this choice, $\varphi_1(r(x), \eta) \equiv 1$. This means the robustness of solutions is not considered at all.

② $0 < \theta < 1$: All solutions with $r(x) \leq \eta$ are maximally desirable in terms of robustness. For non-robust solutions, the desirability decreases exponentially with exceedance of $r(x)$ over η, where smaller values of θ lead to a faster decay. This setting is similar to the simulated annealing approach that will be presented in Section 6.4.3 with two major differences: first, the robustness level is factored in deterministically, and secondly, the robustness level is traded-off with the objective values, meaning a better quality of the latter can compensate for a bad robustness level.

③ $\theta = 0$: In contrast to case ②, all solutions exceeding the robustness constraint are mapped to zero desirability, and therefore do not influence the hypervolume calculation. This corresponds to the original constraint approach from Section 6.3.3.

④ $-1 < \theta < 0$: Negative choices of θ result in robust solutions getting different degrees of desirability, meaning only perfectly robust solutions ($r(x) = 0$) get the maximum value of 1. The value linearly decreases

---

[2] $H_1(x) = \begin{cases} 0 & x < 0 \\ 1 & x \geq 0 \end{cases}$

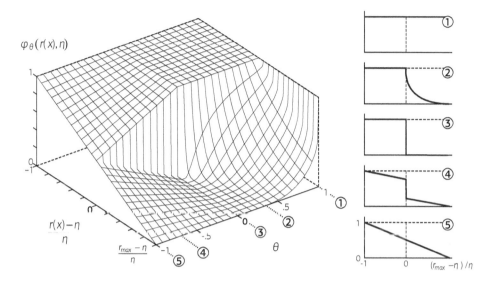

Figure 6.3 Desirability function $\varphi_\theta(r(x),\eta)$ according to Eq. 6.6. By changing the parameter θ, different shapes of φ can be realized as shown in the cross-sectional plots ① to ⑤. The robustness measure $r(x)$ has been normalized to η, such that only solutions with $r(x) \leq o$ are classified robust.

with $r(x)$ and drops passing over the constraint η, where the closer θ is to zero the larger the reduction. The value then further decreases linearly until getting zero for r_{max}.

⑤ $\theta = -1$: In contrast to ④, the desirability φ continuously decreases linearly from $\varphi_{-1}(0, \cdot) = 1$ to $\varphi_{-1}(r_{max}, \cdot) = 0$ without drop at $r(x) = \eta$. This corresponds to considering robustness as an additional objective, see Section 6.3.2.

Calculating the generalized hypervolume indicator in Eq. 6.5 can be done in a similar fashion as for the regular hypervolume indicator, see Figure 6.4 by using the 'hypervolume by slicing objectives' approach [86, 130, 134], where for each box the desirability function needs to be determined. Faster algorithms, for instance Beume and Rudolph [14], can be extended to Definition 6.5 as well; however, it is not clear how the necessary adjustments affect the runtime.

Figure 6.4 Robustness integrating hypervolume calculation for the case $o < \theta < 1$. The box corresponds to the hypervolume, the height being the robustness integrating attainment function $a_A^{\varphi}(z)$. The three solid dots represent robust solutions. According to Eq. 6.6 their dominated area is accounted 100%, i.e., $a_A^{\varphi}(z){=}1$. The non-robust solutions (unfilled dots) contribute less to the hypervolume.

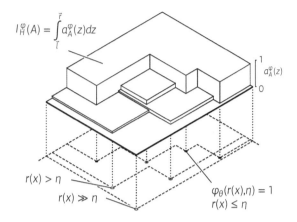

$$I_H^{\varphi}(A) = \int_{\underline{r}}^{\bar{r}} a_A^{\varphi}(z)\,dz$$

$a_A^{\varphi}(z)$

$r(x) > \eta$

$r(x) \gg \eta$

$\varphi_{\theta}(r(x),\eta) = 1$
$r(x) \leq \eta$

6.3.5 · Discussion of the Approaches

All three existing approaches mentioned in the motivation on page 173 can be translated to hypervolume-based search without major modifications necessary. Modifying the objective functions offers a way to account for uncertainty without changing the optimization problem, such that any multiobjective optimization algorithm can be still applied. In particular, the hypervolume indicator is directly applicable. However, no explicit robustness measure can be considered, nor can the search be restricted to certain robustness levels. The latter also holds when treating robustness as an additional objective. The advantage of this approach lies in the diversity of robustness levels that are obtained. On the flip side of the coin, many solutions might be unusable because they are either not robust enough or have very bad objective values to achieve an unessential high robustness. Furthermore, the number of non-dominated solutions increases, which can complicate search and decision making. Realizing robustness as an additional constraint allows to focus on one very specific level of robustness, thereby searching more targeted which potentially leads to a more efficient search. However, focusing can be problematic if the required level can not be fulfilled.

All approaches pursue different optimization goals, such that depending on the decision maker's preference, one or another approach might be appropriate. The extended hypervolume indicator constitutes the most flexible concept, as it allows to realize arbitrary desirability functions the decision maker has with respect to robustness of a solution. All three conventional approaches are thereby special realizations of desirability functions, and can be realized by the robustness integrating hypervolume indicator.

6.4 · Search Algorithm Design

Next, algorithms are presented that implement the concepts presented in Section 6.3. First, the three conventional concepts are considered, where for the constraint approach three modifications are proposed. Secondly, the generalized hypervolume indicator is tackled, and an extension of the Hypervolume Estimation Algorithm for Multiobjective Optimization (HypE) is derived such that the indicator is applicable to many objective problems.

6.4.1 · Modifying the Objective Functions

As discussed in Section 6.3.1, when modifying the objective functions to consider robustness, any multiobjective algorithm—hypervolume-based algorithms in particular—can be applied without any adjustments necessary. Hence, for instance the Regular Hypervolume-based Algorithm (RHV) as outlined in Algorithm 6 on page 114 can be employed as is.

6.4.2 · Additional Objectives

Only minor adjustments are necessary to consider robustness as an additional objective: since the number of objectives increases by one, the reference point or the reference set of the hypervolume indicator need to be changed. In detail, each element of the reference set needs an extra coordinate resulting in $d + 1$ dimensional vectors. Due to the additional objective, the computational time increases, and one might have to switch to approximations schemes, e.g., use HypE (see Chapter 4) instead of the exact hypervolume calculation, as for instance in in RHV or in [14, 129].

6.4.3 · Additional Robustness Constraints

For the constraint concept, first a baseline algorithm is presented that optimizes according to Definition 6.3. Then, three advanced methods are shown that attenuate potential premature convergence. Finally, in Section 6.4.3, a general version is proposed that enables to optimize multiple constraints with predefined number of solutions in parallel.

Baseline Approach

In order to realize the plain constraint approach, as illustrated in Section 6.3.3, in hypervolume-based search, the only change to be made concerns the dominance ranking, where the relation shown in Eq. 6.4 is employed instead of $\preceq_{\text{par}}$, see Figure 6.1(c). In the constraint approach as presented in Section 6.3.3, a robust solution thereby is always preferred over a non-robust solution regardless of their respective objective value. This in turn means, that the algorithm will never accept a non robust solution in favor of a more robust solution. Especially for very rigid robustness constraints $\eta \ll 1$ this carries a certain risk of getting stuck early on in a region with locally minimal robustness, which does not even need to fulfill the constraint η. To attenuate this problem, next three modifications of the baseline algorithm are proposed that loosen up the focus on a robustness constraint.

Advanced Methods

The first modification of the baseline approach is based on relaxing the robustness constraint at the beginning of search; the second algorithm does not introduce robustness into some parts of the set which is thus allowed to converge freely even if its elements exceed the robustness constraint. Finally, a generalization of the constraint method is proposed that allows to focus on multiple robustness constraints at the same time.

Approach 1 | Simulated Annealing. The first algorithm uses the principle of simulated annealing when considering robustness with respect to a constraint η. In contrast to the baseline approach, also solutions exceeding the robustness constraint can be marked robust. The probability in this case

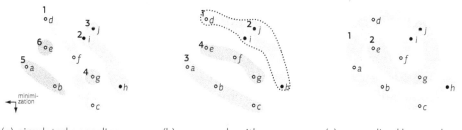

(a) simulated annealing   (b) reserve algorithm   (c) generalized hypervolume

Figure 6.5 Partitioning into fronts of the same ten solutions from Figure 6.1 for the two advanced constraint methods (a), (b), and for the generalized hypervolume indicator. The solid dots represents robust solutions at the considered level of $\eta = 1$ while the unfilled dots represent non-robust solutions. For (a), solutions d, f, and c are classified robust too.

thereby depends on the difference of the robustness $r(x)$ to the constraint level η, and on a temperature T:

$$
P(x \text{ robust}) = \begin{cases} 1 & r(x) \leq \eta \\ u \leq e^{-(r(x)-\eta)/T} & \text{otherwise} \end{cases}
$$

where $u \sim U(0,1)$ is uniformly distributed within 0 and 1. The temperature T is exponentially decreased every generation, i.e., $T = T_0 \cdot \gamma^g$ where g denotes the generation counter, $\gamma \in]0,1[$ denotes the cooling rate, and T_0 the initial temperature. Hence, the probability of non robust solutions being marked robust decreases towards the end of the evolutionary algorithm. In the example shown in Figure 6.5, the solutions d, f, and c are classified as robust—although exceeding the constraint $\eta = 1$. Since these solutions Pareto-dominate all (truly) robust solutions, they are preferred over these solutions unlike in the baseline algorithm, see Section 6.3.3.

Approach 2 | Reserve Approach. The second idea to overcome locally robust regions is to divide the population into two sets: on the first one no robustness considerations are imposed, while for the second set (referred to as the reserve) the individuals are selected according to the baseline constraint concept. This enables some individuals, namely those in the first set, to optimize their objectives values efficiently. Although these individuals are very likely not robust, they can improve the solutions from the second set in two ways: (i) a high quality solution from the first set gets robust through mutation or crossover and thereby improves the reserve, (ii) the objective values of a robust solution are improved by crossover with an individual from the first set. However, since at the end only the reserve is expected to contain individuals fulfilling the constraint, one should choose the size of the reserve β to contain a large portion of the population, and only assign few solutions to the first set where robustness does not matter.

In detail, the reserve algorithm proceeds as follows. First, the membership of a solution to the reserve is determined; a solution x is included in the reserve, denoted by the indicator function $\chi_{\mathrm{rsv}}(x)$, if either it is robust and there are less than $\beta - 1$ other solutions that are also robust and dominate x; or if x is not robust but still is among the β most robust solutions. Hence

$$\chi_{\mathrm{rsv}}(x) = 1 :\Leftrightarrow r(x) \leq \eta \wedge |\{y \preceq_{\mathrm{par}} x \mid y \in X, r(y) \leq \eta| \leq \beta \quad \vee$$
$$r(x) > \eta \wedge |\{y \mid y \in X, r(y) \leq r(x)| \leq \beta$$

Given the membership to the reserve, the preference relation is:

$$\chi_{\mathrm{rsv}}(x) = 1 \wedge \chi_{\mathrm{rsv}}(y) = 0 \quad \wedge$$
$$x \preceq_{\mathrm{rsv}} y :\Leftrightarrow \neg(\chi_{\mathrm{rsv}}(x) = 0 \wedge \chi_{\mathrm{rsv}}(y) = 1) \quad \wedge$$
$$x \preceq_{\mathrm{par}} y$$

For the example in Figure 6.5(b) let the reserve size be $\beta = 4$, leaving one additional place not subject to robustness. Because there are fewer solutions which fulfill the robustness constraint than there are places in the reserve, all three robust solutions are included in the reserve, see dashed border. In addition to them, the next most robust solution (d) is included to complete the reserve. Within the reserve, the solutions are partitioned according to their objective value. After having determined the reserve, all remaining solutions are partitioned based on their objective values.

Approach 3 | Multi-Constraint Approach. So far, robustness has been considered with respect to one robustness constraint η only. However, another scenario could include the desire of the decision maker to optimize multiple robustness constraint at the same time. This can make sense for different reasons: (i) the decision maker wants to learn about the problem landscape, i.e., he likes to know for different degrees of robustness the objective values that can be achieved; (ii) the decision maker needs different degrees of robustness, for instance because the solution are implemented for several application areas that have different robustness requirements, and (iii) premature convergence should be avoided.

To optimize according to multiple robustness constraints, the idea is to divide the population into several groups, which are subject to a given constraint. In the following the baseline algorithm from Section 6.4.3 is used as a basis. The proposed concept not only allows to optimize different degrees of robustness at the same time, but also to put a different emphasis on the individual classes by predefining the number of solutions that should have a certain robustness level. Specifically, let $C = \{(\eta_1, s_1), \ldots, (\eta_k, s_l)\}$ denote a set of l constraints $\eta_1, \ldots, \eta_l$ where for each constraint the user defines the number of individuals $s_i \in \mathbb{N}_{>0}$ that should fulfill the respective constraint η_i (excluding those individuals already belonging to a more restrictive constraint). Hence, $c_1 + \cdots + c_l = |P|$, and without loss of generality let assume $\eta_1 < \eta_2 < \cdots < \eta_l$. The task of an algorithm is then to solve the following problem:

Definition 6.10 (optimal set under multiple robustness constraint): *Consider $C = \{(\eta_1, s_1), \ldots, (\eta_k, s_l)\}$, a set of l robustness constraints η_i with corresponding size s_i. Then a set $A^* \in \Psi_\alpha$, i.e., $|A^*| \leq \alpha$, is optimal with respect to C if it fulfills $A^* \in \{A \in \Psi_\alpha \mid \forall B \in \Psi_\alpha : A \preccurlyeq_C B\}$ where $\preccurlyeq_C$ is given by*

$$A \preccurlyeq_C B :\Leftrightarrow \forall (\eta_i, s_i) \in C : \forall B' \in B_{s_i} \exists A' \in A_{s_i} \text{ s.t. } A' \preccurlyeq_{\eta_i} B'$$

where $\preccurlyeq_{\eta_i}$ denotes the extension of any relation proposed in Section 6.3 to sets, as stated in Eq. 6.4.

In order to optimize according to Definition 6.10, Algorithm 13 is proposed: beginning with the most restrictive robustness level η_i, $i = 1$, one after another s_i individuals are added to the new population. Thereby, the individual increasing the hypervolume at the current robustness level η_i the

Require: Population P, list of constraint classes $C = \{(\eta_1, s_1), \ldots, (\eta_l, s_l)\}$, with $\eta_1 \leq \cdots \leq \eta_l$.

1: $P' = \{\}$
2: **for** $i = 1$ to l **do**   *(iterate over all classes $(\eta_i, s_i) \in C$)*
3:      **for** $j = 1$ to s_i **do**   *(fill current class)*
4:          $x' \leftarrow \arg\max_{x \in P \backslash P'} I_H^{\varphi(\cdot, \eta_i), w}(x \cup P', R)$
5:          **if** $I_H^{\varphi(\cdot, \eta_i), w}(x' \cup P', R) = I_H^{\varphi(\cdot, \eta_i), w}(P', R)$ **then**   *(has no contribution)*
6:              $x' \leftarrow \arg\min_{x \in P \backslash P'} r(x)$ *(get the most robust instead)*
7:          $P' \leftarrow P' \cup x'$
8: **return** P'

Algorithm 13 Classes algorithm based on the greedy hypervolume improvement principle. Beginning with the most robust class, solutions are added to the final population P' that increase the hypervolume at the respective level the most, given the individuals already in P'.

most is selected. If no individual increases the hypervolume, the most robust solution is chosen instead.

6.4.4 · HypE for the Generalized Hypervolume Indicator

To optimize according to the generalized hypervolume indicator, the same greedy procedure as used by the Regular Hypervolume-based Algorithm (RHV) presented in Section 4.1.1 on page 113 can be used. Thereby, two differences arise:

1. first off, non-dominated sorting is done according to $\preceq_\varphi$ (Definition 6.7) and not with respect to $\preceq_{par}$. In Figure 6.6, for instance, the solutions d and e are in different fronts than a for $\preceq_{par}$ (Figure 6.6(a)), but belong to the same front for $\preceq_\varphi$ (Figure 6.6(a));
2. secondly, the hypervolume loss is calculated according to the new indicator, i.e., the loss is $I_H^{\varphi, w}(A, R) - I_H^{\varphi, w}(A \backslash x, R)$, see gray shaded areas in Figures 6.6(a) and 6.6(b).

In this chapter, however, the advanced selection procedure employed by HypE is used (see Chapter 4) which rather than considering the loss when

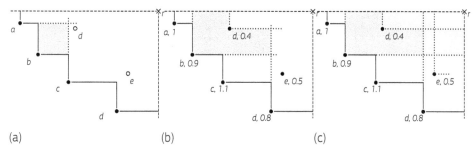

(a)   (b)   (c)

Figure 6.6 In (a) the affected hypervolume region when removing b is shown if robustness is not considered (dark gray). Adding the consideration of robustness (values next to solution labels), the affected region increases (b). Foreseeing the removal of two other solutions apart from b, other regions dominated by b (light gray areas) also need to be considered (c).

removing the respective solution, tries to estimates the expected loss taking into account the removal of additional solutions, see Figure 6.6(c).

Although the exact calculation of this fitness is possible, in this chapter the focus is on its approximation by Monte Carlo sampling, as also implemented in HypE. The basic idea is again to first determine a sampling space S. From this sampling space, m samples then are drawn to estimate the expected hypervolume loss.

Introducing Robustness to HypE. HypE needs to be modified in order to be applicable to the robustness integrating hypervolume indicator (Definition 6.6) due to the following observations. In case of the regular hypervolume indicator, a dominated region is accounted 100% as long as at least one point dominates it. So the only case HypE has to consider is removing all points dominating the portion altogether. For different points having different degrees of robustness, the situation changes: even though a partition dominated by multiple points would stay dominated if one removes not all dominating points, the robustness integrating hypervolume might nevertheless decrease due to the non bivariate attainment function. For example, if the most desirable point in terms of robustness is removed, then the attainment function is decreased and thereby also the robustness integrating hypervolume indicator value, see Theorem 6.8.

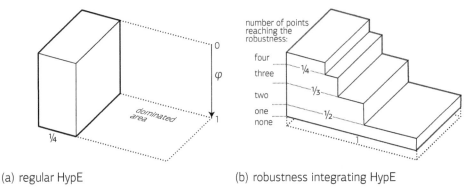

(a) regular HypE   (b) robustness integrating HypE

Figure 6.7 Illustrates how a portion of the objective space U is attributed to the most robust among four points dominating the region. In case of no robustness considerations, the solutions all get ¼ of $\lambda(U)$ as every other solution, see (a). When considering robustness, different layers of robustness have to be distinguished, see (b): the first, and most robust, layer is dominated by no point, and is therefore disregarded. Only the most robust solution dominates the second layer, hence gets the whole slice. The third layer is dominated by an additional point, and both solutions get half of the share. The procedure continues up to the layer where every point reaches the necessary robustness, this layer is distributed evenly among all points.

The second difference to the original HypE algorithm concerns the way the contribution is shared among the dominating point. For the regular hypervolume indicator, all solutions dominating the considered region are equally valuable since they entail the attainment function being 1. Consequently, the region is split equally among all solutions. For example, if four solutions dominate a region, the fitness of each is increased by $1/4$ of the volume of the region, see Figure 6.7(a). For the robustness integrating hypervolume indicator, one has to distinguish different layers of robustness, which are achieved by subsets of all individuals dominating the region. Consequently, the hypervolume of these layers should only be split among those solutions actually reaching that robustness level, see Figure 6.7(b). In the following, first the question is tackled of how to distribute the layers of robustness of a dominated portion among solutions. Then the probability is derived, that each one of these layers is lost.

Distributing Hypervolume among Solutions. Let A denote the set of points and $A_U \subseteq A$ those solutions, that dominate the region U under consideration. To illustrate the extended calculation of the robustness integrating HypE, consider ten points $A = \{x_1, \ldots, x_{10}\}$. The first four points $A_U = \{x_1, \ldots, x_4\}$ dominate the region $U = H(\{x_1, \ldots, x_4\}, \{x_1, \ldots, x_{10}\}, R)$. Additionally, let $r(x_1) \leq r(x_2) \leq r(x_3) \leq r(x_4)$. First, a few simple cases are considered before presenting the final, and rather intriguing, formula to calculate the fitness of a point. First of all, it is investigated how much the robustness integrating hypervolume I_A^φ decreases when removing points from the set A_U and how to attribute this loss to individuals. Assume x_2 or any other point which is less robust than x_1 is removed. In this case, the robustness integrating hypervolume does not decrease at all, since the attainment function depends only on the most robust point dominating the partition, in our case on x_1. Hence, a removal only affects the hypervolume, if no other point dominating the partition U at least as robust as the removed point remains in the population.

On the other hand, lets assume only the most robust solution x_1 is removed. By doing this, the hypervolume decreases by $\lambda(U) \cdot (\varphi(r(x_1)) - \varphi(r(x_2)))$, which is non zero if the robustness of x_1 is more desirable than the one of x_2. Clearly, this loss has to be fully attributed to point x_1, as no other point is removed. Now lets extend this to more than one point being removed. Assume points x_1, x_2, and x_4 are removed. As seen before, the loss of x_4 does not affect the hypervolume since x_3 (which is more robust) stays in the set. So in a set of points remaining in the population, the most robust individual sets a cutoff. For all individuals above this cutoff, i.e., for all individuals being less robust, the hypervolume does not decrease if these individuals are removed. The total loss of $I_H^{\varphi,w}$ is $\lambda(U) \cdot (\varphi(r(x_1)) - \varphi(r(x_3)))$. The question now is, how to distribute the loss among solutions. The share $\lambda(U) \cdot (\varphi(r(x_1)) - \varphi(r(x_2)))$ is only due to x_1, hence it is fully attributed to x_1. The share between $\varphi(x_2)$ and $\varphi(x_3)$ is dominated by both x_1 and x_2, so the portion is evenly split. This procedure continues for all robustness levels below the cutoff, see Figure 6.7(b).

Figure 6.8 Illustration of class c_v: from p points, n dominate the region under consideration. The cutoff point is denoted as v. Besides the considered solution, q points need to be removed below the cutoff. In total k points are removed. In the example, $p = 9$, $v = 2$, $q = 2$, $n = 5$, and $k = 5$.

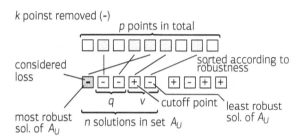

Probability of Loosing Hypervolume. Now that it is known how to distribute the partition U among points for a particular selection of points, one has to consider all possible subsets of A_U, i.e., subsets of points dominating U, and calculate the probability that the subset is lost. Let p denote the total number of points, let $n := |A_U|$ denote the number of points dominating U, and let k denote the number of points to be removed, i.e., $k = p - \alpha$. Not all $\binom{n}{k}$ subsets have to be considered separately, but they can be summarized into classes c_v with $0 \leq v \leq n - 1$, where v denotes the position of the cutoff level, see Figure 6.8. More specifically, c_v contains all subsets where the most robust solution from A_U not being removed is the vth least robust solution among all solutions in A_U. For $v = 0$, all solutions dominating U are removed. For example, let $(\chi_1, \ldots, \chi_p)$ represent different subsets of A, where $\chi_i \in \{0, 1\}$ denotes the absence or presence respectively of solution x_i, and $\chi_i = \times$ denotes both cases (don't care). In the considered example, $c_0 = (0, 0, 0, 0, \times, \ldots, \times)$, $c_1 = (0, 0, 0, 1, \times, \ldots, \times)$, $c_2 = (0, 0, 1, \times, \times, \ldots, \times)$, and $c_3 = (0, 1, \times, \times, \times, \ldots, \times)$. Note that as for the regular HypE calculation, the fitness of a solution is determined under the assumption that this solution is removed, therefore, the subset c_4 (no solution removed from A_U) is not possible.

To derive the probability that a subset being removed belongs to the class c_v, consider one particular way this can happen: the first q individuals are removed from below the cutoff, i.e., are more robust. The remaining $k - q$ points are then removed from above the cutoff or from the set $A \backslash A_U$. This is one of $\binom{k-1}{q}$ equally probable combinations to obtain a cutoff level v, so that the obtained probability has to be multiplied by $\binom{k-1}{q}^3$ in the end.

A cutoff of v means, besides the considered point $q = n - v - 1$ points are removed from below the cutoff level. The probability that these q individuals are removed in the first q removal steps is:

$$P_1 = \frac{q}{p-1} \cdot \frac{q-1}{p-1} \cdots \frac{1}{p-(q-1)} = \frac{q! \cdot (p-q)!}{(p-1)!} \, . \tag{6.7}$$

For the remaining $k-1-q$ points, any of the $p-n$ individuals not dominating the partition may be selected, as well as any of the $v-1$ individuals above the cutoff, i.e., solutions less robust than the cutoff. The cutoff itself may not be removed as this would change the level v. So the probability for the second portion of points to be picked accordingly is:

$$P_2 = \frac{p-n+v-1}{p-q-1} \cdot \frac{p-n+v-2}{p-q-2} \cdots \frac{p-k}{p-k+1} \tag{6.8}$$
$$= \frac{(p-q-2)!(p-k)!}{(p-q-1)!(p-k-1)!}$$

Multiplying P_1 (Eq. 6.7), P_2 (Eq. 6.8) and the number of combinations $\binom{k-1}{q}$ gives the final probability (note that $v = n - q - 1$)

$$P_v(p,q,k) = P_1 \cdot P_2 \cdot \binom{k-1}{q}$$
$$= \frac{q! \cdot (p-q)!}{(p-1)!} \cdot \frac{(p-q-2)!(p-k)!}{(p-q-1)!(p-k-1)!} \cdot \frac{(k-1)!}{q!(k-1-q)!}$$
$$= (p-q)(p-k)\frac{(p-q-2)!}{(p-1)!} \frac{(k-1)!}{(k-1-q)!}$$
$$= (p-1)(p-k) \prod_{i=p-q-1}^{p-1} \frac{1}{i} \prod_{i=k-q}^{k-1} i \, . \tag{6.9}$$

---

[3] Again, note that the solutions whose fitness needs to be determined, is assumed to be removed and belongs to the first q individuals, otherwise it would induce no loss in hypervolume. That is why the binomial coefficient considers the k-1 set instead of k.

For $v = 0$ and $p = n$ the last line is undefined, in this case, $P_0(n, q, k) = 1$ holds.

Example 6.11: Consider four solutions a, b, c and d with robustness $r(a) = 0.8$, $r(b) = 0.9$, $r(c) = 1.05$ and $r(d) = 1.2$. Let the robustness constraint be $\eta = 1$, and let the desirability φ be defined according to Eq. 6.6 with $\theta = 0.1$ and assume two solutions need to be removed. Now consider a sample dominated by a, c and d. This gives $p = 4$, $n = 3$ and $k = 2$. Since only two individuals are to be removed, the probability for having $v = 0$, i.e, all three individuals dominating the sample are removed, is 0. The probability for $v = 1$, i.e., another solution dominating the sample is removed besides the considered individual, is $1/3$. In this case, the first robustness layer extends from $r(a) = .8$ to $r(c) = 1.05$. This gives a value of $\frac{1}{3}\left(\varphi^{0.1}(.8) - \varphi^{0.1}(1.05)\right) = 0.253$ which is completely attributed to a since only this solution reaches the degree of robustness. The second layer extends from $r(c) = 1.05$ to $r(d) = 1.2$ and half of the value $\frac{1}{3}\left(\varphi^{0.1}(1.05) - \varphi^{0.1}(1.2)\right) = 0.079$ is added to the fitness of a and c respectively. The probability for $v = 2$ is $2/3$ (either b or d can be removed, but not c). The contribution $\frac{2}{3}\left(\varphi^{0.1}(.8) - \varphi^{0.1}(1.05)\right) = 0.506$ is completely added to the fitness of a.   ○

Sampling Routine. The HypE routine to consider robustness corresponds to the regular HypE algorithm as listed in Algorithm 9 on page 139. The changes to be made only affect Lines 10 to 20. Algorithm 14 shows the new code replacing Lines 10 to 20 of the original definition. The conditional statement "if $|A_U| \leq k$ then" in Line 12 of the original algorithm is omitted, as the hypervolume might decrease even if not all individuals in A_U are removed. Secondly, the advanced distribution of the sample according to different robustness levels is used (two loops in Line 15 and 18). Thirdly, the probability α is changed and not only depends on k, but also on the population size p and the current cutoff level v.

Desirability Function. The robustness integrating HypE relies on a desirability function φ. This chapter uses the class of functions stated in Eq. 6.6. The parameter θ of this function is thereby either fixed, or geometrically

9: $\cdots$
10: **if** $\exists r \in R : s \leqslant r$ **then**
11: $\quad p \leftarrow |P|$
12: $\quad A_U \leftarrow \bigcup_{a \in P,\ f(a) \leq s} \{f(a)\}$
13: $\quad e \leftarrow$ elements of A_U sorted such that $r(e_1) \leq \cdots \leq r(e_n)$ *(every hit is relevant)*
14: $\quad n \leftarrow |A_U|$ *(number of points dominating the partition)*
15: $\quad$ **for** $v = 0$ to $n - 1$ **do**   *(check all cutoff levels)*
16: $\quad\quad q \leftarrow n - v - 1$
17: $\quad\quad \alpha \leftarrow P_v(p, q, k)$ *(according to Eq. 6.9)*
18: $\quad\quad$ **for** $f = 1$ to $n - v$ **do**   *(update fitness of all contributing solutions)*
19: $\quad\quad\quad$ **if** f equals $n - v$ **then**   *(least robust solution)*
20: $\quad\quad\quad\quad inc \leftarrow \alpha \cdot (\varphi(r(e_f)))$
21: $\quad\quad\quad$ **else**   *(slice to less robust solution $f + 1$)*
22: $\quad\quad\quad\quad inc \leftarrow \alpha \cdot (\varphi(r(e_f)) - \varphi(r(e_{f+1})))$
23: $\quad\quad\quad$ **for** $j = 1$ to f **do**   *(update fitness)*
24: $\quad\quad\quad\quad (a, v) \leftarrow (a, v) \in \mathcal{F}$ where $a \equiv e_f$
25: $\quad\quad\quad\quad \mathcal{F}' \leftarrow (\mathcal{F}' \setminus (a, v)) \cup (a, v + inc/f)$
26: $\quad \mathcal{F} \leftarrow \mathcal{F}'$
27: $\cdots$

Algorithm 14 Hypervolume-Based Fitness Value Estimation for $I_H^{\varphi,w}$-changes to incorporate robustness

decreased in a simulated annealing fashion from 1 to $\theta_{\text{end}} \in]0, 1]$, i.e., in generation g, θ corresponds to $\theta_g = \gamma^g$ with $\gamma = \sqrt[g_{\max}]{\theta_{\text{end}}}$.

6.5 · Experimental Validation

In the following experiments, the algorithms from Section 6.4 are compared on two test problem suites and on a real world bridge truss problem presented in Appendix E.1. The different optimization goals of the approaches rule out a fair comparison as no single performance assessment measure can do justice to all optimization goals. Nonetheless, the approaches are compared on the optimality goal shown in Definition 6.3, which will favor the constraint approach. Yet, the approach presented in Section 6.3.1 is excluded from the experimental comparison, since the approach is not based on a robustness measure $r(x)$.

The following goals will be pursued by visual and quantitative comparisons:

1. the differences between the three existing approaches (see page 173) are shown;
2. it is investigated, how the extended hypervolume approach performs, and how it competes with the other approaches, in particular, the influence of the desirability function is investigated;
3. it is is examined, whether the multi-constraint approach from Section 6.4.3 has advantages over doing independent runs or considering robustness as an additional objective.

6.5.1 · Experimental Setup

The performance of the algorithms is investigated with respect to optimizing a robustness constraint η. The following algorithms are compared:

- as a baseline algorithm, HypE without robustness consideration, denoted $\text{HypE}_{no.\,rob.}$;
- Alg_{ao} using an additional objective;
- the constraint approaches from Section 6.4.3, i.e., baseline Alg_{con}, simulated annealing $Alg_{sim.\,ann.}$, reserve Alg_{rsv}, and multiple classes $Alg_{classes}$;
- HypE using the generalized hypervolume indicator, see Section 6.4.4.

So far, the focus was on environmental selection only, i.e., the task of selecting the most promising population P' of size α from the union of the parent and offspring population. To generate the offspring population, random mating selection is used, although the principles proposed for environmental selection could also be applied to mating selection. From the mating pool Simulated Binary Crossover (SBX) and Polynomial Mutation, see Deb [44], generate new individuals.

The first test problem suite used is by the Walking Fish Group (WFG) [79], and consists of nine well-designed test problems featuring different properties that make the problems hard to solve—like non-separability, bias, many-to-one mappings and multimodality. However, these problems are not created to have specific robustness properties and the robustness landscape is not known. For that reason, six novel test problems are proposed called Bader-Zitzler (BZ) that have different, known robustness characteristics, see Appendix E.2. These novel problems allow to investigate the influence of different robustness landscapes on the performance of the algorithms. In addition to the two test problems suites, the algorithms are compared on a real world truss building problem stated in Appendix E.1, where also additional results on this problem are presented. For the robustness integrating HypE, see Section 6.4.4, the variant using a fixed θ is considered (denoted by HypE$_{\theta f}$), as well as the variant with θ decreasing in each generation to θ_{end}. This latter variant is referred to as HypE$_{\theta_{\text{end}}a}$.

Experimental Settings

The parameters η_{mutation} and $\eta_{\text{crossover}}$ of the Polynomial Mutation, and SBX operator respectively, as well as the corresponding mutation and crossover probabilities, are listed in Table 6.1. Unless noted otherwise, for each test problem 100 runs of 1 000 generations are carried out. The population size α and offspring size μ are both set to 25. For the BZ robustness test problems, see Appendix E.2, the number of decision variables n is set to 10, while for the WFG test problems the recommendations of the authors are used, i.e., the number of distance related parameters is set to $l = 20$ and the number of position related parameters k is set to 4 in the biobjective case, and to $k = 2 \cdot (d - 1)$ otherwise. Except for Figure 6.11, two objectives are optimized.

In all experiments on the two test problem suites, the extend of the neighborhood $\mathcal{B}_\delta$ is set to $\delta = 0.01$. To estimate $f^w(x, \delta)$, for every solution 25 samples are generated in the neighborhood of x and $\hat{f}^w(x, \delta)$ is determined according to Eq. 6.3. After each generation, all solutions are resampled, even those that did not undergo mutation. This prevents that a solution which, only by chance, reaches a good robustness estimate, persists in the population. For the real world bridge problem, on the other hand, a problem

Table 6.1 Parameter setting used for the experimental validation. The number of generations was set to 1 000 for the test problems, and to 10 000 for the bridge problem.

parameter	value	continued	
$\eta_{mutation}$	20	population size a	25
$\eta_{crossover}$	15	number of offspring μ	25
individual mutation prob.	1	number of generations g	1 000/10 000
individual recombination prob.	0.5	perturbation δ	0.01
variable mutation prob.	$1/n$	no. of neighboring points H	25
variable recombination prob.	1	neighborhood size δ	0.01

specific type of noise is used that allows to analytically determine the worst case, see Appendix E.1.

For the $Alg_{sim.\,ann.}$ approach the cooling rate γ is set to 0.99. The reference set of the hypervolume indicator is set to $R = \{r\}$ with $r = (3, 5)$ on WFG, with $r = (6, 6)$ on BZ, and with $r = (0, 2000)$ on the bridge problem[4]. The $Alg_{classes}$-approach proposed in Section 6.4.3 uses the following constraints: for BZ $(\eta_1, \ldots, \eta_5) = (.01, .03, .1, .3, \infty)$. For WFG, due to generally higher robustness levels on these test problems, the classes were set to $(\eta_1, \ldots, \eta_5) = (.001, .003, .01, .03, \infty)$. In both cases, the class sizes were $(s_1, \ldots, s_5) = (4, 4, 6, 4, 6)$ which gives a populations size of 24. For the bridge problem, the classes are set to $(.001, .01, .02, 0.1, \infty)$ with 6 individuals in each class. The size of the bridge is set to 4,6,8,10, and 12 decks, i.e., spanning a width of 40 m up to 120 m. For comparisons with a single robustness constraint, it is set to $\eta = 0.02$. For each comparison, 100 runs of 10 000 generations have been performed.

In this chapter, two types of uncertainty are used. Firstly, for the test problems, where $x \in \mathbb{R}^n$ holds, X^p is assumed to be uniformly distributed within $B_\delta(x)$ according to Eq. 6.1. Random samples are generated within $B_\delta(x)$, and evaluated to obtain an estimate of the robustness measure $r(x)$. Secondly, for the real world application, a problem specific type of noise is considered as outlined in Appendix E.1 on page 264. For this second type

---

[4]For this problem, the first objective is to be maximized.

of noise, along with the structure of the problem, the worst case can be determined analytically.

Performance Assessment

For all comparisons, the robustness of solutions has to be assessed. To this end, 10 000 samples are generated within B_δ. For each objective separately, the 5% largest values are then selected. By these 500 values, the tail of a Generalized Pareto Distribution is fitted, see Kotz and Nadarajah [92]. The method of moments is thereby used to obtain a first guess, which is then optimized maximizing the log-likelihood with respect to the shape parameter k and the logarithm of the scale parameter, $\log(\sigma)$[5]. Given an estimate for the parameters $\hat{k}$ and $\hat{\sigma}$ of the Generalized Pareto Distribution, the worst case estimate $\hat{f}_i^w(x)$ is then given by

$$\hat{f}_i^w(x) = \begin{cases} \hat{\theta} - \hat{\sigma}/\hat{k} & \hat{k} < 0 \\ \infty & otherwise \end{cases}$$

where $\hat{\theta}$ denotes the estimate of the location of the distribution given by the smallest value of the 5% percentile.

The performance of algorithms is assessed in the following manner: at first, a visual comparison takes place by plotting the objective values and robustness on the truss bridge problem (Appendix E.1 on page 264). The influence of θ of the robustness integrating HypE is then further investigated on BZ1. Secondly, all algorithms are compared with respect to the hypervolume indicator at the optimized robustness level η. To this end, the hypervolume of all robust solutions is calculated for each run. Next, the hypervolume values of the different algorithms are compared using the Kruskal-Wallis test and post hoc applying the Conover-Inman procedure to detect the pairs of algorithms being significantly different. The performance $P(\mathcal{A}_i)$ of an algorithm i then corresponds to the number of other algorithms, that are significantly better, see Appendix A on page 225 for

---

[5] Note that the maximum likelihood approximation is only efficient for $k \geq -\frac{1}{2}$ [92]. Preliminary studies, however, not only showed $k \geq -\frac{1}{2}$ for all test problems considered, but also revealed that k is the same for all solutions of a given test problem.

Table 6.2 Comparison of HypE$_{.001a}$ and HypE$_{.1f}$ to different other algorithms for the hypervolume indicator. The number represent the performance score $P(A_i)$, which stands for the number of contenders significantly dominating the corresponding algorithm A_i, i.e., smaller values correspond to better algorithms. Zeros have been replaced by ".".

	Alg_{gao}	Alg_{con}	$Alg_{classes}$	HypE$_{.001a}$	HypE$_{.1f}$	HypE$_{no.rob.}$	Alg_{rsv}	$Alg_{sim.ann.}$
BZ1	6	.	5	.	.	7	3	4
BZ2	4	7	2	2	4	.	.	5
BZ3	.	1	1	2	2	7	3	1
BZ4	2	5	1	3	4	7	.	6
BZ5	4	.	4	.	.	7	1	6
BZ6	.	4	2	4	4	5	1	2
WFG1	4	1	.	1	4	7	1	4
WFG2	5	7	.	1	1	4	1	1
WFG3	1	2	.	2	3	3	2	2
WFG4	6	3	.	1	3	6	2	2
WFG5	6	1	.	1	1	7	2	3
WFG6	6	1	3	.	.	.	.	.
WFG7	7	.	5	.	.	4	3	.
WFG8	6	3	6	.	.	1	.	2
WFG9	6	1	.	1	1	6	4	5
Bridge 4	1	4	1	.	3	7	4	6
Bridge 6	3	4	2	.	.	7	4	6
Bridge 8	3	5	2	1	.	7	4	5
Bridge 10	3	4	2	.	.	7	3	5
Bridge 12	4	4	2	1	.	7	2	4
Total	77	57	38	20	30	106	40	69

a detailed description of the significance ranking. The performance P is calculated for all algorithms, on all test problems of a given suite.

In addition to the significance rank at the respective level η, the mean rank of an algorithm when ranking all algorithms together is reported as well. The reason for plotting the mean rank instead of the significance is to also get an idea of the effect size of the differences—due to the large number of runs (100), differences might show up as significant although the difference is only marginal. The mean rank is reported not only for the optimized level η, but a continuous range of other robustness levels as well to get an idea of the robustness distribution of the different algorithms.

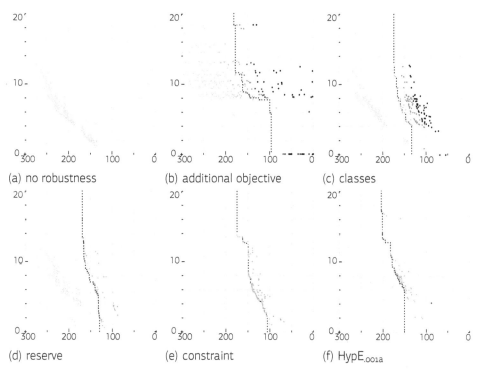

Figure 6.9 Pareto front approximations on the bridge problem for different algorithms. Since the first objective of the bridge problem, the structural efficiency, has to be maximized, the x-axis is reversed such that the figure agrees with the minimization problem. The robustness of a solution is color coded, lighter shades of gray stand for more robust solution. The dotted line represents the Pareto front of robust solutions (for (a), no robust solutions exists).

6.5.2 · Results

Visual Comparison of Pareto fronts

As the Pareto-set approximations in Figure 6.9 show, a comparison of the different approaches is difficult: depending on how robustness is considered, the solutions exhibit different qualities in terms of objective values and robustness. It is up to decision maker to chose the appropriate method for the desired degree of robustness. The existing three approaches thereby constitute rather extreme characteristics. As the name implies, the $\text{HypE}_{no.\,rob.}$ approach only finds non-robust solutions, but in exchange con-

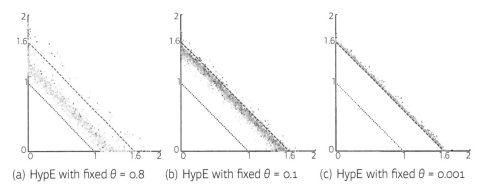

(a) HypE with fixed $\theta = 0.8$ (b) HypE with fixed $\theta = 0.1$ (c) HypE with fixed $\theta = 0.001$

Figure 6.10 Solutions of 100 runs each on BZ1. The dotted line indicates the Pareto front, the dashed line the best robust front.

verges further to the Pareto optimal front. However, the approaches Alg_{ao}, $Alg_{classes}$, and Alg_{rsv} considering robustness (at least for some solutions), outperform $HypE_{no.\,rob.}$ in some regions even with respect to non-robust solutions: the Alg_{rsv} finds better solutions for low values of f_2, while the other two approaches outperform the $HypE_{no.\,rob.}$ algorithm on bridges around $f_2 = 10\,\mathrm{m}$. Considering robustness as an additional objective leads to a large diversity of robustness degrees, however, misses solutions with small values of f_2. This might be due to the choice of the reference point of the hypervolume indicator, and the fact that only 25 solutions are used. $Alg_{classes}$ optimizes five robustness degrees, two of which are classified as non-robust—these two are lying close together because the robustness level of the second last class with $\eta_4 = 0.1$ does barely restrict the objective values. Despite—or perhaps because of—the Alg_{rsv} algorithm also keeping non-robust solutions, the robust front is superior to the one of the Alg_{con} algorithm. The HypE approach with θ decreasing to .001 advances even further. The result of the $Alg_{sim.\,ann.}$ algorithm does not differ much from the Alg_{con} approach and is therefore not shown.

Influence of the Desirability Function φ

As the previous section showed, the robustness integrating HypE seems to, at least for small θ, have advantages over Alg_{con}. Another advantage is its ability to adjust the trade-off between robustness and objective value

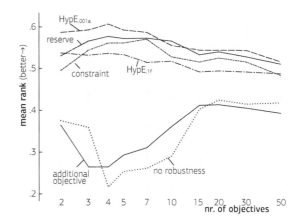

Figure 6.11 Average Kruskal-Wallis ranks over all WFG test problems at the robustness level $\eta = 0.01$ for different number of objectives.

quality. Figure 6.10 shows the influence of different θ on the robustness and quality of the found solutions on BZ1. For this test problem, the robustness of solutions increases with distance to the (linear) Pareto front, see Appendix E.2. Only when choosing $\theta < 0.1$, solutions robust at the constraint level are obtained. In the following a version with θ fixed to 0.1 is used (referred to as HypE$_{.1f}$), and a version with θ decreasing to 0.001 (referred to as HypE$_{.001a}$).

Performance Score over all Testproblems

To obtain a more reliable view of the potential of the different algorithms, the comparison is extended to all test problems. To this end, the performance score $P(\mathcal{A}_i)$ of an algorithm i is calculated as outlined in Section 6.5.1. Table 6.2 shows the performance on the six BZ, the nine WFG, and five instances of the bridge problem. Overall, HypE$_{.001a}$ reaches the best performance, followed by HypE$_{.1f}$, $Alg_{classes}$, and Alg_{rsv}. All four algorithms show a better performance than Alg_{con}.

Hence, not only are two modifications of the constraint approach ($Alg_{classes}$, Alg_{rsv}) able to outperform the existing constraint approach, but the robustness integrating hypervolume indicator as well is overall significantly better than Alg_{con}.

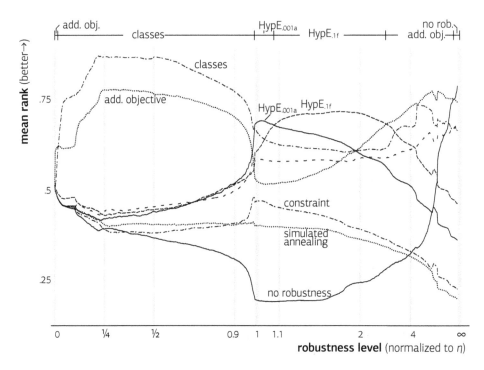

Figure 6.12 Average Kruskal-Wallis ranks over all BZ, WFG, and bridge test problems combined for different degrees of robustness. The best algorithm for a particular robustness level are indicated on top.

On the bridge problem, $HypE_{.001a}$ performs best and is significantly better than the other three algorithms. In case of Alg_{rsv}, and Alg_{con}, it is better in nearly 100% of all runs. On WFG, $Alg_{classes}$ overall performs best. An exception are WFG6-8, where the other three algorithms are all better. On BZ1, 3 and 5, $HypE_{.001a}$ and Alg_{con} perform best, on the remaing BZ problems Alg_{rsv} works best.

Application to Higher Dimensions

All algorithms proposed are not restricted to biobjective problems, but can also be used on problems involving more objectives. Since the runtime increases exponentially with the number of objectives, HypE is applied (Sections 4.3 and 6.4.4) to optimize the hypervolume when facing more than three objectives. Figure 6.11 shows the mean Kruskal-Wallis rank for a selected subset of algorithms at different number of objectives. The algorithm HypE$_{.001a}$ shows the best performance except for 10 objectives, where the mean rank of the Alg_{rsv} approach is larger (although not significantly). Except for 7 and 20 objectives, HypE$_{.001a}$ is significantly better than Alg_{con}. On the other hand, HypE$_{.1f}$ performs worse than the constraint approach for all considered number of objectives except the biobjective case. This might indicate, that the parameter θ in Eq. 6.3 needs to be decreased with the number of objectives, because the trade-off between objective values and robustness is shifted towards objective value in higher dimensions. However, further investigations need to be carried out to show the influence of θ when increasing the number of objectives.

Performance over Different Robustness Levels

In the previous comparisons, solutions robust at the predefined level have been considered. Next, the influence of loosening or tightening up this constraint is investigated. Figure 6.12 illustrates the mean hypervolume rank, normalized such that 0 corresponds to the worst, and 1 to the best quality. The mean ranks are shown for different levels of robustness ρ, normalized such that the center corresponds to the level optimized. For levels of robustness stricter than η, $Alg_{classes}$ reaches the best hypervolume values. Around η, HypE$_{.001a}$ performs best and further decreasing the robustness level, HypE$_{.1f}$ overtakes. Further decreasing the robustness, Alg_{ao}, and finally HypE$_{no.\,rob.}$ are the best choices.

Optimizing Multiple Robustness Classes

Although $Alg_{classes}$ proved useful even when only one of its optimized classes are considered afterwards, the main strength of this approach shows when actually rating the hypervolume of the different classes optimized. Table 6.3 lists the performance scores for the different classes averaged over all test problems of BZ, WFG, and truss bridge. Using $Alg_{ind.\,runs}$ is significantly worse than the remaining approaches considered. This indicates, that optimizing multiple robustness levels concurrently is beneficial regardless of the robustness integration method used. Overall, $Alg_{classes}$ reaches the best

Table 6.3 Comparison of the algorithms: $Alg_{ind.\,runs}$, Alg_{ao}, $HypE_{no.\,rob.}$, and $Alg_{classes}$. For each optimized class the sum of the performance score is reported for each of the three considered problem suites BZ, WFG, and the bridge problem.

		$Alg_{ind.\,runs}$	Alg_{ao}	$HypE_{no.\,rob.}$	$Alg_{classes}$
.01	BZ	0	3	3	3
	Bridge	8	10	3	3
.001	WFG	3	5	8	2
.03	BZ	10	4	17	2
	Bridge	8	10	1	4
.003	WFG	8	11	13	6
.1	BZ	13	4	17	1
	Bridge	8	10	1	4
.01	WFG	13	15	12	5
.3	BZ	10	4	17	2
	Bridge	10	8	0	5
.03	WFG	18	12	12	6
∞	BZ	17	9	3	5
	Bridge	12	6	1	5
	WFG	27	11	1	14
Total		**177**	**135**	**112**	**69**

total performance (69), the algorithms scores best on all classes except the one without robustness ($\eta = \infty$), where $HypE_{no.\,rob.}$ outperforms the other algorithms.

Application to Real World Truss Bridge Problem

In conclusion of this experimental study, the algorithms from Section 6.4 are compared on the truss bridge problem in more detail. First, Figure 6.13 shows the distribution of hypervolume at the optimized robustness level $\eta = 0.02$. In contrast to Section 6.5, the hypervolume is not normalized and larger values correspond to better algorithms.

The two HypE variants $HypE_{.001a}$, and $HypE_{.1f}$ reach the largest hypervolume of 3.37 and 3.28 respectively, the difference not being statistically significant. Both algorithms are significantly better than the $Alg_{classes}$ algorithm, which in turns is better than Alg_{ao}, and Alg_{rsv}. Alg_{con} and $Alg_{sim.\,ann.}$ follow on the last place, only $HypE_{no.\,rob.}$ reaches a lower hypervolume value by only finding non-robust solutions.

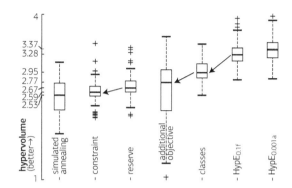

Figure 6.13 Comparison of algorithms on the truss bridge problem. Larger hypervolume values indicate better Pareto set approximations. The HypE$_{no.\,rob.}$ approach reached only unstable bridges, and therefore has obtained a zero hypervolume. Algorithms separated by an arrow are statistically significant, e.g., Alg_{ao} and $Alg_{sim.\,ann.}$.

When relaxing the robustness constraint by 10% to $\eta = 0.022$, the lead of the HypE$_\theta$ algorithms over Alg_{con} even increases: the latter finds no solutions exceeding the constraint, and, consequently, the hypervolume does not further increase. The HypE approaches, on the other hand, trade-off robustness and objective values to a certain extend, such that some solutions slightly exceed the robustness constraint. When relaxing the robustness constraint, these solutions start contributing to the hypervolume: the hypervolume of HypE$_{.1f}$ increases by 1.2%. Because of using a very strict final constraint level, the hypervolume of HypE$_{.001a}$ barely increases (0.006%). Alg_{ao} profits the most (+5%) since the algorithm does not optimize specific to the constraint.

All undominated[6] stable solutions were found by one of the two HypE algorithms (not shown). As far as the best unstable bridges are concerned, most undominated solutions were found by the HypE$_{no.\,rob.}$ algorithm. However, Alg_{rsv} and Alg_{ao} also found Pareto-optimal unstable bridges, e.g., the three cases presented in the following.

Figure 6.14 shows the stable and unstable bridge with the largest structural efficiency. Both solutions are half-through arch bridges crossing the decks with vertical arch ribs, resembling a *Marsh arch bridge* [127]. The unstable bridge uses two chords: the first supports the three joints at the center of the bridge, the second supports the next two joints. The joints closest

---

[6] considering all solutions of all algorithms and runs combined.

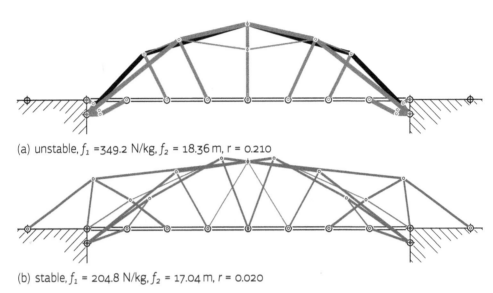

(a) unstable, f_1 = 349.2 N/kg, f_2 = 18.36 m, r = 0.210

(b) stable, f_1 = 204.8 N/kg, f_2 = 17.04 m, r = 0.020

Figure 6.14 Best stable and unstable bridge with large height, the unstable was found by Alg_{ao}, the stable by $HypE_{.001a}$.

to the banks are supported from below. The robust bridge is also a half-through arch bridge, however, uses a different design: first off, all members are thinner, which make them less susceptible to noise, see Eq. E.1. Secondly, the bridge uses a third arch, spanning from the additional nodes. Finally, instead of supporting the decks with only one hanger as for the non-robust solution, two diagonal hangers connect the center decks. These modifications make the bridge ten times more robust than the unstable one, but also decrease the structural efficiency from 349.2 N/kg to 204.8 N/kg.

In Figure 6.15, a stable and an unstable bridge are shown with medium rise. As for the bridges in Figure 6.14, robustness is achieved by decreasing the cross-sectional area of the members, by adding an additional half-through arch, and by rearranging the ribs.

Finally, Figure 6.16 compares the best stable and unstable bridge with minimum rise, i.e., zero height over the middle of the bridge. Both design vary a lot form the half-through bridges shown before. The unstable design

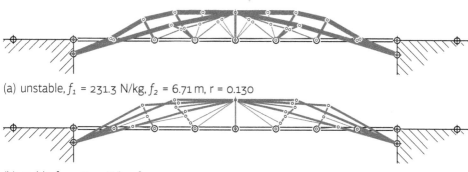

(a) unstable, f_1 = 231.3 N/kg, f_2 = 6.71 m, r = 0.130

(b) stable f_1 = 162.2 N/kg, f_2 = 7.03 m, r = 0.02

Figure 6.15 Best stable and unstable bridge with medium height, the unstable was found by Alg_{rsv}, the stable by $HypE_{.001a}$.

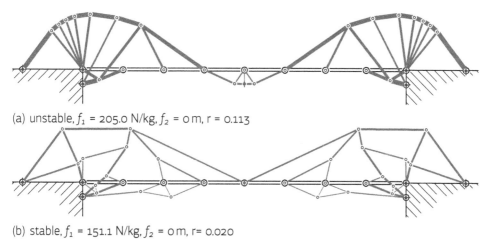

(a) unstable, f_1 = 205.0 N/kg, f_2 = 0 m, r = 0.113

(b) stable, f_1 = 151.1 N/kg, f_2 = 0 m, r = 0.020

Figure 6.16 Best stable and unstable bridge with medium height, the unstable was found by Alg_{rsv}, the stable by $HypE_{.001a}$.

resembles a suspension bridge with pylons at the edge of the abutments. However, the pylons consist of many members that give the suspension cable an arch like shape. An inverted arch supports the two centermost decks, which nicely fits the rest of the structure and gives the bridge not only the largest structural efficiency among all solutions found, but also an aesthetically appealing look.

The robust counterpart also relies on a structure similar to a suspension bridge, but has a less smooth look than the unstable bridge. All members are thinner. In addition to the suspension, the bridge uses a deck truss to support joints from below the roadbed.

6.6 · Summary

This chapter has shown different ways of translating existing robustness concepts to hypervolume-based search, including the traditional approaches: (i) modification of objective values, (ii) considering robustness as an additional objective, and (iii) as an additional constraint. For the latter, three modifications are suggested to overcome premature convergence. Secondly, an extended definition of the hypervolume indicator has been proposed that allows to realize the three approaches, but can also be adjusted to more general cases, thereby flexibly adjusting the trade-off between robustness and objective values while still being able to focus on a particular robustness level. To make this new indicator applicable to problems involving a large number of objectives, an extension of HypE (Hypervolume Estimation Algorithm for Multiobjective Optimization) has been presented.

An extensive comparison has been made on WFG test problems, a novel test problem suite that tests different aspects of robustness, and a new real world bridge problem that provides an intuitive way to assess visually the quality and robustness of solutions. As statistical tests and visual results revealed, the novel hypervolume indicator not only offers more flexibility than traditional approaches, but also outperforms the plain constraint approach. A visual comparisons of the structural properties of the solutions on the bridge problem showed the potential of the proposed approaches even on highly demanding types of problems.

Furthermore, a new algorithm has been proposed to optimize multiple constraints at the same time. In experiments, this approach proved to be beneficial in comparison to doing independent runs.

7

Conclusions

Optimization problems involving many—often conflicting—objectives arise naturally in many practical applications. Multiobjective Evolutionary Algorithms (MOEAs) are one class of search techniques, that has been successfully applied to these types of problems. They aim at approximating the set of Pareto-optimal trade-off solutions, which helps the decision maker in selecting good compromise solution(s), but also to better understand the problem structure.

In recent years, MOEAs based on the Hypervolume Indicator (HI) have become increasingly popular. The hypervolume indicator combines two preferable properties: (i) it transform the multiobjective problem into a single-objective one while taking Pareto dominance into account, (ii) the indicator can express arbitrary user preference.

The aim of the present thesis was to (a) investigate the properties of the HI, (b) generalize its definition to also be able to consider robustness issues, and (c) to widen its application area to problems with large numbers of objectives by proposing a new algorithms.

7.1 · Key Results

In detail, the four major contributions outlined in the following have been made—concerning not only the HI, but also other problems in its context.

7.1.1 · The Hypervolume Indicator as Set Preference Relation

The present thesis has shown that most existing MOEAs can be considered as hill climbers on set problems, implicitly based on preference relations on sets. In this context, the thesis investigated how set preference can be formalized on the basis of quality indicators, and illustrated the importance of generating relations that refine Pareto dominance. A general procedure has been proposed to construct preference relations that fulfill this requirement. Considering the properties of set preference relations has thereby reinforced the usefulness of the HI, as it can be used to refine other indicator-based preference relations.

Moreover, a general algorithm framework has been presented to optimize set preference relations, which separates algorithm design from the articulation of preference relations, thereby providing a great deal of flexibility. This framework has been extended allowing to optimize multiple sets concurrently, showing benefits in terms of the obtained Pareto set approximations but also in terms of simplifying parallelization of the method thus leading to a reduced computation time. A statistical comparison methodology has been proposed that simplifies the performance assessment of algorithms with respect to the underlying preference relation.

7.1.2 · Characterizing the Set Maximizing the Hypervolume

In the light of the growing proliferation of algorithms relying on the HI, it is important to know the *bias* of the indicator. This thesis has provided rigorous results on the question, how Pareto-optimal solutions to biobjective problems are distributed when maximizing the HI. In particular, the influence of (i) the reference point, (ii) the shape of the Pareto front, and (iii) the weight function of the HI has been investigated. The result made evident that the HI is insensitive to the way the front is bent (convex or concave), and that the distribution of solutions only depends on the slope of the front which contradicts previous assumptions. Furthermore, it has been shown that for some front shapes, the extremes are never contained in optimal distributions of solutions, regardless of the choice of the reference point. For the remaining cases, lower bounds for the reference point have been given that guarantee the existence of extremal solutions in optimal distributions.

7.1.3 · Considering Robustness Within Hypervolume-Based Search

While this thesis relied on the existing concept of the weighted HI to express user preference, no method existed so far to consider robustness issues within hypervolume-based search. To this end, an extension of the HI has been proposed. This generalized hypervolume indicator thereby allows to trade-off flexibly the quality of solutions in terms of objective values with their robustness, enabling to consider robustness in many ways. As has been demonstrated, the generalized HI also allows to realize three prevalent existing approaches within hypervolume-based algorithms.

7.1.4 · Fast Algorithms using the Hypervolume Indicator

To employ the beneficial properties of the hypervolume, this thesis has proposed the Hypervolume Estimation Algorithm for Multiobjective Optimization (HypE)—a fast algorithm relying on sampling. This algorithm enables to apply the HI to problems involving large number of objectives, where so far the high computational effort for calculating the hypervolume has prevented the application of the indicator. Furthermore, special attention has been given on how to use the weighted hypervolume indicator in the context of HypE—enabling to incorporate user preference—, and how to use the generalized definition of the HI—enabling to consider the robustness of solutions. Extensive comparisons in the corresponding setting have shown the potential of this novel algorithm.

7.2 · Discussion

The author hopes that the present thesis enhances knowledge of the hypervolume indicator and widens its field of application, thereby contributing to the increasing propagation of the indicator. Most results in this thesis have two aspects: on the one hand, they increase the theoretical knowledge of the indicator or add a new feature, on the other hand they have practical implications.

The new set-based view on MOEAs has investigated theoretically set preference relations, stressing the importance of preference relations being a refinement of Pareto-dominance—which is fulfilled by the Hypervolume Indicator (HI). Being the only indicator known so far, fulfilling the refinement property, gives one reason for the increasing popularity of the indicator. On the other hand, extensive comparisons of MOEAs have shown, that the refinement property of the HI is not only of theoretical interest, but also leads to better Pareto-set approximations on many-objective problems than approaches like NSGA-II or SPEA2 not having the refinement property. Thereby, the proposed algorithm SPAM$^+$, operating on multiple sets of solutions at the same time, might form the basis of other algorithms that pick up the novel set-based perspective.

The benefits of characterizing the optimal set in terms of a density is twofold: first off, it disproved many prevailing beliefs on the HI by describing the bias of the indicator in a concise way hardly to be surpassed by the knowledge of any other MOEA. This knowledge helps to predict the outcome of algorithms. Secondly, the characterization provides a way of translating user preference to a corresponding weighted HI, where arbitrary user preference can be realized in a very concise manner. This might help to develop new preference based algorithms that are both very flexible in terms of the expressed preference, and at the same time very precise.

Proposing a generalized definition of the HI enables the incorporation of the robustness of solutions into the hypervolume in many ways, including three existing possibilities. Moreover, the generalized definition has the potential to open new ways to also incorporate other properties of solutions into hypervolume-based search—an ongoing study by the author and colleagues for instances addresses the consideration of diversity by the generalized HI.

Complementary to the extended definition of the HI and the theoretical investigation of its property, the proposal of HypE widens the area of application of the hypervolume to problems involving a large number of objectives. In the light of the desirable properties of the HI, this new algorithm might help to solve many problems not tackled so far. Hopefully, HypE also forms the basis of development of advanced algorithms addressing preference articulation, robustness consideration or other issues yet to be translated to the HI.

7.3 · Future Perspectives

With respect to the Hypervolume Indicator (HI), still many questions remain open. Some of these question are already subject to ongoing research.

- Probably the most eminent feature of the hypervolume is its property of refining Pareto dominance. Hence, the question arises whether other indicators exist (not based on the hypervolume) that share this property. Such an indicator would be particularly attractive for search, if the indicator were easily calculable even for high dimensional spaces, such that no approximation schemes are necessary as for the HI. Although no proof exists showing that the HI is unique with respect to the refinement property, the author disbeliefs that another such indicator exists, let alone an indicator fast computable and still being as versatile as the HI.
- Seeing the advantages of the hypervolume, an interesting research question is whether other existing approaches—especially in the field of preference articulation—can be expressed by the HI.
- The theoretical results provided with the density hold for biobjective problems only. A conjecture has been stated in this thesis concerning the density for arbitrary number of objectives. However, no proof of the formula has been given. Especially, knowing the influence of the weight function on the density of points is of importance, as this helps expressing user preference by a weighted HI.

- Although the new advanced fitness scheme employed by HypE facilitates approximating the hypervolume, the employed sampling strategy is very basic, as it does not include advanced techniques, e.g., sampling according to Latin Hypercubes, nor does the method use adaptive sampling—although a preliminary procedure has been investigated by the author and colleagues in [7].

Appendix

A · Statistical Comparison of Algorithms

Throughout the present thesis, the following procedure is mostly used to compare different Multiobjective Evolutionary Algorithms (MOEAs). Let A_i with $1 \leq i \leq l$ denote the l algorithms to be compared. For each algorithm A_i, the same number r of independent runs is carried out for g_{max} generations.

A.1 · Step 1: Determining the Hypervolume of All Pareto-Set Approximations

The quality of Pareto-set approximations is assessed using the hypervolume indicator, where for less than 6 objectives the indicator values are calculated exactly and otherwise approximated by Monte Carlo sampling in the following manner: let A denote the set of solutions whose hypervolume needs to be approximated, and let $I_H(A, R)$ denote the hypervolume of A with respect to the reference set R. Then

1. first an axis-aligned hyperrectangle S^r is defined containing the objective vectors of all algorithms, as well as all reference points $r \in R$, see Section 4.1.2 on page 118.
2. Thereafter, m samples s_i, $i \leq 1 \leq m$, are randomly uniformly generated within the hyperrectangle $s_i \in S^r$. For each sample, it is determined whether it is dominated by the set of solutions under consideration, i.e., whether $f(A) \leqslant s_i$ holds.
3. Given the ratio of dominated to undominated samples, an approximation of the hypervolume indicator $\hat{I}_H(A, R)$ then is given by:
   $$\hat{I}_H(A, R) = \frac{|\{t \in \{s_1, \ldots, s_m\} \mid f(A) \leqslant t\}|}{m} \lambda(S^r)$$
   where $\lambda(S^r)$ denotes the Lebesgue measure or hypervolume of S^r.

When sampling is used, uncertainty of measurement is introduced which can be expressed by the standard deviation of the sampled value, which is $\sigma_{\hat{I}} = \lambda(S^r) \sqrt{p(1-p)/m}$, where p denotes the hit probability of the sampling process, i.e., the ratio of dominate samples to the total number of samples used. Unless noted otherwise, 1 000 000 samples are used per Pareto-set approximation. For a typical hit probability between 10% to 90% observed in praxis, this leads to a very small uncertainty below 10^{-3} times $I_H(A, R)$. Hence, it is highly unlikely that the uncertainty will influence the statistical test applyied to the hypervolume estimates, and if it does nonetheless, the statistical tests are over-conservative [39]. Therefore, uncertainty is not considered in the following test.

A.2 · Step 2: Determining Statistically Significant Differences

For formal reason, the null hypothesis that all algorithms are equally well suited to approximate the Pareto-optimal set is investigated first, using the Kruskal-Wallis test at a significance level of α. Let $h_{i,j}$ denote the calculated or approximated hypervolume of the Pareto set approximation of algorithm A_i in run j. Let $N := l \cdot r$ denote the total number of runs. Then, all hypervolume values are rank-ordered, where $R(h_{i,j})$ denotes the rank of value $h_{i,j}$ starting with 1 representing the largest value to N representing the worst hypervolume. If several hypervolume results are equal to each other, the mean rank is assigned to all of them. For each algorithm A_i, the rank sum is then calculated $R_i = \sum_{k=1}^{r} R(h_{i,k})$, $1 \leq i \leq l$.

Given the mean ranks R_i, the test statistic T is

$$T = \frac{1}{S^2} \left(\left(\frac{1}{r} \sum_{i=1}^{l} R_i^2 \right) - \frac{N(N+1)^2}{4} \right)$$

with

$$S^2 = \frac{1}{N-1} \left(\left(\sum_{i=1}^{l} \sum_{j=1}^{r} R(h_{i,j})^2 \right) - \frac{N(N+1)^2}{4} \right)$$

As an approximation for the null distribution of T, the chi-squared distribution with $l - 1$ degrees of freedom is used; if T is greater than the $1 - \alpha$ quantile from the χ_{l-1}^2-distribution, the hypothesis is accepted at the level α, that at least on of the l algorithms yields larger hypervolume values than at least one other algorithm.

When comparing algorithms, to show the sole presence of a difference is insuffient. Rather one wants to know, which one of two algorithms A_i and A_j is better. To this end, for all pairs of algorithms the difference in median of the hypervolume values is compared by the Conover-Inman post-hoc procedure [39], using the same confidence level α as for the Kruskal-Wallis test. This test states, that the difference in hypervolume of two algorithms A_i and A_j is statistically significant, if

$$\left| \frac{R_i - R_j}{r} \right| > t_{1-(\alpha/2)} \sqrt{\left(S^2 \frac{N-1-T}{N-l} \right) \frac{2}{r}} \tag{A.1}$$

holds, where $t_{1-\alpha/2}$ is the $(1 - \alpha/2)$ quantile of the t distribution with $N - l$ degrees of freedom.

A.3 · Step 3: Calculating the Performance Score

Let $\delta_{i,j}$ be 1, if A_i turns out to be significantly better than A_j according to Eq. A.1, and 0 otherwise. Based on $\delta_{i,j}$, for each algorithm A_i the performance index $P(A_i)$ is determined as follows:

$$P(A_i) = \sum_{\substack{j=1 \\ j \neq i}}^{l} \delta_{i,j}$$

Hence, the value $P(A_i)$ reveals, how many other algorithms are significantly better than A_i on the specific test case. The smaller the index, the better the algorithm; an index of zero means that no other algorithm generated significantly better Pareto-set approximations in terms of the hypervolume indicator, while the worst performance of $l-1$ indicates, that all other algorithms are significantly better.

B · Complementary Proofs to Section 2

B.1 · Proof of Theorem 2.15 on page 34

In order to prove Theorem 2.15 on page 34 first a set of smaller results has to be stated:

Lemma B.1: *If all preference relations $\preccurlyeq^j$, $1 \leq j \leq k$ in Definition 2.14 are preorders, then $\preccurlyeq_S$ is a preorder.*

Proof. Reflexivity: As $A \preccurlyeq^i A$ holds for all $1 \leq i \leq k$ (since all $\preccurlyeq^i$ are preorders), it follows $i = k$ in Definition 2.14 (i). Therefore, $(A \preccurlyeq_S A) \Leftrightarrow (A \preccurlyeq^i A)$ and the reflexivity holds. Transitivity is proven by induction. First, it needs to be shown that transitivity holds for $k = 1$. In this case, one has $A \preccurlyeq_S B \Leftrightarrow A \preccurlyeq^1 B$ as $i = k$ in Definition 2.14 (i). Transitivity holds as $\preccurlyeq^1$ is a preorder. Now one has to show that transitivity holds for k if it holds for $k-1$. Let us define the sequence of length $k-1$ as S'. Then one can reformulate Definition 2.14 as follows:

$$(A \preccurlyeq_S B) \Leftrightarrow ((A \equiv_{S'} B) \wedge (A \preccurlyeq^k B)) \vee (A \prec_{S'} B) \tag{B.2}$$

Now, one can show that transitivity holds:

$$(A \preccurlyeq_S B) \wedge (B \preccurlyeq_S C) \Rightarrow$$
$$\Rightarrow [((A \equiv_{S'} B) \wedge (A \preccurlyeq^k B)) \vee (A \prec_{S'} B)] \wedge$$
$$[((B \equiv_{S'} C) \wedge (B \preccurlyeq^k C)) \vee (B \prec_{S'} C)] \Rightarrow$$
$$\Rightarrow ((A \equiv_{S'} B) \wedge (B \equiv_{S'} C) \wedge (A \preccurlyeq^k B) \wedge (\preccurlyeq^k C)) \vee$$
$$((A \prec_{S'} B) \wedge (B \prec_{S'} C)) \Rightarrow$$
$$\Rightarrow ((A \equiv_{S'} C) \wedge (A \preccurlyeq^k C)) \vee (A \prec_{S'} C) \Rightarrow A \preccurlyeq_S C$$

$\square$

Lemma B.3: *If all preference relations $\preccurlyeq^j$, $1 \leq j \leq k$ in Definition 2.14 are total preorders, then $\preccurlyeq_S$ is a total preorder.*

Proof. A preorder $\preccurlyeq$ is called total if $(A \preccurlyeq B) \vee (B \preccurlyeq A)$ holds for all $A, B \in \Psi$. Using the same induction principle as in the proof of B.1 one can notice that for $k = 1$ one has $(A \preccurlyeq_S B) \Leftrightarrow (A \preccurlyeq^1 B)$ and therefore, $\preccurlyeq_S$ is total. For the induction it is known that Eq. B.2 holds. Therefore, it follows

$$(A \preccurlyeq_S B) \vee (B \preccurlyeq_S A) \Leftrightarrow$$
$$\Leftrightarrow ((A \equiv_{S'} B) \wedge (A \preccurlyeq^k B)) \vee ((B \equiv_{S'} A) \wedge (B \preccurlyeq^k A)) \vee$$
$$(A \prec_{S'} B) \vee (B \prec_{S'} A) \Leftrightarrow$$
$$\Leftrightarrow (A \equiv_{S'} B) \vee (A \prec_{S'} B) \vee (B \prec_{S'} A) \Leftrightarrow \text{true}$$

$\square$

Lemma B.5: *If $\preccurlyeq^k$ in Definition 2.14 is a refinement of a given preference relation $\preccurlyeq$ and all relations $\preccurlyeq^j$, $1 \leq j < k$ are weak refinements of $\preccurlyeq$, then $\preccurlyeq_S$ is a refinement of $\preccurlyeq$.*

Proof. Let us suppose that $A \prec B$ holds for some $A, B \in \Psi$. It needs to be shown that $A \prec_{S'} B$ holds. At first note, the $A \preccurlyeq^j B$ holds for all $1 \leq j < k$ as $\preccurlyeq^j$ are weak refinements and $A \prec^k B$ holds as $\preccurlyeq^k$ is a refinement. Let us now consider the sequence S' of length $k - 1$. Because all $\preccurlyeq^j$ are weak refinements, either $A \equiv^j B$ or $A \prec^j B$ holds. Taking into account the construction of S' according to Definition 2.14 one can easily see that $A \preccurlyeq_{S'} B$ holds. Based on the fact that $\preccurlyeq_{S'}$ is a weak refinement it will be shown that $A \prec_S B$ holds, i.e. $\prec_S$ is a refinement. To this end, again Eq. B.2 is used to derive

$$(A \preccurlyeq_S B) \wedge (B \not\preccurlyeq_S A) \Leftrightarrow \qquad\qquad (B.3)$$
$$\Leftrightarrow [((A \equiv_{S'} B) \wedge (A \preccurlyeq^k B)) \vee (A \prec_{S'} B)] \wedge$$
$$((B \not\equiv_{S'} A) \vee (B \not\preccurlyeq^k A)) \wedge (A \not\prec_{S'} B)$$

As $\preccurlyeq_{S'}$ is a weak refinement, two cases need to be considered. If $A \equiv_{S'} B$ holds, then $A \not\prec_{S'} B$ holds as well as $B \not\prec_{S'} A$. In this case, the expression becomes $(A \preccurlyeq^k B) \wedge (B \not\preccurlyeq^k A)$ which yields true. If $A \prec_{S'} B$ holds, then $A \not\equiv_{S'} B$, $B \not\equiv_{S'} A$ and $B \not\prec_{S'} A$ hold. The expression above becomes now $(A \prec_{S'} B) \wedge (B \not\prec_{S'} A)$ which also yields true. $\qquad\square$

Now the proof of Theorem 2.15 can be given.

Proof. Because of Lemma B.5, it is known that the sequence $S' = (\preccurlyeq^1, \preccurlyeq^2, \dots, \preccurlyeq^{k'})$ leads to a refinement of $\preccurlyeq$. One just needs to show that additional preference relations $\preccurlyeq^j$, $k' < j \le k$ in the sequence do not destroy this property. Again the same induction principle is used as in the previous proofs. Let us suppose that S' yields a refinement (as shown above) and S has one additional relation $\preccurlyeq^{k'+1}$, i.e. $k = k' + 1$. Using again Eq. B.2 one can derive the expression for $A \prec_S B$ as in Eq. B.3. Supposing that $A \prec B$ holds in the given preorder, and $\preccurlyeq_{S'}$ is a refinement, the relations $A \not\equiv_{S'} B$, $B \not\equiv_{S'} A$, $A \prec_{S'} A$ and $B \not\prec_{S'} A$ hold. For the expression in Eq. B.3 it follows $(A \preccurlyeq^k B) \wedge (B \not\preccurlyeq^k A)$ which yields true. $\qquad\square$

B.2 · Proof of Theorem 2.19 on Page 36

Proof. Suppose conditions 1 and 2 hold, and let $A, B \in \Psi$ be two arbitrary sets with $A \prec B$, i.e. $(A \preccurlyeq B) \wedge (B \not\preccurlyeq A)$. For the proof, the two local transformations are applied in order to gradually change B to A and show that at each step the indicator value does not decrease and there is at least one step where it increases. First, the elements of B are successively added to A; since for each $b \in B$ it holds $A \preccurlyeq \{b\}$, according to condition 1 the indicator value remains constant after each step, i.e., $I(A) = I(A \cup B)$. Now, the elements of A are successively added to B; since $A \prec B$, there exists an element $a \in A$ such that $B \not\preccurlyeq \{a\}$ according to the conformance of $\preccurlyeq$ with $\preccurlyeq$. That means when adding the elements of A to B the indicator value either remains unchanged (condition 1) or increases (and it will increase at least once, namely for a, according to condition 2), and therefore $I(A \cup B) > I(B)$. Combining the two intermediate results, one obtains $I(A) = I(A \cup B) > I(B)$ which implies $A \preccurlyeq_I B$ and $B \not\preccurlyeq_I A$. Hence, $\preccurlyeq_I$ refines $\preccurlyeq$. For weak refinement, the proof is analogous.

To the prove that the second condition is a necessary condition, suppose $A \not\preccurlyeq \{b\}$. According to Definition 2.11, $(A \cup \{b\}) \prec A$ which implies that $(A \cup \{b\}) \preccurlyeq_I A$ (weak refinement) respectively $(A \cup \{b\}) \prec_I A$ (refinement). Hence, $I(A \cup \{b\}) \ge I(A)$ respectively $I(A \cup \{b\}) > I(A)$ according to Eq. 2.1. $\qquad\square$

C · Complementary Material to Chapter 3

C.1 · Proof of Theorem 3.8 stated on page 80

Before to prove the result, Eq. 3.1 (page 76) is rewritten in the following way

$$I_H^w(u_1, \ldots, u_\mu) = \sum_{i=1}^{\mu} g(u_i, u_{i+1}) \ , \tag{C.4}$$

where g is the 2-dimensional function defined as

$$g(\alpha, \beta) = \int_\alpha^\beta \int_{g(\alpha)}^{g(u_0)} w(u, v) dv \ du \ . \tag{C.5}$$

The derivation of the gradient of I_H^w thus relies on computing the partial derivatives of g. The following lemma gives the expressions of the partial derivative of g:

Lemma C.1: *Let w be a weight function for the weighted hypervolume indicator I_H^w and $g :$ $[u_{min}, u_{max}] \to \mathbb{R}$ be a continuous and differentiable function describing a 2-dimensional Pareto front. Let h be defined as*

$$h(\alpha, \beta) := \int_\alpha^\beta \int_{g(\alpha)}^{g(u_0)} w(u, v) dv du$$

where $g(u_0) = r_2$. Then,

$$\partial_1 h(\alpha, \beta) = -g'(\alpha) \int_\alpha^\beta w(u, g(\alpha)) du - \int_{g(\alpha)}^{g(u_0)} w(\alpha, v) dv \tag{C.6}$$

$$\partial_2 h(\alpha, \beta) = \int_{g(\alpha)}^{g(u_0)} w(\beta, v) dv$$

Proof. To compute the first partial derivative of h, the derivative of the function $h_1 :$ $\alpha \to h(\alpha, \beta)$ has to be computed. Let us define

$$\gamma(l, m) := \int_{g(m)}^{g(u_0)} w(l, v) dv$$

such that

$$h_1(\alpha) := \int_\alpha^\beta \gamma(u, \alpha) du \ .$$

Define

$$K(\bar{u}, \bar{v}) = \int_{\bar{u}}^\beta \gamma(u, \bar{v}) du$$

and be $\Phi : \alpha \in \mathbb{R} \to (\alpha, \alpha) \in \mathbb{R}^2$. Then $h_1(\alpha) = K \circ \Phi(\alpha)$ such that the chain rule can be applied to find the derivative of h_1. Hence, for any $q \in \mathbb{R}$ it holds

$$h_1'(\alpha) q = D_{\Phi(\alpha)} K \circ D_\alpha \Phi(q) \tag{C.7}$$

where $D_\alpha \Phi$ (resp. $D_{\Phi(\alpha)} K$) are the differential of Φ (resp. K) in α (resp. $\Phi(\alpha)$). Therefore, the differentials of Φ and K need to be calculated. Since Φ is linear, $D_\alpha \Phi = \Phi$ and thus

$$D_\alpha \Phi(q) = (q, q) \ . \tag{C.8}$$

Moreover, the differential of K can be expressed with the partial derivatives of K, i.e., $D_{(\bar{u}, \bar{v})} K(q_1, q_2) = (\nabla K) \cdot (q_1, q_2)$ where ∇ is the vector differential operator $\nabla = \left(\frac{\partial}{\partial u_1}, \ldots, \frac{\partial}{\partial u_n} \right) = (\partial_1, \ldots, \partial_n)$ and $(q_1, q_2) \in \mathbb{R}^2$. Hence,

$$D_{(\bar{u}, \bar{v})} K(q_1, q_2) = \partial_1 K(\bar{u}, \bar{v}) \, q_1 + \partial_2 K(\bar{u}, \bar{v}) \, q_2.$$

Thus, the partial derivatives of K is needed. From the fundamental theorem of calculus, $\partial_1 K(\bar{u}, \bar{v}) = -\gamma(\bar{u}, \bar{v})$. Besides, $\partial_2 K(\bar{u}, \bar{v}) = \int_{\bar{u}}^{\beta} \partial_2 \gamma(u, \bar{v}) du$ and therefore

$$D_{(\bar{u}, \bar{v})} K(q_1, q_2) = -\gamma(\bar{u}, \bar{v}) q_1 + \left(\int_{\bar{u}}^{\beta} \partial_2 \gamma(u, \bar{v}) du \right) q_2.$$

Applying again the fundamental theorem of calculus to compute the second partial derivative of γ, one finds that

$$\partial_2 \gamma(u, \bar{v}) = -g'(\bar{v}) w(u, g(\bar{v}))$$

and thus

$$D_{(\bar{u}, \bar{v})} K(q_1, q_2) = \left(- \int_{g(\bar{v})}^{g(u_0)} w(\bar{u}, v) dv \right) q_1 + \left(\int_{\bar{u}}^{\beta} -g'(\bar{v}) w(u, g(\bar{v})) du \right) q_2. \tag{C.9}$$

Combining Eq. C.9 and Eq. C.8 in Eq. C.7 one obtains

$$\partial_1 h(\alpha, \beta) = h_1'(\alpha) = -g'(\alpha) \int_\alpha^\beta w(u, g(\alpha)) du - \int_{g(\alpha)}^{g(u_0)} w(\alpha, v) dv$$

which gives Eq. C.6.

To compute the second partial derivative of h, one needs to compute, for any α, the derivative of the function $h_2 : \beta \to h(\alpha, \beta)$. The function h_2 can be rewritten as $h_2 : \beta \to \int_\alpha^\beta \theta(u) du$ where

$$\theta(u) := \int_{g(\alpha)}^{g(u_0)} w(u, v) dv \ .$$

Therefore, from the fundamental theorem of calculus it follows that $\partial_2 h(\alpha, \beta) = h_2'(\beta) = \theta(\beta)$ and thus

$$\partial_2 h(\alpha, \beta) = \int_{g(\alpha)}^{g(u_0)} w(\beta, v) dv \ .$$

$\square$

Now Theorem 3.8 can be proven

Proof. From the first order necessary optimality conditions follows that if $(v_1^\mu, \ldots, v_\mu^\mu)$ maximizes Eq. 3.1, then either v_i^μ belongs to $]u_{min}, u_{max}[$ and the i-th partial derivative of $I_H^w(v_1^\mu, \ldots, v_\mu^\mu)$ equals zero in v_i^μ, or v_i^μ belongs to the boundary of $[u_{min}, u_{max}]$, i.e., $v_i^\mu = u_{min}$ or $v_i^\mu = u_{max}$. Therefore, the partial derivatives of I_H^w needs to be computed. From Eq. C.4 follows: $\partial_1 I_H^w(v_1^\mu, \ldots, v_\mu^\mu) = \partial_1 h(v_1^\mu, v_2^\mu)$, and from Lemma C.1 therefore follows:

$$\partial_1 I_H^w(v_1^\mu, \ldots, v_\mu^\mu) = -g'(v_1^\mu) \int_{v_1^\mu}^{v_2^\mu} w(u, g(v_1^\mu)) du - \int_{g(v_1^\mu)}^{g(v_0^\mu)} w(v_1^\mu, v) dv$$

and thus if $v_1^\mu \neq u_{min}$ and $v_1^\mu \neq u_{max}$, by setting the previous equation to zero, one obtains the condition

$$-g'(v_1^\mu) \int_{v_1^\mu}^{v_2^\mu} w(u, g(v_1^\mu) du = \int_{g(v_1^\mu)}^{g(v_0^\mu)} w(v_1^\mu, v) dv \ .$$

For $2 \leq i \leq \mu$, $\partial_i I_H^w(v_1^\mu, \ldots, v_\mu^\mu) = \partial_2 h(v_{i-1}^\mu, v_i^\mu) + \partial_1 h(v_i^\mu, v_{i+1}^\mu)$. Using Lemma C.1 one obtains

$$\partial_i I_H^w(v_1^\mu, \ldots, v_\mu^\mu) = \int_{g(v_{i-1}^\mu)}^{g(v_0^\mu)} w(v_i^\mu, v) dv - g'(v_i^\mu) \int_{v_i^\mu}^{v_{i+1}^\mu} w(u, g(v_i^\mu)) du$$

$$- \int_{g(v_i^\mu)}^{g(v_0^\mu)} w(v_i^\mu, v) dv \ .$$

Gathering the first and last term of the right hand side, one obtains

$$\partial_i I_H^w(v_1^\mu, \ldots, v_\mu^\mu) = \int_{g(v_{i-1}^\mu)}^{g(v_i^\mu)} w(v_i^\mu, v) dv - g'(v_i^\mu) \int_{v_i^\mu}^{v_{i+1}^\mu} w(u, g(v_i^\mu)) du \qquad (C.10)$$

and thus if $v_{i+1}^\mu \neq u_{min}$ and $v_{i+1}^\mu \neq u_{max}$, by setting the previous equation to zero, one obtains

$$\int_{g(v_{i-1}^\mu)}^{g(v_i^\mu)} w(v_i^\mu, v) dv = g'(v_i^\mu) \int_{v_i^\mu}^{v_{i+1}^\mu} w(u, g(v_i^\mu)) du \ . \qquad \square$$

C.2 · Proof of Lemma 3.15 stated on page 84

Proof. Let us first note that the Cauchy-Schwarz inequality implies that

$$\int_0^{u_{max}} \frac{|g'(u)w(u, g(u))|}{|\delta(u)|} du \leq \sqrt{\int_0^{u_{max}} \left(g'(u)w(u, g(u))\right)^2 du \int_0^{u_{max}} (1/\delta(u))^2 du} \qquad (C.11)$$

and since $u \to g'(u)w(u, g(u)) \in L^2(0, u_{max})$ and $\frac{1}{\delta} \in L^2(0, u_{max})$, the right-hand side of Eq. C.11 is finite and Eq. 3.8 is well-defined. The proof is divided into two steps.

First, E_μ is rewritten and, in a second step, the limit result is derived by using this new characterization of E_μ.

Step 1: In a first step it is proven that E_μ defined in Eq. 3.7 satisfies

$$E_\mu = \mu \sum_{i=0}^{\mu} \left(-\tfrac{1}{2} g'(v_i^\mu) w(v_i^\mu, g(v_i^\mu))(v_{i+1}^\mu - v_i^\mu)^2 + O\big((v_{i+1}^\mu - v_i^\mu)^3\big) \right) \tag{C.12}$$

To this end, the front is elongated to the right such that g equals $g(u_{max}) = 0$ for $u \in [u_{max}, v_{\mu+1}^\mu]$. Like that,

$$\int_0^{u_{max}} \int_0^{g(u)} w(u,v)dvdu = \sum_{i=0}^{\mu} \int_{v_i^\mu}^{v_{i+1}^\mu} \int_0^{g(u)} w(u,v)\, dv\, du \ , \tag{C.13}$$

while using the fact that $\int_{u_{max}}^{v_{\mu+1}^\mu} \int_0^{g(u)} w(u,v)\, dv\, du = 0$. Using the right hand side of Eq. C.13 in Eq. 3.7, one finds that

$$E_\mu = \mu \left[\sum_{i=0}^{\mu} \int_{v_i^\mu}^{v_{i+1}^\mu} \left(\int_0^{g(v_i^\mu)} w(u,v)\, dv \right) du - \sum_{i=0}^{\mu} \int_{v_i^\mu}^{v_{i+1}^\mu} \left(\int_0^{g(u)} w(u,v)\, dv \right) du \right]$$

and thus

$$E_\mu = \mu \sum_{i=0}^{\mu} \int_{v_i^\mu}^{v_{i+1}^\mu} \int_{g(u)}^{g(v_i^\mu)} w(u,v)\, dv\, du \ . \tag{C.14}$$

At the first order, it follows

$$\int_{g(u)}^{g(v_i^\mu)} w(u,v)dv = w(v_i^\mu, g(v_i^\mu))(g(v_i^\mu) - g(u)) + O((u - v_i^\mu)) \ . \tag{C.15}$$

Since g is differentiable, a Taylor approximation of g can be applied in each interval $[v_i^\mu, v_{i+1}^\mu]$ which gives $g(u) = g(v_i^\mu) + g'(v_i^\mu)(u - v_i^\mu) + O((u - v_i^\mu)^2)$, which thus implies that

$$g(v_i^\mu) - g(u) = -g'(v_i^\mu)(u - v_i^\mu) + O((u - v_i^\mu)^2)$$

and thus the left hand side of Eq. C.15 becomes

$$-w(v_i^\mu, g(v_i^\mu))g'(v_i^\mu)(u - v_i^\mu) + O((u - v_i^\mu)^2) \ .$$

By integrating the previous equation between v_i^μ and v_{i+1}^μ one obtains

$$\int_{v_i^\mu}^{v_{i+1}^\mu} \int_{g(u)}^{g(v_i^\mu)} w(u,v)\, dv\, du = -\frac{1}{2} w(v_i^\mu, g(v_i^\mu))g'(v_i^\mu)(v_{i+1}^\mu - v_i^\mu)^2 + O((v_{i+1}^\mu - v_i^\mu)^3) \ .$$

Summing up for $i = 0$ to $i = \mu$, multiplying by μ and using Eq. C.14, one obtains Eq. C.12, which concludes Step 1.

Step 2: Now, $\frac{1}{2}\int_0^{u_{max}}\frac{g'(u)w(u,g(u))}{\delta(u)}du$ is decomposed into

$$\frac{1}{2}\sum_{i=0}^{\mu-1}\int_{v_i^{\mu}}^{v_{i+1}^{\mu}}\frac{g'(u)w(u,g(u))}{\delta(u)}du + \frac{1}{2}\int_{v_{\mu}^{\mu}}^{u_{max}}\frac{g'(u)w(u,g(u))}{\delta(u)}du \ .$$

For the sake of convenience in the notations, for the remainder of the proof, $v_{\mu+1}^{\mu}$ is redefined as u_{max} such that the decomposition becomes

$$\frac{1}{2}\int_0^{u_{max}}\frac{g'(u)w(u,g(u))}{\delta(u)}du = \frac{1}{2}\sum_{i=0}^{\mu}\int_{v_i^{\mu}}^{v_{i+1}^{\mu}}\frac{g'(u)w(u,g(u))}{\delta(u)}du \tag{C.16}$$

For μ to ∞, the assumption $\mu \sup((\sup_{0\leq i\leq \mu-1}|v_{i+1}^{\mu}-v_i^{\mu}|),|u_{max}-v_{\mu}^{\mu}|)\to c$ implies that the distance between two consecutive points $|v_{i+1}^{\mu}-v_i^{\mu}|$ as well as $|v_{\mu}^{\mu}-u_{max}|$ converges to zero. Let $u\in[0,u_{max}]$ and let us define for a given μ, $\varphi(\mu)$ as the index of the points such that $v_{\varphi(\mu)}^{\mu}$ and $v_{\varphi(\mu)+1}^{\mu}$ surround u, i.e., $v_{\varphi(\mu)}^{\mu}\leq u < v_{\varphi(\mu)+1}^{\mu}$. Because assuming that δ is continuous, a first order approximation of $\delta(u)$ is $\delta(v_{\varphi(\mu)}^{\mu})$, i.e.

$$\delta(u) = \delta(v_{\varphi(\mu)}^{\mu}) + O(v_{\varphi(\mu)+1}^{\mu}-v_{\varphi(\mu)}^{\mu})$$

and therefore by integrating between $v_{\varphi(\mu)}^{\mu}$ and $v_{\varphi(\mu)+1}^{\mu}$ one obtains

$$\int_{v_{\varphi(\mu)}^{\mu}}^{v_{\varphi(\mu)+1}^{\mu}}\delta(u)du = \delta(v_{\varphi(\mu)}^{\mu})(v_{\varphi(\mu)+1}^{\mu}-v_{\varphi(\mu)}^{\mu}) + O(v_{\varphi(\mu)+1}^{\mu}-v_{\varphi(\mu)}^{\mu})^2) \ . \tag{C.17}$$

Moreover by definition of the density δ, Eq. C.17 approximates the number of points contained in the interval $[v_{\varphi(\mu)}^{\mu},v_{\varphi(\mu)+1}^{\mu}[$ (i.e. one) normalized by μ:

$$\mu\int_{v_{\varphi(\mu)}^{\mu}}^{v_{\varphi(\mu)+1}^{\mu}}\delta(u)du = 1 + O((v_{\varphi(\mu)+1}^{\mu}-v_{\varphi(\mu)}^{\mu})) \ . \tag{C.18}$$

Using Eq. C.17 and Eq. C.18, it follows

$$\frac{1}{\delta(v_{\varphi(\mu)}^{\mu})} = \mu(v_{\varphi(\mu)+1}^{\mu}-v_{\varphi(\mu)}^{\mu}) + O(\mu(v_{\varphi(\mu)+1}^{\mu}-v_{\varphi(\mu)}^{\mu})^2) \ .$$

Therefore for every i

$$\frac{1}{\delta(v_i^{\mu})} = \mu(v_{i+1}^{\mu}-v_i^{\mu}) + O(\mu(v_{i+1}^{\mu}-v_i^{\mu})^2) \ . \tag{C.19}$$

Since $u\to g'(u)w(u,g(u))/\delta(u)$ is continuous, one also obtains

$$\int_{v_i^{\mu}}^{v_{i+1}^{\mu}}\frac{g'(u)w(u,g(u))}{\delta(u)}du = \frac{g'(v_i^{\mu})w(v_i^{\mu},g(v_i^{\mu}))}{\delta(v_i^{\mu})}(v_{i+1}^{\mu}-v_i^{\mu}) + O((v_{i+1}^{\mu}-v_i^{\mu})^2) \ .$$

Injecting Eq. C.19 in the previous equation, one obtains

$$\int_{u_i^{\mu}}^{u_{i+1}^{\mu}}\frac{g'(u)w(u,g(u))}{\delta(u)}du = \mu g'(v_i^{\mu})w(v_i^{\mu},g(v_i^{\mu}))(v_{i+1}^{\mu}-v_i^{\mu})^2 + O(\mu(v_{i+1}^{\mu}-v_i^{\mu})^3) \ .$$

Multiplying by $1/2$ and summing up for i from 0 to μ and using Eq. C.12 and Eq. C.16, one obtains

$$\frac{1}{2}\int_0^{u_{max}}\frac{g'(u)w(u,g(u))}{\delta(u)}=-E_\mu+\sum_{i=0}^{\mu}O(\mu(v_{i+1}^\mu-v_i^\mu)^3) \ . \tag{C.20}$$

Let us define Δ_μ as $\sup((\sup_{0\leq i\leq\mu-1}|v_{i+1}^\mu-v_i^\mu|),|u_{max}-v_\mu^\mu|)$. By assumption, it is known that $\mu\Delta_\mu$ converges to a positive constant c. The last term of Eq. C.20 satisfies

$$\left|\sum_{i=0}^{\mu}O(\mu(v_{i+1}^\mu-v_i^\mu)^3)\right|\leq K\mu^2(\Delta_\mu)^3$$

where $K>0$. Since $\mu\Delta_\mu$ converges to c, $(\mu\Delta_\mu)^2$ converges to c^2. With Δ_μ converging to 0, one therefore has that $\mu^2\Delta_\mu^3$ converges to 0. Taking the limit in Eq. C.20 one therefore obtains

$$-\frac{1}{2}\int_0^{u_{max}}\frac{g'(u)w(u,g(u))}{\delta(u)}du=\lim_{\mu\to\infty}E_\mu \ . \qquad\qquad \square$$

C.3 · Proof of Theorem 3.17 on Page 85

Proof. First the differential of E with respect to the density δ is computed, denoted by $DE_\delta(h)$. Let $h\in L^2(0,u_{max})$. Then,

$$E(\delta+h)=-\frac{1}{2}\int_0^{u_{max}}\frac{w(u,g(u))g'(u)}{\delta(u)+h(u)}du$$

$$=-\frac{1}{2}\int_0^{u_{max}}\frac{w(u,g(u))g'(u)}{\delta(u)\left(1+\frac{h(u)}{\delta(u)}\right)}du \ .$$

Due to the Taylor expansion of $\frac{1}{1+y}\overset{y\to0}{=}1-y+O(y)$ this equals

$$E(\delta+h)=-\frac{1}{2}\int_0^{u_{max}}\frac{w(u,g(u))g'(u)}{\delta(u)}\left(1-\frac{h(u)}{\delta(u)}+O\left(\|h(u)\|\right)\right)du$$

$$=-\frac{1}{2}\int_0^{u_{max}}\frac{w(u,g(u))g'(u)}{\delta(u)}du+\frac{1}{2}\int_0^{u_{max}}\frac{w(u,g(u))g'(u)h(u)}{\delta(u)^2}du$$

$$-\frac{1}{2}\int_0^{u_{max}}\frac{w(u,g(u))g'(u)}{\delta(u)}O\left(\|h(u)\|\right)du$$

$$=E(\delta)+\frac{1}{2}\int_0^{u_{max}}\frac{w(u,g(u))g'(u)h(u)}{\delta(u)^2}du+O\left(\|h(u)\|\right) \ .$$

Since $h\to\frac{1}{2}\int_0^{u_{max}}w\frac{g'h}{\delta^2}du$ is linear in h, is is known from differential calculus that

$$DE_\delta(h)=\frac{1}{2}\int_0^{u_{max}}\frac{w(u,g(u))g'(u)}{\delta(u)^2}h(u)du \ .$$

In a similar way,

$$J(\delta + h) = \int_0^{u_{max}} (\delta(u) + h(u))\, du$$

$$= \int_0^{u_{max}} \delta(u)du + \int_0^{u_{max}} h(u)du$$

$$= J(\delta) + \int_0^{u_{max}} h(u)du$$

and as $h \to \int_0^{u_{max}} h(u)du$ is linear, the differential of J equals

$$DJ_\delta(h) = \int_0^{u_{max}} h(u)du \ .$$

From the the Lagrange multiplier theorem for Banach spaces [132], it is known that there exists a $\lambda \in \mathbb{R}$ such that the solution of P satisfies

$$\forall h : DE_\delta(h) + \lambda DJ_\delta(h) = 0$$

that can be rewritten as

$$\forall h : \frac{1}{2} \int_0^{u_{max}} \frac{w(u, g(u))g'(u)}{\delta(u)^2} h(u)du + \lambda \int_0^{u_{max}} h(u)du = 0$$

or

$$\forall h : \int_0^{u_{max}} \left(\frac{1}{2} \frac{w(u, g(u))g'(u)}{\delta(u)^2} + \lambda \right) h(u)du = 0 \ . \tag{C.21}$$

Since a solution for P has to satisfy Eq. C.21 for all h, it is known for the choice of $h(u) = \frac{1}{2}\frac{w(u,g(u))g'(u)}{\delta(u)^2} + \lambda$ that

$$\int_0^{u_{max}} \left(\frac{1}{2} \frac{w(u, g(u))g'(u)}{\delta(u)^2} + \lambda \right)^2 du = 0$$

holds which in turn implies that

$$\frac{1}{2} \frac{g'}{\delta^2} w + \lambda = 0$$

or in other words that

$$\delta(u) = \sqrt{-w(u, g(u))g'(u)}/\sqrt{2\lambda}$$

where the constant λ is still to be determined. It is known that δ is a density and needs therefore to satisfy that $\int_0^{u_{max}} \delta(u)du = 1$. Then, one can determine the missing $\sqrt{2\lambda}$ from

$$1 = \int_0^{u_{max}} \delta(u)du = \int_0^{u_{max}} \frac{\sqrt{-w(u, g(u))g'(u)}}{\sqrt{2\lambda}} du$$

$$= \frac{1}{\sqrt{2\lambda}} \int_0^{u_{max}} \sqrt{-w(u, g(u))g'(u)}du$$

Figure C.1 Illustrates the *shadow* of an objective vector *z*, i.e., the part on the front dominating *z*. In 2d (left) the shadow is a line, while in 3d (right) it is a triangle. In general, the shadow is an affine *d*-1-simplex, given by the vertices b_i.

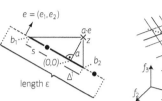

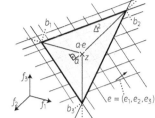

as

$$\sqrt{2\lambda} = \int_0^{u_{max}} \sqrt{-w(u, g(u))g'(u)}\,du$$

which yields then

$$\delta(u) = \frac{\sqrt{-w(u, g(u))g'(u)}}{\int_0^{u_{max}} \sqrt{-w(u, g(u))g'(u)}\,du} \qquad \square$$

C.4 · Considerations Leading to Conjecture 3.22 on Page 90

In the following, the considerations leading to Conjecture 3.22 are presented. The presented content is by no means mathematically formal, however, the considerations might give indications how to formally extend the density formula to arbitrary numbers of objectives.

Biobjective Case

Consider an arbitrary small segment Δ^1 of the front with length $\varepsilon \ll 1$. Provided the front is "smooth", the line segment can be regarded as being linear. Furthermore, let the weight function w and the density δ_{Δ^1}[1] be constant in this region, i.e., the functions must not jump. The hypervolume above the front segment corresponds to the Lebesgue measure of all objective vectors dominated. Consider one such objective vector z at distance a from the front, and the probability of z being dominated. Let the *shadow* Δ^1 of z be the line segment on the front dominating z, see Figure C.1. The objective vector z is dominated, iff at least one point of the optimal μ-distribution lies in the shadow. The number of points in the shadow is thereby given by $\mu\delta_{\Delta^1} \cdot s$, where s denotes the length of Δ^1, i.e., $s = \lambda(\Delta^1)$. If this number is greater 1, then the objective vector is dominated. If the number is smaller 1, it gives the percentage of objective vectors at distance a, that are dominated. For instance, if $\mu\delta_{\Delta^1} \cdot s = 0.2$, then for 20%

---

[1]The notation δ_{Δ_1} is used here for short to refer to the density on the front segment, i.e., $\delta_{\Delta_1} = \delta(x)$, $x \in \Delta_1$

of considered line segments the objective vector will be dominated, or in other words, the probability of a given z at distance a being dominated is **20%**.

The length of a segment can be determined by considering the extremes of the line denoted b_1, b_2 with the smallest f_1 and f_2 value respectively. Let the line segment be determined by the normal vector (e_1, e_2), i.e., $(z_1^\Delta, z_2^\Delta)(e_1, e_2) = 0$ holds for all points (z_1^Δ, z_2^Δ) on the front segment, and let the point $(0,0)$ lie on the line segment Δ^1. Furthermore, let the considered objective vector z lie at $a \cdot (e_1, e_2)$. Then, $b_1 = a(-e_2^2/e_1, e_2)$, and $b_2 = a(e_1, -e_1^2/e_2)$ respectively, see Figure C.1. Hence, the length of shadow Δ^1 of an objective z at distance a from the front segment, given by the normal vector (e_1, e_2) is:

$$s_e(a) = \|b_1 - b_2\| = a \frac{(e_1^2 + e_2^2)^{3/2}}{e_1 e_2} = a \frac{1}{e_1 e_2} =: a \cdot \gamma \quad \gamma := \frac{1}{e_1 e_2}$$

(The last step follows from the fact, that e is a unit vector and $e_1^2 + e_2^2 = 1$). Hence, the shadow linearly increases with distance a. Let $\tilde{a} = 1/(\mu \delta_{\Delta 1} \gamma)$ denote the distance for which the number of points on the line segment becomes 1. All objective vectors at distance $a \geq \tilde{a}$ will be dominated, while for the remaining cases the probability is $\mu \delta_{\Delta 1} s_e(a)$. Hence, the undominated area K above the line segment is:

$$K = \varepsilon \int_0^{\tilde{a}} (1 - \mu \delta_{\Delta 1} s_e(x)) w \, dx = \varepsilon \int_0^{\tilde{a}} (1 - \mu \delta_{\Delta 1} x \gamma) w \, dx = \varepsilon \frac{w}{2 \mu \delta_{\Delta 1} \gamma}$$

Now consider a second line segment on a different part of the front. Let superscripts $'$, and $''$ refer to variables of the first and second segment. Then the overall undominated area becomes $K_{\text{total}} = K' + K'' = \varepsilon w'/(2\mu \delta'_{\Delta 1} \gamma') + \varepsilon w''/(2\mu \delta''_{\Delta 1} \gamma'')$. Let the total number of points in both segments is $\mu \delta'_{\Delta 1} \varepsilon + \mu \delta''_{\Delta 1} \varepsilon$ be constant. Given this constraint, the undominated area K_{total} must be minimal for the given densities, otherwise one could increase the hypervolume by moving points from one segment to the other, hence

$$\delta'_{\Delta 1}, \delta''_{\Delta 1} = \arg \min_{\delta'_{\Delta 1}, \delta''_{\Delta 1}} K_{total}, \text{ given } \mu \delta'_{\Delta 1} \varepsilon + \mu \delta''_{\Delta 1} \varepsilon = C \ .$$

Using the Lagrange multiplier $\nabla_{x,y,l} \Lambda(x, y, l) = 0$, with

$$\Lambda(\delta'_{\Delta 1}, \delta''_{\Delta 1}, l) = \varepsilon w'(2\mu \delta'_{\Delta 1} \gamma')^{-1} + \varepsilon w''(2\mu \delta''_{\Delta 1} \gamma'')^{-1} + l(\delta'_{\Delta 1} + \delta''_{\Delta 1} - C)\mu \varepsilon \ ,$$

one obtains the following two equations

$$\frac{\partial K_{\text{total}}}{\partial \delta'_{\Delta 1}} = -\frac{\varepsilon w'}{2\gamma' \mu (\delta'_{\Delta 1})^2} + l \mu \varepsilon \stackrel{!}{=} 0 \qquad \frac{\partial K_{\text{total}}}{\partial \delta''_{\Delta 1}} = -\frac{\varepsilon w''}{2\gamma'' \mu (\delta''_{\Delta 1})^2} + l \mu \varepsilon \stackrel{!}{=} 0$$

hence

$$\frac{\gamma'(\delta'_{\Delta 1})^2}{w'} = \frac{\gamma''(\delta''_{\Delta 1})^2}{w''} \Rightarrow \frac{\delta'_{\Delta 1}}{\delta''_{\Delta 1}} = \frac{(w'/\gamma')^{1/2}}{(w''/\gamma'')^{1/2}}$$

Since this holds for all line segment pairs $'$, and $''$, one obtains

$$\delta_F(z^*) \propto (w(z^*)/\gamma^*)^{1/2} = \sqrt{w(z^*) \cdot e_1^* e_2^*}$$

where z^* denotes a point on the Pareto-front, while $w(z^*)$ and (e_1^*, e_2^*) denote the weight and normal vector at z^* respectively.

Example C.6: Consider the formulation $(u, g(u))$ for fronts as introduced in Section 3.2. Then $e = \frac{1}{\sqrt{1+g'^2}}(-g', 1)$ and

$$\delta_F(u) \propto \sqrt{w(u)\frac{-g'(u)}{(1+g'(u)^2)} \cdot 1} \ .$$

Hence, the result agrees with Eq. 3.10 on page 86.   o

Arbitrary Dimensionality d

Consider an arbitrary number of objectives d, and a d-1 dimensional front. Consider again an arbitrary small portion Δ^{d-1} of the front. Again let w and δ_Δ be constant in the considered region and the front be linear, expressed by the normal vector $e = (e_1, \cdots, e_d)$. Let the considered objective vector z be at $a(e_1, \ldots, e_d)$. Then the vertices of the shadow Δ^{d-1} are obtained by intersecting $a(e_1, \cdots, e_{i-1}, \beta, e_{i+1}, \cdots, e_d)$, $1 \leq i \leq d$, $\beta \in \mathbb{R}$ with the front, which gives the vertices

$$b_i = a(e_1, \ldots, e_{i-1}, e_i - 1/e_i, e_{i+1}, \cdots, e_d)$$
$$= ae + (0, \ldots, 0, -a/e_i, 0, \ldots, 0) \tag{C.22}$$

From Eq. C.22 it follows, that the vertices give an affine $(d-1)$-simplex. For example, the case $d = 3$ shown in Figure C.1 leads to a triangular shadow, while for $d = 4$ the shadow is a tetrahedron. Hence, the (hyper-)volume of Δ^{d-1} is

$$s_e(a) = \lambda(\Delta^{d-1}) = a^{d-1}\frac{1}{(d-1)! \prod_{i=1}^{d} e_i} =: a^{d-1} \cdot \gamma \quad \gamma := \frac{1}{(d-1)! \prod_{i=1}^{d} e_i}$$

The distance $\tilde{a}$, for which the number of points in the simplex becomes 1, is

$$\mu\delta_\Delta s_e(a) \overset{!}{=} 1 \Rightarrow \tilde{a} = (\mu\delta_\Delta\gamma)^{-1/(d-1)}$$

and the undominated area becomes

$$K = \varepsilon \int_0^{\tilde{a}} (1 - \mu\delta_\Delta a^{d-1}\gamma)w dx = \frac{\varepsilon(d-1)w}{d(\mu\delta_\Delta\gamma)^{1/d-1}}$$

Determining K for two different regions on the front and taking the sum again gives the minimization problem

$$\min_{\delta_\Delta', \delta_\Delta''} K_{\text{total}} = K' + K'' = \frac{\varepsilon(d-1)w'}{d(\mu\delta_\Delta'\gamma')^{1/(d-1)}} + \frac{\varepsilon(d-1)w''}{d(\mu\delta_\Delta''\gamma'')^{1/d-1}} \text{ given } \mu\varepsilon(\delta_\Delta' + \delta_\Delta'') = C$$

Using Lagrange multipliers as for the biobjective case, and with

$$\frac{\partial K}{\partial \delta_\Delta} = -\frac{\varepsilon w}{d(\mu\delta_\Delta\gamma)^{1/(d-1)}\delta_\Delta}$$

the following equation results

$$-\frac{\varepsilon w'}{d(\mu \delta'_\Delta \gamma')^{1/(d-1)} \delta'_\Delta} + \lambda \mu \varepsilon = -\frac{\varepsilon w''}{d(\mu \delta''_\Delta \gamma'')^{1/(d-1)} \delta''_\Delta} + \lambda \mu \varepsilon ,$$

and therefore

$$\frac{\delta'_\Delta}{\delta''_\Delta} = \frac{w'/(\gamma')^{1/d}}{w''/(\gamma'')^{1/d}} \tag{C.23}$$

Since Eq. C.23 holds for all considered pairs of front segments, the density is

$$\delta(z^*) \propto (w(z^*)/\gamma^*)^{1/d} \propto \sqrt[d]{w(z^*) \cdot \prod_1^d e_i^*}$$

C.5 · Proof of Theorem 3.26 on Page 92

In order to proof the theorem, the following corollary is stated which directly follows from the continuity of the density:

Corollary C.7: *As the number of point μ increases to infinity, the hypervolume contribution $C_a = I_h(a, A)$ of all points $a \in A$ approaches zero.*

Proof. Let the contribution of a point a be denoted as C_a. Then, C_a is given by Eq. C.24, see Figure C.2. By the continuity of the density, both ε_a and ζ_a converge to zero. Since by assumption $|g'(u_a)| < \infty$ also $g(u_a - \varepsilon_a) - g(u_a)$ converges to zero, such that integration domain converges to a null set. Because the weight function is finite, C_a therefore converges to 0. □

The previous corollary will be used in the following to proof Theorem 3.26:

Proof. Let $g(u)$ denote the Pareto front and let $(v_i^\mu, g(v_i^\mu))$, $(v_j^\mu, g(v_j^\mu))$ be two points that belong to an optimal distribution of μ points on the front g. Let the distances to the left neighbor (v_{i-1}^μ resp. v_{j-1}^μ) of these points be ε_i and ε_j respectively and the distances to the right neighbor (v_{i+1}^μ resp. v_{j+1}^μ) be ζ_i and ζ_j respectively, see Figure C.2. Let $w(u, v)$ denote the weight function. Let C_i and C_j denote the contribution of the points v_i^μ and v_j^μ to the overall hypervolume, i.e.

$$C_a = \int\limits_{g(u_a)}^{g(u_a - \varepsilon_a)} \int\limits_{u_a}^{u_a + \zeta_a} w(u, v) du dv \qquad a \in \{i, j\} \tag{C.24}$$

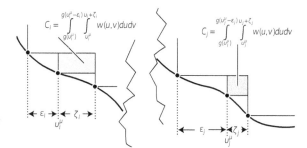

Figure C.2 Two hypervolume contributions C_i and C_j on different parts of the same front $g(u)$.

and let $\overline{w_a}(u,v)$ and $\underline{w_a}(u,v)$ with $a = \{i,j\}$ denote the supremum and infimum respectively of $w(u,v)$ inside the domain of C_a, i.e.,

$$w_a(u,v) := \sup_{\substack{u_a \leq u \leq u_a+\zeta_a \\ g(u_a) \leq v \leq g(u_a-\varepsilon_a)}} w(u,v) \qquad\qquad a \in \{i,j\} \tag{C.25}$$

$$\underline{w_a}(u,v) := \inf_{\substack{u_a \leq u \leq u_a+\zeta_a \\ g(u_a) \leq v \leq g(u_a-\varepsilon_a)}} w(u,v). \tag{C.26}$$

Using Eq. C.25 and Eq. C.26, the contribution C_a according to Eq. C.24 can be upper and lower bounded by

$$C_a \in \left[\Omega \underline{w_a}(u,v), \Omega_a \overline{w_a}(u,v)\right] \text{ with } \Omega_a := \zeta_a \cdot (g(u_a - \varepsilon_a) - g(u_a)), a \in \{i,j\}$$

hence

$$\frac{\Omega_i \underline{w_i}(u,v)}{\Omega_j \overline{w_j}(u,v)} \leq \frac{C_i}{C_j} \leq \frac{\Omega_i \overline{w_i}(u,v)}{\Omega_j \underline{w_j}(u,v)} \ . \tag{C.27}$$

In the following, the left hand side of Eq. C.27 is considered as $\mu \to \infty$; the same derivations will also hold analogously for the right hand side. Injecting Ω_a into the left hand side of Eq. C.27 gives

$$\frac{\Omega_i \underline{w_i}(u,v)}{\Omega_j \overline{w_j}(u,v)} = \frac{\zeta_i \cdot (g(v_i^\mu - \varepsilon_i) - g(v_i^\mu))\underline{w_i}(u,v)}{\zeta_j \cdot (g(v_j^\mu - \varepsilon_j) - g(v_j^\mu))\overline{w_j}(u,v)}$$

and replacing $g(v_a^\mu - \varepsilon_a) - g(v_a^\mu)$ by a Taylor approximation leads to

$$= \frac{\zeta_i \cdot (-\varepsilon_i g'(v_i^\mu) + \varepsilon_i^2 g''(v_i^\mu) + \ldots) \cdot \underline{w_i}(u,v)}{\zeta_j \cdot (-\varepsilon_j g'(v_j^\mu) + \varepsilon_j^2 g''(v_j^\mu) + \ldots) \cdot \overline{w_j}(u,v)} \ .$$

According to the definition of the density $\delta(u)$ (see Theorem 3.17 on page 85) ζ_a and ε_a are given by $\zeta_a = 1/\mu\delta(v_a^\mu)$ and $\varepsilon_a = 1/\mu\delta(v_{a-1}^\mu)$ respectively, where $a = \{i, j\}$. Hence,

$$\lim_{\mu\to\infty} \frac{\Omega_i \underline{w_i}(u,v)}{\Omega_j \overline{w_j}(u,v)} = \lim_{\mu\to\infty} \frac{\frac{1}{\mu\delta(v_i^\mu)} \cdot (-\frac{1}{\mu\delta(v_{i-1}^\mu)} g'(v_i^\mu) + \frac{1}{\mu^2\delta(v_{i-1}^\mu)^2} g''(v_i^\mu) - \ldots) \cdot \underline{w_i}(u,v)}{\frac{1}{\mu\delta(v_j^\mu)} \cdot (-\frac{1}{\mu\delta(v_{j-1}^\mu)} g'(v_j^\mu) + \frac{1}{\mu^2\delta(v_{j-1}^\mu)^2} g''(v_j^\mu) - \ldots) \cdot \overline{w_j}(u,v)}$$

$$= \lim_{\mu\to\infty} \frac{\delta(v_j^\mu)\delta(v_{j-1}^\mu) \cdot (-g'(v_i^\mu) + \frac{1}{\mu\delta(v_{i-1}^\mu)} g''(v_i^\mu) - \ldots) \cdot \underline{w_i}(u,v)}{\delta(v_i^\mu)\delta(v_{i-1}^\mu) \cdot (-g'(v_j^\mu) + \frac{1}{\mu\delta(v_{j-1}^\mu)} g''(v_j^\mu) - \ldots) \cdot \overline{w_j}(u,v)}$$

$$= \lim_{\mu\to\infty} \frac{\delta(v_j^\mu)\delta(v_{j-1}^\mu) \cdot g'(v_i^\mu) \cdot \underline{w_i}(u,v)}{\delta(v_i^\mu)\delta(v_{i-1}^\mu) \cdot g'(v_j^\mu) \cdot \overline{w_j}(u,v)} \; ,$$

and provided that both limits exist (they do as shown below) one can write

$$= \frac{g'(v_i^\mu)}{g'(v_j^\mu)} \cdot \lim_{\mu\to\infty} \frac{\delta(v_j^\mu)\delta(v_{j-1}^\mu)}{\delta(v_i^\mu)\delta(v_{i-1}^\mu)} \cdot \lim_{\mu\to\infty} \frac{\underline{w_i}(u,v)}{\overline{w_j}(u,v)} \; . \tag{C.28}$$

Due to the continuity of $\delta(u)$ as the number of points increases to infinity one has $\delta(v_a^\mu) \to \delta(v_{a-1}^\mu)$ for $a = i, j$. Hence the first limit becomes

$$\lim_{\mu\to\infty} \frac{\delta(v_j^\mu)\delta(v_{j-1}^\mu)}{\delta(v_i^\mu)\delta(v_{i-1}^\mu)} = \frac{\delta(v_j^\mu)^2}{\delta(v_i^\mu)^2}$$

which is according to the density formula in Eq. 3.9 on page 85

$$= \frac{g'(v_j^\mu) w(v_j^\mu, g(v_j^\mu))}{g'(v_i^\mu) w(v_i^\mu, g(v_i^\mu))} \; . \tag{C.29}$$

For the second limit, from Corollary C.7 and the assumption of a continuous weight function it follows

$$\lim_{\mu\to\infty} \frac{\underline{w_i}(u,v)}{\overline{w_j}(u,v)} = \frac{w(v_i^\mu, g(v_i^\mu))}{w(v_j^\mu, g(v_j^\mu))} \; . \tag{C.30}$$

Injecting Eq. C.29 and Eq. C.30 into Eq. C.28 finally gives

$$\lim_{\mu\to\infty} \frac{\Omega_i \underline{w_i}(u,v)}{\Omega_j \overline{w_j}(u,v)} = \frac{g'(v_i^\mu)}{g'(v_j^\mu)} \cdot \frac{g'(v_j^\mu) w(v_j^\mu, g(v_j^\mu))}{g'(v_i^\mu) w(v_i^\mu, g(v_i^\mu))} \cdot \frac{w(v_i^\mu, g(v_i^\mu))}{w(v_j^\mu, g(v_j^\mu))} = 1 \; .$$

Therefore, $C_i/C_j \geq 1$. By exchanging the supremum and infimum in Eq. C.30, it follow also that $C_i/C_j \leq 1$. From the squeeze theorem one therefore obtains $\lim_{\mu\to\infty} C_i/C_j = 1$ which means that every point has the same hypervolume contribution. $\square$

C.6 · Proof of Theorem 3.29 Stated on Page 96

Before to state and prove Theorem 3.29, one needs to establish a technical lemma.

Lemma C.10: *Let assume that g is continuous on $[u_{min}, u_{max}]$ and differentiable on $]u_{min}, u_{max}[$. Let $u_2 \in]u_{min}, r_1]$ and let us define the function $\Theta : [0, u_{max} - u_{min}] \to \mathbb{R}$ as*

$$\Theta(\varepsilon) = \int_{u_{min}+\varepsilon}^{u_2} \left(\int_{g(u_{min}+\varepsilon)}^{g(u_{min})} w(u, v)dv \right) du$$

and $\Gamma : [0, u_2 - u_{min}] \to \mathbb{R}$ as

$$\Gamma(\varepsilon) = \int_{u_{min}}^{u_{min}+\varepsilon} \int_{g(u_{min})}^{r_2} w(u, v) \, dv \, du \ .$$

If w is continuous, positive and $\lim_{u \to u_{min}} g'(u) = -\infty$ then for any $r_2 > g(u_{min})$

$$\lim_{\varepsilon \to 0} \frac{\Theta(\varepsilon)}{\Gamma(\varepsilon)} = +\infty \ .$$

Proof. The limits of Θ and Γ for ε converging to 0 equal 0. Therefore, the l'Hôpital rule is applied to compute $\lim_{\varepsilon \to 0} \frac{\Theta(\varepsilon)}{\Gamma(\varepsilon)}$. First of all, note that since g is differentiable on $]u_{min}, u_{max}[$, Θ and Γ are differentiable on $]0, u_{max} - u_{min}[$. Moreover, it follows that $\Theta(\varepsilon) = g(u_{min} + \varepsilon, u_2)$ where g is defined in Eq. C.5 except for the change from $g(v_0^\mu)$ to $g(u_{min})$. The proof of Lemma C.1, however, does not change if exchanging the constant $g(v_0^\mu)$ to the constant $g(u_{min})$, and one can deduce

$$\Theta'(\varepsilon) = -g'(u_{min} + \varepsilon) \int_{u_{min}+\varepsilon}^{u_2} w(u, g(u_{min} + \varepsilon))du - \int_{g(u_{min}+\varepsilon)}^{g(u_{min})} w(u_{min} + \varepsilon, v) \, dv \ .$$

From the fundamental theorem of calculus, one also has that

$$\Gamma'(\varepsilon) = \int_{g(u_{min})}^{r_2} w(u_{min} + \varepsilon, v) \, dv \ .$$

From the l'Hôpital rule, it is deduced that

$$\lim_{\varepsilon \to 0} \frac{\Theta(\varepsilon)}{\Gamma(\varepsilon)} = \lim_{\varepsilon \to 0} \frac{\Theta'(\varepsilon)}{\Gamma'(\varepsilon)} \ . \tag{C.31}$$

By continuity of w, it is deduced that

$$\lim_{\varepsilon \to 0} \Gamma'(\varepsilon) = \lim_{\varepsilon \to 0} \int_{g(u_{min})}^{r_2} w(u_{min} + \varepsilon, v) \, dv = \int_{g(u_{min})}^{r_2} w(u_{min}, v) \, dv$$

and by continuity of g and w, it is deduced that

$$\lim_{\varepsilon \to 0} \int_{u_{min}+\varepsilon}^{u_2} w(u, g(u_{min} + \varepsilon))du = \int_{u_{min}}^{u_2} w(u, g(u_{min}))du$$

obviously, the term is not zero since $w > 0$ and $u_2 > u_{min}$ and

$$\lim_{\varepsilon \to 0} \int_{g(u_{min}+\varepsilon)}^{g(u_{min})} w(u_{min} + \varepsilon, v) \, dv = 0 \ .$$

Therefore $\lim_{\varepsilon \to 0} \Theta'(\varepsilon) = \lim_{\varepsilon \to 0} -g'(u_{min} + \varepsilon) \cdot \int_{u_{min}}^{u_2} w(u, g(u_{min}))du = +\infty$ because u_2 is fixed, i.e., independent of ε, and therefore, the integral is constant. By Eq. C.31 one obtains the result. $\square$

Now, Theorem 3.29 can finally be proven.

Proof. First, the result for the left extreme is proven. Let v_1^{μ} and v_2^{μ} denote the two leftmost points of an optimal μ-distribution for I_H^w if $\mu \geq 2$. In case of $\mu = 1$, let v_1^{μ} be the optimal position of the (single) point. In this case, the contribution of v_1^{μ} in the first dimension extends to the reference point, which is represented by setting $v_2^{\mu} = r_1$ such that from now on, it is assumed $\mu \geq 2$. Furthermore, let $\lim_{u \to u_{min}} g'(u) = -\infty$ and let $v_1^{\mu} = u_{min}$ in order to get a contradiction. Let $I_h^w(u_{min})$ be the hypervolume solely dominated by the point u_{min}. Shifting v_1^{μ} to the right by $\varepsilon > 0$ (see Figure C.3), then the new hypervolume contribution $I_h^w(u_{min} + \varepsilon)$ satisfies

$$I_h^w(u_{min} + \varepsilon) = I_h^w(u_{min}) + \int_{u_{min}+\varepsilon}^{v_2^{\mu}} \int_{g(u_{min}+\varepsilon)}^{g(u_{min})} w(u, v)dvdu$$
$$- \int_{u_{min}}^{u_{min}+\varepsilon} \int_{g(u_{min})}^{r_2} w(u, v)dvdu \ .$$

Identifying u_2 with v_2^{μ} in the definition of Θ in Lemma C.10, the previous equation can be rewritten as

$$I_h^w(u_{min} + \varepsilon) = I_h^w(u_{min}) + \Theta(\varepsilon) - \Gamma(\varepsilon) \ .$$

From Lemma C.10, for any $r_2 > g(u_{min})$, there exists an $\varepsilon > 0$ such that $\frac{\Theta(\varepsilon)}{\Gamma(\varepsilon)} > 1$ and thus $\Theta(\varepsilon) - \Gamma(\varepsilon) > 0$. Thus, for any $r_2 > g(u_{min})$, there exists an ε such that $I_h^w(u_{min} + \varepsilon) > I_h^w(u_{min})$ and thus $I_h^w(u_{min})$ is not maximal which contradicts the fact that $v_1^{\mu} = u_{min}$. In a similar way, the result for the right extreme can be proven. $\square$

C.7 · Proof of Theorem 3.39 on Page 102

Proof. The proof is analogous to Theorem 3.32 setting

$$I_h^w(u_{\mu}; u_{\mu-1}, r_1) = \int_{u_{\mu}}^{r_1} \int_{g(u_{\mu})}^{g(u_{\mu-1})} w(u, v) \, dv \, du \tag{C.32}$$

and proofing a proposition analogous to Proposition 3.33 stating that if $u_{\mu} \to I_h^w(u_{\mu}; u_{min}, r_1)$ is maximal for $u_{\mu} = u_{max}$, then for any $u_{\mu-1} \in [u_{min}, u_{\mu-1}]$ the contribution $I_h^w(u_{\mu}; u_{\mu-1}, r_1)$ is maximal for $u_{\mu} = u_{max}$ too. Equation 3.23 then follows taking the partial derivative of Eq. C.32 according to Lemma C.1. $\square$

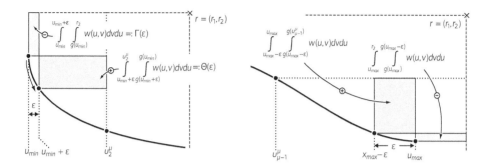

Figure C.3 If the function $g(u)$ describing the Pareto front has an infinite derivative at its left extreme, the leftmost Pareto-optimal point at u_{min} will never coincide with the leftmost point v_1^μ of an optimal μ-distribution for I_h^w (left); similarly, if the derivative is zero at the right extreme, the rightmost Pareto-optimal point at u_{max} will never coincide with the rightmost point v_μ^μ (right). The reason is in both cases that for any finite r_1, and r_2 respectively, there exists an $\varepsilon > 0$, such that the dominated space gained ($\oplus$) when moving v_1^μ from u_{min} to $u_{min}+\varepsilon$, and v_μ^μ from u_{max} to $u_{max} - \varepsilon$ respectively, is larger than the space no longer dominated ($\ominus$).

C.8 · Proof of Corollary 3.41 on Page 102

Proof. Setting $w(u,v)$ to 1 in Eq. 3.24 of Theorem 3.32 gives

$$-g'(u_\mu)(\mathcal{K}_1 - u_\mu) > g(u_{min}) - g(u_\mu), \quad \forall u_\mu \in [u_{min}, u_{max}[$$

with any $r_1 \geq \mathcal{K}_1$, the rightmost extreme is included. The previous equation writes

$$\mathcal{K}_1 > (g(u_\mu) - g(u_{min}))/g'(u_\mu) + u_\mu \text{ for all } u_\mu \in [u_{min}, u_{max}[, \tag{C.33}$$

Since $\mathcal{K}_1$ has to be larger than the right-hand side of Eq. C.33 for all u_μ in $[u_{min}, u_{max}[$, it has to be larger than the supremum of the left hand side of Eq. C.33 for u_μ in $[u_{min}, u_{max}[$ and thus

$$\mathcal{K}_1 > \sup\{u + \frac{g(u) - g(u_{min})}{g'(u)} : u \in]u_{min}, u_{max}]\} \tag{C.34}$$

$\mathcal{R}_1$ is defined as the infimum over $\mathcal{K}_1$ satisfying Eq. C.34 in other words

$$\mathcal{R}_1 = \sup\{u + \frac{g(u) - g(u_{min})}{g'(u)} : u \in]u_{min}, u_{max}]\} \ . \qquad \square$$

C.9 · Proof of Theorem 3.44 on page 104

Proof. Let $v_1^\mu(R^1)$ (resp. $v_1^\mu(R^2)$) be the leftmost point of an optimal μ-distribution for I_H^w where the hypervolume indicator is computed with respect to the reference point R^1 (resp. R^2). Similarly, let $v_\mu^\mu(R^1)$ (resp. $v_\mu^\mu(R^2)$) be the rightmost point associated with

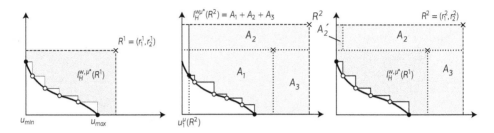

Figure C.4 If the optimal distribution of μ points contains the extremes (left-hand side), then after increasing the reference point from R^1 to R^2 the extremes are still included in the optimal μ-distribution (right-hand side). This can be proven by contradiction (middle).

an optimal μ-distribution for I_H^w where the hypervolume is computed with respect to the reference point R^1 (resp. R^2). By assumption, $v_1^\mu(R^1) = u_{min}$ and $v_\mu^\mu(R^1) = u_{max}$.

Assume, in order to get a contradiction, that $v_1^\mu(R^2) > u_{min}$ (i.e., the leftmost point of the optimal μ-distribution for I_H^w and R^2 is not the left extreme) and assume that $v_\mu^\mu(R^2) = u_{max}$ for the moment. Let $I_{H,\mu}^{w*}(R^2)$ (resp. $I_{H,\mu}^{w*}(R^1)$) be the hypervolume associated with an optimal μ-distribution for I_H^w computed with respect to the reference point R^2 (resp. with respect to R^1). Then $I_{H,\mu}^{w*}(R^2)$ is decomposed in the following manner (see Figure C.4)

$$I_{H,\mu}^{w*}(R^2) = A_1 + A_2 + A_3 \tag{C.35}$$

where, A_1 is the hypervolume (computed with respect to the weight w) enclosed in between the optimal μ-distribution associated with R^2 and the reference point R^1, A_2 is the hypervolume (computed with respect to w) enclosed in the rectangle whose diagonal extremities are R^2 and $(v_1^\mu(R^2), r_2^1)$ and A_3 is the hypervolume (again computed with respect to w) enclosed in the rectangle with diagonal $[(r_1^1, g(u_{max})), (r_1^2, r_2^1)]$. Let us now consider an optimal μ-distribution for I_H^w associated with the reference point R^1 and denote this optimal μ-distribution $(v_1^\mu(R^1), \ldots, v_\mu^\mu(R^1))$. The weighted hypervolume enclosed by this set of points and R^2 equals $I_{H,\mu}^{w*}(R^1) + A_2 + A_2' + A_3$ where A_2' is the hypervolume (computed with respect to w) enclosed in the rectangle whose diagonal is $[(u_{min}, r_2^1), (v_1^\mu(R^2), r_2^2)]$ (Figure C.4). By definition of $I_{H,\mu}^{w*}(R^2)$ one obtains

$$I_{H,\mu}^{w*}(R^2) \geq I_{H,\mu}^{w*}(R^1) + A_2 + A_2' + A_3 \ . \tag{C.36}$$

However, since $I_{H,\mu}^{w*}(R^1)$ is the maximal hypervolume value possible for the reference point R^1 and a set of μ points, it follows

$$A_1 \leq I_{H,\mu}^{w*}(R^1)$$

and thus with Eq. C.36

$$I_{H,\mu}^{w*}(R^2) \geq A_1 + A_2 + A_2' + A_3 \ .$$

From Eq. C.35, it can be deduced that

$$I_{H,\mu}^{w*}(R^2) \geq I_{H,\mu}^{w*}(R^2) + A_2' \ . \tag{C.37}$$

Since having assumed that $v_1^\mu(R^2) > u_{min}$ and that $r_2^2 > r_2^1$, if follows $A_2' > 0$. And thus, Eq. C.37 implies that $I_{H,\mu}^{w*}(R^2) > I_{H,\mu}^{w*}(R^2)$, which contradicts the initial assumption. In a similar way, a contradiction can be shown if assuming that both $v_1^\mu(R^2) > u_{min}$ and $v_\mu^\mu(R^2) < u_{max}$, i.e., if both extremes are not contained in an optimal μ-distribution for I_H^w and the reference point R^2. Also the proof for the right extreme is similar.   □

C.10 · Proof of Theorem 3.46 on Page 105

Proof. Let $\varepsilon_2 \in \mathbb{R}_{>0}$ bc fixed and let $R = (R_1, R_2) = (r_1, \mathcal{R}_2^{\text{Nadir}} + \varepsilon_2)$ for r_1 be arbitrarily chosen with $r_1 \geq \mathcal{R}_1^{\text{Nadir}}$. The optimal μ-distributions for I_H^w and the reference point R obviously depend on μ. Let $v_2^\mu(R)$ denote the second point of an optimal μ-distribution for I_H^w when R is chosen as reference point. It is known that for μ to infinity, $v_2^\mu(R)$ converges to u_{min}. Also, because g' is continuous on $[u_{min}, u_{max}]$, the extreme value theorem implies that there exists $\theta > 0$ such that $|g'(u)| \leq \theta$ for all $u \in [u_{min}, u_{max}]$. Since g' is negative one therefore obtains

$$\forall u \in [u_{min}, u_{max}] : -g'(u) \leq \theta \ . \tag{C.38}$$

In order to prove that the leftmost point of an optimal μ-distribution is u_{min}, it is enough to show that the first partial derivative of I_H^w is non-zero on $]u_{min}, v_2^\mu(R)]$. According to Eq. 3.1 and Lemma C.1, the first partial derivative of $I_H^w((v_1^\mu, \ldots, v_\mu^\mu))$ equals (omitting the dependence in R for the following equations)

$$\partial_1 I_H^w = -g'(v_1^\mu) \int_{v_1^\mu}^{v_2^\mu} w(u, g(v_1^\mu)) du - \int_{g(v_1^\mu)}^{R_2} w(v_1^\mu, u) du$$

$$= (-g'(v_1^\mu)) \int_{u_{min}}^{v_2^\mu} w(u, g(v_1^\mu)) du - (-g'(v_1^\mu)) \int_{u_{min}}^{v_1^\mu} w(u, g(v_1^\mu)) du$$

$$- \int_{g(v_1^\mu)}^{\mathcal{R}_2^{\text{Nadir}}} w(v_1^\mu, v) dv - \int_{\mathcal{R}_2^{\text{Nadir}}}^{\mathcal{R}_2^{\text{Nadir}} + \varepsilon_2} w(v_1^\mu, v) dv \ .$$

Since the second and third summand are non-positive due to w being strictly positive it follows

$$\leq (-g'(v_1^\mu)) \int_{u_{min}}^{v_2^\mu} w(u, g(v_1^\mu)) du - \int_{\mathcal{R}_2^{\text{Nadir}}}^{\mathcal{R}_2^{\text{Nadir}} + \varepsilon_2} w(v_1^\mu, v) dv \tag{C.39}$$

and because $w \leq W$ and with Eq. C.38, Eq. C.39 can be upper bounded by

$$\leq \theta W(v_2^\mu - u_{min}) - \int_{\mathcal{R}_2^{\text{Nadir}}}^{\mathcal{R}_2^{\text{Nadir}} + \varepsilon_2} w(v_1^\mu, v)dv \ . \tag{C.40}$$

Since v_2^μ converges to u_{min} for μ to infinity, and $-\int_{\mathcal{R}_2^{\text{Nadir}}}^{\mathcal{R}_2^{\text{Nadir}} + \varepsilon_2} w(v_1^\mu, v)dv < 0$ we deduce that there exists μ_1 such that for all μ larger than μ_1, Eq. C.40 is strictly negative and thus for all μ larger than μ_1, the first partial derivative of I_H^w is non zero, i.e. $v_1^\mu = u_{min}$. With Lemma 3.44 it follows that all reference points dominated by R will also allow to obtain the left extreme.

The same steps lead to the right extreme. Let $\varepsilon_1 \in \mathbb{R}_{>0}$ be fixed and let $R = (\mathcal{R}_1^{\text{Nadir}} + \varepsilon_1, r_2)$ for $r_2 \geq \mathcal{R}_2^{\text{Nadir}}$. Following the same steps for the right extreme, one needs to prove that the μ-th partial derivative of I_H^w is non zero for all $v_\mu^\mu \in [v_{\mu-1}^\mu, u_{max}[$. According to Eq. C.10,

$$\partial_\mu I_H^w(v_1^\mu, \ldots, v_\mu^\mu) = - \int_{g(v_\mu^\mu)}^{g(v_{\mu-1}^\mu)} w(v_\mu^\mu, v)dv - g'(v_\mu^\mu) \int_{v_\mu^\mu}^{\mathcal{R}_1^{\text{Nadir}} + \varepsilon_1} w(u, g(v_\mu^\mu))du$$

$$\geq - W(f(v_{\mu-1}^\mu) - f(v_\mu^\mu)) - g'(v_\mu^\mu) \int_{v_\mu^\mu}^{\mathcal{R}_1^{\text{Nadir}} + \varepsilon_1} w(u, g(v_\mu^\mu))du$$

and since $v_\mu^\mu \leq \mathcal{R}_1^{\text{Nadir}}$, one obtains

$$\geq - W(f(v_{\mu-1}^\mu) - f(v_\mu^\mu)) - g'(v_\mu^\mu) \int_{\mathcal{R}_1^{\text{Nadir}}}^{\mathcal{R}_1^{\text{Nadir}} + \varepsilon_1} w(u, g(v_\mu^\mu))du$$

By continuity of f and the fact that both v_μ^μ and $v_{\mu-1}^\mu$ converge to u_{max} the term $W(f(v_{\mu-1}^\mu) - f(v_\mu^\mu))$ converges to zero. Since $-g'(v_\mu^\mu) \int_{\mathcal{R}_1^{\text{Nadir}}}^{\mathcal{R}_1^{\text{Nadir}} + \varepsilon_1} w(u, g(v_\mu^\mu))du$ is strictly positive, it can be deduced that there exists μ_2 such that for all $\mu \geq \mu_2$, $\partial_\mu I_H^w(v_1^\mu, \ldots, v_\mu^\mu)$ is strictly positive and thus for all μ larger than μ_2 the μ-th partial derivative of I_H^w is non zero, i.e. $v_\mu^\mu = u_{max}$. With Lemma 3.44 it can be deduced that all reference points dominated by R will also allow to obtain the right extreme. $\qquad\square$

C.11 · Derivation of Results in Table 3.1 on Page 104 and Figure 3.4 on page 88

In this section, the results presented in Section 3.3 and 3.4 are applied to the test problems in the ZDT [138], the DTLZ [54], and the WFG [79] test function suites. The results are derived for the unweighted case of I_H, i.e., a weight function $w(u, v) = 1$, but they can also be derived for any other weight function w. In particular, the function $g(u)$ describing the Pareto front is derived, and its derivative $g'(u)$ which directly leads to the density $\delta_F(u)$. Furthermore, a lower bound $\mathcal{R}$ is derived for the choice of the reference point such that the extremes are included, and compute an approximation of the optimal μ-distribution for $\mu = 20$ points is compared. For the latter, the approximation schemes as proposed in [4], a paper by the author and colleagues, are used to get a precise picture for a given μ. The densities and the lower bounds $\mathcal{R}$ for the reference point are obtained by the commercial computer algebra system Maple 12.0.

Table 3.1 on Page 104 summarizes the results on the density and the lower bounds for the reference point for all problems investigated in the following. Moreover, Figure 3.4 on page 88 shows a plot of the Pareto front, the obtained approximation of an optimal μ-distribution for $\mu = 20$, and the derived density $\delta_F(u)$ (as the hatched area on top of the front $g(u)$) for all investigated test problems.

The presented results show that for several of the considered test problems, analytical results for the density and the lower bounds for the reference point can be given easily—at least if a computer algebra system such as Maple is used. Otherwise, numerical results can be provided that approximate the mathematical results with an arbitrary high precision (up to the machine precision) which also holds for the approximations of the optimal μ-distributions shown in Figure 3.4.

Definitions and Results for the ZDT Test Function Suite
There exist six ZDT test problems—ZDT1 to ZDT6—of which ZDT5 has a discrete Pareto front and is therefore excluded from our investigations [138]. In the following let $x = (x_1, \ldots, x_n) \in \mathbb{R}^n$ denote the decision vector of n real-valued variables. Then, all ZDT test problems have the same structure

minimize $f_1(x_1)$

minimize $f_2(x) = h(x_2, \ldots, x_n) \cdot h\big(f_1(x_1), h(x_2, \ldots, x_n)\big)$

where $0 \leq x_i \leq 1$ for $i \in \{1, \ldots, n\}$ except for ZDT4. The distance to the Pareto front is determined by the functional $h(x) \geq 1$. Based on this observation, the Pareto front $g(u)$ is obtained by setting $h(x) = 1$.

ZDT1: For the definition of the problem, refer to Example 3.31 on page 97 and only recapitulate the front shape of $g(u) = 1 - \sqrt{u}$ with $u_{min} = 0$ and $u_{max} = 1$, see Figure 3.4(a) on page 88. From $g'(u) = -1/(2\sqrt{u})$ the density on the front according to Eq. 3.10 is

$$\delta_F(u) = \frac{3\sqrt[4]{u}}{2\sqrt{4u+1}}$$

Since $g'(u_{min}) = -\infty$, the left extreme is never included as stated already in Example 3.31. The lower bound of the reference point $\mathcal{R} = (\mathcal{R}_1, \mathcal{R}_2)$ to have the right extreme, according to Eq. 3.25, equals

$$\mathcal{R}_1 = \sup_{u \in]u_{min}, u_{max}]} u + \frac{1 - \sqrt{u} - 1}{-1/(2\sqrt{u})} = \sup_{u \in]0,1]} 3u = 3 \ .$$

ZDT2: For the definition of the ZDT2 problem, refer to Example 3.20 on page 86 and recapitulate the front shape of $g(u) = 1 - u^2$ with $u_{min} = 0$ and $u_{max} = 1$ and the density of $\delta_F(u) = \frac{3\sqrt{u}}{2\sqrt{1+4u^2}}$ only (see Figure 3.4(b)). The lower bounds for the reference point $\mathcal{R} = (\mathcal{R}_1, \mathcal{R}_2)$ to obtain the extremes are according to Eq. 3.25 and Eq. 3.17 on pages 102 and 102 respectively.

$$\mathcal{R}_1 = \sup_{u \in]u_{min}, u_{max}]} u + \frac{1 - u^2 - 1}{-2u} = \sup_{u \in]0,1]} \frac{3}{2} u = \frac{3}{2} \qquad \text{and}$$

$$\mathcal{R}_2 = \sup_{u \in [u_{min}, u_{max}[} -2u \cdot (u - 1) + 1 - u^2 = \sup_{u \in [0,1[} 2u - 3u^2 + 1 = \frac{4}{3}$$

respectively.

ZDT3: The problem formulation of ZDT3 is

$$\text{minimize} \quad f_1(x_1) = x_1$$

$$\text{minimize} \quad f_2(x) = h(x) \cdot \left(1 - \sqrt{f_1(x_1)/h(x)} - (f_1(x_1)/h(x)) \sin(10\pi f_1(x_1)) \right)$$

$$h(x) = 1 + \frac{9}{n-1} \sum_{i=2}^{n} x_i$$

$$\text{subject to} \quad 0 \le x_i \le 1 \text{ for } i = 1, \ldots, n$$

Due to the sine-function in the definition of f_2, the front is discontinuous: $g : D \to [-1, 1], u \mapsto 1 - \sqrt{u} - u \cdot \sin(10\pi u)$ where $D = [0, 0.0830] \cup (0.1823, 0.2578] \cup (0.4093, 0.4539] \cup (0.6184, 0.6525] \cup (0.8233, 0.8518]$ is derived numerically. Hence $u_{min} = 0$ and $u_{max} = 0.8518$. The density is:

$$\delta_F(u) = C \cdot \frac{\sqrt{\frac{1}{2\sqrt{u}} + \sin(10\pi u) + 10\pi u \cos(10\pi u)}}{\sqrt{1 + \left(\frac{1}{2\sqrt{u}} + \sin(10\pi u) + 10\pi u \cos(10\pi u) \right)^2}} \qquad C \approx 1.5589$$

where $u \in D$ and $\delta_F(u) = 0$ otherwise. Figure 3.4(c) shows the Pareto front and the density. Since $g'(u_{min}) = -\infty$ and $g'(u_{max}) = 0$, the left and right extremes are never included.

ZDT4: The problem formulation of ZDT4 is

$$\text{minimize} \quad f_1(x_1) = x_1$$

$$\text{minimize} \quad f_2(x) = h(x) \cdot \left(1 - \sqrt{f_1(x_1)/h(x)}\right)$$

$$h(x) = 1 + 10(n-1) + \sum_{i=2}^{n}(x_i^2 - 10\cos(4\pi x_i))$$

$$\text{subject to} \quad 0 \le x_1 \le 1, \quad -5 \le x_i \le 5 \text{ for } i = 2, \ldots, n \ .$$

The Pareto front is again reached for $h(x) = 1$ which gives $g(u) = 1 - \sqrt{u}$. Hence, the density and the choice of the reference point is the same as for ZDT1.

ZDT6: The sixth problem of the ZDT family is defined as

$$\text{minimize} \quad f_1(x_1) = 1 - e^{-4x_1}\sin^6(6\pi x_1)$$

$$\text{minimize} \quad f_2(x) = h(x) \cdot \left(1 - (f_1(x_1)/h(x))^2\right)$$

$$h(x) = 1 + 9\left((\sum_{i=2}^{n} x_i)/(n-1)\right)^{1/4}$$

$$\text{subject to} \quad 0 \le x_i \le 1 \text{ for } i = 1, \ldots, n \ .$$

The Pareto front is $g : [u_{min}, u_{max}] \to [0,1], u \mapsto 1 - u^2$ with $u_{min} \approx 0.2808$ and $u_{max} = 1$, see Figure 3.4(d). Hence, the Pareto front coincides with the one of ZDT2 except for u_{min} which is shifted slightly to the right. From this, it follows that also the density is the same except for a constant factor, i.e., $\delta_F(u)$ is larger than the density for ZDT2 by a factor of about 1.25. For the lower bound $\mathcal{R}$ of the reference point, one obtains

$$\mathcal{R}_1 = \sup_{u \in]u_{min}, u_{max}]} u + \frac{1 - u^2 - (1 - u_{min}^2)}{-2u}$$

$$= \sup_{u \in]0.2808, 1]} \frac{u_{min}^2 - 3u^2}{-2u} = \frac{3 - u_{min}^2}{2} \approx 1.461$$

and

$$\mathcal{R}_2 = \sup_{u \in [u_{min}, 1[} -2u(u - u_{max}) + 1 - u = \sup_{u \in [u_{min}, 1[} 2u - 3u^2 + 1 = \frac{4}{3} \ .$$

Hence, the lower bound $\mathcal{R}_2$ is the same as for ZDT2, but $\mathcal{R}_1$ differs slightly from ZDT2.

Definitions and Results for the DTLZ Test Function Suite

The DTLZ test suite offers seven test problems which can be scaled to any number of objectives [54]. For the biobjective variants, DTLZ5 and DTLZ6 are degenerated, i.e., the Pareto fronts consist of only a single point and are therefore not examined in the following.

The DTLZ test problems share—for the biobjective case—the following generic structure

$$\text{minimize} \quad f_1(x) = \big(1 + h(x_M)\big)h_1(x)$$
$$\text{minimize} \quad f_2(x) = \big(1 + h(x_M)\big)h_2(x)$$

where x_M denotes a subset of the decision variables x with $h(x_M) \geq 0$ and the Pareto-optimal points being achieved for $h(x_M) = 0$.

DTLZ1: The problem formulation for DTLZ1 is

$$\text{minimize} \quad f_1(x) = \big(1 + h(x)\big)1/2x_1$$
$$\text{minimize} \quad f_2(x) = \big(1 + h(x)\big)1/2(1 - x_1)$$

$$h(x_M) = 100 \left(n + \sum_{x_i \in x_M} (x_i - 0.5)^2 - \cos(20\pi(x_i - 0.5)) \right)$$

$$\text{subject to} \quad 0 \leq x_i \leq 1 \text{ for } i = 1, \dots, n \ .$$

The Pareto front is obtained for $h(x) = 0$ which leads to $g(u) = 1/2 - u$ with $u_{min} = 0$ and $u_{max} = 1/2$, see Figure 3.4(e) on page 88. According to Eq. 3.10, the density on the front is $\delta_F(u) = \sqrt{2}$. A lower bound for the reference point is given by

$$\mathcal{R}_1 = \sup_{u \in]0, 1/2]} 1 - u = 1$$

and $\mathcal{R}_2 = \mathcal{R}_1$ for symmetry reasons.

DTLZ2: For the definition of the problem, refer to Example 3.1 on page 75 and only recapitulate the front shape of $g(u) = \sqrt{1 - u^2}$ with $u_{min} = 0$ and $u_{max} = 1$, see Figure 3.4(f). According to Eq. 3.10, the density on the front is

$$\delta_F(u) = \frac{\sqrt{\pi}}{\Gamma(3/4)^2} \sqrt{u\sqrt{1 - u^2}}$$

where Γ denotes the gamma-function, i.e., $\Gamma(3/4) \approx 1.225$. A lower bound for the reference point is given by

$$\mathcal{R}_1 = \sup_{u \in]u_{min}, u_{max}]} u + \frac{\sqrt{1 - u^2} - \sqrt{1 - u_{min}^2}}{-u/\sqrt{1 - u^2}}$$

$$= \sup_{u \in]0, 1]} \frac{\sqrt{1 - u^2} - 1 + 2u^2}{u} = 1/2 \left(\sqrt{3} - 1 \right) 3^{3/4} \sqrt{2} \approx 1.18$$

and for symmetry reasons $\mathcal{R}_2 = \mathcal{R}_1$.

DTLZ3: The problem formulation of DTLZ3 is the same as for DTLZ2 except for the function $h(x)$. However, the Pareto front is formed by the same decision vectors as for DTLZ2, i.e., for $h(x) = 1$ and the fronts of DTLZ2 and DTLZ3 are identical. Hence, also the density and the choice of the reference point are the same as for DTLZ2.

DTLZ4: In DTLZ4, the same functions as in DTLZ2 are used with an additional meta-variable mapping $m : [0,1] \rightarrow [0,1]$ of the decision variables, i.e., the decision variable $m(x_i) = x_i^\alpha$ is used instead of the original decision variable x_i in the formulation of the DTLZ2 function. This transformation does not affect the shape of the Pareto front and the results on optimal μ-distributions for the unweighted hypervolume indicator again coincide with the ones for DTLZ2.

DTLZ7: The problem formulation of DTLZ7 is

$$\text{minimize} \quad f_1(x) = x_1$$

$$\text{minimize} \quad f_2(x) = (1 + h(x)) \left(2 - \frac{x_1}{1 + h(x)} (1 + \sin(3\pi x_1)) \right)$$

$$h(x_M) = 1 + \frac{9}{|x_M|} \sum_{x_i \in x_M} x_i$$

subject to $\quad 0 \leq x_i \leq 1$ for $i = 1, \dots, n$.

The corresponding Pareto front is discontinuous and described by the function $g : D \rightarrow [0,4]$, $u \mapsto 4 - u(1 + \sin(3\pi u))$ where $D = [0, 0.2514] \cup (0.6316, 0.8594] \cup (1.3596, 1.5148] \cup (2.0518, 2.1164]$ is derived numerically, see Figure 3.4(g). Hence, $u_{min} = 0$ and $u_{max} \approx 2.1164$. The derivative of $g(u)$ is $g'(u) = -1 - \sin(3\pi u) - 3\pi u \cos(3\pi u)$ and the density therefore is

$$\delta_F(u) = C \cdot \frac{\sqrt{1 + \sin(3\pi u) + 3\pi u \cos(3\pi u)}}{\sqrt{1 + \left(1 + \sin(3\pi u) + 3\pi u \cos(3\pi u)\right)^2}}$$

with $C \approx 0.6566$. For $\mathcal{R}$, one finds by numerical methods $\mathcal{R}_1 \approx 2.481$ and $\mathcal{R}_2 \approx 13.3720$.

Definitions and Results for the WFG Test Function Suite

The WFG test suite offers nine test problems which can be scaled to any number of objectives. In contrast to DTLZ and ZDT, the problem formulations are build using an arbitrary number of so-called *transformation functions*. These functions are not stated here, the interested reader is refered to [79]. The resulting Pareto front shape is determined by parameterized *shape functions* t_i mapping $x_i \in [0,1]$ to the ith objective in the range $[0,1]$. All test functions WFG4 to WFG9 share the same shape functions and are therefore examined together in the following.

WFG1: For WFG1, the shape functions are convex and mixed respectively, i.e.

$$t_1(x) = 1 - \cos(x_1\pi/2)$$

$$t_2(x) = 1 - x_1 - \frac{\sin(10\pi x_1)}{10\pi}$$

which leads to the Pareto front

$$g(u) = \frac{2\rho - \sin(2\rho)}{10\pi} - 1$$

with $\rho = 10\arccos(1 - u)$, $u_{min} = 0$ and $u_{max} = 1$, see Figure 3.4(h). The density becomes

$$\delta_F(u) = C \cdot \sqrt{\frac{2(1 - \cos(2\rho))\pi}{\sqrt{u(2-u)}\left(\pi^2 - 4\frac{(1-\cos(2\rho))^2}{u(u-2)}\right)}}$$

with $C \approx 1.1569$. Since $g'(u_{max}) = 0$ the rightmost extreme point is never included in an optimal μ-distribution for I_H^w. For the choice of $\mathcal{R}_2$ the analytical expression is very long and therefore omitted. A numerical approximation leads to $\mathcal{R}_2 \approx 0.9795$.

WFG2: For WFG2, the shape functions are convex and discontinuous respectively, i.e.,

$$t_1(x) = 1 - \cos(x_1\pi/2)$$

$$t_2(x) = 1 - x_1 - \frac{\cos(10\pi x_1 + \pi/2)}{10\pi}$$

which leads to the discontinuous Pareto front $g : D \to [0, 1]$,

$$u \mapsto 1 - 2\frac{(\pi - 0.1\rho)\cos^2(\rho)}{\pi}$$

where $\rho = \arccos(u - 1)$, and with a numerically derived domain $D = [0, 0.0021] \cup (0.0206, 0.0537] \cup (0.1514, 0.1956] \cup (0.3674, 0.4164] \cup (0.6452, 0.6948] \cup (0.9567, 1]$, such that $u_{min} = 0$ and $u_{max} = 1$, see Figure 3.4(i). The density becomes

$$\delta_F(u) = C \cdot \frac{\sqrt{-g'(u)}}{\sqrt{1 + g'(u)^2}}$$

with $C \approx 0.44607$, and

$$g'(u) = -2\frac{\cos(\rho)(\cos(\rho) + 20\sin(\rho)\pi - 2\sin(\rho)\rho)}{\sqrt{u(2-u)}\pi}$$

$\forall u \in D$ and $\delta_F(u) = 0$ otherwise. Again, $g'(0) = -\infty$ such that the leftmost extreme point is never included in an optimal μ-distribution for I_H^w. For the rightmost extreme one finds $\mathcal{R}_1 \approx 2.571$.

WFG3: For WFG3, the shape functions are both linear, i.e.

$$t_1(x) = x_1$$
$$t_2(x) = 1 - x_1$$

which leads to the linear Pareto front $g(u) = 1 - u$ with $u_{min} = 0$ and $u_{max} = 1$. Hence, the density is $\delta_F(u) = 1/\sqrt{2}$, see Figure 3.4(e) for a scaled version of this Pareto front. For the choice of the reference point the same arguments as for DTLZ1 hold, which leads to $\mathcal{R} = (2, 2)$.

WFG4 to WFG9: For the six remaining test problems WFG4 to WFG9, the shape functions t_1 and t_2 are both concave, i.e.,

$$t_1(x) = \sin(x_1 \pi/2)$$
$$t_2(x) - \cos(x_1 \pi/2)$$

which leads to a spherical Pareto front $g(u) = \sqrt{1 - u^2}$ with $u_{min} = 0$ and $u_{max} = 1$. Hence, the Pareto front coincides with the front of DTLZ2, and consequently also the density and the choice of the reference point are the same as for DTLZ2.

D · Complementary Material to Chapter 4

D.1 · Solving the Hypervolume Subset Selection Problem (HSSP) in 2d

Several evolutionary algorithms aim at maximizing the hypervolume indicator in their environmental selection step which can be formulated as solving the Hypervolume Subset Selection Problem (HSSP): given a set of solutions A and $0 \le q \le |A|$, find a subset $A^* \subseteq A$ with $|A^*| = q$, such that the weighted hypervolume indicator of A^* is maximal.

While for more than two objectives the HSSP problem is expected to be difficult and for this reason greedy heuristics are used to tackle the HSSP, e.g., in [16, 82, 141], here an efficient exact algorithm is proposed for the case of 2 objectives—using the fact that the hypervolume contribution of an objective vector only depends on its two adjacent neighbors[2]. Exploiting this property, *dynamic programming* [40] can be used to solve the problem exactly in time $\mathcal{O}(|A|^3)$ as opposed to $\mathcal{O}(|A|^2)$ for the greedy approach by combining solutions of smaller subproblems P_c^{t-1} in a bottom-up fashion to solutions for larger subproblems P_c^t: for a fixed solution $a_c \in A$ and a $t \in \{0, \ldots, |A|\}$, the subproblem P_c^t is defined as finding the set $A_c^t \subseteq A$ of t solutions maximizing

---

[2] For example, on the left hand side of Figure D.1 the hypervolume contribution of o_2 is bounded by o_1 and o_3 but not by o_4, o_5 or o_6. This in turn means, that the increase in hypervolume, when adding o_2 to any subset whose left-most element is o_3, is equal.

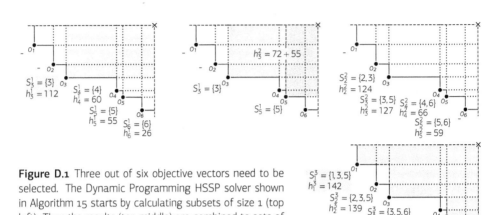

Figure D.1 Three out of six objective vectors need to be selected. The Dynamic Programming HSSP solver shown in Algorithm 15 starts by calculating subsets of size 1 (top left). Then the results (top middle) are combined to sets of size of 2 (top right) and finally of size 3 (left).

the hypervolume such that A_c^t contains a_c and in addition, only elements a_k, $k \in \{1, \ldots, |A|\}$, lying to the right of a_c, i.e., $f_1(a_c) \leq f_1(a_k)$.

Obviously, $\{a_c\}$ is the solution for P_c^1. According to the above made statement, the solution for P_c^t with $t > 1$ can now be easily found when considering the unions of $\{a_c\}$ with the solutions of all P_k^{t-1} with $f_1(a_c) \leq f_1(a_k)$ and taking the resulting solution set with the highest hypervolume. Once the solutions for $t = q$ are determined, the subset which then has the largest hypervolume corresponds to the solution to the overall problem. Algorithm 15 shows the pseudo code of the procedure where sets S_c^t of indices instead of the sets A_i^t are considered for clarity. The algorithm is illustrated by means of an example:

Example D.1: Consider six objective vectors o_1 to o_6 of which one likes to choose those $q = 3$ that maximize the hypervolume, see Figure D.1. In the first stage (a), the optimal subsets of size 1 and their hypervolume value are calculated (Lines 1 and 2 in Algorithm 15). Please note that some subsets do not exist or will not be used to build the overall solution and can therefore be neglected (dashes).

In the next stages, the subsets of size $t = 2$ to q (Lines 3-10) are determined for all individuals o_c (Lines 4-10). To this end, the hypervolume of combining o_c with any subset to its right of size $t - 1$ (Lines 6-7) are calculated. For example, in the top middle of Figure D.1 o_3 is combined with the subset S_5^1 to form $S_3^2 = \{3, 5\}$ with hypervolume $h_3^1 = 127$. In this way, all subsets of size 2 (c) and then of size 3 (d) are determined.

1: $h_i^1 \leftarrow h_i := C_H^w\big((o_{i,1}, o_{i,2}), r\big) \quad \forall 1 \leq c \leq p$
2: $S_c^1 \leftarrow \{c\} \quad \forall q \leq c \leq p$ *(optimal subsets)*
3: **for** $t = 2$ to q **do**   *(bottom-up approach)*
4:     **for** $c = q - t + 1$ to $p - t + 1$ **do**   *(subproblem)*
5:         $l \leftarrow (0, \ldots, 0)$
6:         **for** $d = c + 1$ to $p - t + 1$ **do**
7:             $l_d = h_d^{t-1} + C_H^w\big((o_{c,1}, o_{c,2}), (o_{d,1}, r_2)\big)$
8:         $m \leftarrow \arg\max_i l_i$
9:         $S_c^t \leftarrow \{c\} \cup S_m^{t-1}$ *(merge c with S_m and ...)*
10:        $h_c^t \leftarrow l_m$ *(...update hypervolume)*
11: $m \leftarrow \arg\max_i h_i^q$ *(pick best subset)*
12: **return** S_m^q *(solution to overall problem)*

Algorithm 15 HSSP-Solver. Requires a matrix $O := (o_{i,j})_{p \times 2}$, where the rows represent the objective vectors sorted in ascending order according to the first objective, a subset size $q \geq 1$, and a reference point $r = (r_1, r_2)$. The function $C_H^w(l, u)$ returns the weighted hypervolume of the rectangle from the lower left corner $l = (l_1, l_2)$ to the upper right corner $u = (u_1, u_2)$. The algorithm returns a set S that references rows of O that maximize the weighted hypervolume.

Reaching $t = q$, the optimal solution to the overall problem corresponds to the set with the largest hypervolume, in this example $S_1^3 = \{1, 3, 5\}$ with value $h_1^3 = 142$ (Line 11).∘

Note that the advantage of the exact algorithm over often used greedy approaches for HSSP is that it overcomes the non-convergence of greedy algorithms, see [17] for details.

D.2 · Proof of Theorem 4.3 on page 120

Proof. (i) It needs to be shown that no objective vector outside the hyperrectangle $S^r(x)$ is solely dominated by x. Assume to the contrary that there were an objective vector z outside $S^r(x)$ that is dominated by x exclusively. The vector can lie outside the hyperrectangle for two reasons: Firstly, because z is smaller than $f(x)$ in at least one objective, say s. This means that $z_s < f_s(x)$ which contradicts $f(x) \leq z$. Secondly, because $f(x)$ is larger than the upper vertex u of $S^r(x)$ in at least one objective t, i.e., $f_t(x) > u_t$. In the last case—according to Definition 4.2—there has to be an decision vector $x' \in A \setminus x$ with $f_t(x') = u_t$ and $x' \preceq_{|t} x$. Moreover, $f(x) \leq z$ by assumption. Hence, $f(x') \leq z$ and z is not solely dominated by x ($f_i(x') \leq f_i(x) \forall i \in \{1, \ldots, t-1, t+1, \ldots, d\}$ due to $x' \preceq_{|t} x$, and $f_t(x') = u_t < f_t(x)$ because $f_t(x) > u_t$).

(ii) The sampling hyperrectangle of x is defined by the lower vertex $l := f(x)$ and the upper vertex u, see Eq. 4.2. There are two ways to decrease the volume of the hyperrectangle: Firstly, at least one coordinate, say s, of the lower vertex l is increased. This would imply, however, that $f(x)$ is not included in the sampling space anymore since $l_s > f_s(x)$. Secondly, at least one coordinate of the upper vertex u is decreased. Consider decreasing element u_t by $\varepsilon < u_t - f_t(x)$ to get the new upper vertex $u' := (u_1, \ldots, u_t - \varepsilon, \ldots, u_d)$ where $u_t - \varepsilon > f_t(x)$. Let $e := (f_1(x), \ldots, f_{t-1}(x), u_t, f_{t+1}(x), \ldots, f_d(x))$ denote one of the vertices adjacent to z. On the one hand does e, because of coordinate t, not belong to the sampling space. On the other hand, e is still dominated by x since $f_t(x) < u'_t$. Hence, there needs to be another point $x' \in A \setminus x$ that dominates e (If not, x would be the only point dominating e, which therefore needed to be included in the sampling hyperrectangle). But x' would then as well dominate x in all but coordinate t. This contradicts Eq. 4.3 and therefore no such vector x' exists. Hence, no other decision vector apart from x dominates point e and the sampling hyperrectangle is not compliant with Eq. 4.2. $\qquad\square$

D.3 · Sampling-Based Hypervolume-Oriented Algorithm (SHV)

In order to implement the sampling procedure derived in Section 4.1.2 into an algorithm, the Regular Hypervolume-based Algorithm (RHV) shown in algorithm 6 is used. The only modification with respect to the original proposition based on the exact hypervolume calculation concerns the fitness calculation (Lines 14 and 15) which is replaced by an approximation scheme. The modified algorithm is shown in Algorithm 16.

Step 1: Drawing Initial Samples
First, the sampling spaces S_i^r are calculated for all solutions x_i according to Definition 4.2, see Lines 4 to 8 of Algorithm 16. Then a few initial samples m_{por} are drawn for each individual. Based on that, the contributions are estimated (Line 10) according to Eq. 4.1. Given the initial estimates, the following statistical test is used to determine the probability, that the solution with the smallest contribution has obtained also the smallest contribution estimate.

Step 2: Determining the Probability of Correct Selection
Consider k decision vectors x_i, $1 \le i \le k$, with contribution estimates $\hat{\lambda}(C_i)$, and let m_i and H_i denote the underlying number of samples and hits respectively[3]. Without loss of generality, let x_k be the decision vector with the smallest estimate (or one of the

---

[3] The first time the test is applied, $m_i = m_{por}$ holds.

1: $U \leftarrow A$ *(sampling has to be redone for all individuals $x_i \in U$)*
2: **while** $|A| > k'$ **do**
3:      $m_{total} \leftarrow 0$
4:      **for all** $x_i \in U$ **do**   *(reset sampling information)*
5:          $S_i^r \leftarrow CalculateSamplingHyperrectangle(A, i)$
6:          $I_i = (0, 0, S_i^r)$ *(triple of sampling statistics: (m_i, H_i, S_i^r))*
7:          $I_i \leftarrow MonteCarloSampling(I_i, m_{por})$
8:          $m_{total} \leftarrow m_{total} + m_{por}$
9:      $\mathcal{I} \leftarrow \{I_1, \dots, I_{|A|}\}$ *(set containing all sampling triples)*
10:     $w, c \leftarrow GetIndexOfWorstIndividualAndConfidence(\mathcal{I})$
11:     **while** $c < \alpha$ and $m_{total} < m_{max}$ **do**
12:        $i \leftarrow GetIndexOfNextIndividualToBeSampled(A, \mathcal{I})$
13:        $I_i \leftarrow MonteCarloSampling(I_i, m_{por})$
14:        $\mathcal{I}_i \leftarrow I_i$ *(update sampling information)*
15:        $m_{total} \leftarrow m_{total} + m_{por}$
16:        $w, c \leftarrow GetIndexOfWorstIndividualAndConfidence(\mathcal{I})$
17:     $A \leftarrow A \setminus x_w$ *(Remove the worst individual)*
18:     $U \leftarrow AffectedIndividuals(A, x_w)$
19: **return** A

Algorithm 16 Environmental Selection Truncation of Sampling-based Hypervolume-oriented Algorithm (SHV). Requires a set A, a desired size k', the number of samples per step m_{por}, the maximum allowed number of samples per removal m_{max}, and the desired confidence level α.

decision vectors that share the same minimal value). The probability, that x_k really has the smallest contribution can be lower bounded by [27, 34]:

$$P_{\hat{\lambda}(C_i)} \left(\bigcap_{i=1}^{k-1} \lambda(C_k) \leq \lambda(C_i) \right) \geq \prod_{i=1}^{k-1} P_{\hat{\lambda}(C_i)} \big(\lambda(C_k) \leq \lambda(C_i) \big) \tag{D.41}$$

where $P_{\hat{\lambda}(C_i)}(\cdot) := P(\cdot | \hat{\lambda}(C_1), \dots, \hat{\lambda}(C_k))$ denotes the conditional probability given the contribution estimates $\hat{\lambda}(C_1)$ to $\hat{\lambda}(C_k)$.

To determine the probability of $\lambda(C_k) \leq \lambda(C_i)$ given the estimates $\hat{\lambda}(C_k)$ and $\hat{\lambda}(C_i)$, the confidence interval proposed by Agresti and Coull [2] is considered:

$$P_{\hat{\lambda}(C_i)} \left(\lambda(C_k) \leq \lambda(C_i) \right) \approx \Phi \left(\frac{\hat{\lambda}(C_i) - \hat{\lambda}(C_k)}{\sqrt{\frac{\tilde{p}_k(1-\tilde{p}_k)}{m_k+2} \lambda(S_k)^2 + \frac{\tilde{p}_i(1-\tilde{p}_i)}{m_i+2} \lambda(S_i)^2}} \right) \tag{D.42}$$

where $\tilde{p}_i := (H_i + 1)(m_i + 2)$, and Φ denotes the cumulative standard normal distribution function. Based on this confidence level, also the next individual to be sampled can be determined as shown in the following.

Step 3: Resampling or Removing

If the confidence according to Eq. D.41 of removing the individual with the smallest estimate, say x_w, attains the user defined level α then x_w is removed (Line 17). Otherwise,
one individual is selected of which the estimate is refined by drawing m_{por} additional
samples (Lines 12 and 13); the individual to be sampled next is thereby determined by
two equiprobable options: either the individual with the smallest estimate is sampled
or one of the other individuals $x_c \in A \setminus x_w$. In case of the latter, the chance that x_c is
selected is proportional to the probability that $\lambda(C_c)$ is smaller or equal $\lambda(C_w)$, i.e.,

$$P(x_c \text{ selected}) \propto P(\lambda(C_c) < \lambda(C_w))$$

which is approximated by Eq. D.42. After sampling x_c or x_w took place, the confidence
according to Eq. D.41 is checked again, and as long as the desired confidence level is
not reached sampling continues, see Lines 11 to 18.

Since the difference between two contributions can be arbitrarily small, the procedure
may continue forever. In order to prevent this, a maximum number of samples m_{max} is
defined after which the individual x_w with the smallest estimated contribution $\hat{\lambda}(C_w)$
is removed regardless of the confidence level this decision reaches.

Step 4: Next Iteration Step

Instead of discarding all sampling statistics including the sampling hyperrectangles after
removing solution x_w, first it is determined which contributions are actually affected
by the removal of x_w. Those which are not affected keep both their sampling box
and sampling statistics. The potential influence of the removal of an individual x_w
on the contribution of another individual x_a can be checked by noting the following:
the removal clearly cannot decrease the contribution $\lambda(C_a)$ of x_a. On the other hand,
$\lambda(C_a)$ only possibly increases when x_w dominates part of C_a, which is not the case if
x_w does not dominate the upper vertex u_a of the sampling hyperrectangle S_a^r of x_a.
Hence, the set U_w of potentially affected points by the removal of x_w is:

$$U_w = \{x_a \in A \mid x_w \preceq u_a\}$$

where u_a is the upper vertex of the sampling hyperrectangle S_a^r according to Eq. 4.2.

D.4 · Proof of Theorem 4.6 on page 126

Proof. According to Eq. 4.4 it holds:

$$I_H(A, R) = \lambda\big(H(A, R)\big)$$
$$= \lambda\bigg(\dot{\bigcup_{T \subseteq A}} H(T, A, R)\bigg) .$$

By dividing the subsets into groups of equal size, one obtains

$$= \lambda\left(\overset{\textbf{.}}{\bigcup_{1\leq i \leq |A|}} \overset{\textbf{.}}{\bigcup_{\substack{T\subseteq A \\ |T|=i}}} H(T, A, R) \right)$$

which can be rewritten as

$$= \sum_{i=1}^{|A|} \lambda\left(\bigcup_{\substack{T\subseteq A \\ |T|=i}} H(T, A, R) \right)$$

because the inner unions are all disjoint. Now, for each subset of size i the Lebesque measure is counted once for each element and then divide by $1/i$:

$$= \sum_{i=1}^{|A|} \frac{1}{i} \sum_{a\in A} \lambda\left(\bigcup_{\substack{T\subseteq A \\ |T|=i \\ a\in T}} H(T, A, R) \right) .$$

Changing the order of the sums results in

$$= \sum_{a\in A} \sum_{i=1}^{|A|} \frac{1}{i} \lambda\left(\bigcup_{\substack{T\subseteq A \\ |T|=i \\ a\in T}} H(T, A, R) \right)$$

and using Definition 4.5 one obtains

$$= \sum_{a\in A} I_h(a, A, R)$$

which concludes the proof. $\square$

D.5 · Proof of Theorem 4.7 on page 127

Proof. From Theorem 4.6 it is known that

$$\sum_{b_1\in\{a\}\cup B_1} I_h(b_1, \{a\}\cup B_1, R) = I_H(\{a\}\cup B_1, R)$$

which—following Definition 2.20—equals

$$= \lambda\big(H(\{a\}\cup B_1, R) \big) .$$

Since $\{a\} \preccurlyeq B_1$, it holds $H(b, R) \subseteq H(\{a\}, R)$ for all $b \in B_1$ and therefore the above formula can be simplified to

$$= \lambda\big(H(\{a\}, R) \big)$$

The same holds analogically for the right-hand side of the equation in Theorem 4.7 which proves the claim. □

D.6 · Proof of Theorem 4.9 on page 130

Proof. Definition 4.8 states that

$$I_h^k(a, A, R) = \frac{1}{|\mathcal{T}|} \sum_{T \in \mathcal{T}} \left[\sum_{\substack{U \subseteq T \\ a \in U}} \frac{1}{|U|} \lambda\big(H(U, A, R)\big) \right]$$

where $\mathcal{T}$ denotes the set of subsets of A, that contain k elements, one of which is individual a, i.e., $\mathcal{T} = \{T \subseteq A; a \in T \wedge |T| = k\}$. Inserting the definition of $\mathcal{T}$ leads to

$$= \frac{1}{|\mathcal{T}|} \sum_{\substack{T \in A \\ |T|=k \\ a \in T}} \sum_{\substack{U \subseteq T \\ a \in U}} \frac{1}{|U|} \lambda\big(H(U, A, R)\big) \ . \tag{D.43}$$

To combine the two summations of the previous equation, let $o(U)$ denote the number of times the summand $\frac{1}{|U|}\lambda\big(H(U, A, R)\big)$ is added for the same set U, which yields

$$= \frac{1}{|\mathcal{T}|} \sum_{\substack{U \subseteq A \\ a \in U}} o(U) \frac{1}{|U|} \lambda\big(H(U, A, R)\big) \ .$$

Splitting up this result into summation over subsets of equal size gives

$$= \frac{1}{|\mathcal{T}|} \sum_{i=1}^{k} \frac{1}{i} \sum_{\substack{U \subseteq A \\ |U|=i \\ a \in U}} o(U) \lambda\big(H(U, A, R)\big) \ .$$

For symmetry reasons, each subset U with cardinality $|U| = i$ has the same number of occurences $o(U) =: o_i$

$$= \frac{1}{|\mathcal{T}|} \sum_{i=1}^{k} \frac{o_i}{i} \sum_{\substack{U \subseteq A \\ |U|=i \\ a \in U}} \lambda\big(H(U, A, R)\big) \ ,$$

and since all $H(U, A, R)$ in the sum are disjoint, according to Eq. 4.4 one obtains

$$= \frac{1}{|\mathcal{T}|} \sum_{i=1}^{k} \frac{o_i}{i} \lambda\Big(\bigcup_{\substack{U \subseteq A \\ |U|=i \\ a \in U}} H(U, A, R) \Big) \ ,$$

Figure D.2 U is a subset of T, which in turn is a subset of A; all three sets contain a. Given one particular U of size i there exist $\binom{|A|-i}{k-i}$ subsets $T \subseteq A$ of size k which are a superset of U. In the example shown, there exist $\binom{10-4}{6-4} = 15$ sets $U \subseteq A$ of size 6 which are a superset of T with $|T| = 4$.

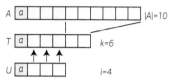

which is according to Eq. 4.5

$$= \sum_{i=1}^{k} \frac{o_i}{i \cdot |\mathcal{T}|} \lambda\big(H_i(a, A, R)\big) \ .$$

After having transformed the original equation, the number o_i is determined, i.e., the number of times the term $\frac{1}{|U|}\lambda\big(H(U, A, R)\big)$ appears in Eq. D.43. The term is added once every time the corresponding set U is a subset of T. Hence, $o(U)$ with $|U| - i$ corresponds to the number of sets T that are a superset of U. As depicted in Figure D.2, U defines i elements of T and the remaining $k - i$ elements can be chosen freely from the $|A| - i$ elements in A that are not yet in T.

Therefore, there exist $\binom{|A|-i}{k-i}$ subsets $T \in \mathcal{T}$ that contain one particular U with $|U| = i$ and $a \in U$. Therefore, $o(U) = o_i = \binom{|A|-i}{k-i}$. Likewise, the total number of sets T is $|\mathcal{T}| = \binom{|A|-1}{k-1}$.

Hence

$$\frac{o_i}{|\mathcal{T}|} = \frac{\binom{|A|-i}{k-i}}{\binom{|A|-1}{k-1}} = \frac{(|A| - i)!(k - 1)!((|A| - 1) - (k - 1))!}{(k - i)!((|A| - i) - (k - i))!(|A| - 1)!}$$

$$= \frac{(|A| - i)!(k - 1)!}{(|A| - 1)!(k - i)!} = \frac{(k - 1)(k - 2)\cdots(k - (i - 1))}{(|A| - 1)(|A| - 2)\cdots(|A| - (i - 1))}$$

$$= \prod_{j=1}^{i-1} \frac{k - j}{|A| - j} = \alpha_i \ .$$

Therefore

$$I_h^k(a, A, R) = \sum_{i=1}^{k} \frac{\alpha_i}{i} \lambda\big(H_i(a, A, R)\big)$$

which concludes the proof.   □

D.7 · Comparison of HypE to different MOEAs–Detailed Results

Table D.1 on pages 265, 266, 267, and 268 reveals the performance score on every testproblem of the DTLZ [54], the WFG [79], and the knapsack [137] test problem

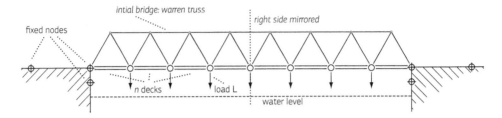

Figure E.1 Illustration of the truss bridge problem. Between the two banks with predefined abutments, n decks with equal load have to be supported by a steel truss. As starting point, the individuals of the evolutionary algorithm are initialized to the shown Warren truss without verticals. At each bank, two supplementary fixed nodes are available to support the bridge additionally.

suites for different number of objectives ranging from 2 to 50 (see Section 4.5.2 on page 146).

E · Complementary Material to Chapter 6

In this appendix two new classes of problems for robustness investigations are presented: first, in Section E.1 a real world mechanical problem is stated. Secondly, in Section E.2 a novel test problem suite is presented to test the performance of algorithms with respect to different robustness landscapes.

E.1 · Truss Bridge Problem

First, the truss bridge problem is stated. Then, a problem-specific evolutionary algorithm is presented to find good solutions of this mechanical problem.

Problem Statement

The task of the truss bridge problem is to build a bridge over a river. Between two banks, n equally long decks have to be supported by a steel truss[4]. A uniform load is assumed over the decks that leads to $n - 1$ equal force vectors, see Figure E.1. The first objective of the truss bridge problem is to maximize the structural efficiency—the ratio of load carried by the bridge without elastic failure to the total bridge mass, i.e., costs. The river is considered environmentally sensitive and therefore no supporting structures are allowed below the water level. Furthermore, to limit the intervention in

---

[4] The decks are of 5 meters long.

Table D.1 Comparison of HypE to different MOEAs with respect to the hypervolume indicator. The first number represents the performance score P, which stands for the number of participants significantly dominating the selected algorithm. The number in brackets denote the hypervolume value, normalized to the minimum and maximum value observed on the test problem.

	Problem	SHV	IBEA	NSGA-II	RS	SPEA2	HypE	HypE*
2 objectives	DTLZ 1	3 (0.286)	0 (0.667)	2 (0.441)	3 (0.306)	3 (0.343)	1 (0.545)	3 (0.279)
	DTLZ 2	2 (0.438)	0 (0.871)	5 (0.306)	5 (0.278)	2 (0.431)	1 (0.682)	4 (0.362)
	DTLZ 3	6 (0.265)	0 (0.759)	1 (0.596)	3 (0.452)	1 (0.578)	3 (0.454)	2 (0.483)
	DTLZ 4	1 (0.848)	0 (0.928)	3 (0.732)	3 (0.834)	2 (0.769)	1 (0.779)	3 (0.711)
	DTLZ 5	2 (0.489)	0 (0.931)	5 (0.361)	6 (0.279)	2 (0.463)	1 (0.724)	4 (0.428)
	DTLZ 6	2 (0.670)	0 (0.914)	5 (0.326)	4 (0.388)	6 (0.229)	1 (0.856)	2 (0.659)
	DTLZ 7	0 (0.945)	1 (0.898)	6 (0.739)	2 (0.818)	4 (0.817)	2 (0.853)	1 (0.876)
	Knapsack	2 (0.523)	0 (0.631)	0 (0.603)	3 (0.493)	0 (0.574)	0 (0.633)	0 (0.630)
	WFG 1	4 (0.567)	0 (0.949)	1 (0.792)	6 (0.160)	1 (0.776)	2 (0.744)	4 (0.557)
	WFG 2	1 (0.987)	4 (0.962)	3 (0.974)	6 (0.702)	4 (0.969)	0 (0.990)	0 (0.989)
	WFG 3	2 (0.994)	0 (0.997)	4 (0.991)	6 (0.559)	4 (0.990)	0 (0.997)	2 (0.994)
	WFG 4	0 (0.964)	0 (0.969)	4 (0.891)	6 (0.314)	4 (0.898)	0 (0.968)	0 (0.963)
	WFG 5	3 (0.994)	0 (0.997)	5 (0.992)	6 (0.402)	2 (0.995)	0 (0.998)	2 (0.995)
	WFG 6	2 (0.945)	0 (0.975)	4 (0.932)	6 (0.418)	4 (0.930)	1 (0.955)	2 (0.942)
	WFG 7	3 (0.929)	0 (0.988)	1 (0.946)	6 (0.294)	2 (0.939)	1 (0.947)	4 (0.920)
	WFG 8	3 (0.431)	0 (0.675)	1 (0.536)	3 (0.367)	1 (0.514)	0 (0.683)	1 (0.549)
	WFG 9	1 (0.920)	0 (0.939)	4 (0.891)	6 (0.313)	4 (0.878)	1 (0.924)	0 (0.931)
3 objectives	DTLZ 1	3 (0.313)	1 (0.505)	6 (0.168)	0 (0.607)	5 (0.275)	1 (0.395)	3 (0.336)
	DTLZ 2	2 (0.995)	0 (0.998)	5 (0.683)	6 (0.491)	4 (0.888)	1 (0.996)	3 (0.994)
	DTLZ 3	3 (0.210)	1 (0.495)	3 (0.179)	0 (0.679)	3 (0.216)	2 (0.398)	3 (0.196)
	DTLZ 4	1 (0.945)	0 (0.989)	3 (0.777)	3 (0.774)	2 (0.860)	0 (0.987)	2 (0.922)
	DTLZ 5	1 (0.991)	0 (0.994)	5 (0.696)	6 (0.374)	4 (0.882)	2 (0.990)	3 (0.989)
	DTLZ 6	2 (0.971)	0 (0.990)	6 (0.151)	5 (0.237)	4 (0.266)	0 (0.991)	3 (0.967)
	DTLZ 7	0 (0.993)	1 (0.987)	6 (0.633)	4 (0.794)	5 (0.722)	3 (0.970)	2 (0.980)
	Knapsack	2 (0.441)	0 (0.544)	1 (0.462)	6 (0.322)	1 (0.441)	0 (0.550)	0 (0.473)
	WFG 1	4 (0.792)	3 (0.811)	3 (0.827)	6 (0.207)	1 (0.881)	0 (0.985)	1 (0.894)
	WFG 2	0 (0.556)	3 (0.475)	3 (0.406)	6 (0.261)	2 (0.441)	0 (0.446)	0 (0.372)
	WFG 3	2 (0.995)	3 (0.981)	4 (0.966)	6 (0.689)	4 (0.966)	0 (0.999)	1 (0.998)
	WFG 4	0 (0.978)	3 (0.955)	5 (0.708)	6 (0.220)	4 (0.740)	1 (0.975)	0 (0.979)
	WFG 5	2 (0.988)	3 (0.952)	4 (0.884)	6 (0.343)	5 (0.877)	0 (0.991)	0 (0.991)
	WFG 6	2 (0.959)	2 (0.955)	4 (0.914)	6 (0.415)	5 (0.879)	0 (0.987)	1 (0.981)
	WFG 7	1 (0.965)	3 (0.950)	5 (0.770)	6 (0.183)	4 (0.858)	0 (0.988)	2 (0.958)
	WFG 8	2 (0.887)	0 (0.922)	4 (0.842)	6 (0.301)	5 (0.780)	0 (0.906)	3 (0.870)
	WFG 9	1 (0.954)	3 (0.914)	5 (0.735)	6 (0.283)	4 (0.766)	0 (0.972)	1 (0.956)

continued

Table D.1 continued from page 265

	Problem	SHV	IBEA	NSGA-II	RS	SPEA2	HypE	HypE*
5 objectives	DTLZ 1	2 (0.927)	3 (0.905)	5 (0.831)	6 (0.548)	4 (0.869)	0 (0.968)	1 (0.961)
	DTLZ 2	1 (0.998)	0 (0.999)	4 (0.808)	6 (0.324)	5 (0.795)	2 (0.998)	3 (0.998)
	DTLZ 3	2 (0.754)	1 (0.786)	6 (0.365)	4 (0.529)	4 (0.520)	0 (0.824)	1 (0.768)
	DTLZ 4	1 (0.997)	0 (0.998)	4 (0.749)	5 (0.558)	6 (0.537)	2 (0.992)	2 (0.992)
	DTLZ 5	0 (0.997)	0 (0.998)	4 (0.854)	6 (0.403)	5 (0.841)	2 (0.996)	2 (0.995)
	DTLZ 6	3 (0.964)	1 (0.979)	5 (0.428)	6 (0.311)	4 (0.597)	0 (0.988)	1 (0.977)
	DTLZ 7	0 (0.988)	0 (0.986)	6 (0.478)	4 (0.672)	5 (0.569)	2 (0.868)	2 (0.862)
	Knapsack	0 (0.676)	0 (0.862)	2 (0.163)	2 (0.235)	1 (0.369)	2 (0.242)	2 (0.256)
	WFG 1	4 (0.766)	5 (0.703)	2 (0.832)	6 (0.291)	2 (0.820)	0 (0.973)	1 (0.951)
	WFG 2	0 (0.671)	0 (0.533)	0 (0.644)	6 (0.351)	0 (0.624)	0 (0.557)	3 (0.503)
	WFG 3	6 (0.339)	0 (0.974)	3 (0.946)	5 (0.760)	4 (0.932)	0 (0.977)	0 (0.971)
	WFG 4	0 (0.965)	3 (0.894)	5 (0.711)	6 (0.241)	4 (0.741)	1 (0.948)	1 (0.949)
	WFG 5	5 (0.754)	1 (0.971)	4 (0.892)	6 (0.303)	3 (0.911)	0 (0.978)	1 (0.975)
	WFG 6	0 (0.953)	0 (0.949)	4 (0.913)	6 (0.392)	5 (0.872)	1 (0.948)	2 (0.940)
	WFG 7	0 (0.921)	1 (0.822)	2 (0.774)	6 (0.157)	4 (0.745)	2 (0.784)	5 (0.700)
	WFG 8	0 (0.847)	0 (0.856)	4 (0.685)	6 (0.309)	5 (0.588)	2 (0.825)	3 (0.809)
	WFG 9	5 (0.496)	2 (0.720)	4 (0.645)	6 (0.138)	3 (0.667)	0 (0.937)	0 (0.956)
7 objectives	DTLZ 1	2 (0.962)	2 (0.960)	5 (0.950)	6 (0.563)	2 (0.961)	0 (0.995)	0 (0.995)
	DTLZ 2	3 (0.998)	0 (1.000)	5 (0.808)	6 (0.340)	4 (0.850)	1 (0.999)	1 (0.999)
	DTLZ 3	1 (0.951)	1 (0.958)	5 (0.589)	6 (0.438)	4 (0.723)	0 (0.973)	1 (0.952)
	DTLZ 4	1 (0.999)	0 (1.000)	4 (0.902)	6 (0.569)	5 (0.814)	2 (0.999)	2 (0.999)
	DTLZ 5	1 (0.997)	0 (0.997)	4 (0.888)	6 (0.502)	4 (0.899)	0 (0.997)	1 (0.997)
	DTLZ 6	3 (0.954)	2 (0.983)	5 (0.635)	6 (0.397)	4 (0.756)	0 (0.993)	1 (0.988)
	DTLZ 7	0 (0.981)	1 (0.958)	5 (0.348)	4 (0.559)	5 (0.352)	2 (0.877)	2 (0.870)
	Knapsack	0 (0.745)	0 (0.768)	2 (0.235)	2 (0.226)	2 (0.272)	2 (0.276)	4 (0.212)
	WFG 1	4 (0.647)	5 (0.649)	2 (0.814)	6 (0.189)	2 (0.812)	0 (0.956)	1 (0.937)
	WFG 2	0 (0.632)	0 (0.747)	1 (0.409)	5 (0.155)	0 (0.837)	0 (0.528)	0 (0.630)
	WFG 3	6 (0.105)	2 (0.975)	3 (0.961)	5 (0.709)	4 (0.958)	0 (0.983)	0 (0.982)
	WFG 4	3 (0.888)	2 (0.919)	4 (0.688)	6 (0.200)	4 (0.694)	0 (0.956)	0 (0.952)
	WFG 5	6 (0.042)	2 (0.982)	4 (0.905)	5 (0.406)	3 (0.938)	0 (0.986)	0 (0.987)
	WFG 6	0 (0.978)	0 (0.967)	4 (0.940)	6 (0.453)	5 (0.921)	0 (0.974)	3 (0.967)
	WFG 7	1 (0.688)	3 (0.657)	0 (0.813)	6 (0.207)	3 (0.658)	1 (0.713)	5 (0.606)
	WFG 8	0 (0.933)	1 (0.905)	4 (0.709)	6 (0.366)	5 (0.537)	2 (0.863)	2 (0.874)
	WFG 9	5 (0.385)	2 (0.681)	3 (0.679)	6 (0.119)	3 (0.683)	0 (0.928)	0 (0.943)

continued

Table D.1 continued from page 265

	Problem	SHV	IBEA	NSGA-II	RS	SPEA2	HypE	HypE*
10 objectives	DTLZ 1	3 (0.981)	5 (0.971)	4 (0.986)	6 (0.590)	2 (0.990)	0 (0.999)	0 (0.999)
	DTLZ 2	3 (0.999)	2 (1.000)	5 (0.825)	6 (0.290)	4 (0.868)	0 (1.000)	0 (1.000)
	DTLZ 3	3 (0.951)	1 (0.990)	5 (0.676)	6 (0.358)	4 (0.750)	0 (0.994)	1 (0.990)
	DTLZ 4	2 (1.000)	0 (1.000)	4 (0.988)	6 (0.560)	5 (0.960)	1 (1.000)	0 (1.000)
	DTLZ 5	3 (0.951)	0 (0.998)	4 (0.899)	6 (0.471)	4 (0.892)	0 (0.998)	1 (0.997)
	DTLZ 6	4 (0.497)	2 (0.987)	4 (0.706)	6 (0.276)	3 (0.769)	0 (0.994)	1 (0.992)
	DTLZ 7	0 (0.986)	1 (0.831)	4 (0.137)	6 (0.057)	4 (0.166)	2 (0.744)	1 (0.781)
	Knapsack	0 (0.568)	0 (0.529)	2 (0.149)	4 (0.119)	2 (0.173)	5 (0.068)	5 (0.060)
	WFG 1	6 (0.402)	4 (0.843)	2 (0.932)	5 (0.562)	2 (0.937)	0 (0.977)	0 (0.975)
	WFG 2	0 (0.971)	0 (0.988)	0 (0.978)	5 (0.020)	2 (0.962)	0 (0.981)	1 (0.966)
	WFG 3	6 (0.088)	1 (0.973)	3 (0.947)	5 (0.792)	4 (0.933)	0 (0.980)	1 (0.976)
	WFG 4	3 (0.698)	2 (0.896)	3 (0.708)	6 (0.207)	5 (0.669)	0 (0.950)	0 (0.955)
	WFG 5	6 (0.014)	2 (0.979)	4 (0.832)	5 (0.365)	3 (0.913)	0 (0.987)	0 (0.989)
	WFG 6	3 (0.934)	1 (0.949)	4 (0.896)	6 (0.449)	5 (0.865)	0 (0.959)	1 (0.949)
	WFG 7	1 (0.686)	4 (0.464)	1 (0.604)	6 (0.077)	4 (0.473)	0 (0.683)	3 (0.548)
	WFG 8	0 (0.956)	1 (0.903)	4 (0.689)	6 (0.221)	5 (0.438)	2 (0.883)	2 (0.875)
	WFG 9	5 (0.222)	3 (0.584)	3 (0.644)	6 (0.109)	2 (0.676)	1 (0.893)	0 (0.925)
25 objectives	DTLZ 1	4 (0.994)	5 (0.987)	2 (1.000)	6 (0.657)	3 (0.998)	0 (1.000)	0 (1.000)
	DTLZ 2	3 (0.999)	2 (1.000)	4 (0.965)	6 (0.301)	5 (0.882)	0 (1.000)	0 (1.000)
	DTLZ 3	3 (0.967)	2 (0.999)	4 (0.930)	6 (0.455)	5 (0.827)	0 (0.999)	0 (1.000)
	DTLZ 4	3 (1.000)	2 (1.000)	4 (1.000)	6 (0.546)	5 (0.991)	0 (1.000)	0 (1.000)
	DTLZ 5	5 (0.781)	2 (0.996)	3 (0.949)	6 (0.457)	4 (0.808)	0 (0.999)	1 (0.999)
	DTLZ 6	6 (0.286)	2 (0.993)	3 (0.957)	5 (0.412)	4 (0.830)	0 (0.999)	0 (0.998)
	DTLZ 7	0 (0.973)	0 (0.966)	3 (0.856)	2 (0.893)	4 (0.671)	2 (0.889)	3 (0.825)
	Knapsack	0 (0.000)	4 (0.000)	5 (0.000)	3 (0.000)	6 (0.000)	1 (0.000)	2 (0.000)
	WFG 1	6 (0.183)	4 (0.930)	0 (0.971)	5 (0.815)	3 (0.965)	0 (0.972)	0 (0.973)
	WFG 2	0 (0.951)	0 (0.951)	2 (0.935)	6 (0.072)	2 (0.933)	2 (0.934)	2 (0.928)
	WFG 3	6 (0.037)	0 (0.983)	3 (0.965)	5 (0.758)	3 (0.963)	1 (0.974)	1 (0.977)
	WFG 4	6 (0.063)	2 (0.890)	3 (0.541)	5 (0.170)	4 (0.432)	0 (0.941)	0 (0.945)
	WFG 5	6 (0.003)	3 (0.832)	4 (0.796)	5 (0.227)	2 (0.915)	0 (0.989)	0 (0.989)
	WFG 6	3 (0.932)	0 (0.959)	5 (0.913)	6 (0.579)	3 (0.926)	0 (0.961)	0 (0.962)
	WFG 7	3 (0.286)	4 (0.183)	2 (0.386)	6 (0.081)	4 (0.185)	0 (0.707)	1 (0.479)
	WFG 8	0 (0.924)	0 (0.909)	4 (0.517)	6 (0.189)	5 (0.305)	2 (0.817)	3 (0.792)
	WFG 9	5 (0.118)	3 (0.531)	3 (0.580)	5 (0.133)	2 (0.681)	0 (0.893)	1 (0.848)

continued

Table D.1 continued from page 265

	Problem	SHV	IBEA	NSGA-II	RS	SPEA2	HypE	HypE*
50 objectives	DTLZ 1	4 (0.992)	5 (0.985)	2 (1.000)	6 (0.566)	3 (0.999)	1 (1.000)	0 (1.000)
	DTLZ 2	3 (1.000)	2 (1.000)	4 (0.998)	6 (0.375)	5 (0.917)	0 (1.000)	0 (1.000)
	DTLZ 3	3 (0.984)	2 (1.000)	3 (0.988)	6 (0.518)	5 (0.891)	0 (1.000)	0 (1.000)
	DTLZ 4	2 (1.000)	2 (1.000)	4 (1.000)	6 (0.517)	5 (0.999)	0 (1.000)	0 (1.000)
	DTLZ 5	5 (0.477)	2 (0.996)	3 (0.954)	5 (0.425)	4 (0.752)	0 (0.999)	0 (0.999)
	DTLZ 6	6 (0.112)	2 (0.995)	3 (0.979)	5 (0.399)	4 (0.839)	0 (0.998)	1 (0.998)
	DTLZ 7	1 (0.767)	0 (0.966)	5 (0.233)	4 (0.254)	6 (0.020)	2 (0.684)	3 (0.675)
	Knapsack	0 (0.000)	4 (0.000)	5 (0.000)	3 (0.000)	6 (0.000)	1 (0.000)	2 (0.000)
	WFG 1	6 (0.210)	4 (0.869)	2 (0.962)	4 (0.823)	2 (0.961)	0 (0.971)	0 (0.970)
	WFG 2	3 (0.538)	0 (0.962)	0 (0.959)	6 (0.076)	0 (0.952)	2 (0.945)	3 (0.943)
	WFG 3	6 (0.059)	0 (0.981)	2 (0.972)	5 (0.731)	2 (0.973)	0 (0.976)	0 (0.979)
	WFG 4	6 (0.011)	2 (0.783)	3 (0.268)	5 (0.118)	3 (0.258)	0 (0.944)	1 (0.908)
	WFG 5	6 (0.003)	2 (0.940)	4 (0.789)	5 (0.416)	3 (0.913)	1 (0.987)	0 (0.989)
	WFG 6	4 (0.933)	2 (0.963)	4 (0.941)	6 (0.663)	2 (0.961)	0 (0.974)	0 (0.976)
	WFG 7	1 (0.312)	5 (0.026)	3 (0.208)	5 (0.022)	4 (0.034)	0 (0.581)	1 (0.378)
	WFG 8	1 (0.669)	0 (0.913)	4 (0.341)	6 (0.147)	5 (0.233)	1 (0.602)	2 (0.579)
	WFG 9	5 (0.250)	3 (0.597)	3 (0.559)	6 (0.166)	2 (0.727)	0 (0.907)	0 (0.903)

the natural scenery, the second objective is to minimize the rise of the bridge, measured from the decks at the center of the bridge[5].

The bridge is considered two dimensional, i.e., the entire structure lies in a two dimensional plane. The slender members (referred to as bars) are connected at revolute joints (referred to as nodes). Half of the external load on the decks is applied to each of the two end joints and the weight of the members is considered insignificant compared to the loads and is therefore omitted. Hence, no torsional forces are active and all forces on members are tensile or compressive. For detailed information on these types of truss bridges see W.F. Chen and L. Duan [127].

In contrast to other well known truss problems, like for instance the ten bar truss problem [44], the nodes or bars are not specified in advanced, neither are they restricted to discrete positions like as in [13]. In fact, all kinds of geometries are possible which renders the problem much harder than the above mentioned ten bar truss problem. The only restriction is, that the predefined decks can not be changed in any way. In

---

[5] The height is arbitrarily defined at the middle of the bridge and not over the entire span width, to promote bridges very different to those optimizing the structural efficiency—which tend to have the largest height at the center of the bridge.

addition to the two endpoints, two additional fixed nodes at each bank can, but do not need to be, added to the truss[6].

The truss is made only from steel with yield strength 690 MPa and density $7\,800\,\text{kg/m}^3$. The maximum area of the members allowed is $0.04\,\text{m}^2$, and the minimum area is set to $2.5 \cdot 10^{-5}\,\text{m}^2$. The decks have a fixed cross-sectional area of $0.02\,\text{m}^2$.

Evolutionary Algorithm

In the following an evolutionary algorithm is presented tailored to the steel truss bridge problem stated above. The algorithm consists of: (i) a general representation which can model all possible bridges, (ii) an initialization of solutions, (iii) the calculation of the objective values, and (iv) different mutation operators to generate new solutions.

Representation. The representation consists of variable length lists. The first list contains all nodes. A node is thereby determined by its position (x, y), the degrees of freedom of the node (i.e., whether the node is fixed or not), and the load attached to this node—the latter is non-zero only for the $n-1$ predefined joints between the decks. The second list contains the members that consist of references to the two endpoints of the bar, and the cross-sectional area of the bar. Since the problem is mirror-symmetrical, only the left half of the bridge is represented and solved, see below.

Initialization. As a starting point, all solutions are set to a Warren truss without verticals, and with equilateral triangles. This ensures that the initial bridges are statically determinate and stable. Of course, the risk increases that the diversity of solutions is limited unnecessarily. As the results in Section 6.5.2 on page 207 show this is not the case though—the solutions found vary a lot from the initial Warren truss.

Calculating the Objective Function. To determine the first objective function, the structural efficiency, matrix analysis of the truss is performed; more specifically, the matrix force method is used to determine the internal forces of all members. Given their area, the weakest link can then be identified which defines the maximum load of the bridge. If the bridge is statistically undetermined, i.e., the matrix becomes singular, the bridge is classified infeasible. No repairing mechanism is used in this case. The weight of the bridge, on the other hand, is determined by summing up the product of length, area, and density of all bars. For the weight, the members constituting the deck of the bridge are also included. Finally, dividing the maximum load by the total weight gives the first objective, i.e., the structural efficiency.

---

[6] The additional fixed nodes are located 2.5 m below the edge of the abutment and 7.5 m to the left and right of the edge respectively.

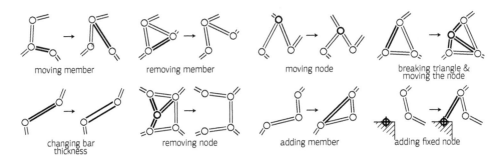

moving member   removing member   moving node   breaking triangle & moving the node

changing bar thickness   removing node   adding member   adding fixed node

Figure E.2 Illustrates the eight mutation operators used to optimize the bridge problem.

The maximum vertical distance of a member or node above the deck level, measured at the center of the bridge, gives the second objective. The rise of the bridge is to be minimized.

Because of the symmetry of the problem, only the left half of the bridge is represented and solved. To this end, all nodes lying on the mirror axis, the center of the bridge, are fixed in the horizontal dimension. This models the fact, that due to symmetry, the horizontal component of the force vectors at these nodes is zero. All members except those on the mirror axis are considered twice in terms of cost, since they have a symmetric counterpart. On the other hand, the internal load of members on the symmetry axis is doubled after matrix analysis, since the right, not considered, half of the bridge will contribute the same load as the left half.

Mutation Operators. Due to the complex representation of the bridges no crossover but only mutation operators are applied to generate new bridges. In each generation, one of the following eight mutation functions is used, where the probability of an operator being applied is evolved by self-adaptation [44]:

moving member: A member is randomly picked and its endpoints are changed, such that the member ends up at a different place.

removing member: A randomly chosen member is removed. Nodes that are no longer connected are removed too.

adding member: Two nodes are picked randomly and a member is added between them.

moving nodes: The location of a node is moved uniformly within the interval $[-1\,m, 1\,m] \times [-1\,m, 1\,m]$.

removing node: A randomly chosen node is removed; all members connected to that node are removed as well.

adding fixed node: A node from the set of fixed nodes is picked, and connected to a randomly chosen (non-fixed) node.

breaking triangle and moving node: This mutation operator should help the formation of repeated triangular patterns, which are known to be beneficial because triangles can not be distorted by stress. An existing triangle is chosen, then one of its three sides is divided in the middle by adding a new node. This node is then connected by the corresponding median of the triangle. Since this new member would get zero internal force, the new node is moved additionally by the operator *moving node*.

changing member area: This mutation operator randomly picks a member and changes its area by factor ρ, where $\rho \sim U(0.5, 1.5)$ is randomly distributed between 0.5 and 1.5.

Figure E.2 illustrates the eight mutation operators. In addition to these operators, with a probability of 50% the cross-sectional areas of the bridge are optimized according to matrix analysis, i.e., each cross-sectional area is decreased as far as the maximum load carried does not decrease.

Noise

Many different sources of uncertainty are conceivable for the truss problem, e.g., differing location of the nodes due to imprecise construction, and varying member areas because of manufacturing imperfection or changing external load distributions. The present thesis considers random perturbations of the yield strength of members. The thicker a bar thereby is, the larger the variance of the noise. The reasoning behind this assumption is that material properties are harder to control the larger a structure is. The model $\sigma_{UTS} \sim \sigma_{UTS} \cdot U(1 - (r^2)\delta, 1 + (r^2)\delta)$ is used, where r is the radius of the bar and σ_{UTS} denotes the yield strength of a member. As robustness measure, the maximum deviation according to Eq. 6.2 is used. However, in contrast to Section 6.5 where a sampling procedure is used to estimate the worst case, the worst case is determined analytically: for each member, the yield strength is set to the minimum value according to the noise model, i.e., $\sigma_{UTS}^w = \sigma_{UTS} \cdot (1 - (r^2))\delta$. In all experimental comparisons, δ was set to 100.

E.2 · BZ Robustness Testproblem Suite

Existing test problem suites like Walking Fish Group (WFG) [79] or Deb-Thiele-Laumanns-Zitzler (DTLZ) [52] feature different properties—like non-separability, bias, many-to-one mappings and multimodality. However, these problems have no specific robustness properties, and the robustness landscape is not known. For that reason, six novel test problems are proposed denoted as Bader-Zitzler (BZ) that have different, known robustness characteristics. These problems, BZ1 to BZ6, allow to investigate the influence of different robustness landscapes on the performance of the algorithms. All, except for BZ5, share the following simple structure:

$$
\left.
\begin{aligned}
\text{Minimize} \quad & f_i(x) = \frac{x_i}{\left\| \sum_{i=1}^{k} x_i \right\|_\beta} \cdot \left(1 + S(g(x))\right) \quad 1 \le i \le d \\
\text{with} \quad & g(x) = \frac{1}{n-k} \sum_{i=k+1}^{n} x_i \\
\text{subject to} \quad & 0 \le x_i \le 1 \text{ for } i = 1, 2, \ldots, n
\end{aligned}
\right\}
\qquad \text{(E.44)}
$$

The first k decision variables are position related, the last $n-k$ decision variables determine the distance to the Pareto front. The Pareto front is reached for $x_i = 0$, $k+1 \le i \le n$, which leads to $S(g(x)) = 0$. The front has has the form $\left(f_1(x)^\beta + \ldots + f_d(x)^\beta\right)^{1/\beta} = 1$. The parameter β thereby specifies the shape of the Pareto front: for $\beta > 1$ the shape is convex, for $\beta = 1$ it is linear and for $0 < \beta < 1$ the shape is concave. The distance to the Pareto front is given by $S(g(x))$, where $g(x)$ is the mean of the distance related decision variables $x_{k+1}, \ldots, x_n$ (an exception is BZ5, where S is a function of $g(x)$ and the variance $\sigma^2 = \text{Var}(\{x_1, \ldots, x_k\})$).

The distance to the front, i.e., $S(g(x))$, depends on a fast oscillating cosine function that causes the perturbations of the objective values and where its amplitude determines the robustness of a solution. In the following, realization of S are listed, and choice of parameter β for the six test problems BZ1 to BZ6 and discuss their robustness landscape is discussed. In the following for the sake of simplicity, let $h := g(x)$

BZ1

For the first test problem, the distance to the front subject to $h := g(x)$ is

$$
S(h) = h + \left((1-h) \cdot \cos(1000h)\right)^2 .
$$

Figure 3(a) shows the function S as a function of h, as well as the maximum and minimum within a neighborhood of B_δ (see Section 6.2). As for all BZ test problems, the (best case) distance to the front linearly decreases with decreasing d. The difference to the worst case, on the other hand, goes in the opposite direction and increases. This gives a continuous trade-off between the objective values $f(x)$ (better for smaller values of h) and the robustness $r(x)$ (better the larger h). The parameter β is set to 1 which gives a linear front shape.

BZ2

For the second test problem, $\beta = 2$ describing a sphere-shaped Pareto front, the distance to which is given by:

$$
S(h) = 3h + \frac{1}{1 + \exp(-200(h - 0.1))} \cdot \left((1-h) \cdot \cos(1000h)\right)^2 .
$$

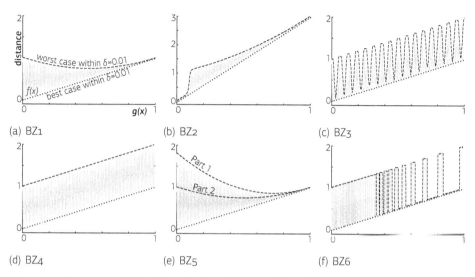

Figure E.3 Distance to the front (gray line) as a function of $g(x)$ (abscissa), see Eq. E.44. The solid and dashed line represent the minimal and maximal distance respectively within the interval $[g(x-\delta), g(x+\delta)]$ with $\delta = 0.01$.

Figure 3(b) shows the distance as a function of h. As in BZ1, the robustness first decreases with decreasing h. However, around $h = 0.1$ the exponential distribution kicks in, and the amplitude of the cosine function becomes very small such that the Pareto front and its adjacencies are robust. BZ2 tests, whether an algorithm is able to overcome the decreasing robustness as approaching the Pareto front, or if the solutions are driven away from the Pareto front to increase their robustness.

BZ3

For the third instance of BZ the distance to the front is a product of two cosine terms:

$$S(h) = h + \big(\cos(50h)\cos(1000h)\big)^4 \ .$$

The concave Pareto front ($\beta = 0.5$) is non robust. However, by increasing the distance to the front the term $\cos(50h)$ periodically leads to robust fronts, see Figure 3(c). An algorithm therefore has to overcome many robust local fronts before reaching the robust front that is closest to the Pareto front.

BZ4

For BZ4, the amplitude of the oscillation term does not change, see Figure 3(d):

$$S(h) = h + \cos(1000h)^2 \ .$$

Therefore, the robustness does not change with h. The only way to minimize $r(x)$ (Eq. 6.2) is to choose a h for which $\cos(1000h)^2$ is close to the worst case. The shape of the Pareto front is convex with $\beta = 3$.

BZ5

The distance to the front for the fifth BZ not only depends on the aggregated variable h, but also on the variance of the distance related decision variables $\sigma^2 = \mathrm{Var}(\{x_1, \ldots, x_k\})$:

$$S(h, \sigma^2) = \begin{cases} h + \big((1-h)\cos(1000h)\big)^2 & \sigma^2 < 0.04 \\ h + 1.8\big((1-h)\cos(1000h)\big)^2 & \text{otherwise} \end{cases}$$

This gives two different degrees of robustness for any choice of h. Depending on the location in the objective space, the distance to the Pareto front (given by $\beta = 0.3$) therefore varies for a given robustness level: it is smaller where $\sigma^2 < 0.04$ and larger where the variance exceeds 0.04.

BZ6

The last instance of the BZ suite uses a step function as distance $S(h)$, see Figure 3(f),

$$S(h) = \begin{cases} h + 1 & \cos\left(\frac{1000.0}{(0.01 + h)h\pi}\right) > 0.9 \\ h & \text{otherwise} \end{cases}.$$

This leads to different robust regions whose width decrease with decreasing distance to the front. Therewith, the ability of an algorithm to determine the robustness of a solution is tested. For example, when the number of samples to determine the robustness is small, the edges of a robust region might not be detected and a non-robust solutions is misclassified as robust. As for BZ2 the Pareto front is a sphere ($\beta = 2$).

Bibliography

1 B. Abraham, editor. *Quality Improvement Through Statistical Methods (Statistics for Industry and Technology)*. Birkhäuser Boston, 1 edition, 1998.

2 A. Agresti and B. A. Coull. Approximate is Better than "Exact" for Interval Estimation of Binomial Proportions. *The American Statistician*, 52(2):119–126, 1998.

3 F. J. Aherne, N. A. Thacker, and P. I. Rockett. Optimising Object Recognition Parameters using a Parallel Multiobjective Genetic Algorithm. In *Proceedings of the 2nd IEE/IEEE International Conference on Genetic Algorithms in Engineering Systems: Innovations and Applications (GALESIA'97)*, pages 1–6. IEEE, 1997.

4 A. Auger, J. Bader, D. Brockhoff, and E. Zitzler. Theory of the Hypervolume Indicator: Optimal μ-Distributions and the Choice of the Reference Point. In *Foundations of Genetic Algorithms (FOGA 2009)*, pages 87–102, New York, NY, USA, 2009. ACM.

5 A. Auger, J. Bader, D. Brockhoff, and E. Zitzler. Articulating User Preferences in Many-Objective Problems by Sampling the Weighted Hypervolume. In G. Raidl et al., editors, *Genetic and Evolutionary Computation Conference (GECCO 2009)*, pages 555–562, New York, NY, USA, 2009. ACM.

6 A. Auger, J. Bader, D. Brockhoff, and E. Zitzler. Investigating and Exploiting the Bias of the Weighted Hypervolume to Articulate User Preferences. In G. Raidl et al., editors, *Genetic and Evolutionary Computation Conference (GECCO 2009)*, pages 563–570, New York, NY, USA, 2009. ACM.

7 J. Bader and E. Zitzler. HypE: An Algorithm for Fast Hypervolume-Based Many-Objective Optimization. TIK Report 286, Computer Engineering and Networks Laboratory (TIK), ETH Zurich, November 2008.

8 J. Bader and E. Zitzler. A Hypervolume-Based Optimizer for High-Dimensional Objective Spaces. In *Conference on Multiple Objective and Goal Programming (MOPGP 2008)*, Lecture Notes in Economics and Mathematical Systems. Springer, 2009. to appear.

9 J. Bader and E. Zitzler. HypE: An Algorithm for Fast Hypervolume-Based Many-Objective Optimization. *Evolutionary Computation*, page no appear, 2009. to appear.

10 J. Bader, D. Brockhoff, S. Welten, and E. Zitzler. On Using Populations of Sets in Multiobjective Optimization. In M. Ehrgott et al., editors, *Conference on Evolutionary Multi-Criterion Optimization (EMO 2009)*, volume 5467 of *LNCS*, pages 140–154. Springer, 2009.

11 J. Bader, K. Deb, and E. Zitzler. Faster Hypervolume-based Search using Monte Carlo Sampling. In *Conference on Multiple Criteria Decision Making (MCDM 2008)*, pages 313–326. Springer, 2010.

12 M. Beer and M. Liebscher. Designing Robust Structures–a Nonlinear Simulation Based Approach. *Computers and Structures*, 86(10):1102–1122, 2008.

13 A. Ben-Tal and A. Nemirovski. Robust Optimization – Methodology and Applications. *Mathematical Programming*, 92(3):453–480, 2003.

14 N. Beume and G. Rudolph. Faster S-Metric Calculation by Considering Dominated Hypervolume as Klee's Measure Problem. Technical Report CI-216/06, Sonderforschungsbereich 531 Computational Intelligence, Universität Dortmund, 2006. shorter version published at IASTED International Conference on Computational Intelligence (CI 2006).

15 N. Beume, C. M. Fonseca, M. Lopez-Ibanez, L. Paquete, and J. Vahrenhold. On the Complexity of Computing the Hypervolume Indicator. Technical Report CI-235/07, University of Dortmund, December 2007.

16 N. Beume, B. Naujoks, and M. Emmerich. SMS-EMOA: Multiobjective Selection Based on Dominated Hypervolume. *European Journal on Operational Research*, 181:1653–1669, 2007.

17 N. Beume, B. Naujoks, M. Preuss, G. Rudolph, and T. Wagner. Effects of 1-Greedy $\mathcal{S}$-Metric-Selection on Innumerably Large Pareto Fronts. In M. Ehrgott et al., editors, *Conference on Evolutionary Multi-Criterion Optimization (EMO 2009)*, volume 5467 of *LNCS*, pages 21–35. Springer, 2009.

18 H.-G. Beyer and B. Sendhoff. Robust optimization - A comprehensive survey. *Computer Methods in Applied Mechanics and Engineering*, 196(33-34):3190–3218, 2007.

19 S. Bleuler, M. Laumanns, L. Thiele, and E. Zitzler. PISA—A Platform and Programming Language Independent Interface for Search Algorithms. In C. M. Fonseca et al., editors, *Conference on Evolutionary Multi-Criterion Optimization (EMO 2003)*, volume 2632 of *LNCS*, pages 494–508, Berlin, 2003. Springer.

20 L. Bradstreet, L. Barone, and L. While. Maximising Hypervolume for Selection in Multi-objective Evolutionary Algorithms. In *Congress on Evolutionary Computation (CEC 2006)*, pages 6208–6215, Vancouver, BC, Canada, 2006. IEEE.

21 J. Branke. Creating Robust Solutions by Means of Evolutionary Algorithms. In A. E. Eiben and T. Bäck and M. Schoenauer and H.-P. Schwefel, editor, *Parallel Problem Solving from Nature – PPSN V*, pages 119–128, Berlin, 1998. Springer. Lecture Notes in Computer Science 1498.

22 J. Branke and K. Deb. Integrating User Preferences into Evolutionary Multi-Objective Optimization. Technical Report 2004004, Indian Institute of Technology, Kanpur, India, 2004. also published as book chapter in Y. Jin, editor: *Knowledge Incorporation in Evolutionary Computation*, pages 461–477, Springer, 2004.

23 J. Branke and C. Schmidt. Selection in the Presence of Noise. *Lecture Notes in Computer Science*, pages 766–777, 2003.

24 J. Branke, T. Kaußler, and H. Schmeck. Guidance in Evolutionary Multi-Objective Optimization. *Advances in Engineering Software*, 32:499–507, 2001.

25 J. Branke, K. Deb, H. Dierolf, and M. Osswald. Finding Knees in Multi-objective Optimization. In X. Yao et al., editors, *Conference on Parallel Problem Solving from Nature (PPSN VIII)*, volume 3242 of *LNCS*, pages 722–731. Springer, 2004.

26 J. Branke, H. Schmeck, K. Deb, and M. Reddy. Parallelizing Multi-Objective Evolutionary Algorithms: Cone Separation. In *Congress on Evolutionary Computation (CEC 2004)*, volume 2, pages 1952–1957, Portland, Oregon, USA, 2004. IEEE Service Center.

27 J. Branke, S. E. Chick, and C. Schmidt. New developments in ranking and selection: an empirical comparison of the three main approaches. In *Proceedings of the 37th conference on Winter simulation (WSC 2005)*, pages 708–717. Winter Simulation Conference, 2005.

28 K. Bringmann and T. Friedrich. Approximating the Volume of Unions and Intersections of High-Dimensional Geometric Objects. In S. H. Hong, H. Nagamochi, and T. Fukunaga, editors, *International Symposium on Algorithms and Computation (ISAAC 2008)*, volume 5369 of *LNCS*, pages 436–447, Berlin, Germany, 2008. Springer.

29 K. Bringmann and T. Friedrich. Approximating the Least Hypervolume Contributor: NP-hard in General, But Fast in Practice. In M. Ehrgott et al., editors, *Conference on Evolutionary Multi-Criterion Optimization (EMO 2009)*, volume 5467 of *LNCS*, pages 6–20. Springer, 2009.

30 D. Brockhoff and E. Zitzler. Improving Hypervolume-based Multiobjective Evolutionary Algorithms by Using Objective Reduction Methods. In *Congress on Evolutionary Computation (CEC 2007)*, pages 2086–2093. IEEE Press, 2007.

31 D. Brockhoff, T. Friedrich, N. Hebbinghaus, C. Klein, F. Neumann, and E. Zitzler. Do Additional Objectives Make a Problem Harder? In D. Thierens et al., editors, *Genetic and Evolutionary Computation Conference (GECCO 2007)*, pages 765–772, New York, NY, USA, 2007. ACM Press.

32 E.K. Burke, P. De Causmaecker, G. De Maere, J. Mulder, M. Paelinck, and G. Vanden Berghe. A Multi-Objective Approach for Robust Airline Scheduling. *Computers and Operations Research*, pages 822–832, 2009.

33 R. E. Caflisch. Monte Carlo and Quasi-Monte Carlo Methods. *Acta Numerica*, 7:1–49, 1998.

34 C.-H. Chen. A lower bound for the correct subset-selection probability and its application to discrete event simulations. *IEEE Trans. Auto. Control*, 41(8):1227–1231, 1996.

35 W. Chen, J.K. Allen, K.-L. Tsui, and F. Mistree. A Procedure For Robust Design: Minimizing Variations Caused By Noise Factors And Control Factors. *ASME Journal of Mechanical Design*, 118:478–485, 1996.

36 C. A. Coello Coello. Handling Preferences in Evolutionary Multiobjective Optimization: A Survey. In *Congress on Evolutionary Computation (CEC 2000)*, pages 30–37. IEEE Press, 2000.

37 C. A. Coello Coello, G. B. Lamont, and D. A. Van Veldhuizen. *Evolutionary Algorithms for Solving Multi-Objective Problems*. Springer, Berlin, Germany, 2007.

38 R. Cohen and L. Katzir. The Generalized Maximum Coverage Problem. *Inf. Process. Lett.*, 108(1): 15–22, 2008.

39 W. J. Conover. *Practical Nonparametric Statistics*. John Wiley, 3rd edition, 1999.

40 T. H. Cormen, C. E. Leiserson, R. L. Rivest, and C. Stein. *Introduction to Algorithms*. The MIT Press, 2nd edition edition, 2001.

41 D. Cvetković and I. C. Parmee. Preferences and their Application in Evolutionary Multiobjective Optimisation. *IEEE Transactions on Evolutionary Computation*, 6(1):42–57, February 2002.

42 I. Das. On Characterizing the "Knee" of the Pareto Curve Based on Normal-Boundary Intersection. *Structural and Multidisciplinary Optimization*, 18(2–3):107–115, 1999.

43 I. Das. Robustness Optimization for Constrained Nonlinear Programming Problems. *Engineering Optimization*, 32(5):585–618, 2000.

44 K. Deb. *Multi-Objective Optimization Using Evolutionary Algorithms*. Wiley, Chichester, UK, 2001.

45 K. Deb. Current Trends in Evolutionary Multi-Objective Optimization. *International Journal for Simulation and Multidisciplinary Design Optimization*, 1:1–8, 2007.

46 K. Deb and H. Gupta. Searching for Robust Pareto-Optimal Solutions in Multi-objective Optimization. In *Evolutionary Multi-Criterion Optimization*, volume 3410/2005 of *Lecture Notes in Computer Science*, pages 150–164. Springer, 2005.

47 K. Deb and H. Gupta. Introducing Robustness in Multi-Objective Optimization. *Evolutionary Computation*, 14(4):463–494, 2006.

48 K. Deb and A. Kumar. Interactive Evolutionary Multi-Objective Optimization and Decision-Making using Reference Direction Method. In *Genetic and Evolutionary Computation Conference (GECCO 2007)*, pages 781–788. ACM, 2007.

49 K. Deb and J. Sundar. Reference Point Based Multi-Objective Optimization Using Evolutionary Algorithms. In Maarten Keijzer et al., editors, *Conference on Genetic and Evolutionary Computation (GECCO 2006)*, pages 635–642. ACM Press, 2006. also published as journal version dsrc2006a.

50 K. Deb, S. Agrawal, A. Pratap, and T. Meyarivan. A Fast Elitist Non-Dominated Sorting Genetic Algorithm for Multi-Objective Optimization: NSGA-II. In M. Schoenauer et al., editors, *Conference on Parallel Problem Solving from Nature (PPSN VI)*, volume 1917 of *LNCS*, pages 849–858. Springer, 2000.

51 K. Deb, A. Pratap, S. Agarwal, and T. Meyarivan. A Fast and Elitist Multiobjective Genetic Algorithm: NSGA-II. *IEEE Transactions on Evolutionary Computation*, 6(2):182–197, 2002.

52 K. Deb, L. Thiele, M. Laumanns, and E. Zitzler. Scalable Multi-Objective Optimization Test Problems. In *Congress on Evolutionary Computation (CEC 2002)*, pages 825–830. IEEE Press, 2002.

53 K. Deb, M. Mohan, and S. Mishra. Evaluating the ε-Domination Based Multi-Objective Evolutionary Algorithm for a Quick Computation of Pareto-Optimal Solutions. *Evolutionary Computation*, 13(4): 501–525, Winter 2005.

54 K. Deb, L. Thiele, M. Laumanns, and E. Zitzler. Scalable Test Problems for Evolutionary Multi-Objective Optimization. In A. Abraham, R. Jain, and R. Goldberg, editors, *Evolutionary Multiobjective Optimization: Theoretical Advances and Applications*, chapter 6, pages 105–145. Springer, 2005.

55 K. Deb, J. Sundar, U. B. Rao N., and S. Chaudhuri. Reference Point Based Multi-Objective Optimization Using Evolutionary Algorithms. *Int. Journal of Computational Intelligence Research*, 2(3):273–286, 2006.

56 L. Devroye. *Non-Uniform Random Variate Generation*. Springer, 1986.

57 I.N. Egorov, G.V. Kretinin, and I.A. Leshchenko. How to Execute Robust Design Optimization. In *9th AIAA/ISSMO Symposium and Exhibit on Multidisciplinary Analysis and Optimization*, 2002.

58 M. Ehrgott. *Multicriteria Optimization*. Springer, Berlin, Germany, 2nd edition, 2005.

59 M. Emmerich, N. Beume, and B. Naujoks. An EMO Algorithm Using the Hypervolume Measure as Selection Criterion. In *Conference on Evolutionary Multi-Criterion Optimization (EMO 2005)*, volume 3410 of *LNCS*, pages 62–76. Springer, 2005.

60 M. Emmerich, A. Deutz, and N. Beume. Gradient-Based/Evolutionary Relay Hybrid for Computing Pareto Front Approximations Maximizing the S-Metric. In *Hybrid Metaheuristics*, pages 140–156. Springer, 2007.

61 R. Everson, J. Fieldsend, and S. Singh. Full Elite-Sets for Multiobjective Optimisation. In I.C. Parmee, editor, *Conference on adaptive computing in design and manufacture (ADCM 2002)*, pages 343–354, London, UK, 2002. Springer.

62 M. Fleischer. The measure of Pareto optima. Applications to multi-objective metaheuristics. In C. M. Fonseca et al., editors, *Conference on Evolutionary Multi-Criterion Optimization (EMO 2003)*, volume 2632 of *LNCS*, pages 519–533, Faro, Portugal, 2003. Springer.

63 C. M. Fonseca and Peter J. Fleming. Genetic Algorithms for Multiobjective Optimization: Formulation, Discussion and Generalization. In Stephanie Forrest, editor, *Conference on Genetic Algorithms*, pages 416–423, San Mateo, California, 1993. Morgan Kaufmann.

64 C. M. Fonseca and Peter J. Fleming. Multiobjective Optimization and Multiple Constraint Handling with Evolutionary Algorithms—Part I: A Unified Formulation. *IEEE Transactions on Systems, Man, and Cybernetics*, 28(1):26–37, 1998.

65 C. M. Fonseca and Peter J. Fleming. Multiobjective Optimization and Multiple Constraint Handling with Evolutionary Algorithms—Part II: Application Example. *IEEE Transactions on Systems, Man, and Cybernetics*, 28(1):38–47, 1998.

66 C. M. Fonseca, L. Paquete, and M. López-Ibáñez. An Improved Dimension-Sweep Algorithm for the Hypervolume Indicator. In *Congress on Evolutionary Computation (CEC 2006)*, pages 1157–1163, Sheraton Vancouver Wall Centre Hotel, Vancouver, BC Canada, 2006. IEEE Press.

67 T. Friedrich, C. Horoba, and F. Neumann. Multiplicative Approximations and the Hypervolume Indicator. In G. Raidl et al., editors, *Genetic and Evolutionary Computation Conference (GECCO 2009)*, pages 571–578. ACM, 2009.

68 P. Ge, C.Y.L. Stephen, and S.T.S. Bukkapatnam. Supporting Negotiations in the Early Stage of Large-Scale Mechanical System Design. *Journal of Mechanical Design*, 127:1056, 2005.

69 C.-K. Goh and K.C. Tan. *Evolutionary Multi-objective Optimization in Uncertain Environments*, volume 186 of *Studies in Computational Intelligence*. Springer, 2009.

70 D. E. Goldberg. *Genetic Algorithms in Search, Optimization, and Machine Learning*. Addison-Wesley, Reading, Massachusetts, 1989.

71 F.G. Guimaraes, D.A. Lowther, and J.A. Ramirez. Multiobjective Approaches for Robust Electromagnetic Design. *Magnetics, IEEE Transactions on*, 42(4):1207–1210, 2006.

72 S. Gunawan and S. Azarm. On a Combined Multi-Objective and Feasibility Robustness Method for Design Optimization. *Proceedings of 10th AIAA/ISSMO MDO*, 2004.

73 S. Gunawan and S. Azarm. Multi-objective robust optimization using a sensitivity region concept. *Structural and Multidisciplinary Optimization*, 29(1):50–60, 2005.

74 A. Hamann, R. Racu, and R. Ernst. Multi-Dimensional Robustness Optimization in Heterogeneous Distributed Embedded Systems. In *13th IEEE Real Time and Embedded Technology and Applications Symposium, 2007. RTAS'07*, pages 269–280, 2007.

75 M. P. Hansen and A. Jaszkiewicz. Evaluating the quality of approximations of the non-dominated set. Technical report, Institute of Mathematical Modeling, Technical University of Denmark, 1998. IMM Technical Report IMM-REP-1998-7.

76 T. Hiroyasu, M. Miki, and S. Watanabe. The new model of parallel genetic algorithm in multi-objective optimization problems—divided range multi-objective genetic algorithm. In *Congress on Evolutionary Computation (CEC 2000)*, pages 333–340, Piscataway, NJ, 2000. IEEE Service Center.

77 W. Hoeffding. Probability Inequalities for Sums of Bounded Random Variables. *J Am Stat Assoc*, 58 (301):13–30, 1963.

78 S. Huband, P. Hingston, L. White, and L. Barone. An Evolution Strategy with Probabilistic Mutation for Multi-Objective Optimisation. In *Congress on Evolutionary Computation (CEC 2003)*, volume 3,

pages 2284–2291, Canberra, Australia, 2003. IEEE Press.

79 S. Huband, P. Hingston, L. Barone, and L. While. A Review of Multiobjective Test Problems and a Scalable Test Problem Toolkit. *IEEE Transactions on Evolutionary Computation*, 10(5):477–506, 2006.

80 E. J. Hughes. Evolutionary multi-objective ranking with uncertainty and noise. In *Evolutionary Multi-Criterion Optimization*, Lecture Notes in Computer Science, pages 329–343. Springer Berlin, 2001.

81 E. J. Hughes. Evolutionary Many-Objective Optimisation: Many Once or One Many? In *Congress on Evolutionary Computation (CEC 2005)*, pages 222–227. IEEE Press, 2005.

82 C. Igel, N. Hansen, and S. Roth. Covariance Matrix Adaptation for Multi-objective Optimization. *Evol Comput*, 15(1):1–28, 2007.

83 L. Jaulin, M. Kieffer, O. Didrit, and E. Walter. *Applied Interval Analysis*. Springer London, 2001.

84 Y. Jin and J. Branke. Evolutionary Optimization In Uncertain Environments—A Survey. *IEEE Transactions on Evolutionary Computation*, 9(3):303–317, 2005.

85 Y. Jin and B. Sendhoff. Trade-Off between Performance and Robustness: An Evolutionary Multiobjective Approach. In C. M. Fonseca et al., editors, *EMO 2003*, volume 2632, pages 237–251. Springer, 2003.

86 J. Knowles. *Local-Search and Hybrid Evolutionary Algorithms for Pareto Optimization*. PhD thesis, University of Reading, 2002.

87 J. Knowles. ParEGO: A Hybrid Algorithm With On-Line Landscape Approximation for Expensive Multiobjective Optimization Problems. *IEEE Transactions on Evolutionary Computation*, 10(1):50–66, 2005.

88 J. Knowles and D. Corne. On Metrics for Comparing Non-Dominated Sets. In *Congress on Evolutionary Computation (CEC 2002)*, pages 711–716, Piscataway, NJ, 2002. IEEE Press.

89 J. Knowles and D. Corne. Properties of an Adaptive Archiving Algorithm for Storing Nondominated Vectors. *IEEE Transactions on Evolutionary Computation*, 7(2):100–116, 2003.

90 J. Knowles, D. Corne, and M. Fleischer. Bounded Archiving using the Lebesgue Measure. In *Congress on Evolutionary Computation (CEC 2003*, pages 2490–2497, Canberra, Australia, 2006. IEEE Press.

91 J. Knowles, L. Thiele, and E. Zitzler. A Tutorial on the Performance Assessment of Stochastic Multiobjective Optimizers. TIK Report 214, Computer Engineering and Networks Laboratory (TIK), ETH Zurich, February 2006.

92 S. Kotz and S. Nadarajah. *Extreme Value Distributions: Theory and Applications*. World Scientific Publishing Company, 1st edition, 2001.

93 P. Kouvelis and G. Yu. *Robust Discrete Pptimization and its Applications*. Kluwer Academic Publishers, 1997.

94 A. Kunjur and S. Krishnamurty. A Robust Multi-Criteria Optimization Approach. *Mechanism and Machine Theory*, 32(7):797–810, 1997.

95 M. Laumanns, G. Rudolph, and H.-P. Schwefel. Approximating the Pareto Set: Concepts, Diversity Issues, and Performance Assessment. Technical Report CI-7299, University of Dortmund, 1999.

96 M. Laumanns, L. Thiele, K. Deb, and E. Zitzler. Combining Convergence and Diversity in Evolutionary Multiobjective Optimization. *Evolutionary Computation*, 10(3):263–282, 2002.

97 J. Lee and P. Hajela. Parallel Genetic Algorithm Implementation in Multidisciplinary Rotor Blade Design. *Journal of Aircraft*, 33(5):962–969, 1996.

98 M. Li, S. Azarm, and V. Aute. A Multi-objective Genetic Algorithm for Robust Design Optimization. In *GECCO 2005*, pages 771–778. ACM, 2005.

99 G. Lizarraga-Lizarraga, A. Hernandez-Aguirre, and S. Botello-Rionda. G-Metric: an M-ary quality indicator for the evaluation of non-dominated sets. In *Genetic And Evolutionary Computation Conference (GECCO 2008)*, pages 665–672, New York, NY, USA, 2008. ACM.

100 M. Mezmaz and N. Melab and E.-G. Talbi. Using the Multi-Start and Island Models for Parallel Multi-Objective Optimization on the Computational Grid. In *eScience*, page 112. IEEE Computer Society, 2006.

101 J. Mehnen, H. Trautmann, and A. Tiwari. Introducing User Preference Using Desirability Functions in Multi-Objective Evolutionary Optimisation of Noisy Processes. In *Congress on Evolutionary Compuation (CEC 2007)*, pages 2687–2694. IEEE Press, 2007.

102 K. Miettinen. *Nonlinear Multiobjective Optimization*. Kluwer, Boston, MA, USA, 1999.

103 S. Mostaghim, J. Branke, and H. Schmeck. Multi-objective Particle Swarm Optimization on Computer Grids. In *Proceedings of the 9th annual conference on Genetic and evolutionary computation (GECCO 2007)*, pages 869–875, New York, NY, USA, 2007. ACM.

104 J.M. Mulvey, R.J. Vanderbei, and S.A. Zenios. Robust Optimization of Large-Scale Systems. *Operations research*, pages 264–281, 1995.

105 M. Nicolini. A Two-Level Evolutionary Approach to Multi-criterion Optimization of Water Supply Systems. In *Conference on Evolutionary Multi-Criterion Optimization (EMO 2005)*, volume 3410 of *LNCS*, pages 736–751. Springer, 2005.

106 S. Obayashi, K. Deb, C. Poloni, T. Hiroyasu, and T. Murata, editors. *Conference on Evolutionary Multi-Criterion Optimization (EMO 2007)*, volume 4403 of *LNCS*, Berlin, Germany, 2007. Springer.

107 A. Parkinson, C. Sorensen, and N. Pourhassan. A General Approach for Robust Optimal Design. *Journal of Mechanical Design*, 115(1):74–80, 1993.

108 C. Poloni. Hybrid GA for Multi-Objective Aerodynamic Shape Optimization. In G. Winter, J. Periaux, M. Galan, and P. Cuesta, editors, *Genetic Algorithms in Engineering and Computer Science*, pages

397–416. John Wiley & Sons, 1995.

109 R. C. Purshouse. *On the Evolutionary Optimisation of Many Objectives*. PhD thesis, The University of Sheffield, 2003.

110 R. C. Purshouse and P. J. Fleming. An Adaptive Divide-and-Conquer Methodology for Evolutionary Multi-criterion Optimisation. In C. Fonseca et al., editors, *Conference on Evolutionary Multi-Criterion Optimization (EMO 2003)*, number 2632 in LNCS, pages 133–147. Springer, 2003.

111 L. Rachmawati and D. Srinivasan. Preference Incorporation in Multi-objective Evolutionary Algorithms: A Survey. In *Congress on Evolutionary Computation (CEC 2006)*, pages 962–968. IEEE Press, July 2006.

112 H. Sawai and S. Adachi. Effects of Hierarchical Migration in a Parallel Distributed Parameter-free GA. In *Congress on Evolutionary Computation (CEC 2000)*, pages 1117–1124, Piscataway, NJ, 2000. IEEE Press.

113 J. Scharnow, K. Tinnefeld, and I. Wegener. The Analysis of Evolutionary Algorithms on Sorting and Shortest Paths Problems. *Journal of Mathematical Modelling and Algorithms*, 3(4):349–366, 2004. Online Date Tuesday, December 28, 2004.

114 J. Schott. Fault tolerant design using single and multicriteria genetic algorithm optimization. Master's thesis, Department of Aeronautics and Astronautics, Massachusetts Institute of Technology, 1995.

115 G. L. Soares, R. L. S. Adriano, C. A. Maia, L. Jaulin, and J. A. Vasconcelos. Robust Multi-Objective TEAM 22 Problem: A Case Study of Uncertainties in Design Optimization. *IEEE Transactions on Magnetics*, 45:1028–1031, 2009.

116 G. L. Soares, R. O. Parreiras, L. Jaulin, and J. A. Vasconcelos C. A. Maia. Interval Robust Multi-objective Algorithm. *Nonlinear Analysis*, 71:1818–1825, 2009.

117 N. Srinivas and K. Deb. Multiobjective Optimization Using Nondominated Sorting in Genetic Algorithms. *Evolutionary Computation*, 2(3):221–248, 1994.

118 T. J. Stanley and T. Mudge. A Parallel Genetic Algorithm for Multiobjective Microprocessor Design. In L. J. Eshelman, editor, *Proceedings of the Sixth International Conference on Genetic Algorithms*, pages 597–604. University of Pittsburgh, Morgan Kaufmann Publishers, 1995.

119 G. Taguchi. *Introduction to Quality Engineering: Designing Quality into Products and Processes*. Quality Resources, 1986.

120 E.-G. Talbi, S. Mostaghim, T. Okabe, H. Ishibuchi, G. Rudolph, and C. A. Coello Coello. Parallel Approaches for Multiobjective Optimization. In J. Branke et al., editors, *Multiobjective Optimization: Interactive and Evolutionary Approaches*, pages 349–372. Springer, 2008.

121 J. Teich. Pareto-Front Exploration with Uncertain Objectives. In *Conference on Evolutionary Multi-Criterion Optimization (EMO 2001)*, pages 314–328, London, UK, 2001. Springer.

122 K.L. Tsui. Robust Design Optimization for Multiple Characteristic Problems. *International Journal of Production Research*, 37(2):433–445, 1999.

123 S. Tsutsui and A. Ghosh. Genetic Algorithms with a Robust Solution Searching Scheme. *IEEE Trans. on Evolutionary Computation*, 1(3):201–208, 1997.

124 D. A. Van Veldhuizen. *Multiobjective Evolutionary Algorithms: Classifications, Analyses, and New Innovations.* PhD thesis, Graduate School of Engineering, Air Force Institute of Technology, Air University, 1999.

125 D. A. Van Veldhuizen and G. B. Lamont. Multiobjective Evolutionary Algorithms: Analyzing the State-of-the-Art. *Evolutionary Computation*, 8(2):125–147, 2000.

126 T. Wagner, N. Beume, and B. Naujoks. Pareto-, Aggregation-, and Indicator-based Methods in Many-objective Optimization. In S. Obayashi et al., editors, *Conference on Evolutionary Multi-Criterion Optimization (EMO 2007)*, volume 4403 of *LNCS*, pages 742–756, Berlin Heidelberg, Germany, 2007. Springer. extended version published as internal report of Sonderforschungsbereich 531 Computational Intelligence CI-217/06, Universität Dortmund, September 2006.

127 W.F. Chen and L. Duan. *Bridge Engineering Handbook.* CRC, 1 edition, 1999.

128 L. While. A New Analysis of the LebMeasure Algorithm for Calculating Hypervolume. In *Conference on Evolutionary Multi-Criterion Optimization (EMO 2005)*, volume 3410 of *LNCS*, pages 326–340, Guanajuato, México, 2005. Springer.

129 L. While, L. Bradstreet, L. Barone, and P. Hingston. Heuristics for Optimising the Calculation of Hypervolume for Multi-objective Optimisation Problems. In *Congress on Evolutionary Computation (CEC 2005)*, pages 2225–2232, IEEE Service Center, Edinburgh, Scotland, 2005. IEEE Press.

130 L. While, P. Hingston, L. Barone, and S. Huband. A Faster Algorithm for Calculating Hypervolume. *IEEE Transactions on Evolutionary Computation*, 10(1):29–38, 2006.

131 Q. Yang and S. Ding. Novel Algorithm to Calculate Hypervolume Indicator of Pareto Approximation Set. In *Advanced Intelligent Computing Theories and Applications. With Aspects of Theoretical and Methodological Issues, Third International Conference on Intelligent Computing (ICIC 2007)*, volume 2, pages 235–244, 2007.

132 E. Zeidler. *Applied Functional Analysis: Main Principles and Their Applications.* Applied Mathematical Sciences 109. Springer, 1995.

133 E. Zitzler. *Evolutionary Algorithms for Multiobjective Optimization: Methods and Applications.* PhD thesis, ETH Zurich, Switzerland, 1999.

134 E. Zitzler. Hypervolume metric calculation. *ftp://ftp.tik.ee.ethz.ch/pub/people/zitzler/hypervol.c*, 2001.

135 E. Zitzler and S. Künzli. Indicator-Based Selection in Multiobjective Search. In X. Yao et al., editors, *Conference on Parallel Problem Solving from Nature (PPSN VIII)*, volume 3242 of *LNCS*, pages 832–842. Springer, 2004.

136 E. Zitzler and L. Thiele. Multiobjective Optimization Using Evolutionary Algorithms - A Comparative Case Study. In *Conference on Parallel Problem Solving from Nature (PPSN V)*, pages 292–301, Amsterdam, 1998.

137 E. Zitzler and L. Thiele. Multiobjective Evolutionary Algorithms: A Comparative Case Study and the Strength Pareto Approach. *IEEE Transactions on Evolutionary Computation*, 3(4):257–271, 1999.

138 E. Zitzler, K. Deb, and L. Thiele. Comparison of Multiobjective Evolutionary Algorithms: Empirical Results. *Evolutionary Computation*, 8(2):173–195, 2000.

139 E. Zitzler, M. Laumanns, and L. Thiele. SPEA2: Improving the Strength Pareto Evolutionary Algorithm for Multiobjective Optimization. In K.C. Giannakoglou et al., editors, *Evolutionary Methods for Design, Optimisation and Control with Application to Industrial Problems (EUROGEN 2001)*, pages 95–100. International Center for Numerical Methods in Engineering (CIMNE), 2002.

140 E. Zitzler, L. Thiele, M. Laumanns, C. M. Fonseca, and V. Grunert da Fonseca. Performance Assessment of Multiobjective Optimizers: An Analysis and Review. *IEEE Transactions on Evolutionary Computation*, 7(2):117–132, 2003.

141 E. Zitzler, D. Brockhoff, and L. Thiele. The Hypervolume Indicator Revisited: On the Design of Pareto-compliant Indicators Via Weighted Integration. In S. Obayashi et al., editors, *Conference on Evolutionary Multi-Criterion Optimization (EMO 2007)*, volume 4403 of *LNCS*, pages 862–876, Berlin, 2007. Springer.

142 E. Zitzler, L. Thiele, and J. Bader. SPAM: Set Preference Algorithm for Multiobjective Optimization. In G. Rudolph et al., editors, *Conference on Parallel Problem Solving From Nature (PPSN X)*, volume 5199 of *LNCS*, pages 847–858. Springer, 2008.

143 E. Zitzler, L. Thiele, and J. Bader. On Set-Based Multiobjective Optimization (Revised Version). TIK Report 300, Computer Engineering and Networks Laboratory (TIK), ETH Zurich, December 2008.

144 E. Zitzler, L. Thiele, and J. Bader. On Set-Based Multiobjective Optimization. *IEEE Transactions on Evolutionary Computation*, 2009. to appear.

Curriculum Vitae

Personal Information

Johannes Michael Bader
Born April 6, 1981 in Jegenstorf, Switzerland
Citizen of Basel, BS

Education

2006–2009 Doctoral student at Computer Engineering and Networks Laboratory (TIK), ETH Zurich, Switzerland

2001–2006 Master studies in information technology and electrical engineering at ETH Zurich, Switzerland

2001 Matura at Mathematisch-Naturwissenschaftliches Gymnasium Bern Neufeld

www.ingramcontent.com/pod-product-compliance
Lightning Source LLC
Chambersburg PA
CBHW080354060326
40689CB00019B/4005